PRACTICAL GUILT

PRACTICAL GUILT

Moral Dilemmas, Emotions, and Social Norms

P. S. GREENSPAN

New York   Oxford
OXFORD UNIVERSITY PRESS
1995

Oxford University Press

Oxford   New York
Athens   Auckland   Bangkok   Bombay
Calcutta   Cape Town   Dar es Salaam   Delhi
Florence   Hong Kong   Istanbul   Karachi
Kuala Lumpur   Madras   Madrid   Melbourne
Mexico City   Nairobi   Paris   Singapore
Taipei   Tokyo   Toronto

and associated companies in
Berlin   Ibadan

Published by Oxford University Press, Inc.,
200 Madison Avenue, New York, New York 10016

Library of Congress Cataloging-in-Publication Data
Greenspan, Patricia S., 1944–
Practical guilt : moral dilemmas, emotions, and social norms /
P. S. Greenspan.
p.   cm.
Includes bibliographical references and index.
ISBN 0–19–508762–3; ISBN 0–19–509090–X (pbk.)
1. Guilt.   2. Emotions (Philosophy)   3. Social norms.   4. Ethics.
I. Title
BJ1471.5.G74   1994
128′.3—dc20   93-40067

1 3 5 7 9 8 6 4 2
Printed in the United States of America
on acid-free paper

In memory of
ALAN DONAGAN

The fox condemns the trap, not himself.

William Blake
The Marriage of Heaven and Hell

Acknowledgments

The sources of my thinking on the several subjects of this essay go back many years, but its first full draft was written during 1990–91 at the National Humanities Center in Research Triangle Park, North Carolina. I am indebted to the other fellows in residence at the center for historical and literary discussion of guilt, and to the center staff for sustaining the more upbeat emotions that allowed for my unusual productivity over the year. Let me also thank the National Endowment for the Humanities for providing my funding and the University of Maryland, which provided supplementary support. Two terms off at Maryland during the preceding two years enabled me to write drafts of some initial sections and to work out a detailed plan of argument. I owe special thanks to colleague James Lesher, then acting dean of the College of Arts and Humanities, for arranging my leave during autumn 1988; I was awarded another leave by the Graduate Research Board at Maryland during autumn 1989.

I am also grateful to a number of people who supported my work on this project or provoked my thinking with correspondence or conversation on the subjects it brings together. Alan Donagan, to whom the book is dedicated, was my colleague at the University of Chicago and the mainstay of my grant referees for many years thereafter, switching over to this project despite his sharply opposing view on moral dilemmas. His letters on the subject determined the basic shape of my argument and its ultimate focus on metaethics—to use a term still out of favor for a set of issues in the foundations of ethics that concerned me most as a student of philosophy but became unfashionable at about the time I left school. Much of this essay emerged in an attempt to answer Alan's insistent and impassioned questions about how ethics could accommodate dilemmas while amounting to something more than a simple codification of emotions.

Alan's prodding served to draw me back to a number of earlier interests, with dilemmas providing a helpfully narrow angle of approach to topics too large to deal with effectively head-on. At one point during the planning of this essay, upon reviewing some of my old student papers and other course materials while packing up to move, I even found some anticipations of my specific theses. There was a long-forgotten defense of guilt for the unavoidable written up for a seminar at Harvard in 1970 and a critique of W. D. Ross for a 1967 ethics course whose main line of argument I decided to incorporate into chapter 4, section 3, of this essay. Some of these topics, which at that point were rather off-center, have since come into their own in contemporary moral philosophy. However, they have mainly been linked with the Aristotelian approach to ethics that stresses notions of virtue and character over obligation and action. My argument here is in part an attempt to show what sort of role emotions also play on the modern approach we associate with Kant, once we detach it from some of the more extreme elements of a Kantian approach, as brought out by my treatment of dilemmas.

Some features of this project are due to conversations with Maryland colleague and department chair Michael Slote that encouraged me to bring my work on dilemmas and emotions to bear on more mainstream issues in ethics. To highlight the connection, I decided to present my argument as it emerged, in discussion of the views of a number of central contemporary authors, to whom I also owe a debt of thanks for providing me with materials I sometimes use in ways quite other than what they intended. Among authors on dilemmas, a particular influence was Ruth Marcus, whose paper I responded to at the 1980 Chapel Hill Colloquium in Philosophy. Three conversations with Bernard Williams in October 1989 also helped me clarify his views on dilemmas and related subjects.

Besides Donagan and Slote, a number of people wrote letters in support of my numerous grant applications for this project: Annette Baier, Simon Blackburn, Richard Brandt, John Cooper, Jonathan Glover, Mary Mothersill, Thomas Nagel, and Philip Quinn. What emerged from my year at the National Humanities Center was a social view of the bases of ethics that I came to see as the central result of my work on this subject. Colleagues who provided comments on drafts of part or all of the essay include Kent Bach, David Copp, Jonathan Dancy, Stephen Leighton, Geoffrey Sayre-McCord, Walter Sinnott-Armstrong, the late Michael Woods, several anonymous reviewers, and students in some of my classes, especially Lawrence Dobbs, Richard Fyfe, Scott Gelfand, David Hull, and Stephen Tighe.

I also received comments on drafts of particular sections at a number of oral presentations (at Philosophy Department Colloquia, unless otherwise noted): Chapter 5, section 1, "Subjective Guilt and Responsibility," was read at the University of Rochester in 1988, then at Indiana University in 1989; part of chapter 4, section 1, at North Carolina State University in 1991 under the title "Guilt and Virtue"; chapter 4, section 2, "Guilt as an Identificatory Mechanism," at the University of North Carolina at Chapel Hill and at the National Humanities Center Seminar on the Concept of a Person in 1991; part of chapter 5, sections 2–3, at a symposium in honor of Ruth Marcus at the Pacific Division meetings of the American Philosophical Association in 1992 under the title "Perspectival Guilt"; and a selection from chapter 3, section 3, at Georgetown University and Queen's University (Kingston, Ontario) in 1993 under the title "Protagorean Realism." Chapter 3, section 1, was discussed at a meeting of the Georgetown/ Maryland Moral Psychology Reading Group in 1991.

Later drafts of some of these pieces, along with some related selections, have appeared in print: "Subjective Guilt and Responsibility," in *Mind* 101 (1992):

287–303; "Guilt as an Indentificatory Mechanism," in *Pacific Philosophical Quarterly* 74 (1993): 46–59; "Guilt and Virtue," in *Journal of Philosophy* 91 (1994): 57–70; and a longer version of "Perspectival Guilt," in *Modality, Morality and Belief: Essays in Honor of Ruth Barcan Marcus*, ed. W. Sinnott-Armstrong (Cambridge: Cambridge University Press, 1994 [copyright © Cambridge University Press; reprinted by permission]).

For secretarial support at various stages, let me also thank Marsha Brown, Richard Fyfe, and Katie Kight. I owe particular thanks at Oxford University Press to Angela Blackburn for painstaking editorial help and advice.

Washington, D.C.   P.S.G.
August 1993

Contents

Contents

PRACTICAL GUILT

Introduction

In what follows I deal with a number of diverse issues of interest to philosophers (and others) in several areas and of different intellectual bent. I explain the connections among these topics in chapter 1, but since my discussion quickly enters the thick of metaethical debate, it might be helpful at this point to present an overall map of my argument so that readers may chart alternative paths through it.

My argument begins with issues in the foundations of ethics, with an eye to determining the place of moral emotion. However, many readers might prefer to begin with my treatment of a specific emotion, guilt, in part II, possibly doubling back later as needed to make full sense of the general points I extract from that discussion for moral dilemmas, toward the end of chapter 5, or the role of emotion in ethics, in chapter 6. I have provided index references to cases discussed, along with other background information that should help to clear up any initially obscure passages, but I think that the bulk of chapters 4 and 5 can be read independently by readers with a special interest in emotion.

For readers of part I, I shall give more specific advice as my discussion there proceeds about how they might bypass the more technical treatment of deontic logic in chapter 2. It should also be possible to proceed directly to chapter 3, and thence to chapter 6, for an account of my proposals on metaethics that bypasses details of the literature on moral dilemmas along with the treatment of guilt. The index will supply references to some terminology explained in chapter 1; and the second section of chapter 1 might be read on its own, for a fuller account of my overall argument in relation to metaethics. At this point I want just to give an outline that indicates the main topics to be covered in each chapter but leaves explanations until later.

I begin in chapter 1 with a review of philosophers' treatment of dilemmas, attempting to show why they are thought to pose a problem for the coherency of ethics. On my account they call into question the motivational force of "ought" and similar deontic terms, taken as essentially practical or action-guiding. They pose a metaethical dilemma of sorts, between "subject-independent" views of moral motivation, which apparently make moral dilemmas impossible, and "subject-dependent" views, which seem to be unable to capture the motivational difficulty of dilemmas.

3

In chapter 2 I deal with some of the standard questions raised for dilemmas in connection with deontic logic, though I come at them from a direction that I hope will bring out their metaethical relevance. First I address questions raised by Bernard Williams's dismissal of dilemmas involving practical oughts as conclusions of deliberation. I argue that an investigation of some presuppositions about the weighing of moral reasons favors a redefinition of dilemmas in terms of prohibitions rather than positive oughts. I then apply this negative formulation to the choice dilemmas apparently force between standard deontic principles, most notably "ought"-implies-"can" and agglomeration, with some comments about the implications of the choice for the unifiability of action-guiding ethics, understood as based on practical "ought."

Chapter 3 begins with a shift to contemporary versions of the question of motivational force introduced in chapter 1. On the basis of some of Philippa Foot's comments about moral teaching, I suggest a way of undermining the standard dichotomy between internalism and externalism in contemporary metaethics by connecting motivational force to the general moral function of "ought," as presupposed in teaching the term, rather than to its meaning in a given judgment. The resulting view, which I call "general internalism," amounts to a modification of externalism to provide a nonaccidental link between moral judgment and motivation. I attempt to show that it yields a more plausible account of various problematic metaethical issues than standard internalism or externalism.

In particular, I argue that the view is needed to make sense of moral dilemmas. Standard versions of internalism, as represented by the views of John McDowell and J. L. Mackie, seem to be unable to account for dilemmas adequately. By switching to general internalism, however, I show how we can extract from elements of both views an explanation of dilemmas in terms of the conception of ethics as a social artifact with a link to individual motivation provided by emotion. Part I ends with some of the implications of my proposed metaethical alternative, which I defend as a version of moral realism.

Part II turns to guilt and related reactions to moral wrong, initially considered without distinction, as emotional residues of moral conflict or more generally of "moral failure" in the sense of ought-violation. In chapter 4 I show the significance of guilt feelings as a link between virtue and duty ethics. I then attempt a more specific account of the nature and function of guilt as an identificatory mechanism, eventually distinguishing it from shame and other similar moral feelings that do not necessarily involve identification with others, though my view allows for their overlap with guilt in some cases.

Next I turn to questions about the sense in which guilt or any emotional reaction can be morally required—as guilt seems to be in typical cases of moral failure—in light of the principle that "ought"-implies-"can." In application to dilemmas, these are questions about a judgment of "ought-to-feel" that might be thought of as offering a way out—an indirect way of satisfying the ought that is not acted on—for agents with enough control to generate the requisite emotion. I argue, however, that this suggestion needs to be qualified in important ways. Among other things, there are second-order dilemmas in some cases, in which guilt feelings would interfere with effective action on the ought that is supposed to be satisfied directly, by taking action.

In chapter 5 I address objections to classifying the agent's reaction as guilt in situations of dilemma on the grounds that guilt implies a judgment of culpability. In application initially to nondilemmatic cases of guilt for the unavoidable, I defend a view of the propositional content of guilt according to which the emotion involves an "as if" version of the corresponding evaluative judgment, not necessarily an evaluation that the agent believes. On the question of appropriateness, my approach yields an asymmetry between guilt and emotional blame that I take to explain any reluctance we may have to impose guilt on the agent in a dilemma. The different position of the subject in relation to guilt as opposed to blame licenses a different sort of assessment of emotional warrant, so that less is required to warrant guilt. I go on to defend a corresponding objective notion of guilt in application to moral dilemmas, thought of as cases where all the agent's options for action are wrong.

In chapter 6 I focus again on the metaethical position emerging from my argument, as introduced in chapter 1 and developed in chapter 3. After drawing out some of the implications of my motivational interpretation of the role of moral emotion, I attempt to show how the "social artifact" version of moral realism can allow for an element of expressivism and other views commonly thought of in contrast to realism—most notably relativism—without entailing acceptance of those views. On its most general characterization, the result of my argument is thus a defense of commonsense ethics against the problems raised by dilemmas, by way of an extended treatment of the bases of ethics in moral emotion.

I

BETWEEN THE HORNS

1

Defusing Dilemmas

In the past twenty-five years or so a number of philosophers have argued for the possibility of full-blown moral dilemmas: cases in which all of the agent's alternatives, through no fault of his own, turn out to be morally wrong. Other authors have attempted to dismiss such cases as undermining the rational coherency of ethics, on the modern conception of ethics as essentially a system of rules meant to guide action. A good specimen of the sort of case at issue in the literature is provided by one of Michael Walzer's examples in his contribution to a 1973 symposium on the rules of war with Thomas Nagel, Richard Brandt, and R. M. Hare.[1] The case assumes that torture is necessary to get a terrorist to give away the whereabouts of bombs set to go off throughout the city but that torture still remains wrong under these circumstances—along with the agent's only other alternative, which involves letting the bombs destroy many innocent civilians.

The case is one in which our ordinary moral code fails to yield coherent moral advice—in Nagel's words it sets the agent in a "moral blind alley"—since it apparently rules out all alternatives.[2] Brandt and Hare argue in opposition to this account that such acts as torturing the terrorist, even if normally wrong, do not really count as wrong under the circumstances.[3] Instead of relying on general rules such as the one prohibiting torture, we should appeal in a case of conflict to straightforward utilitarian assessments of the acts in question. But note that someone on either side of this dispute could agree with Brandt and Hare that utilitarian considerations outweigh principled objections to torture in Walzer's case when it comes to a practical decision. The dispute concerns not what to do in such cases but whether the action one must do, morally speaking, can still be wrong.

For a case that poses the issue more sharply, we might set up alternatives of roughly the same sort and attempt to bring them into balance. Walzer's case involves doing active harm in order to save lives, but consider a possible case from spy fiction in which someone has stumbled across plans for a political assassination and is threatened with the murder of a family member unless she remains silent. Here the agent may be made out as choosing between two failures to save a life—on the assumption that she is all set to inform on the assassins when they reveal that the family member is under threat and will be killed unless she holds back. Each of her alternatives—failing to save the family member and failing to save the assassin's intended victim—would seem to be forbidden by the moral rules. By adjusting amounts of harm that would ensue and similar morally significant features of the case, we could presumably make both alternatives come out as about equally wrong on the view that allows for dilemmas—or not wrong after all, apparently, on the view favored by Brandt and Hare.

At issue in this "balanced" assassination case, on my understanding of dilemmas, is whether the term "wrong" makes sense apart from a comparison of options in which at least one act comes out as right. Proponents of dilemmas interpret "wrong" as applying to some property of acts that is not essentially comparative, and the phenomenology of moral experience seems to bear them out. Though in some cases the availability of a better alternative may be all that makes us count an act as wrong, that is not our initial reason for holding in the assassination case that it would be wrong to allow a murder. It also seems that, whatever the agent decides to do here, it will be reasonable for her to feel a sense of guilt for allowing a murder. On the other hand, the logic of moral discourse may seem to require taking the comparative point about "wrong" as understood and dismissing guilt feelings as inappropriate where an agent makes the best choice possible under the circumstances.

I shall eventually argue, in the chapters that follow, that guilt can indeed be made out as appropriate in such cases—not just an understandable spillover from more normal cases but rather a warranted reaction to whichever act the agent decides to do. This account will yield a way of making sense of the possibility of dilemmas, for no comparison of alternatives seems to be built into the claim that a virtuous agent would view some act as a stain on her moral record. Just as every one of a set of exhaustive alternatives can be ugly or upsetting or in some other way repugnant, so there is no strictly logical problem in supposing that all of an agent's alternatives warrant guilt.

There might seem to be a logical problem with conflicting ought-judgments themselves, but in the contemporary debate over dilemmas to be outlined in the present chapter this at any rate has been shown to be false: It begs the question at issue in dilemmas to suppose that the prohibition of an act implies that some alternative to it is *not* prohibited—as we would need to say in order to derive a straightforward logical contradiction from the prohibition of all alternatives. However, even if dilemmas involve no contradiction, they seem to make impossible demands of an agent. In warranting guilt for unavoidable wrong, they subject an agent to "moral luck," meaning moral responsibility for factors beyond his control.[4] More fundamentally, they seem to pose a threat to the very intelligibility of ethics as a system of rules meant to guide action. It is unclear how moral judgments can be thought of as telling an agent what to do in a case of practical deadlock, where everything he *can* do is forbidden.

In this chapter, I hope to bring out some more particular questions raised by dilemmas for the view of ethics as essentially action-guiding. I take these to be variants of a historical problem about the motivational force of obligation. In fact, I shall suggest that dilemmas also reveal the main lines of an answer to these more general metaethical questions in the role they assign to guilt. Let me first fill in some of the philosophical background on dilemmas and attempt to show how the issue bears on metaethics (section 1). I shall then be in a position to give an idea of my own intended argument and its implications for ethics and moral psychology (section 2). In general terms, I think we can use dilemmas to exhibit the motivational structure of an ethics that in some sense rests on psychology yet escapes between the horns of some standard ways of making out the relation between the two. It does so on my account by reference to the social role and origins of moral motivation.

1. Moral Dilemmas and Motivational Force

Dilemmas first surface as problems for the coherency of action-guiding ethics in the modern literature, with its emphasis since Kant on notions of obligation. Aquinas had earlier restricted conflict to cases of prior wrongdoing on the part of the agent, apparently in answer to questions of moral luck raised by Gregory the Great's view of dilemmas as traps set by the devil.[5] If the devil could trap an innocent agent into doing wrong, then presumably not all evildoers would deserve eternal punishment. But the claim that all alternatives are wrong is not thus problematic as applied to an author of prior evil, already consigned to hell by a just god.

Instead, the claim seems to raise problems for the view of an agent as "bound" to act by obligation independently of some sanction like the threat of divine punishment. Thus, Kant denied the possibility of moral dilemmas, seen as conflicting obligations, on a notion of obligation as "moral necessity."[6] Though it might make sense to say of Aquinas's evil agent in a dilemma that he has to do two incompatible acts in order to get to heaven—at least as a way of saying that heaven is by now beyond his reach—the claim that he "has to" *simpliciter* would just seem incoherent. Such metaphors of necessity refer to obedience to law as a kind of compulsion, and for Kant they also have a literal application to the holy or perfectly rational will, which is moral by nature. The moral law simply describes the natural behavior of a holy will, so any obligations derived from it on Kantian assumptions must be capable of joint fulfillment.

Moral philosophers after Kant allow for and often emphasize conflict of obligations, but not of a sort that clearly involves dilemmas. In most cases dilemmas are ruled out: Ross, for instance, limits conflict to prima facie duties, only one of which in any conflicting set can amount to an actual duty in the sense that implies really being in force.[7] The suggestion that there might be genuine dilemmas seems to have emerged only in recent years as a product of the attempt to formalize Kantian assumptions about moral necessity in deontic logic.

Deontic logic, the logic of obligation, was set up on the model of alethic modal logic, the logic of necessity and possibility, with moral requirement taken as analogous to necessary truth except for its failure to imply truth; but a number of paradoxical consequences immediately raised questions about the analogy.[8] Undermining it opened the door to the possibility of dilemmas, not as a further problem for deontic logic—except insofar as the standard system lacked the resources to capture dilemmas—but rather as an insight into the nature of the ethics of duty, the modern approach to ethics exemplified by Kant. The suggestion was picked up by moral philosophers and interpreted as in some way problematic for ethics, but with disagreement about the extent to which it undermined ethical rationality. Let us take a look at the highlights of that debate, in enough detail for a reconception of the problem.

Dilemmas in Contemporary Duty Ethics

Dilemmas were introduced into the nontechnical literature by a logician, E. J. Lemmon, in an article published in *The Philosophical Review* in 1962.[9] Lemmon understood dilemmas as cases in which an agent both ought and ought not to do the same thing. In typical cases he took them to be explained by the derivation of oughts from three different sources: duties (based on the agent's position or status), obligations (based instead on acts of commitment), and general moral principles. Thus, in Plato's well-known case of weapons borrowed from someone who then goes mad and demands their return, the agent has to choose between fulfilling an obligation based on his promise and satisfying the more general obligation to prevent harm.[10]

Lemmon treats Plato's case as resolvable by appeal to a higher-order utilitarian principle, but he also brings up Sartre's case of a young man in occupied France who has to choose between joining the resistance and staying home to support his dependent mother.[11] This case apparently involves a choice between two oughts of the same sort: duties based on the agent's different roles as son and citizen. Lemmon treats the evidence bearing on the choice as inconclusive, but the case provides at least the framework for a full-blown dilemma to the extent that it is not clearly decidable by appeal to the agent's preexisting moral attitudes. In a full-blown dilemma on Lemmon's account, the agent has to develop a new moral outlook in deciding what to do—which in this case would seem to mean identifying himself with one of his conflicting roles.

Lemmon's account leaves a number of questions unanswered: It is unclear, in particular, whether the choice of a new moral outlook is supposed to resolve a dilemma or to leave it in force. At any rate, Lemmon makes out the problem raised by dilemmas as a problem for the adequacy of general philosophical approaches to ethics: approaches he sees as tailored to "the easy, rule-guided moral situation."[12] In strictly logical terms, he takes dilemmas to be unproblematic, as he thinks can be shown by contrasting "ought" with "must." That "must" and "must not" are incompatible he takes to follow from the fact (or presumed fact; I shall question it in chapter 2) that "must" implies "will." "He will" and "he will not" cannot both be true, so neither can "He must" and "He must not." But the argument does not apply to "ought": The possibility of violating an ought amounts to the basic point of disanalogy between deontic and alethic modal logic.

The next major discussion of dilemmas occurs in Bernard Williams's defense of the consistency of conflicting oughts, initially published in the *Proceedings of the Aristotelian Society* in 1965.[13] Williams argues that dilemmas violate standard deontic assumptions to the extent that they force a choice between the principle that "ought" implies "can" and a principle of deontic distribution that he refers to as "agglomeration" and decides to drop—in contrast to Lemmon, who instead rejects "ought"-implies-"can."[14] With O as an operator for "ought" and A and B as variables describing possible acts, we may symbolize agglomeration as: OA and OB imply O(A & B). In dilemmatic cases, where A and B are assumed to be incompatible, it will not be possible to satisfy their conjunction, so O(A & B) will violate "ought"-implies-"can."

Williams's article has been widely disputed in the ethics literature for his apparent argument to the existence of dilemmas from moral emotion and for the metaethical conclusions he uses dilemmas to support. He sets up dilemmas a bit differently from Lemmon, focusing on cases of contingent conflict, where the several things one ought to do are not logically incompatible but are jointly unrealizable in the world as it happens to be. The case Williams presents as a full-blown dilemma is one in which there may be no uncertainty about what to do, assuming that one ought to do what is "for the best": the case of Aeschylus' Agamemnon, who as military commander has to sacrifice his daughter Iphigenia to secure the success of the Greek fleet.[15]

Despite its false religious assumptions, Agamemnon's case is well chosen to illustrate the basis of dilemmas in moral emotion. Having killed his daughter, Agamemnon is expected to feel bad about his action even in the absence of reasons for doubt about whether it was for the best. His conflict cannot be resolved "without remainder" insofar as it leaves a kind of affective residue that Williams identifies as regret and defends as a rationally appropriate moral reaction. What Williams wants to say on this basis is that the "ought" that Agamemnon has to violate is still in force rather than being canceled or qualified in the way that ethical theories often assume. Agamemnon's conflict therefore resembles a conflict of desires, in which the rejected element does not simply vanish but may reappear in affective form—or sometimes with a different object, as in cases involving obligations to make up for a violation of obligation.

In more general terms, the case of Agamemnon is supposed to exhibit a disanalogy between ought-judgments and beliefs that Williams takes in a later article as undermining moral realism, understood as involving commitment to an independent reality that makes moral judgments true or false.[16] On Williams's account, in contrast to a conflict of desires, a conflict of beliefs is decided by eliminating one of the conflicting elements. The conflict between beliefs means that one of them must be wrong, unlike ought-judgments, which may both remain in force despite a conflict.

This point against moral realism has received critical attention from Philippa Foot and other authors[17] as the upshot of Williams's treatment of dilemmas. But dilemmas surface often in Williams's writings, along with other cases of conflict—in discussions of utilitarianism, "dirty hands" in political life, and incommensurable values—apparently as basic ethical data with diverse implications.[18] In the first instance, they are used just to provide an extreme contrast to cases of conflict in which one of the conflicting oughts is canceled.

On Williams's view, dilemmatic oughts are neither canceled nor overridden. He later distinguishes an intermediate sort of case that also involves a moral remainder, albeit one characterized somewhat differently in terms of feeling. In contrast to dilemmas—which are now set up negatively, as "tragic" cases in which all alternatives are wrong—there are fairly common cases of utilitarian trade-offs in political life in which right action still incurs a "moral cost." Though the agent does not do wrong *simpliciter*, he has to wrong someone—there is a victim of his action, who has a justified complaint—and his act retains an "uncancelled moral disagreeableness," reflected in an appropriate reaction of disquiet or distaste.[19] A deeper form of regret is apparently reserved for dilemmatic cases, though Williams stops short of ascribing guilt to the agent in a dilemma.

Guilt may be thought to be irrational in a case where, through no fault of his own, the agent cannot avoid doing wrong, on the assumption that the reaction can be justified only if one *is* guilty. However, some later essays by logicians do defend guilt, in different ways, as the appropriate reaction to dilemmas. Bas van Fraassen takes appropriate feelings of guilt to depend on actual or objective guilt, but he holds that guilt for the unavoidable is shown to be coherent in objective terms by the doctrine of original sin; Ruth Marcus expresses doubts about this but notes that the object of guilt in a dilemma, the particular alternative that is rejected, is not unavoidable in itself. Van Fraassen is one of a number of authors who follow Lemmon in attributing dilemmas to multiple sources or grounds of obligation, extending Lemmon's account with a notion of incommensurable values or reasons, whereas Marcus defends the possibility of single-principle conflicts at least for deontological conceptions of the right. Van Fraassen takes dilemmas to call into question presuppositions of standard deontic logic, seen as including an assumption linking "ought" to what is for the best.[20]

A more detailed account in terms of incommensurability is provided by Nagel in a discussion identifying five fundamental types of value—and ultimately the clash between agent- and outcome-centered standpoints of evaluation—as sources of dilemma.[21] On Nagel's view, dilemmas undermine the unifiability of ethics conceived as the search for general principles, as opposed to a "fragmentary" approach to the subject relying on the exercise of judgment in particular cases.

However, dilemmas attributable to multiple standpoints, or grounds of obligation or social roles, could be handled by keying oughts to these different sources, as in Hector-Neri Castañeda's alternative system of deontic logic with its subscripted version of O.[22] So it is important that Nagel briefly allows for conflicts *within* his several categories[23] and hence between unqualified (or at any rate, similarly qualified) ought-judgments. The common reaction that dilemmas as thus understood would make ethics in some way incoherent or inconsistent gets its first sustained argument in an article by Terrance McConnell.[24] McConnell cites John Rawls along with Castañeda and David Lyons to illustrate the widespread assumption that an adequate moral theory must exclude dilemmas; Marcus adds Donald Davidson to the list of well-known contemporary philosophers who treat conflicting oughts as evidence of a contradiction in the existing moral code.[25] But against these authors Marcus defends the code that yields dilemmas as indeed consistent.

For our purposes, what McConnell picks out as his second sense of ethical inconsistency is what is relevant: On the standard assumption that an obligation to do B entails an obligation to do whatever B requires, dilemmas involve commitment to both OA and O~A. This is to say that Williams's contingent notion of dilemmas yields dilemmas in Lemmon's sense, in which the same act is both required and forbidden—a strange consequence that violates some highly intuitive principles of standard deontic logic, though it may not be logically questionable in itself.

On the other hand, Marcus essentially argues that the general rules that give rise to contingent dilemmas need not be inconsistent even in practical terms, so that ethics conceived as a system of rules is not undermined by the derivation of incompatible directives. She does so by putting forth a definition of consistency for rules that counts as consistent any set of rules that can be obeyed in all circumstances in *some* possible world, even if not in the actual world.[26] Our moral code will not be deficient as a guide to action in the actual world as long as it meets this weaker requirement of consistency, since Marcus takes the code to include a second-order regulative principle enjoining the avoidance of conflict. This is the action required of us in dilemmatic cases, and feelings of guilt are justified by the role they play in motivating it—at any rate in future cases, or before a given dilemma becomes unavoidable. Assuming that violating any obligation incurs at least a small burden of guilt—a need to make explanations and excuses—Marcus extends the account of dilemmas in terms of unerased obligations beyond those cases Williams acknowledges, to include even trivial ought-conflicts. The result would seem to be a view of dilemmas and guilt as pervading the moral life.

In defense of a Kantian approach to ethics, however, Alan Donagan reformulates McConnell's charge of practical inconsistency against proponents of dilemma who reject the principle of agglomeration—including all authors after Lemmon in this overview—by comparing the ultimate moral authority on any such account to Captain Queeg in *The Caine Mutiny*.[27] Captain Queeg was found mentally incompetent, partly on the grounds that he issued conflicting orders. By the same token, morality would be "absurd," even if not inconsistent, if it subjected us to conflicting commands. On Donagan's rationalist assumptions, then, we may reject a moral system as "ill constructed" if its precepts cannot be agglomerated. Donagan sees Marcus as instead modifying "ought"-implies-"can," since she restricts the principle to first-order rules, but as thus interpreted her appeal to the second-order regulative principle that tells us to avoid conflict involves treating morality as an unreachable ideal.[28] Essentially, then, our choice between the two principles, "ought"-implies-"can" and agglomeration, amounts to a choice between the action-guiding function of ethics and its rationality or coherency as a product of human thought.

The bulk of Donagan's argument against dilemmas amounts to an attempt to account for the facts of moral conflict within his rationalist preconceptions.

Like McConnell (following Aquinas), he exempts the evildoer's self-imposed conflicts as no threat to ethical consistency, but he handles other cases either by challenging the validity of one of the conflicting considerations or by denying that the choice between them can be moral. Other authors have added a positive account of the emotional facts of conflict; the best known is Hare's two-level utilitarian explanation in terms of general habits of emotional response instilled in us as the most efficient way of motivating moral behavior under normal circumstances.[29] But the main charge against dilemmas seems to be some version of incoherency of the sort illustrated by Donagan's Captain Queeg case.

There are other, more specialized treatments of dilemma.[30] I have presented only highlights of the debate in order to exhibit the central problem dilemmas seem to raise for moral theory. In the first instance, it is a problem about whether "ought" can play the strong action-guiding role, as a vehicle for expressing moral commands, that appears to be assigned to it by the modern ethics of duty. For the assumption behind the charge of practical incoherency is that conflicting moral judgments cannot make sense if taken at face value as telling the agent what to do, in contrast to their interpretation in the cases Aquinas accepted, as essentially serving to punish an agent for prior wrong.

That the derivation of conflicting commands amounts to a perfectly intelligible foul-up of an ethical system or its fit to the world—one that may not be fully attributable to problems in assessing *value*—seems to be an overlooked alternative. Indeed, as I shall go on to indicate, even Williams fails to leave room for this possibility. Marcus's view makes room for something like it, but declines to acknowledge it as a foul-up. I take it to be based on a view of ethics as a necessarily imperfect human product, but no more incoherent than a hypothetical pinball machine that registers "tilt" under circumstances other than player error. This results in a nasty surprise, as on the view of dilemmas as traps of the devil. On my own account, though, dilemmas are explained by limitations of the mechanism rather than by fiendish intention.

My overview here also omits some of the meatier cases of dilemma: newsworthy cases of "moral blackmail" on the model of the choice between letting hostages be killed and encouraging further terrorism by negotiating for their release, and various other real-life and literary cases such as (in one example) the woman's choice between family duty and duty to self in Ibsen's *A Doll's House*.[31] I focus instead throughout this essay on variants of a few cases dealt with at length in the philosophical literature, plus some rather streamlined additions like the case of Captain Queeg, to illustrate the problem dilemmas seem to pose for action-guiding duty ethics. I shall later argue that it is a soluble problem, if we make a number of important distinctions on the understanding of action-guiding status. At this point, however, I want to identify it *as* a problem and to show how it bears on more general concerns in the history of moral philosophy.

The Problem for Practical "Ought"

Donagan uses the Captain Queeg case against a command-based view of ethics like van Fraassen's. But it is worth noting that a moral legislator responsible for dilemmas need not come out with straightforwardly conflicting commands—to swab and not to swab the deck, say—but only with ought-judgments that imply such commands, given further facts about the world and a strong interpretation of "ought." We would be less likely to question Queeg's sanity or legal competence—more likely to attribute the conflict to change of mind, forgetfulness, and similar normal mental imperfections—if he had issued two contingently conflicting commands, as on Williams's account of dilemmas. The conflict might even be rather obvious: Imagine a harried mother's commands to her children to clean up and (in the same breath) to keep still.

Donagan's analogy seems to mix together different sorts of criticism, then. I want to disentangle one of them, the one corresponding to the charge of incoherency, for discussion in what follows. His statement of the Captain Queeg analogy in terms of commands masks a distinction between irrationality and unreasonableness: If Queeg had simply come out with conflicting requirements—requirements for adequate performance in a certain rank, say (perhaps as criteria for promotion)—the fact that it would be impossible to act on both of them might be seen as canceling the natural interpretation of his statements as commands. Issuing them would still undermine his authority to some extent, since it would show him to be an impossible person to satisfy. But it is another question whether his statements make no sense, as one might want to say of the conflicting commands issued by the mother in my example.

Of course, morality or the moral code might be said to be in a special position, since it is not subject to the mental limitations—of knowledge and memory, of change in perspective over time—that characterize human legislators and judges. Morality presumably means what it says, along with all the consequences of what it says, at any given time. Similarly for God. But Donagan needs the sort of distinction just illustrated in order to make an exception of Aquinas's dilemmas for the evildoer. How would God be cleared of incoherency in his commands at a given time—where that implies a failure to make sense, or irrationality—by the fact that the conflict between them is attributable to the agent's prior moral error? The agent is punished in such cases with unreasonable requirements—or with requirements that would be unreasonable if he were innocent. Imposing them on an innocent person in full-fledged cases of dilemma would presumably support an objection from unfairness, or moral luck, which Donagan and others might see as involving an incoherency in our moral concepts or in the nature and purposes attributed to God as a moral judge. So this more general incoherency rather than incoherency in the conflicting commands themselves seems to be what is in question.

However, what if one thinks of ethics or morality—I shall use the two terms interchangeably—as primarily an instrument of *social* rationality, either manmade or designed with human limitations in mind? Dilemmas might then be explained as side effects of the pursuit of perfectly coherent general purposes with a moral code tailored to reflect these limitations, and we might deny any possibility of appeal beyond them to some more ultimate level of moral truth that would resolve the conflict.[32] With moral luck thus accepted as a fact of ethical life, dilemmas may still be said to undermine the authority of the moral code to some extent by revealing its fallibility as a guide to choice. But it is a further step to the charge that it is incompetent to legislate, on the model of Captain Queeg.

Williams is one author who seems to be eager to make room for moral luck, and in recent writings he attempts to undermine the notion of moral blame; yet even he denies all-things-considered or "conclusive" practical status to the ought that is not acted on in a dilemma.[33] This may surprise some readers; he is usually and naturally interpreted as holding that dilemmas involve action-guiding oughts.[34] I attempt to shed light on this issue in chapter 2. For the moment, however, let us just note that other putative senses of "ought," distinguished for other purposes, might be called into service to capture dilemmas but do not seem to be adequate to capture their problematic aspect. A merely classificatory ought that might be thought of as "critical" or "judgmental"—labeling alternatives to a certain action as wrong but not actually telling the agent what to do—would not seem to capture the sense in which an agent in the grips of a dilemma is motivationally "torn." Moreover, various weaker but still action-guiding senses of "ought" might be distinguished from the strong or imperatival sense that yields commands; these include commendatory or ideal "ought" and a prima facie or other "ought" that records a commitment or other practical reason but without final judgment as to whether it requires action. Just because they are in themselves relatively inert in motivational terms, though, these substitutes for conclusive practical "ought" seem to yield too easy a picture of dilemmatic choice.

This problem is brought out in its sharpest form by what I call "balanced" dilemmas, where the alternatives in question are about equally wrong—and seriously so, enough to justify taking both of the conflicting oughts as conclusive in a moral sense. Of course they cannot both determine action, nor can they coherently be meant to do so in conjunction. This is essentially why Williams denies them conclusive practical status. But his view here seems to cut against the characterization of dilemmas on Nagel's account, say, as cases in which there is "decisive support" for incompatible alternatives: If an ought that seems to express "decisive and sufficient" reasons for action[35] has practical or motivational force at all, how can the rational agent who accepts it forgo action on it in favor of its competitor?

Williams cannot mean to say merely that its competitor in fact wins the day. We shall have to ask what he does (or should) mean by inquiring into some of the notions of deontic comparison that come up in an attempt at explanation. More generally, though, we need to ask whether it is possible to accommodate dilemmas within a coherent motivational picture of the moral "ought." The question that seems to emerge from the debate over the rationality of two competing (and in some sense conclusive) practical oughts can be made out as a new version of an old question in moral philosophy about the motivational force of obligation: How can the reason that "binds" an agent to the performance of an obligatory act be seen as compelling action?

The question for dilemmas is how "compulsive" moral motivation can pull in opposing directions. We might think of motivational force in terms of vectors, which in dilemmatic cases apparently are not canceled or even weakened by opposition. In mathematical terms, they do not combine to yield a single product. To retain their problematic aspect—to defuse dilemmas as a threat to ethics rather than merely debunk or deflate them—we need to retain this difficult motivational property. It is unclear how we can do this, however, on standard accounts of the relation of ethics to psychology.

In motivational terms, standard accounts divide into those that make out the motivational force of moral judgments as dependent on some extracognitive psychological state of the agent, typically desire, and those that insist that belief is sufficient to generate the necessary motivation for action. Accounts of the latter sort might be said to make moral motivation "subject-independent," meaning that its source is independent of the particular mind that holds a moral judgment (rather than minds generally). Subject-independent accounts are given by authors who would be classified in contemporary terminology as "internalist realists" (sometimes "cognitivists"). These authors hold, that is, both that the motivation to act on a moral judgment is implied by its meaning, so that a rational agent who holds it necessarily acts on it (internalism), and that moral judgments describe some subject-independent facts about the world (realism).[36] Accounts of motivational force that make it subject-dependent, on the other hand, are given by authors who deny either one of these positions—holding either that moral motivation is provided by something besides the content of a moral judgment (externalism) or that moral judgments either have no subject-independent content or are false (antirealism).

These terms are not without problems, but on the assumption that Hume falls into the externalist-or-antirealist category insofar as he gives a subject-dependent account of moral motivation, the main positions on motivational force can be illustrated by the contrast between his view and Kant's.[37] Because of its link to obligation, which for Hume is secondary to virtue, the notion of motivational force comes up more explicitly in Kant, though Hume's talk of practical force and of the dependence of morality on sentiment (including desire) can be understood as contrasting with Kant's position. Roughly speaking, then, I want to say that the choice between Humean and Kantian, or subject-dependent and subject-independent, approaches to moral motivation amounts to a choice between making dilemmas implausibly easy on the agent in motivational terms and making them hard to the point of impossibility.

Let us begin with Kant, whose position is more clear-cut. It is summed up in general terms by his claim, shortly before he rules out conflicting obligations, that "in discussing practical laws of reason we do not take [moral] feeling into account, since it does not concern the *ground* of these laws but only the subjective *effect* which they have on our mind."[38] He goes on to give a version of a common objection to emotion-based theories of ethics—what I shall call the charge of "subject-relativity"—in view of the fact that emotional motivation varies from one mind to the next. However, for Kant—and in the general historical tradition of discussion of motivational force, which goes back to natural law theorists—talk of motivation is not limited to subjective causation of the sort the objection questions, but rather refers in the first instance to the determination to act by considerations of reason.[39] The point for our purposes is that motivational force in this sense, if built into the meaning of a moral judgment, would indeed seem to rule out belief in conflicting judgments on the part of an agent who is fully rational. To hold both of two ought-judgments known to be in conflict would be to attempt to act on both of them and hence to attempt to do what one knew to be impossible.

At any rate, this holds for "conclusive" ought-judgments, on an all-or-nothing interpretation of their motivational force. But on Kantian cognitivist assumptions, the connection between belief in and action on a given ought-judgment would not seem to allow for any independent variation in degree. So a less than firm tendency to act, on the part of a rational agent (rational in a sense that rules out weakness of will), would have to be explained in terms of some similarly qualified belief—not the sort of conclusive or "all-things-considered" judgment we have in a full-blown dilemma.

Do dilemmas set up in terms of practical "ought" fare any better on a Humean or other subject-dependent approach? Here we have a wider range of possibilities to consider, but if we limit ourselves for the moment to standard forms of subject-dependence, it is hard to see how they can yield an adequate motivational picture of dilemmas. What is in question, let us assume, is the strength of an agent's desires to act on each of the oughts in conflict. Subject-dependent views divide, though, over the question whether this connection to desire is in some sense given in the content of an ought-judgment. At this point, let us assume that it is, in line with the standard reading of Hume as an internalist antirealist. Now, if an agent were fully attuned in these terms to both sides of a conflict, the problem just outlined for subject-independent views would seem to apply here too. So instead we need to assume that the agent's motivation to act on one of the oughts in conflict is weak enough to permit action on the other. In that case, on our current understanding of the content of an ought-judgment, at least one of the judgments in question would itself be weakened accordingly to a prima facie ought-judgment, and we would lose the sense of "all-things-considered" conflict that accounts for the motivational difficulty of dilemmas.

This is to say that dilemmas become too unproblematic on a standard sort of Humean approach. They apparently are assimilated to cases of prima facie ought-conflict. But the resultant picture of choice in a dilemma seems in a certain sense to be too easy: It is as if Agamemnon or the agent in my balanced assassination case in section 1 had simply to weigh up pros and cons and decide, flipping a coin or the like to break any ties, with various compensatory acts and feelings seen as called for by the act thus chosen but with any opposing *motives* under the circumstances canceled out. The agent ought to feel something like horror at the choice, perhaps; but this and similar moral reactions on the standard picture seem to be felt more or less on the side, not as part of his current motivation to take action but rather as contemplative responses to action on the model of an aesthetic reaction.

In fact, I shall go on to suggest ways of modifying this picture in defense of a roughly Humean approach, though one whose content I shall understand as subject-independent, in a sense sufficient to answer the charge of subject-relativity. At this point, however, I want to blur over some distinctions I make later, to set up the problem my argument is meant to address. In short, the standard approaches available in the literature to handle moral dilemmas face us with a metaethical dilemma: They make dilemmas either too problematic, in the sense of being practically difficult to the point of impossibility, or too unproblematic: too easy on the agent in motivational terms to capture the difficulty of dilemmatic choice.

The second horn of this metaethical dilemma covers several distinguishable sorts of inadequacies in accounts of dilemma. As a further instance of it, suppose we now try the other Humean view I allowed for and think of subject-dependent motivational force as extrinsic to the meaning of an ought-judgment. This amounts in contemporary terms to a shift from internalism to externalism. But it would seem to attribute to the agent in a dilemma the kind of motivational detachment from a moral judgment that in extreme form amounts to motivational "amoralism" (sometimes called *accidie*)—the lack of any inclination to do what one believes to be required—here explained just by the impossibility of satisfying all requirements. On the resulting account, dilemmatic oughts could both be recognized as all-things-considered, but we would have to deny that they could both be practical—meant to guide action, that is to say, as used by the agent who *ex hypothesi* holds both of them.

The agent might still feel morally torn between alternatives, but the point is that this motivational effect would no longer be attributable to the judgments he applies to the case. It seems to be an accidental effect, dependent on what a particular agent happens to feel, and hence to be vulnerable to the charge of subject-relativity. Even if we grant that a normal agent will feel pulled in both directions in the situation of dilemmatic choice—or in Humean terms that it is part of human nature to feel that way—we cannot conclude that such feelings are appropriate to the situation or in some way called for by it.[40] This version of the Humean account, then, seems not to have the resources to represent the authoritative status of moral claims, as imposing requirements upon minds rather than merely allowing for whatever desires minds happen to have.[41] So again (but in another sense) dilemmas seem to be made too easy.

What if we respond to these difficulties in the obvious way, by rejecting the possibility of dilemmas? In fact, I think that problems similar to those just noted can be seen to arise in another form for an attempt to capture the psychological phenomena of ought-conflict without recognizing dilemmas. Consider Hare's attempt to explain the agent's reactions in cases of conflict as appropriate to more normal sorts of cases, cases covered by the simple rules we learn as children and generally find adequate to the moral life, though we also can appeal beyond them to utilitarian considerations where they conflict. In the rare situation of conflict on Hare's account, guilt, remorse, and similar moral reactions to wrong would actually be inappropriate in representational terms—one of the agent's options would not really be wrong—but the feelings would still be valuable as signs of a good moral upbringing.[42] Indeed, some form of moral distress at what he has to do seems to be required of the agent in a dilemma if we are to think well of him.

That last claim may seem to be borne out by Aeschylus' treatment of Agamemnon, for instance.[43] In general, Hare's account of the feelings expected of a moral agent in many ways resembles my own intended account in this essay, but his metaethical presuppositions yield a different view of conflict—a view I take to be inadequate in the end to capture even the subjective aspect of dilemmas across the board. To see this, let us first ask how the emotional requirements Hare would impose on the agent in a case of conflict are supposed to fit into his utilitarianism. Hare's discussion of moral education suggests a justification of emotion as a precondition of personal virtue, but his overall view is put forth as a two-level version of act-utilitarianism. Emotions would seem to come out, in that case, as required only in light of the generally good effects of inculcating virtue. But it does not seem obvious that this approach would yield a requirement of emotion in all cases of putative dilemma—or specifically a requirement to feel guilt or some similar negative self-directed emotion of the sort that the relevant cases assume.

We would not be satisfied, that is, by an Agamemnon who reacted simply with horror or some other form of anxiety at his action viewed externally, without evaluative focus on his own role in it as agent. We seem to demand the negative self-focus of guilt and related emotions—at a minimum, Williams's "agent-regret"—in response to a seriously wrong act.[44] But it is unclear whether we can always justify this in utilitarian terms, in part just because the situation of dilemma is so rare. A reasonable set of utilitarian rules prescribing moral feelings would presumably make exceptions for cases that can be seen not to support the usual role of feeling as a goad to moral behavior. But there might have been no reason to think that Agamemnon or anyone affected by his actions would be likely to suffer specifically as a result of his failure to feel guilt—enough so, at any rate, to justify the unpleasantness of that emotion as something required above and beyond any public atonement he might offer.

The most Hare's account can provide, it seems, in the way of a requirement to feel guilty in such cases is another simple rule on the level of those that are superseded by act-utilitarian calculations in cases of dilemma. The requirement to feel would itself be superseded, then, in the event of conflict—as might well occur in a case like Agamemnon's, where guilt feelings would be likely to undermine the performance of act-utilitarian obligations. Moreover, these remarks apply not just to agents like Agamemnon who happen not to feel what is generally required of agents who have acted similarly but also to some agents who do meet the normal expectations. It is sometimes possible, that is, to talk oneself out of feeling guilty in cases where the emotion is understood to be just an unfortunate side effect of oversimplified rules learned in childhood but later refined so as not to apply. In such cases, part of what one does to get rid of the feeling is to point to the evidence for its inappropriateness—where that means its failure to represent accurately the particular situation at hand. On the sort of view Hare recommends, we apparently lose the sense that guilt or the like is a correct response to the agent's situation in the sense that implies accurate representation of it—what I call rational (as distinct from moral or social) appropriateness.[45] So where the moral requirement to feel is superseded by act-utilitarian considerations, an agent ought simply to forgo guilt if he can manage it.

In my own argument I assume that the rational appropriateness of guilt is in question unless otherwise noted. I shall later have much more to say about the emotional requirements of cases like Agamemnon's, which might be thought of as yielding a subjective notion of dilemmas. Subjectively speaking, dilemmas involve the appropriateness of guilt for all alternatives, taking guilt broadly at this point to include remorse and similar reactions to an act thought of as wrong, though I later make some more detailed distinctions. Apart from this subjective sense, however, I do not intend to argue here for the existence of dilemmas. Instead, my central question is whether dilemmas as cases of unavoidable wrong threaten the coherency of ethics. To address that question, I shall often assume in what follows that dilemmas in this objective sense exist, but the reader is free to conditionalize my argument, taking it as an indication of the problems to which acceptance of dilemmas would give rise.

In the first instance, then, my aim here is to escape the metaethical dilemma set up in this section by showing how a reasonably authoritative conception of ethics can coherently allow for dilemmas, without making them motivationally flaccid or in some other way implausibly undemanding. I shall not attempt to convert the reader to a particular view on the question of dilemmas but just to provide a sensible rationale for such a view. This is also my aim with respect to the broader questions, such as that of emotional appropriateness, that come up in connection with my treatment of dilemmas. Since these broader questions are important to my argument—they eventually will displace dilemmas, in fact, as its central focus—they require separate discussion.

2. Motivating Moral "Ought"

The general problem of motivational force was posed in contemporary terms by Elizabeth Anscombe in an argument for the abandonment of the specifically moral sense of "ought" in modern duty ethics.[46] Anscombe favored an interpretation derived from the Aristotelian ethics of virtue, and a contemporary move back to Aristotle's approach, with evaluations of persons and personal traits replacing act-requirements as the primary ethical judgments, now seems to be in full swing.[47] The problem just posed for dilemmas as practical conflicts fits into this trend in the literature to the extent that it cuts against a strong action-guiding sense of "ought." Anscombe's argument calls into question the moral sense of "ought" on the grounds that it is at this point merely "emphatic": It rests on a mere appearance of force left over from the earlier use of the word on natural law accounts in connection with divine judgment.[48] Without the view of ethics as based on laws promulgated by God, so that motivational force could be understood concretely in terms of a threat of God's displeasure or of punishment, there is nothing to support the heavy stress laid on "ought" as a distinctively moral notion.

Moral dilemmas can now be seen as providing a logically vivid illustration of the impossible demands on the moral "ought" according to this view of modern ethics. The problem they raise for the practical coherency of ethics—taken as something over and above problems of moral luck—results from a secular Kantian conception of obligation as moral necessity. A strong interpretation of "ought" in terms of divine punishment, though it would of course raise questions about God's justice, might in principle be handled by hesitating to attribute to God our notion of individual responsibility. On the other hand, a weaker secular interpretation as merely judgmental or at any rate not conclusively practical—as referring simply to a commitment, say, or to liability to social condemnation—would make dilemmas in a sense too easy, if my preceding argument is correct. It is emphatic "ought" that is in question here, too, but in its action-guiding role, as providing the motivational force that Anscombe dismisses as "purely psychological" (p. 41), now that the term itself has been drained of content.

The extended argument that follows amounts to a defense of "ought" against the motivational problem raised by dilemmas along with some other cases in metaethical dispute. But rather than attempting to answer Anscombe's challenge by supplying the missing content of "ought," I shall suggest a two-component view of moral meaning that separates the question of the meaning of a given judgment from the question of its motivational force. My argument on motivational force will allow for different interpretations of the content of "ought" rather than pinning it down precisely, though I shall also give an indication of my own favored view if only to exhibit its departure from Anscombe on the connection of "ought" to natural law.

Anscombe's claim that the motivational force of "ought" is undermined by the abandonment of belief in natural law, the belief supporting its original interpretation, assumes that motivational force is determined by meaning. This amounts to a version of internalism. Internalism seems to have emerged, in fact, during the seventeenth- and eighteenth-century transformations of the natural law approach within British moral philosophy. Motivational force was initially understood as something like a causally effective version of what Philippa Foot calls "reason-giving" force.[49] A moral judgment has reason-giving force for a certain agent if it supplies her with a reason for doing what it prescribes—a reason that has to make sense in light of her interests and desires, though she need not therefore be motivated by them to act on it. On natural law accounts, for instance, perhaps we could say that the threat of divine punishment would count as a reason for obeying the law, even though some basically rational agents with insufficient fear of divine punishment might not be motivated to do so, instead choosing to incur the punishment. This allows that a rational agent's desires and other motivating states such as emotions may fail to reflect her interests—in other words, that there may be a gap between accepting an ought-judgment and being motivated to act on it.

However, the gap is closed by a different way of understanding motivational force that seems to have become standard in Anglo-American moral philosophy by the time we get to the contemporary debate over internalism versus externalism. The shift is presupposed by eighteenth-century moral philosophy, especially "moral sense" theories, which began to focus on emotion as the critical factor in moral motivation, though this was soon overshadowed by an emphasis on its role in moral knowledge.[50] In effect, reason-giving force was made to depend on motivational force rather than the other way around: It was benevolence or conscience or some other internal motive that supplied the agent with a reason for action on a moral judgment. But the reversal made it seem plausible to take holding a moral judgment as implying motivation to act on it.

Hence Anscombe finds "ought" empty of content if it lacks motivational force; on the other hand, she assumes that its force must be more than psychological in order to capture the authority we ascribe to moral judgment. She quickly disposes of Butler, for instance, on the grounds that he does not make room for an immoral conscience.[51] Her argument is essentially a version of the Kantian objection from subject-relativity, but a central purpose of my own argument in what follows is to assign emotion a role in modern duty ethics that escapes reasonable forms of this objection.

I shall approach the problem of motivational force through dilemmas, taking dilemmas as a way of posing the problem in sharp form. My ultimate aim, as I have noted, is not to convert the reader to my own view of dilemmas; rather, I hope to use dilemmas as a way of exhibiting the connections among a number of central issues in metaethics—taking the term broadly to refer to the study of the foundations of ethics.[52] I think we can establish a new angle of view on this subject, away from its previous focus on metaphysical, epistemological, and semantic issues, by assigning a central position to issues in moral psychology, as raised by the question of dilemmas. I shall begin, then, in chapter 2 by considering some fairly narrowly defined questions about dilemmas and moral reasoning in connection with deontic logic, but my concerns will soon branch out from that starting point.

In effect, this essay will have three main topics: dilemmas, guilt, and metaethics —or, more specifically, the role of emotion in the foundations of ethics, which I take to be that of supplying motivational force. My initial focus will be relatively narrow, with dilemmas serving as a way in and guilt as a bridge to my ultimate topic, the role of emotion in ethics. Similarly for authors considered: I shall begin with Williams as my central example since his work covers the various topics I want to bring together, though he often fails to connect them clearly or to go as far as I would like on key issues. On two issues concerning dilemmas—whether they are conflicts between conclusive practical oughts and whether guilt as opposed to some weaker form of regret is appropriate for the ought not acted on—my own position comes closer to some of the other authors discussed in my initial overview, especially Nagel and Marcus.

Once my argument turns to general metaethical issues, as it will fairly quickly on the basis of the opposition Williams sets up between dilemmas and moral realism, I shall discuss some other authors whose overall approaches stand in sharp contrast to Williams's: Philippa Foot and John McDowell. J. L. Mackie's view, which is one of the main contemporary examples of antirealism, provides both a contrast to McDowell (in a contemporary version of the Hume/Kant contrast in the preceding section) and some materials for constructing the sort of two-component realist view that I want to defend here as able to handle dilemmas. I refer to this view as "social artifact realism." It is realist at any rate in a somewhat extended sense that seems to fit current definitions.

The view essentially puts social rationality in the role Anscombe assigns to a divine lawgiver. A moral code or other normative system (for simplicity's sake, I shall mainly speak in terms of a code of rules) is something man-made but subject to constraints dictated by social ends and the nature and functions of society—as if the standard Aristotelian arguments about virtue were modified to apply to groups. Its content is therefore not fixed by the rules a group happens to have—the norm-based alternative that Anscombe at one point considers and rejects—but it is *real* in the way that artifacts are real, though their original existence is of course dependent on minds. It is also imperfect—as a product of human imperfection in general terms, but more specifically because it is subject to limitations in the ordinary human capacity to master rules. For a fundamental social constraint on the code is the requirement of teachability.

The moral code on this account is not unlike what Hare describes as the simpler set of rules that we ordinarily go by, but it is not superseded in moral terms when it yields a conflict. Rather, cases of conflict involve real motivational deadlock, indicating a breakdown of the moral code that my own view will try to explain as a side effect of the mechanism that allows the code to function properly in normal cases. For what makes the rules action-guiding in general is the sort of internal goad to action that is provided by teaching them in conjunction with guilt and similar moral emotions. This motivational role of emotion favors what I call a "perspectival" notion of appropriateness that is weaker than the one Hare takes for granted, since it assesses emotions as warranted relative to a partial subset of the total body of evidence in light of which we would assess a corresponding belief. Thus, guilt may be appropriate as a feeling even where the agent is not objectively at fault all things considered, as we assume in a case of dilemma.

I shall not give a detailed account of the nature and justification of the moral code in what follows, since I want my argument to apply to various different approaches to ethics. Those contemporary approaches I am familiar with all seem to allow for dilemmas at least on something like Hare's "intuitive" level of simple rules—though sometimes with a higher level deus ex machina (whether act-utilitarianism or God himself) brought in to save the day. On a rule-utilitarian view, for instance, the rules that would have the best consequences overall if generally adhered to presumably must be consistent, but they might still come into contingent conflict as a result of some unusual event or in cases where the assumption of general adherence is not satisfied. On a divine command view, we could get similar results by thinking of God as a kind of moral watchmaker whose commands amount to a code of rules meant to serve for all time rather than specific directives, without an option of direct appeal where they conflict. And even on a Kantian view, applying the categorical imperative to a set of maxims simple enough to yield teachable rules might also be held to generate conflicts.

Such theories need not treat dilemmas as an embarrassment. Rather, dilemmas amount to the sorts of exceptions that can be said to "prove" the moral rules. They exhibit the general mechanism of action-guidance by blocking its usual direct effects, displaying a residue of guilt or some similar negative moral emotion that usually functions in anticipatory form, before action, to ensure compliance with the rules. This emotion is what yields the appearance of binding force in cases where compliance is reluctant.

The discussion of guilt, then, will connect my initial topic, moral dilemmas, with the general issue I expect it to illuminate: the role of emotion in moral motivation. Through most of this argument, I understand "guilt" rather broadly, using the term at the outset to cover various distinguishable emotions such as shame and remorse, and even later for the most part ignoring its religious and psychoanalytic associations. No doubt in reaction to one or both of the latter, the very idea of guilt is an object of amusement or aversion in some quarters, and very few mainstream moral philosophers make mention of it. But I think there is something to be said in defense of the emotion—or, rather, the emotional mechanism. For guilt on the view I shall defend here, even guilt in the narrow sense, is not really a single emotion but a tendency to take on various different identificatory emotions involving a negative self-evaluation.

Within philosophy, this view gets support from Jonathan Edwards's explanation of conscience in his 1755 treatise on ethics, and it is also borne out by recent psychological studies of guilt.[53] In fact, the term "guilt" seems not to have been used as an emotion term at all until the late sixteenth century—and then only in error, as a substitute for "sense of guilt," with "guilt" on its accepted use taken as referring to an objective state of affairs.[54] The religious notion, at least in the first instance, involves an extraemotional state of the self—a variant of primitive ideas of "tainting," analogous to a disease that will spread unless one takes steps to prevent it, as spelled out for guilt by rules of ritual atonement.[55] Atonement as originally conceived might or might not involve a notion of some feeling one ought to have—fear of God's wrath, say, or contrition. But the gradual internalization of religious focus associated particularly with the period of the Reformation seems to have led to the idea of a general feeling or sense of guilt as the appropriate response to wrongdoing.[56] Later I attempt to show how the emotional mechanism I equate with (subjective) guilt preserves some of these historical associations.

I shall also have to say something about the pitfalls of the emotion, and at least by implication those of emotional response generally, since guilt in some of its manifestations seems to represent an extreme case of emotional uncontrol. The widespread view of guilt as a personally destructive psychological force—a mechanism of social control that essentially inflicts damage on the individual—is due to Freud's influence and among philosophers may be traced back to Nietzsche.[57] Even within the psychoanalytic literature, however, one can find the defense of a psychologically beneficial form of guilt in the work of Melanie Klein.[58] My own defense of the emotion in common sense terms will focus on the social bases that give it value as a moral motivator.

My interpretation of guilt as an identificatory mechanism will allow for its attribution beyond Judeo-Christian religious culture and its historical heirs to cultures that lack our emphasis on guilt, sometimes thought of by anthropologists following Ruth Benedict as "shame-cultures."[59] I shall eventually argue that guilt has some advantages over shame and other related emotions as a source of moral motivation. To some extent, however, the central role I assign to guilt is an accidental function of my focus on the problem of moral dilemmas. My detailed account of its role in moral motivation is intended as exemplary—a way into the general question of the role of emotion in ethics. It is a moral (or specifically deontic) emotion par excellence, but it shares with other emotions on my account a motivational function that stands in contrast to the perceptual analogy applied to emotions on other emotion-based but nondismissive accounts of ethics. That is, Hume and other moral "sentimentalists" seem to see moral emotions as recording evaluative information (or possibly misinformation) about the world. The standard contrasting account—besides emotivism and similar dismissive accounts—is Mill's utilitarian treatment of "internal sanctions," which assigns emotions a motivational role without effect on the content of moral judgment.[60] I hope in what follows to exhibit a further metaethical option, one that gets in between the horns of the standard alternatives with its focus on the social standpoint of evaluation. I shall do so by digging deeply into the motivational questions raised by dilemmas.

2

Practical Oughts
and Prohibitions

Let us first turn to the problems raised by dilemmas for the logical principles governing ought-judgment. Williams's early article focused attention on the clash between the principle that "ought" implies "can" and the principle of agglomeration—that OA and OB imply O(A & B)—both of which seem intuitively to characterize a strong action-guiding sense of "ought." The same can be said of two other principles of standard deontic logic that later authors have brought into conflict on the assumption that dilemmas exist: the principle that "ought" implies "permissible" and the principle of deontic closure.

The latter principle essentially tells us that anything necessary to fulfill an obligation is itself obligatory; with ~M as the alethic modal operator for possibility, we may symbolize this as: OA and ~M(A & ~B) imply OB.[1] Some such principle along with agglomeration would seem to be needed to support the derivation of one ought-statement from another and hence the systematic project of deontic logic. On the other hand, the two principles governing the implications of the term "ought" seem to be needed to support a notion of prescriptive "ought," taken as an ought that is both practical and positive, or meant to tell an agent what to do. We seem to be forced to choose, then, between the systematic aims of deontic logic and its relevance to action-guiding ethics.

In fact, I think that something like this will turn out to be true. However, we need not deal here in full detail with the problems raised by the two pairs of principles within deontic logic. Instead, let us look at some central deontic notions and principles in application to moral reasoning, with deontic logic understood as a failed attempt at systematization whose grounds for failure may be illuminating. I shall occasionally use the resources of deontic logic to symbolize the principles and other assumptions under scrutiny; but the main thing I expect my argument on this subject to reveal is that an attempt to handle dilemmas by working out some alternative deontic system would at best be impossibly complicated.

I shall begin by focusing on the problem posed in chapter 1 for conflicts between practical oughts (section 1). The principle that "ought" implies "can" would seem to be defensible by appeal to the notion of a practical ought as one that is intended to guide action: What would be the point, in short, of trying to

29

guide an agent in a direction he cannot go? Yet Williams's explanation of conclusive practical "ought" apparently makes the notion inapplicable to dilemmas. It has to apply in some form, however, in order to make sense of our reasoning about the fulfillment of conflicting oughts at times before they actually
come into conflict.

My argument involves a closer look at the interpretation of practical "ought"
and related notions, including notions of deontic weight such as "all-things-
considered." In section 2 I raise some more general questions about the picture
of the logical structure of ought-conflict that is presupposed by deontic logic in
common with much of contemporary moral philosophy, as derived from Ross's
account of the balancing of prima facie duties. Among other things, I hope to
bring out a way of assessing the comparative strength of oughts that favors a
negative characterization of dilemmas in terms of prohibitions, or action-guiding
judgments of moral wrong, rather than positive ought-judgments. In short, I
argue that accepting the principle that "ought" implies "permissible" means
taking positive ought-conflicts as merely prima facie—and to that extent granting Williams's point—whereas cases of exhaustive prohibition may still come
out as dilemmatic in the fullest sense.

The defense of negative action-guiding dilemmas is the main result of my
argument in this chapter. In response to the literature on dilemmas, however,
the second half of the chapter turns to somewhat more technical discussion.
For those who prefer to shortcut details this is summed up in a final subsection
beginning on p. 62. My full argument in section 3 focuses on the changes in
deontic logic and ultimately in our picture of moral reasoning that would be
needed to accommodate dilemmas on my account. To let the operator O cover
our ordinary ought-judgments, with "ought" taken in a strong action-guiding
sense, I retain the two ought-implication principles "ought"-implies-"can" and
"ought"-implies-"permissible." In light of my treatment of dilemmas, the latter
principle is limited to positive ought-judgments, so closure can also be retained
with appropriate limitations. On the other hand, I attempt to show how we
might indeed find grounds for dropping the other ought-derivation principle,
agglomeration, and what results the change would have for the logical structure of ethics. Broadly speaking, on the view that will emerge here, ethics comes
out as fragmented—as Nagel puts it in his treatment of dilemmas in terms of
incommensurable values. My own account will involve a specifically deontic
form of fragmentation, a splintering into practical subsystems; but one line of
attack on the coherency of ethics as thus construed will be met by showing the
rationale behind the denial of agglomeration.

1. Practical Oughts in Conflict

In this section I want to defend the practical status of dilemmatic oughts against
some implications of Williams's view.[2] I take it that denying the practical status of dilemmas would leave us without the aspect of motivational conflict that
we need in order to capture what is troubling about them as problems of moral

choice. First I focus on a particular argument that seems to show that practical force has to be attributed to dilemmatic oughts in order to account for the force of some oughts derived from them: oughts prescribing actions needed to prepare to satisfy the first set, or what I shall call "preparatory" oughts. At any rate, this conclusion follows from a natural understanding of practical force in terms of meaning. I go on to defend that interpretation as an alternative to taking practical force as a function of the speaker's intentions. I then begin to respond to the various reasons my discussion brings to light for denying "all-things-considered" status to conflicting practical oughts.

Throughout this argument, I assume that there are or at any rate can be genuine dilemmas—meaning (for purposes of the present discussion) dilemmas of the "balanced" variety in which the two oughts in conflict are of roughly equal weight. I also assume that the cases under consideration involve "time-bound" oughts, in contrast to the timeless obligations sometimes taken for granted in discussions of deontic logic.[3] This means essentially that whether a given ought is in force depends on when it is evaluated—a time that need not be the same as the date (implicit or explicit) on its object, or what it tells the agent he ought to do. If yesterday I promised, for instance, to do act A tomorrow, it is already true today that I ought to do A tomorrow. In my central argument in this section I hope to show that these assumptions favor an interpretation of dilemmatic "ought" as practical, in order to make sense of the advance deliberation that fulfilling it may entail.

Deliberation in Dilemmas

Consider the case of dilemma set up by Sartre: The man who must choose between joining the French resistance and staying home to support his dependent mother might very well represent both of his options as things he ought to do. That is, we can imagine him prescribing each of them, as he weighs the relevant considerations. Of course he would not come out with a conjoint ought-statement prescribing both, but we can follow Williams and other authors on dilemmas in allowing for a distinction here by rejecting the principle of agglomeration. However, one might be moved to ask how the agent in Sartre's case could coherently prescribe even each of his options without a change of mind—in the same breath, as it were—given that his combined prescriptions would be unfulfillable.

Should we avoid this problem by representing the oughts in conflict as not really meant to elicit action and in that sense not *practical* oughts? Perhaps we might characterize dilemmas instead in terms of oughts that simply classify various possible acts with respect to moral reasons, telling us that there are decisive moral reasons for each of two exclusive alternatives rather than presuming to tell the agent what to do under the circumstances. However, this would leave out the kind of active motivational conflict that moral reasons seem to generate in typical cases of dilemma. It would make dilemmas too easy: We would lose the sense of the rational agent as practically "torn," or subject to contrary motivational vectors, to the extent that she appreciates the reasons bearing on her choice of action. Instead, the case would be assimilated to one in which an agent could not decide what to do, at any rate on moral grounds—a case in which she was *intellectually* torn, though not because of any defect in her practical reasoning.

We would also seem to lack the resources to capture an agent's earlier reasoning in cases of dilemma. That is, we sometimes have to derive practical directives from dilemmatic ought-statements before they come into conflict—for instance, where their fulfillment requires advance preparation. If the oughts in a dilemmatic pair were not practical, however, it is unclear how they could support the derivation of practical preparatory oughts. An attempt to take the dilemmatic oughts as practical only at an earlier time when they yielded such preparatory oughts without conflict would seem to undermine the very point of practical force by letting it lapse unaccountably before the time the ought-statement in question assigns to action.

This is my argument for dilemmatic practical "ought" in a nutshell; now let me illustrate it with a version of Sartre's case. For the agent to be able to support his mother financially, say, in 1942—taking a simple-minded view of the sort of support that is in question here just for purposes of easy illustration—it might be necessary for him to start saving in 1932. So in 1932 we apparently could derive a claim that he ought to save some money.[4] But then one of the ought-statements that conflict in 1942 would seem to involve a practical ought at least from the standpoint of 1932. Moreover, if we say that its practical force somehow lapses by 1942, that would seem to undermine any practical force ascribed to it earlier. Presumably, the reason for the earlier advice was just to enable the agent to support his mother later, but supporting her in 1942 requires further action at that time. What would be the point in practical terms of giving advice that will just be withdrawn before the time to act on it arrives?

Someone raising objections to this argument might defend the notion of earlier practical force that simply lapses as familiar enough in other cases: What about obligations that become unfulfillable before the time of action, say—assuming a tensed version of the principle that "ought" implies "can" as applying to practical "ought"? However, since "can" in the principle implies that fulfillment is possible through the agent's own efforts, I would reply that the obligations in question here are those that the agent essentially *makes* unfulfillable by doing or failing to do something earlier, as opposed to any that lapse because of events he cannot prevent, including actions of other agents. For instance, we might suppose that our agent's obligation to support his mother in 1942 would lapse in practical force before then if he did not save money in 1932, since on our hypothesis the later obligation is fulfillable only with ten years of savings behind him. Here a practical ought lapses by the time assigned to action because the agent fails to act in light of it at earlier times. In the case of dilemma, by contrast, on the assumption of lapsed practical force, it would seem that the agent could follow our advice to the letter until the time for action arrives and still have it withdrawn at the last minute.

My argument can also be extended to meet various more sophisticated objections. I do not want to pause for a full treatment, but it is worth noting that the oughts the argument turns on are not supposed to be relative to the agent's state of knowledge, in particular whether the dilemma can be foreseen. For instance, someone might suggest that we could explain the practical force of the 1932 oughts in terms of some sort of epistemic claim about the 1942 oughts—about their *probable* practical force, say, relative to what is known in 1932—without taking the 1942 oughts to be practical as well. However, it is not clear why the agent actually (and not just probably) ought to prepare to satisfy an ought that is merely probable.

The claim that an ought is practical, though, which I interpreted above as a claim that it is meant to elicit action, naturally suggests that it is offered as advice to a given agent (possibly by the agent himself), so that its force would vary with contextual factors including what is known at the time. However, unless we are concerned with the agent's blameworthiness for failing to act (with subjective rather than objective "ought," in the usual terminology), a practical ought is assumed to hold whether or not the agent knows or has reason to think that it does. Whether an ought is practical or "action-guiding" in this sense depends only on how it is intended, not on whether circumstances are such that the intention is fulfillable, including whether it gets through to the agent, as required for actually guiding his action. In order to cover oughts in the third person we might think of this as an ought that is "suited to" action-guidance.

The problem with dilemmatic oughts, it seems, is with the *speaker's* state of knowledge: The fact that he knows that two of his intentions are not jointly fulfillable would seem to make a rational speaker retract one of them. My present argument is not designed to answer this problem but to show that denying practical force to dilemmatic oughts does not yield a satisfying answer, given the other things we want to say in such cases. My answer to the problem in later chapters will involve assessing the rationality of ethics—of a moral code or system of norms (what actually gives rise to these oughts, even if in the deliberative voice of some individual speaker)—in social terms. What one is assessing, in short, is something general: a set of general social rules or guidelines designed to be teachable on the basis of general emotional response tendencies. This is the source of various specific practical directives that may not always be rational considered in themselves, as utterances of some individual agent or other speaker.

The practical force of the dilemmatic oughts in my example can thus be understood as derivative from the moral system that yields them. To say that they are meant to elicit action, then, is ultimately to say something about the intent of the system—about the role such a system assigns to moral judgments—rather than about the intentions of a particular speaker. I now want at least to allow for some of the larger points I have in mind by defending my interpretation of practical force as something that is not simply supplied by the speaker.

Practical Force and Meaning

My argument above from preparatory "ought" seems to depend on thinking of practical "force" in a linguistic sense, as a function of meaning. This is what makes it puzzling to think of a practical ought as derived from another ought that is *not* practical: Where could it get its practical force except from the ought it is derived from? But if practical or action-guiding force is a function of the speaker's intention, one might want to think of it as contextual: a matter of what the speaker in a given case uses an ought-statement to do, which is a function of what he thinks it *can* do and varies with the circumstances—with whether the ought is fulfillable in itself and whether it has competition as in dilemmas. On this account a speaker supplies practical force to an ought that is itself motivationally inert—so that he might just supply it to a derivative ought like those in my example. It is his "speech act" rather than the meaning of the term that makes "ought" practical.

This account makes sense in light of all the cases in common language that fail to obey the principle that "ought" implies "can." There are other senses of "ought" in play besides the practical—most notably ideal "ought," which is meant to commend some action or state of affairs. In another version of the case from Sartre, for instance, we might want to say that the agent ought to be less attached to his mother, without supposing that he has very much control over his degree of attachment and hence without meaning to get him to change it. However, we need not assume that these different uses of "ought" are distinct enough to count as different senses. We have something more general than a particular speech act on a particular occasion (an utterance) to appeal to—a recognized use (meaning a mode of use rather than an instance) obeying logical principles of its own—as an alternative to descriptive meaning. We may still think of this as a form of "meaning" in the wider sense of general linguistic intent suggested at the end of the preceding subsection.[5] That is, a term may be linked nonaccidentally to the pursuit of certain purposes by a general role or function (even if one among several) in the language, in a way that controls what a given speaker uses it to do rather than simply emerging from his speech act. If we think of the language as already fixed by past usage, we can say that the term is "meant," in the sense of "designed," to fulfill a certain function.

This notion of a general recognized use of a term, which itself has a kind of functional meaning, will accommodate third-person practical oughts as instances of practical "ought" that are not actually intended to fulfill its defining function. What makes them practical, we want to say, is the fact that they are *suited* to action-guidance—capable of eliciting action by virtue of their general role in the language—as would not be the case, for instance, if they were not really about action but rather were meant to commend some personal trait or state of affairs. Of course, it may sometimes be indeterminate whether a given third-person ought is an instance of practical "ought" in this sense. The only test would seem to be a more general sort of appeal to the intentions of a given speaker— what he *would* try to do with it in the presence of the agent, say, at any rate under ideal conditions (where interference would not be resented and so forth)— and speakers' intentions may be indeterminate. But although the notion of a general use of the term is something we extract from such particular instances— much as we extract the notion of a language from a history of individual utterances—it may be set up in normative terms as something independent, a system dictating correct use on a given occasion.

This suggestion leaves it open that an ought may count as practical even if it is not in fact used to fulfill the defining function of practical "ought" on a given occasion, and even if for extrinsic reasons it could not be so used. It is enough that it be part of a systematic use of the term that has that function in general. Whatever the limitations on our ability to tell when this is so, the point gives us a rough argument for counting dilemmatic oughts as practical, just insofar as they are logically linked to clear-cut cases of practical "ought" in the way that makes them part of the same general use of the term.

We also want to say more than this, for the practical force of the preparatory ought in my example seemed to be something imposed on the agent or other speaker, not something he supplied, even by choosing a certain form of words. To withhold it in light of the later dilemma would have been an error, tantamount to plumping for one side of the dilemma in advance. In effect, I argue in chapter 4 that there is a way of taking dilemmatic oughts in most cases as practical in a fuller sense—albeit an indirect sense, in which emotion may be elicited as a substitute for action—even on the level of individual utterance. For the moment, however, let me reinforce my general suggestions on the meaning of practical "ought" with some speculations on the origins of the notion.

One possible source is our talk of the practical "force" of moral terms, used more or less interchangeably with "motivational" force, though it refers to the speaker as opposed to the agent. This usage traces back most notably to Hume's discussion in the *Treatise* of morality as practical, in the sense of being meant to influence action; the notion of "force" that later authors have supplied here seems essentially to combine Hume's talk of influence or impulsion with the linguistic concerns of our own times.[6] The link was effected by noncognitivist accounts of moral meaning in terms of practical function but is by now a feature of the terms in which the metaethical debate is set up, even if one rejects noncognitivism.

What Hume had in mind, however, was a branch of philosophy tied to a certain faculty of the mind: practical as opposed to speculative or theoretical reason. But practical "ought" also has a plausible interpretation in terms of practical reasons that might be thought to reflect this earlier notion rather than the idea of "force" as something a term might have by virtue of its function in the language. Whether a given use of "ought" counts as a practical reason may indeed seem to be something that is settled case by case, depending in the first instance on the intentions of the speaker. Thus, Williams, taking the first-person use as primary, understands a practical "ought" as one that plays a certain role in deliberation; it answers the deliberative question, "What ought I to do?"[7] What is in question here in denying this function to the oughts in a dilemma is whether the agent can reasonably use them to conclude deliberation under certain circumstances—where he cannot act on both—and not whether they are oughts of a sort that play that role in general.

This understanding of practical "ought" makes sense in connection with the attempts of some contemporary authors to define "ought" in terms of reasons.[8] However, the intuitive appeal of the denial of practical "ought" in dilemmas may also depend on the common view of a (conclusive) practical reason as motivationally sufficient—as providing sufficient reason for action in causal terms—assuming rationality.[9] A practical reason on this interpretation requires nothing further to produce action. The interpretation comes ultimately from Aristotle on deliberation, especially his claim that the conclusion of the practical syllogism is an action.[10] We might want to say that an ought that is practical in this sense is one that would produce action in a rational agent if only certain external conditions were met. In that case, if conflicting oughts were both practical, they would produce incompatible actions. Since that result is impossible, it follows that conflicting oughts cannot both be practical.

This argument rests on taking "practical" as meaning something like "sufficient to determine the will to action," with the phrase understood to imply motivational effectiveness in the absence of external barriers. The phrase echoes Kant; and the reading of "practical" seems to be borne out by Kant's identification of practical reason with the will.[11] But I think we can see that it would not survive the shift from Kantian—and originally Aristotelian—talk of a general faculty of practical reason to the contemporary discussion of *a* practical reason and of ought-statements as practical. Of practical reason it might of course be said that it would not be the faculty it is unless it in fact produces action. But it is a further step to make the same claim of a given practical reason. To say that an ought-statement is practical or action-guiding need not be to say that it actually motivates action in a given case but just that it is meant to—in a sense distinct from what its speaker has in mind, as well as from the descriptive meaning of the statement.

"All Things Considered"

The notion of motivational sufficiency suggests an idea of a practical ought as representing the output of deliberation, or an "all-out" judgment, on the model of the unconditional judgment in Davidson's treatment of weakness of will.[12] It may be natural to equate this with the all-things-considered or "all-in" ought-judgment on Williams's account,[13] but Davidson interprets the latter as conditional. It essentially sums up the evidence, or the input of deliberation, on the assumption that all the facts are in. But in between input and output falls the shadow of redeliberation: deliberation from contrary reasons. In cases of dilemma, moreover, redeliberation need not be irrational. Assuming that dilemmas exist, then, a process of deliberation that is rationally sufficient—sufficient to justify action and in that sense complete—need not be motivationally so, even in a rational agent, in the sense that implies causal efficacy.

This conception of practical reasoning can be reconciled with Aristotle's view—even his view of the practical syllogism as entailing action, the source of Davidson's unconditional reading of the "all-out" judgment. John Cooper, for instance, treats the conclusion of practical reasoning as a decision to perform a specific *type* of action, with the practical *syllogism* as a reconstruction of the further perceptual processes needed to produce a particular action.[14] It would thus be possible to reach a conclusion of practical reasoning or deliberation and yet fail to act, as happens in cases of weakness of will but also at least arguably in some cases of moral conflict.[15] The conclusion of deliberation need not be taken as a here-and-now judgment prescribing "this" action but rather as one that narrows things down to an act of a certain kind, with some time left before action for the agent to apply or fail to apply the judgment to what lies before him. In that case, it seems, there will be room for contrary reasons to get a grip.

On my account, it is Kantian necessitarianism—what might be called "rational" necessitarianism, though in application to moral judgments it yields the notion of moral necessity—that stands in the way of making sense of dilemmas. In the present connection, Kantian talk of the will or practical reason as "determining" action is often used without question even by opponents of Kantian ethics. I shall have more to say later on this general issue, but here I want to focus on the notion of an "all-things-considered" practical ought. In response to the argument just outlined, one might want to say that the claim that deliberation yields an all-things-considered conclusion implies a kind of rational completeness that rules out conflicting conclusions; it amounts to a claim that there are no further reasons to take into account. So deliberation in a case of dilemma may fail to yield an all-things-considered conclusion, but it cannot yield two such conclusions.

What happens, then, in a case like Sartre's? One might be tempted to handle the case by taking even an arbitrary resolution of the conflict to turn on something like a choice of "projects"[16]—an implicitly general act of self-legislation with implications for the agent's future choices—that could be represented as a further step in practical reasoning. If the agent chooses to stay with his mother, say, he will effectively be committing himself to a future mode of life containing further choices in harmony with that one. He will be ruling out options such as quitting his job the following year to pursue his goals as an artist. It is important, however, that this sort of deliberative conclusion would be limited to the first person, with the implication that others could not prescribe for the agent the choice he is entitled to make for himself in the situation of dilemma.[17]

Still, there seem to be cases unlike Sartre's case whose resolution does not or should not involve a decision of principle, even an arbitrary decision with implications for the future. Consider the case of dilemma in the novel *Sophie's Choice*, where Sophie is forced by a concentration camp guard to choose one of her children, lest both be taken to the gas chamber.[18] Even if, morally speaking, Sophie must choose one child to save, but supposing that the choice of her son over her daughter cannot really be justified by appeal to some relevant distinguishing feature of the sort she in fact relies on, the choice she makes should not be taken as constraining future choices. She is not henceforth committed to action consistent with it such as some sort of special attention to male children—or for that matter, to action with the opposite tendency, as if to compensate.

The point is that not every decision to act, and hence not every practical resolution of a dilemma, involves appeal to an ought-judgment. Thus, Williams allows for an alternative version of the deliberative question, as "What *am* I to do?",[19] which would seem to apply to decisions bearing on only one case. With the deliberative question framed in terms of "ought," though, so that the conclusion of deliberation is supposed to be an ought-judgment—what we might think of as a "principled" rather than an arbitrary answer to the deliberative question—why should we not say that Sophie's deliberation terminates in a dilemma?

The denial that dilemmatic ought-statements can both hold all-things-considered is a standard response from opponents of dilemma to cases like Sophie's. What they would say is that the conflicting ought-judgments at issue in the case—one prescribing that she save her daughter and the other that she save her son—are not final judgments but merely prima facie; so the case may be assimilated to Ross's cases of prima facie duties. The only duty that Sophie has "all things considered" is the disjunctive duty to save *either* her daughter or her son, for it is of overriding importance that she save one of them, and under the circumstances she cannot save both.

It is odd to find Williams in agreement on this point with the opponents of dilemma, even if only with reference to practical oughts. In application to cases of the sort I call "weighted," on the model of Agamemnon's case, Williams wants to say that neither ought in conflict is overridden: Though all things considered it may be *better* to fulfill one of them, its fulfillment "does not adequately meet the claims involved in the conflict,"[20] so the other ought remains in force. In balanced cases like Sophie's, then, where neither alternative is better, we would seem to have all the more reason to say that the two oughts in conflict are neither overriding nor overridden.[21]

Williams briefly suggests a reason for denying that they are in force all things considered when he notes that "the process of deliberation . . . involves narrowing down, by rejection, the answers to 'What ought I to do?'"[22] On this account, an all-things-considered answer would evidently be an answer based on ruling out all other answers—all other alternatives to action, that is—so of course there can be only one. In a case of balanced dilemma, the only candidate for this status is the disjunctive ought that prescribes fulfilling one or the other of the two oughts in conflict.

However, I think we should look again at this apparently trivial point. There is another way of making out an all-things-considered answer—namely, as one based on ruling out all other answers *that can be ruled out*. If the evidence in a given case does not support a unique answer, then *two* answers to the deliberative question may be said to hold all things considered. In light of all the evidence, that is—the set of "principled" appeals available to justify an ought-judgment—we seem to have sufficient reason for concluding both that Sophie ought to save her daughter and that she ought to save her son.

Both pieces of action-guidance are independently warranted, in short—a fact that would not be captured if we stopped at the judgment that Sophie ought to save one child or the other. Williams's explanation of why neither of the conflicting oughts in weighted cases counts as overriding also reveals the inadequacy of this stronger disjunctive ought. Presumably, each child has an independent claim on its mother to be saved—not just a claim for fair consideration in the choice of one to save—that the disjunctive ought fails to answer. Of course the disjunctive ought may still be said to be in force "all things considered," but it would be question-begging to assume that it is in competition with the conflicting oughts for that status. So we have no real justification for letting it displace them as deliberative conclusions. This also holds for an ought resulting from an arbitrary decision procedure that might be used to satisfy the disjunctive ought: the outcome of a coin-flip, say.

What I think we ultimately need is another look at notions of deontic weight. I shall attempt this in the next section, but at this point we can already see at least in rough outline how all-things-considered status may apply to each of two conflicting practical ought-judgments. First, we need to recognize that even reasons already acknowledged as bearing on a given case may be reconsidered from another evaluative standpoint. There can be different ways of assessing reasons, that is, both of which take in *all* the reasons, at least as background considerations, if we allow for "gestalt shifts" determining which reasons stand out against the overall background. The all-things-considered evaluation of action need not be governed by a single standard of what is "for the best," on the model that Williams applies to Agamemnon's case,[23] but can also appeal to various independent standards, as Williams and other proponents of dilemma recognize.

Second, we should note that the "core" meaning of an ought-judgment involves a *negative* evaluation—a judgment that all alternatives to action are ruled out—so that deliberation involves narrowing down one's options in a more fundamental sense than Williams indicates. It does not just involve rejecting answers to the question "What ought I to do?"; rather, an answer to this question itself rests on rejecting the agent's other options. If there can be two such answers, then, that together would rule out all the agent's options, we would have a case in which the same total body of reasons, assessed according to two different standards, yields conflicting negative all-things-considered ought-judgments.

Let us return to Sartre's case for a simple example that allows for the plausibility of an appeal to reasons. On an account that denies practical status to the oughts in a dilemma, what the agent in such a case is doing is considering only a limited subset of the reasons bearing on his action as he frames his two conclusions: "I've got to join the resistance," say, and "I can't leave Mother." However, one could just as easily represent the same chain of reasoning as involving an evaluative "gestalt shift" in his view of the full set of reasons bearing on the case. That is, instead of reaching different conclusions on the basis of a limited set of reasons about whether it would be better to join the resistance or to support his mother, the agent might be seen as concluding that a failure to do either would be *bad enough*.

It would be bad enough to count as morally unthinkable, let us say, for a negative version of the "satisficing" account of moral deliberation that has been suggested by recent authors on utilitarianism and related subjects.[24] The case of course is one in which the agent has to decide in practical terms to *do* the unthinkable; but this decision need not rest on the sorts of reasons whose conclusion can be translated into a third-person ought-judgment. A general principle of action of the sort that in some extramoral sense resolves the dilemma would be limited to the first person in the way noted earlier and may sometimes involve a step beyond deliberation in terms of "ought."

This negative model of deliberation in dilemmas will let us see the agent as motivationally torn rather than simply left up in the air, as we might expect if deliberation failed to terminate. However, it is important that "ought" in standard deontic logic also has positive implications insofar as it is assumed to imply "permissible."[25] In fact, this seems to me to reflect the most common use of "ought" in everyday speech and to be tied to the prescriptive function often assigned to the term. Examples like those just given for Sartre's case—"I've got to join the resistance" and "I can't leave Mother"—suggest that the point does not hold for "must," though "must" is sometimes thought of as a stronger form of the same concept.[26] At any rate, with "ought" understood as prescriptive in this sense, it would indeed seem to be impossible for practical reasoning to generate conflicting ought-judgments as conclusions.

This is one of those points that are obvious once seen, and it may explain the plausibility of the rejection of practical "ought" in dilemmas. It is the combination embodied in the meaning of prescriptive "ought" of a positive claim that its object is permissible with the negative "core" claim that everything else is impermissible that disallows conflict. In intuitive terms: To say that an all-things-considered review of the reasons rules out everything is just to say that nothing is permissible. But in that case, the requirements of prescriptive "ought" will not be met.

So it is for prescriptive "ought," not just practical "ought"—for "ought" that is assumed to be positive in its practical role, to the extent that it points the agent *toward* some action—that Williams's denial of practical "ought" in dilemmas seems to be defensible. In that case, however, in order to capture the motivational conflict involved in dilemmas—to make them out as involving more than a conflict between prima facie ought-judgments—we can move to a negative characterization of them in terms of prohibitions, or action-guiding judgments of moral wrong.

Williams himself seems in later writings to prefer a negative characterization.[27] Taking the distinction to have the implications for practical "ought" that my argument here suggests means violating some other assumptions of standard deontic logic, in the first instance that "forbidden" implies the permissibility of some alternative to action. But those assumptions essentially just beg the question of dilemmas, presumably on grounds of systematic simplicity. I examine these deontic assumptions in more detail later in this chapter, but we can see the significance of my positive/negative distinction in nontechnical terms at this point in relation to Williams's deliberative question "What ought I to do?" In one sense, indeed, this question would not be answered adequately by a prohibition—it would be raised again, just as it would be if answered with two conflicting positive oughts—unless it is understood in relation to a particular act, so that the context supplies a positive ought-judgment. In that case "You ought not to do A" will amount to advice to do B, where A and B exhaust the field of alternatives. But this implication of positive practical force trades on our ordinary assumption that *some* act of those open to the agent is permissible, which of course is just what dilemmas call into question.

2. Deontic Strength and Value

The attempt to confine moral conflict to conflict between prima facie ought-judgments harks back to Ross's theory. Despite many authors' objections to the term "prima facie" and Ross's own qualms about his use of it as an adjective modifying "duty," the Latin term seems irreplaceably handy for making an easy switch to adverbial status in application to "ought" and related expressions. We can speak of an ought or an ought-judgment as merely prima facie— or within one, of what its agent ought prima facie to do. The term is also familiar from its use in law with reference to partial evidence. Ross at one point gives "parti-resultant" as a more informative substitute for it.[28] We apply it on the assumption that the reasons or evidence bearing on an ought-judgment can be broken down into distinguishable grounds, pro and con, so that a judgment based on only some of them can be said to result from a partial subset of the total body of evidence.

Although Ross himself contrasted prima facie with actual or absolute duties, in the contemporary literature the term seems to have two contraries, used more or less interchangeably in application to oughts that result from a weighing of all relevant evidence: "overriding" and "all-things-considered." These terms of deontic weight or strength are equivalent, however, only on the assumption that there are no full-fledged action-guiding dilemmas. In this section I show how the underlying notions come apart and examine the consequences of prising them apart for the resolution of dilemmas.

Contemporary accounts of the meaning of "ought" suggest that many of the nondilemmatic cases for which "ought" has more or less become canonical in moral philosophy are really more appropriately described by "must."[29] But my discussion here of deontic dominance, as we might call the property of an ought that wins the weighing process, will also yield a more complicated picture of this stronger form of "ought." In application to an ought of normal strength, my discussion of dominance will bring out reasons for the differential treatment of positive and negative dilemmas that began to emerge in the last section. I then consider some questions about the resolvability of dilemmas conceived in positive or negative terms. By singling out negative dilemmas as irresolvable in a stronger sense, I shall be defending a conception of dilemmas that fits their use in logic and mathematics in addition to the everyday picture of them as practical choice-conflicts. Dilemmatic reasoning involves showing that all alternatives have contradictory or otherwise unacceptable consequences. Similarly, as a moral concept the notion has its clearest application to cases in which all alternatives count as wrong.

Forms of Dominance

The difference between all-things-considered and overriding ought-judgments can be brought out most sharply by way of a look at their application to judgments of permission. The operator P (for "it is permissible that") is taken as primitive in one approach to standard deontic logic, with O defined in terms of it as denying the permissibility of the negation of the object of obligation. An axiom of the standard system yields the principle that "ought" implies "permissible," so that "ought" is doubly linked to permissibility: negatively, since $Op = \sim P\bar{p}$, and positively, since Op implies Pp. However, a positive judgment of permission can be thought of as holding all things considered but not as overriding: It just makes no sense to say that something is overridingly permissible.

The reason for this seems to be that two different kinds of deontic weight or dominance are assessed by the two notions. For "all-things-considered" the relevant sort of weight is at least partly evidential: the weight of the evidence or reasons for holding the deontic judgment in question considered against the background of the total body of evidence.[30] This applies readily enough to a positive judgment of permissibility, if only by negating its application to the negative judgment of impermissibility. The positive judgment may be said to hold "all things considered" as long as the negative judgment does not.

By contrast, for a judgment of overridingness the relevant sort of weight is specifically practical, since it measures something like the importance of acting on the deontic judgment in question. This may be thought of as the practical "strength" of a requirement or prohibition. However, it does not apply to a permission, as a judgment that simply allows some action. An action and the alternatives to it may both be permitted, and there is no inference from a denial that an action is prohibited with such-and-such a strength to a claim that the action is permitted with the same strength. Permissions have no particular practical strength but would seem just to hold in the absence of any prohibition, however weak, that meets the requisite level of strength to count as "all-things-considered."

This distinction between evidential backing and practical strength seems to hold up, moreover, if we understand ought-judgments in terms of practical reasons. A permission would then amount to a denial that there are such reasons in sufficient strength to yield an ought. Reasons *for* it could not be practical in the relevant sense, since there is nothing in particular that amounts to action in fulfillment of a permission. Besides reasons for belief in a permission, or as a way of analyzing such reasons, there might be said to be reasons for issuing a permission that are practical in a more general or indirect sense; they may appeal, say, to the value of morally unconstrained choice with respect to the action in question. But these are not reasons for action in the sense that applies to a requirement or prohibition, where what is in question is action on the part of the agent to whom the judgment applies, as opposed to the speaker's act in issuing the judgment.

The distinction between the two sorts of assessment in application to permissions introduces complexities that are increased in application to the compound judgments taken as corresponding to positive oughts. Presumably, both elements of the judgment Op, ~Pp̄ and Pp, would have to be weighed in an all-things-considered assessment, whereas if permissions cannot be overriding, only the negative "core" element of the meaning of the judgment can be taken into account by a claim of overridingness. But the point for my purposes here is that on the assumption of dilemmas the all-things-considered assessment of the two elements will itself come apart. Supposing that all alternatives in a given case are prohibited strongly enough to count as impermissible all-things-considered—and that the case can be described (granting closure) as one in which both Op and Op̄ hold—the negative but not the positive element of the meaning of each of the ought-judgments bearing on the case would seem to be satisfied.

That all alternatives are ruled out all things considered amounts, of course, to the sort of assumption whose coherency is in question in the debate over dilemmas. But I think we can now see a way of interpreting "all things considered" that allows for its coherency. Let us think of an all-things-considered prohibition in the first instance as one that is important enough—or the reasons for which are important enough—to stand in light of the total body of evidence. This amounts to a kind of perceptual or figure-ground dominance—of the reasons for prohibiting something against the general background of reasons bearing on action—and hence allows for gestalt shifts in a way that is not possible for practical motives. The reasons for prohibiting something and the reasons for prohibiting its contrary may both be important enough to stand out against the field, that is, assuming that neither overrides the other, as in cases of dilemma.

In the case drawn from Sartre, for instance, it seems to make perfect sense for the agent to say that the reasons against abandoning his mother and the reasons against letting down the resistance are important enough to be unaffected by each other. Both prohibitions hold, that is, in light of all the evidence bearing on action—assuming (as the case demands) that the resistance needs this particular agent no less than his mother does. Neither prohibition is overriding, on our assumption that the case is a balanced dilemma, so each prohibition is sufficiently serious to remain in force despite the conflict.

The "weighted" cases that Williams discusses may not seem at first glance to allow for a shift in evidential perspective; but they turn out to be amenable to the same general treatment. Williams wants to say that neither obligation is really overriding in a case like Agamemnon's, even though one of his options is clearly better, on the grounds that the reasons for preferring one to the other fail to answer adequately the reasons on the other side—or in Williams's terms "the claims involved in the conflict."[31] That is, as utilitarian considerations, they fail to answer the nonutilitarian reasons for the ought that is not acted on; and presumably the same could be said of any resolution of the dilemma that appealed to reasons different in kind from those the agent chooses to act against. If Agamemnon decided that his duties as military commander were more important under the circumstances than his role as a father—whether on utilitarian grounds or something else—that would still leave his paternal obligations with enough importance, of a sort incommensurable with that of his military role, to remain in force despite the conflict.

The basic notion that lies behind the all-things-considered weighing of evidence seems to be that of a *sufficiently serious* reason—to prohibit something, in the first instance, with permission defined in terms of the absence of a sufficiently serious reason to prohibit something and obligation defined as indicated above. This notion must have comparative content of the sort that comes into the notion of overridingness, if we assume that some reasons can be serious enough to cancel out others, at least below a certain threshhold level of absolute seriousness. It cannot be purely comparative, though, on the assumption that it yields dilemmas for prohibitions that are supported by reasons above the threshhold level—reasons that are serious *enough*. If we understand dilemmas in terms of the notion, we can rule out the sorts of conflicts among trivial obligations that are plausibly dismissed as prima facie.[32] I appealed to the notion at the end of my preceding section as providing a way around Williams's ban on conclusive dilemmatic oughts—supposing that oughts include "ought-nots," or prohibitions.

Our intuitive talk of practical necessity corresponding to the modal auxiliary "must"—for which "ought" often functions as a weaker substitute in the discourse of moral philosophy—seems to fit the notion rather nicely. Talk of what one "cannot" do on moral grounds—in simplistic terms, the idea of something "taboo" (without the overtones the word sometimes has of absolute or groundless prohibition)—may be taken as indicating the absolute seriousness of a prohibition. The prohibition in question is serious enough, that is, to persist in the face of extreme barriers to action in accordance with it, including moral barriers of the sort one encounters in dilemmas.

It does sound natural, as I noted at the end of the last section, for the agent in Sartre's case to use variants of "must" to express the two oughts bearing on his decision: "I've got to join the resistance" and "I can't leave Mother." Each statement evinces a kind of moral urgency; and neither, not even the positive statement, seems to imply "permissible." One can easily imagine the agent, in response to a review of the reasons against joining the resistance, protesting that he *has* to. "Must" is stronger than "ought" in the suggestion it gives of moral catastrophe if unsatisfied—as opposed to doing less than one's best in moral terms—and in cases of dilemma there is catastrophe either way.

However, some authors hold that "must" has strong enough implications to provide a way out of dilemmas. The view is suggested by Lemmon's argument for their logical coherency, which depends on contrasting "ought" with "must," and by Williams's account of practical necessity, in which he argues for a version of Lemmon's assumption that "must" implies "will," or actuality.[33] But Williams's account is importantly limited—to intentional action, as he notes, but also to what he calls "incapacities of character."[34] The latter represent only one sort of application of "must," the sort exemplified by the Sophoclean tragic hero that he picks out at the beginning of his treatment as one of the two main examples of its moral use—with the other example provided by the Kantian moral agent. Faced with a dilemma the Sophoclean hero cannot do otherwise, given his character, than act on a certain one of the oughts in conflict. The claim that he cannot do otherwise, then, is a claim that his character is such that he cannot—which would be falsified, of course, by his doing otherwise after all.

It should be obvious that there cannot be two incompatible actions of which this claim is true, for reasons resembling the argument from motivational sufficiency that I considered and rejected toward the end of my preceding section as an interpretation of Williams's notion of conclusive practical "ought." Does the interpretation instead fit the notion of "must," which Williams takes as stronger? It could fit the notion in general terms, I think, only if all decisions in cases of dilemma could be made out as determined by the agent's preestablished character. But in Sartre's case the causal relation between character and choice is supposed to run in reverse. At any rate, reference to character in a sense that allows for development over the time in question—as at least partly constituted by the agent's current projects and the like, assumed to preexist his choice but also to be subject to change in the situation that requires choice—cannot play a *causal* role here. Does the truth of the agent's claim that he "had to" choose a certain option simply depend, then, on what he goes on to do, in something like the way that a claim of knowledge depends on truth: not because his character makes him act as he does, but rather because our notion of it refers in part to future action?

It seems wrong, first of all, to reject as false an agent's claim that he "has to" do something he later fails to do. Consider "I have to go now," as said by a guest who is persuaded to linger on. Though we might respond in conversation with a denial of his statement, our counterclaim can also be read as a way of pointing out that practical necessity does not imply necessity. We need not be denying, that is, that the guest's reasons for leaving are strong enough to support the statement; we might just be telling him to ignore them or acknowledging after the fact that he did ignore them. Similarly, the reason why the agent in Sartre's case cannot say at a later time that he had to take the option he in fact rejected is not that one of his original statements has turned out to be false but rather that the moral importance of action on it has become a thing of the past. Moral catastrophe has already occurred and been assimilated into the background of action.

In any case, there are "must"-claims that do not fit the character model at all. "I have to pay my rent on the first of the month" need not be taken as attributing to its speaker a high degree of conscientiousness in financial matters. Instead, it is naturally read as elliptical for a claim that something bad will happen if the rent is not paid by the time indicated. This may be something specific—the agent will be subject to a fine, say—but it need not be. Perhaps the only penalty for tardy payment is failure to meet a certain standard of performance in financial matters or failure to conform to the rules, something that is perfectly possible, on the model of "moral catastrophe."

A simplification of deontic logic sometimes called "escapism" applies this reading to oughts generally, with the role of the threatened bad state of affairs assigned to "the sanction," symbolized by a constant S referring to whatever is

entailed by the nonfulfillment of obligation and presumably is escaped by fulfillment.[35] On this account a statement like the one just above might be read as
"If I don't pay my rent by the fifth of the month, I incur the sanction." The
further "escapist" assumption that the sanction is avoidable makes this approach
unsuitable for our purposes, since it begs the question of dilemmas. However,
it provides a reasonable model for interpreting individual "must"-claims of the
sort just illustrated: as ought-statements that threaten the agent with a morally
catastrophic sanction.

Will the sanctions model let us assimilate "must"-claims to the perceptual
picture of figure-ground dominance I have sketched in application to all-things-
considered prohibition? Not without some differences, it seems; for besides its
failure to imply "permissible" but for similar reasons "must" also fails to imply "can" in intuitive terms. The agent may protest that he has to support his
mother, for instance, in response to reasons for thinking it impossible at this
point—without ten years of savings behind him, say—as well as in response to
reasons for some conflicting obligation. I would explain this by taking "must"
as resting on a *partial* view of the evidence rather than on an all-things-considered view. That is, it rests on reasons that are thought to be important enough
to stand on their own, blotting out contrary reasons rather than simply domi-
nating the field. The agent's protest amounts to a denial of any contrary reasons—for the moment, anyway—as he asserts the strength of the reasons he
chooses to focus on. It isolates the latter from the evidential background, instead of picking them out from a background that remains within view, as
indicated by the fact that he could not have said, in light of the reasons for joining the resistance, "*Even so*, I can't leave Mother."

On this account "must" is not just a strengthened form of "ought" but rather
presupposes a different way of dealing with the reasons for an ought-judgment,
where these are assumed to be particularly strong. If we also assume that the
same body of evidence admits of gestalt shifts, on the other hand, the "even
so" statement just above would be acceptable as rephrased in terms of "ought":
"Even so, I shouldn't leave Mother." Nor does its naturalness depend on a
weaker reading of "ought" as merely recommending rather than requiring
action; it would sound most natural as "Even so, it would be *wrong* to leave
Mother." This grants the contrary reasons rather than denies them, but asserts
in the face of them that the prohibition in question holds "all things considered."

Can the prohibition be practical if the contrary prohibition is, too? I see no
barrier to taking contrary prohibitions as *meant* to guide action, when they
follow from rules designed for that purpose in general terms, though the specific directives derived from the rules on a given occasion are not jointly fulfillable
and hence would be unreasonable as commands. With agglomeration out of
the picture, they are not therefore logically incoherent in combination. For that
matter, they may in fact guide action at least indirectly, on the sanctions model,
by making out nonfulfillment as morally unacceptable or as incurring some sort
of specific sanction rather than by directly bringing about fulfillment. On this
interpretation, "Don't do X" is elliptical for "Don't do X *or* you will incur S."

In cases of dilemma, of course, the agent will have no way of avoiding S altogether; in opting for a particular horn of the dilemma, however, he chooses to accept a particular instance of S. Putting up with a sanction, then, or accepting it—or something more active, such as subjecting oneself to it—might be thought of as an indirect way of satisfying the ought that loses out.

However, this possibility—to be considered in more concrete form later, when I turn to guilt as an example of what philosophers call "internal sanctions"—can hold only for negative oughts or prohibitions, if my preceding argument is correct. Insofar as a positive ought also implies that fulfillment is permissible—in other words, insofar as it does not simply reduce to a negative ought—it rules out the competing all-things-considered ought as interpreted on the sanctions model, with a statement of permission taken as denying that its object will incur a sanction.[36] Further, on the account just given, the corresponding "must," positive *or* negative, turns a blind eye to contrary reasons in a way that undermines the support for its competitor. By contrast, a negative ought exhibits a kind of perceptual dominance that admits contrary reasons into the field of view and hence allows its competitor a basis in it as well.

In maintaining a prohibition "all-things-considered" even in light of equally strong prohibitions of alternatives, we are exhibiting what might be called the intractability of moral wrong: the relative imperviousness of judgments of wrong to the sorts of further practical calculations that affect positive or nonmoral action-guidance. The claim that there are important enough reasons for requiring some act, by contrast—or on the other hand, for ruling it out in prudential terms as irrational or the like—will not make sense as an all-things-considered judgment in combination with an admission that there are equally strong reasons on the other side. The evidential assessment of negative ought-judgments thus seems to allow them uniquely the sort of noncomparative content that is needed for full-fledged moral dilemmas.

Resolvability and Wrong

Williams and other proponents of moral dilemmas make them out as resolvable only nonmorally, by appeal to a practical ought reflecting the agent's personal projects and the like. Morally speaking, they are irresolvable, in the sense that morality fails to provide a basis for resolving them. Once we distinguish between positive and negative dilemmas, however, I think we can see that full-fledged dilemmas—those that fit the negative conception in terms of exhaustive prohibitions—will be irresolvable in a stronger sense: They will admit of no morally *acceptable* resolution, whether or not morally based. The agent has to violate moral norms, not just to reach beyond them, in order to resolve a negative dilemma in practical terms, as he must in one way or another, since the prohibitions bearing on his decision are assumed to exhaust the field.

For dilemmas characterized positively, on the other hand, we seem to have to yield to the insistence of opponents of dilemmas that what we really have are prima facie oughts in conflict; otherwise, the same acts would come out as both permissible and impermissible. This follows from the assumption that separates positive from negative oughts: that "ought" implies "permissible." Whether or not one of the conflicting oughts can be taken as overriding, it seems that neither can count as all-things-considered on this positive formulation. This was the kernel of truth I found in Williams's argument for denying that both can be conclusive. Rather than excluding dilemmas from the practical sphere, however, my account allows for a separate treatment of dilemmas set up negatively.

As noted in my initial overview of the literature on dilemmas, moral philosophers have sometimes stressed the negative characterization, but as far as I know the distinction was not given any attention until my own treatment in 1983 of the case from *Sophie's Choice*.[37] The positive characterization is emphasized in the literature on deontic logic; with the exception of Von Wright in 1968 none of the classic papers on the subject discusses dilemmas in negative terms, and the distinction is first noted in a piece published in 1987.[38] Here I want essentially to revise my earlier argument for the distinction in light of later developments, especially my current suggestions on deontic strength and value, by taking a fresh look at the notion of a disjunctive ought brought in to resolve a dilemma. Readers who wish to bypass technical discussion should at this point skip to p. 62 for the summary and transitional comments at the end of this chapter.

In attempting to resolve Sophie's dilemma, then, one might appeal to an ought that prescribes saving at least one child, which under the circumstances requires choosing a particular one. I think of this as a disjunctive ought—on a use of the term that covers inclusive "or"—since it amounts to an indefinite prescription to save one child or other. On the assumption that the dilemmatic oughts that prescribe saving each child are in balance, the disjunctive ought might naturally be taken as outweighing either of them. It is most important that Sophie not let both children be killed, so on this account what she ought to do all things considered is to make a choice between them and save one of them—choosing one by some fair method. What the disjunctive ought prescribes, in effect, is a *practical* resolution of the dilemma: action in accordance with a tiebreaking ought, presumably arbitrary, of the sort that might result from flipping a coin in circumstances that allow for it. In order to satisfy the minimal moral demands of the case, Sophie is advised to appeal beyond strictly moral considerations.

However, Williams's view on overridingness seemed to rule out that account of Sophie's choice. Supposing that a mother has serious and separate moral obligations to preserve each of her children, not just her progeny considered collectively, Sophie's satisfaction of the disjunctive obligation would not adequately meet the claims involved in the conflict. Unlike Agamemnon's choice between his daughter and the expedition under his command, Sophie's choice might be said to involve commensurable (equal) claims, but on the assumption that they do not permit trade-offs, a fair decision between them will still leave one of them unsatisfied. It is not enough that both be taken into account on the model of political representation.

On the other hand, we can now see grounds for accepting the conclusion of opponents of dilemmas—and Williams's conclusion for conflicting practical oughts—that neither of the conflicting positive oughts in Sophie's case is in force all things considered. Though neither is overridden, each implies a claim of permissibility that is contradicted by the other. Can we then say that it is all-things-considered status rather than overridingness that distinguishes the disjunctive ought? There may be no ought in force all things considered to contradict the implied claim that it is permissible for Sophie to save one child or the other.

To say this, we would have to reject at least some strong forms of the principle of deontic closure, assuming that the negative oughts or prohibitions bearing on the case *are* in force all things considered. As the case is set up, saving one child requires letting one be taken to the gas chamber—whichever one is not picked out by the tiebreaker Sophie uses. If the necessary means to satisfying an ought are themselves obligatory—as closure over causal relations would have it—and "ought" implies "permissible," the disjunctive ought presumably combines with the tiebreaker (at any rate after the latter is decided upon) to imply the permissibility of failing to save a particular child. So it cannot hold all things considered along with a prohibition of that failure.

In any case, what the disjunctive ought gives us is not quite a resolution of the dilemma. On the positive account of the case, we do not have a dilemma in the first place but instead just a prima facie ought-conflict. And on the negative account, the disjunctive ought does not yield a morally acceptable resolution, despite its moral basis, since we also have all-things-considered prohibitions ruling out each of the actions that would satisfy it. Closure over causal relations would yield explicit prohibitions of saving either child, and even without closure we have to conclude that any particular acts that would satisfy the disjunctive obligation are morally prohibited under some other description.[39] They may not be prohibited with equal force—we can say that the disjunctive ought is weightier than the dilemmatic prohibitions and hence in one sense "outweighs" them—but the prohibitions are serious enough in absolute terms to count as all-things-considered.

In short, though it is perfectly clear what Sophie must do, and on moral grounds, in response to the dilemma, there seems to be no way out of the dilemma that can count as morally permissible. I have framed this conclusion in terms of "must" rather than "ought," since the use of "ought" might be taken to entail that some act is permissible after all, on our assumption that "ought" implies "permissible." Whether it does have that consequence depends on whether we accept closure over causal relations. For reasons like those just indicated, if we do accept closure, there will be nothing that Sophie morally ought to do, at any rate all things considered, in response to the dilemma—not even the disjunctive act of saving one child or the other, despite its overriding moral importance, as one might say. At any rate, even without closure we would have to deny that any particular act done to satisfy the disjunction can possibly pass muster in moral terms.

There will be other balanced cases, like the assassination case in chapter 1, that do not allow for a disjunctive ought in the first place, since all the alternatives in them, including inaction, are prohibited with equal force. Sophie's choice might be made into such a case if we assume that she has to do something morally worse to either child in order to save the other than simply failing to save it. At a certain level—if Sophie had to torture one child, say—the wrongness of these acts might be thought of as balancing the wrongness of violating the disjunctive obligation and failing to save either one. However, even without an exhaustively *balanced* case of exhaustive prohibition, dilemmas on the negative characterization will still have problematic consequences of the sort just indicated.

We can already begin to see some of the complications for deontic logic that dilemmas introduce. I shall postpone to my next section further comments on closure and the other standard principles that dilemmas call into question. The important thing to note at this point is that much depends on how we decide to describe a given case—both the choices and the reasons for them that are thought to be at issue in the dilemma. In the first instance, our decision will affect the plausibility of the case as set up in negative terms: the plausibility of the claim that there is reason enough for prohibiting all options in it. Consider Sartre's case, once again: A serious question might be raised about counting as wrong or impermissible in its own right the agent's failure to join the resistance. It sounds plausible in positive terms to say that he ought to join the resistance; and on standard deontic assumptions this implies that it would be impermissible for him not to. But in this case the reasons *for* the act in question would normally be taken as primary, it seems, with reasons against omitting the act seen as derived from them. To get around this problem and continue to use the case for purposes of illustration, I specified that the resistance needs this agent in particular. To support the claim that he would be doing something wrong by staying home—in a sense that does not reduce to a failure to satisfy a positive duty—we might suppose that he is the one person who possesses certain skills with explosives, so that the resistance depends on him no less than his mother does.

Our ordinary assumption about the case, by contrast, would be just that the agent ought to volunteer for a task that is required of some indefinite set of members of a group he belongs to—in a commendatory sense of "ought" that does not really have the imperatival force of an ought based on prohibition. We sometimes blur the distinction between these different levels or strengths of action-guiding force to get practical results. But it is important that with any weaker assumptions than those just indicated Sartre's case would no longer count as a full-fledged dilemma in my terms, however neatly balanced the alternatives it presents, or however balanced they seem to be if we consider deontic strength independently of positive or negative value. The crucial thing for the question of resolvability is that the agent's alternatives each be prohibited by strong enough reasons for the prohibitions to stand in light of each other.

On the other hand, the cases I have referred to as weighted dilemmas, such as Agamemnon's case, will fit my account of dilemmas irresolvable by permissible means, assuming that the prohibitions they involve are in force all things considered. Even in light of all the evidence—in light of what we might suppose to be the overriding importance of the success of the Greek military expedition—Agamemnon's sacrifice of Iphigenia remains prohibited; it still counts as morally wrong, and indeed in the strongest terms, in a sense meant to guide action. Here it is even clear which alternative the agent must choose for a practical resolution of the dilemma like that given by the disjunctive ought in Sophie's case, whereas in Sophie's case the disjunctive ought needed supplementation by a tiebreaker selecting a specific option. So the case does not involve a moral quandary, but it still seems to amount to a moral dilemma.

Since balanced dilemmas pose further problems of choice, they might seem to be dilemmatic in a fuller sense. But the term "fatal" dilemma seems apt for any cases that exhibit the property of allowing no morally acceptable resolution. Fatal dilemmas are those that exhibit Nagel's "moral blind alley": They offer the agent no way out of a forced choice among moral wrongs. To describe even Sophie's case in these terms, however, requires some care. Her prohibited alternatives have to be thought of as acts of failing to save either child—standing idly by while a child is taken—rather than as the acts of saving one child that they also amount to in fact, for the acts of saving also come out as permissible under that description. Moreover, if it does not seem plausible that there are strong enough reasons against each act of omission for the two prohibitions to hold in light of each other—and even in light of the weightier disjunctive requirement to save at least one of her children—the case could always be strengthened. We might suppose that Sophie actually has to harm one child to save the other, as in the exhaustively balanced variant case I described. My suggestion is just that on some version the case will exhibit the sort of fatal dilemmatic structure that poses problems for the practical coherency of ethics.

For an example that does not require compounding the wrongs the agent has to choose between, we might turn back to my assassination case. Here the agent faces a choice between allowing the assassination of an important political figure by her silence and letting the assassins murder one of her relatives, if she fails to cooperate and informs on them. To balance the agent's responsibility to her family, we might suppose that the political figure represents a major force for good under urgent circumstances. However, even if the case is not a balanced dilemma, it will come out as a fatal dilemma along with Walzer's torture case, according to the treatment just given of weighted cases like Agamemnon's. In common with Agamemnon's case and at least some variants of Sophie's, it admits of no morally acceptable resolution; unlike all but exhaustively balanced variants of Sophie's case, it does not even allow for the sort of morally mandated, though still impermissible, way out that is provided by a weightier disjunctive requirement.

In short, no matter what the agent does here, she does wrong, and neither of her options seems to be any better or morally more important than the other. What can it mean, then, to offer her all-things-considered moral advice—or for that matter, to decline to do so, stopping at the claim that each of her alternatives is prima facie prohibited? The case seems to undermine not just the agent's choice of action but our own account of it in action-guiding terms. It therefore poses in particularly stark form the problem of practical "ought" in dilemmas.

I want now to consider some of the general consequences for deontic logic of my own attempt to make room for such cases within action-guiding ethics.

3. Problems for Practical Ought-Systems

On the view I set out to defend here, the statements that seem to apply to dilemmas are odd and in many ways unsettling but not incoherent. They make sense as results of applying teachable practical rules to situations of intractable wrong, even if they may be said to make no sense as concrete pieces of practical advice in those situations. I now want to pinpoint some of the ways in which dilemmas on the account just given are unsettling, particularly for systematic approaches to moral reasoning that purport to capture our ordinary notion of practical "ought." I shall focus on a few central problems raised by dilemmas for deontic logic, without much technical detail on alternative systems. My aim is just to indicate in broad outline the degree of complication that would result from an attempt to stretch the materials provided by the standard system to fit our ordinary moral thought.

I shall assume on the basis of my understanding of the action-guiding function assigned to "ought"—or to the particular sense or use of "ought" that deontic logic as here interpreted is meant to capture—that both of the ought-implication principles picked out earlier do apply. For practical "ought," that is, it is essentially a matter of definition that "ought" implies "can" and that positive (and hence prescriptive) "ought" implies "permissible"; but this is of course compatible with the claim that other uses of "ought" have different functions and hence do not obey the two principles.[40] My central task in this section will be to suggest ways of handling the two further principles that seemed to conflict with these in application to dilemmas: the ought-derivation principles, agglomeration and closure.

Closure will naturally come up first because of its relation as indicated in my last section to some of the odder results of the distinction I have defended between positive and negative dilemmas. In fact, before we get to the clash between principles, we need to raise some questions about the results of that distinction for deontic logic. So far, I have blurred over problems about permission and negation in the standard system that now need to be considered. Once they are dealt with, I shall claim, dilemmas themselves will not give us reason to restrict the principle of closure. However, there are other reasons having to do with the interpretation of the deontic operator that will be worth discussing here at least briefly.

On the other hand, agglomeration will still be called into question by dilemmas, and I shall go on to suggest a rationale for dropping it that makes sense on our assumption of a strong action-guiding interpretation of "ought," now thought of in negative terms. Without agglomeration we seem to end up with a collection of subsystems of practical "ought" designed to rule out dilemmas within any single system. Along with dilemmas, though, this picture also seems to rule out the sort of interplay between ought-judgments that deontic logic has to capture if it is to represent any of the more interesting cases of moral reasoning.

Proscriptive "Ought"

Standard deontic logic derives the principle that "ought" implies "permissible" from an axiom that essentially begs the question against dilemmas: Pp ∨ Pp̄.[41] Even without this assumption, however, a version of "ought"-implies-"permissible" might seem to rule out the distinction underlying our negative definition of dilemmas because the principle applies to negative oughts as well as positive. That is, if "ought-not" also implies "permissible-not," we would seem to have incompatible judgments of permissibility in negative cases as well as positive. In the assassination case, for instance, if the agent ought neither to inform on the assassins nor to remain silent, we seem to have it that she is permitted to do either, given that not doing one amounts to doing the other. But our negative ought-judgments presumably tell us that she is *not* permitted to do either. Since "ought" involves both a positive and a negative permission, in short, the case yields a contradiction, assuming closure. Even without closure it yields an implausible set of permissions.

Perhaps the simplest way of avoiding this problem would be to take "ought-not," or F (for "it is forbidden that"), as primitive in deontic logic rather than O or P and to build "ought"-implies-"permissible" into the definition of Op. With Pp defined as ~Fp, Op would then come out as Fp̄ & ~Fp; and "ought"-implies-"permissible" would not apply to Fp to yield Pp̄. The principle would still apply to Op̄, but the point is that on this approach Op̄ would no longer be equivalent to Fp. It would no longer amount to a negative ought, or "ought-not," a prohibition, but instead, one might say, to "ought not-"—with "not" understood as negating the object of "ought," so that the resulting ought-statement requires some alternative action, rather than as yielding a negative version of the operator, so that the statement forbids action.

This negative approach therefore involves complicating one of the underlying grammatical assumptions of deontic logic, which treats "ought-not" and "ought not-" as interchangeable. However, it does seem to fit the picture of all-things-considered practical oughts and reasons that emerged from my treatment of dilemmas in this chapter. The notion of sufficient reason for prohibiting some action came out as fundamental in the sense of not reducing to reasons in favor of some alternative action, since it is not undercut by decisive reasons against alternatives. This picture captures something intuitively basic, moreover, to the extent that the notion of a "taboo"—ruling out certain actions on the basis of authoritative command—might be thought of as a primitive "ought" in historical or developmental terms as well as logically.

On the other hand, the picture might seem to violate the standard interpretation of negation, derived from Frege, as modifying the content of a proposition rather than amounting to a further operator on propositions—denial, say— on a par with assertion. For instance, Frege insists that no distinction between positive and negative propositions (in his terms, "thoughts") is needed to make sense of any logical principle he knows of.[42] Would this rule out principles of deontic logic that distinguish between positive and negative deontic operators? In fact, Michael Dummett suggests that we add to Frege's stated remarks some corresponding points about prohibition: To avoid overcomplication in the way Frege has in mind when he takes the denial of a proposition as asserting its negation, we also need to take prohibition as commanding a negation.[43] But this is apparently to grant that Fp amounts to O$\bar{p}$.

This application of Frege's view is less straightforward than it appears, however. First, we should note that the deontic operators are not themselves "force operators" on the model of assertion. They can be understood as propositional operators, forming compound propositions from propositional variables—"it ought to be the case that p" from "it is the case that p"—so that negative force can still modify the content of a proposition: It would be built into the content of the compound proposition formed by a negative deontic operator. We now need to drop the assumption that this is expressible in terms of the negation of the simpler component proposition, however. Instead, we have to recognize a distinction for a statement with imperatival force between negating the description of the state of affairs it commands the agent to bring about and issuing a negative version of the command—in other words, substituting "prevent" for "bring about."

We should grant, of course, that packing negation into the operator as on this account will indeed complicate matters in a way that is contrary to the spirit of Frege's approach. But against the simple application of Frege's views on affirmation and negation to the deontic modalities, we should note that the latter are already complicated by the presence of permission as an intermediate possibility between command and prohibition. There are two different ways of negating the imperatival content of a command, one might say: issuing a countercommand and simply retracting the command.[44]

In fact, "entertaining" a proposition might be suggested in place of assertion as providing a mentalistic parallel to command that more accurately represents the real complications to be found in our use of the notion, including the logical space it leaves for permission. Here there seem to be several possibilities: (1) One can hold a proposition in mind, or actively entertain it, by analogy to a command. (2) One can block it out or exclude it from consciousness—the analogue of prohibition—possibly but not necessarily by entertaining some other proposition that excludes it. But (3) one can also simply fail to entertain it, not necessarily by blocking it out but perhaps just because one is unreceptive to it in some more passive way. The sort of assumption marking off the third possibility from the second is that being unprepared to think about something, being uninterested in it, or the like is not always explainable in terms of some competing mental activity. For similar reasons, (4) one can also in some cases do nothing to prevent a certain proposition from coming to mind and yet just fail to entertain it. So failing to block out a propositional thought counts as a distinguishable possibility—amounting to the analogue of permission in my treatment of the logic of practical "ought."

The complications introduced by my approach, then, are not without parallel in moral psychology, and my approach is founded on moral psychology insofar as it rests on the perceptual or figure/ground assessment of deontic weights that was outlined in the preceding section. We can see further reasons for complicating this account if we now take a look at the problems with closure, the principle called into question by dilemmas in standard deontic logic on the assumption that "ought" implies "permissible." Since my account effectively limits the latter principle to positive oughts—those expressed by the operator O, including oughts with negated propositions as their objects—and at the same time limits dilemmas to negative oughts, it keeps dilemmas from posing any special problem with respect to closure. We no longer have to worry, that is, about applying closure to a statement granting the permissibility of satisfying a conflicting ought—about whether we could derive from it a contradiction of the statement of impermissibility that follows by definition from the ought with which it conflicts. For all-things-considered conflicting oughts will now be limited to prohibitions, which do not imply "permissible."

Closure may be questioned, however, on independent grounds that bring to light important general problems with the interpretation of the deontic operator—or operators, we now should say, since the ambiguities in our reading of O will be exhibited somewhat differently by F, which does not provide a parallel to the distinction between "ought" and "obligation." As previously stated in positive form, closure allows us to derive obligations to do anything necessary to fulfill our obligations. To the extent that the unrestricted principle is plausible, however, it really seems to apply to oughts rather than to obligations strictly construed—at any rate, obligations whose objects amount to acts—for reasons we may illustrate with the assassination case.

In intuitive terms, with "obligation" taken broadly to include requirements imposed by moral principles as well as specific commitments, the agent in the assassination case may be said to have an obligation to protect her country or even to save a certain political figure from assassination in addition to the obligation to protect her family. To fulfill this obligation under the circumstances, she is required to inform on the assassins. Fulfilling the latter requirement in turn imposes on her any number of further requirements in context, most notably that she fail to prevent the murder of the family member under threat but also, for instance, that she move her lips and other trivial presuppositions of action on her original obligation that have nothing to do with the conflict.

Whether O applies to any of these putatively derived obligations, however—whether we can speak of them plausibly as "obligations"—depends very much on the terms in which we decide to interpret the operator. The word "ought" applies fairly readily to the results of closure—we may grant that the agent *ought* to move her lips, say—but "obligation" appears to be sensitive to instrumental remoteness and changes in wording of a sort that would make it hard to formulate a qualified version of the principle. We might grant, for instance, that the agent has an obligation that requires her to move her lips—or even that it is obligatory *that* she move her lips—but surely not that she has an obligation *to* move her lips. On the other hand, I think we would allow that she has an obligation to say something, for instance, even though this already involves going somewhat beyond the stated contents of her original obligation and certainly of the general moral principle from which it was derived by closure.[45] The best we can say, I think, is that closure does not hold generally for obligation, at any rate as applied directly to acts.

Standard deontic logic reads O in a way that mixes "ought" and "obligation," but as applied to propositional variables on assumptions that do seem to allow for closure—though they also seem to keep deontic logic from capturing practical "ought." The readings usually given for the operator are "it is obligatory that" or "it ought to be (the case) that," taken as interchangeable. Both phrases, but especially the latter, are naturally read in light of the sort of ideal interpretation of ought-judgments that corresponds to the "ideal world" semantics of standard deontic logic.[46] What ought to be the case, according to this approach, is what *is* the case in all deontically perfect or ideal worlds, worlds in perfect conformity to the moral rules. In recognizing dilemmas, of course, we recognize that the real world is not in this sense ideal: Any world compatible with what is now irrevocably the case will have to be seriously flawed in moral terms. Even apart from dilemmas, moreover, our real-world obligations will sometimes rest on the assumption of a less than perfect moral world to the extent that they include "contrary-to-duty" obligations, obligations to make up for moral wrongs.[47] What is in question here is what a given agent ought to do, not what ought to be, but although "ought-to-do" seems to cover more of our ordinary practical ought-judgments, deontic logic seems to fit "ought-to-be."

Even read in terms of "obligation," then, but applied to propositional variables, O can be expected to support closure, as it seemed to in the examples drawn from the assassination case just above. That anything logically or causally required by what is true of all ideal worlds will be true of them as well presumably would follow from the definition of a morally ideal world as satisfying logical and causal laws. As applied to acts, on the other hand, examples like those just cited suggest that closure holds for "ought" but not for "obligation," so it seems we have to choose between "ought" and "obligation" in interpreting the deontic operator. Where they introduce an infinitive phrase rather than "that," terms based on "obligation" appear to be more tightly tied to the wording of the principles, commitments, or the like from which particular requirements are derived.

To avoid these complications, I have mainly stuck to "ought" in this chapter, supplying its missing noun form with the verb even in some cases where "obligation" might sound more natural. For we seem to need both the principle of closure and statements of "ought-to-do" in order to capture the practical reasoning involved in dilemmas—including most notably the derivation of preparatory oughts that came into my initial argument against Williams. In a case like Sartre's, that is, even if there are no positive dilemmatic oughts in force all things considered, we still want to be able to derive obligations requiring the agent to take any necessary *and permissible* means to satisfying the corresponding prohibitions. If it is forbidden for the agent to fail to support his mother in 1942, say, and financial as well as personal support is intended, then he ought to start saving as early as 1932 on the assumption that saving in no way interferes with the ability to satisfy his other obligations. That we now need to spell out the latter assumption, of permissibility, is a complication introduced by my negative formulation of deontic principles. With permissibility granted, however, closure does seem to apply to the case in negative form and to yield a positive preparatory ought-judgment.

In negative "ought-to-do" terms, closure says that it is forbidden to do anything that entails doing something forbidden: FA and ~M(B & ~A) imply FB. The principle seems at least not to clash with intuition, whose deliverances are less firm for the less familiar negative operator. "Forbidden" may sound odd in application to acts whose logical or causal tie to a violation of obligation is relatively remote, but it is not clearly ruled out, and we seem to have no less awkward phrase except "ought not," which does apply. It also is worth noting that "forbidden" clearly means something stronger than "nonideal," even where it is used in a phrase that suggests "ought-to-be." Similarly for "prohibited," which I shall continue to use here.

The distinction between "ought-to-do" and "ought-to-be," considered as extending to "forbidden" and related negative ought-terms, might now help us to deal with some of the odd results noted (and some others that were blurred over) in the preceding section. On the present account we would seem to be limited to a negative version of the disjunctive ought that was brought in to resolve Sophie's dilemma at least in practical terms: a conjunctive prohibition— on letting both children be killed, say—that would not be subject to "ought"-implies-"permissible." Otherwise, the principle of closure, or closure plus agglomeration, would apparently classify the same act as both permissible and forbidden: A positive disjunctive ought would imply the permissibility of saving a particular child in accordance with some sort of tiebreaker, while the original dilemmatic prohibitions would imply that this is forbidden.

Without the disjunctive ought, though, there will be nothing that Sophie ought to do. We now have to deny, that is, that she ought (all things considered) to save at least one child—just because there is no permissible means to doing so—even assuming that the prohibition on letting both be killed is clearly stronger than either of the dilemmatic prohibitions. The point is that Sophie is given no moral permission to act in this case. Any particular act she might perform—meaning any act-token (whether or not we should take this to include disjunctive and other compound acts)—is prohibited with sufficient independent strength to remain in force even in light of the conjunctive prohibition.

Although this result may sound odd, we can mute its oddness by granting that it still ought to *be the case* that Sophie save at least one child, since there ought to be some permissible way of doing so—even in the less-than-ideal world in which she has to act to save a child at all. There is still a distinguishable type of act that is required of her (and hence permitted) under the circumstances; it is merely a contingent matter that this coincides with a prohibited act-type, as her choice-situation is in fact set up. However, prohibition might be said to "dominate" permission for "ought-to-do": If an act-token is prohibited under some description, then it is prohibited *tout court*, whether or not it is also permitted under some other description. What this means is that all of Sophie's particular options come out as prohibited. At the same time, there still will be some to which "ought-to-be" applies, to yield not just a version of the disjunctive ought (and its particular conclusion by way of the tiebreaker) but also of the original dilemmatic oughts whose positive "ought-to-do" versions we had to drop. We can also say that it ought to be the case that Sophie save *each* child, that is, given that "ought-to-be" can be limited fairly naturally to acts under different descriptions.

With different background conditions presupposed by different ought-statements as on dyadic systems of deontic logic, "ought-to-be" should accommodate all of the various statements we want to make about cases of moral dilemma.[48] Relative to the fact that Sophie has to act to save one child, that is, it ought to be the case that she does—compatibly with the fact that it really ought not to be the case (and would not be the case in a world that was ideal without qualification) that she have to act to save one child. Different conditions would yield different and sometimes conflicting obligations, but on this account the statements expressing them would essentially be insulated from each other by their different presuppositions in a way that would make it impossible for them to capture the motivational conflict characteristic of dilemmas.

This sort of fragmentation of deontic logic into separate subsystems is the main threat posed by dropping the principle of agglomeration, as I go on to argue. In any case, it is "ought-to-do" rather than "ought-to-be" that would seem to have even a chance of capturing action-guiding dilemmas. It is also "ought-to-do" that coincides with the sort of everyday practical use of "ought" that deontic logicians generally seem to be after, despite their usual reading of the operator. The basis of standard deontic logic in ideal conceptions of "ought" seems to undermine any claims it might make to capture the elements of ordinary moral reasoning. Nonstandard approaches in the field seem to be able to capture them only by disconnecting them, cutting off possibilities of mutual influence, as we shall see.

Deontic Fragmentation

Williams defends his decision to drop the principle of agglomeration by noting that many of the act-evaluations that might be thought to entail ought-statements—"desirable," "advisable," "sensible," and "prudent" are his examples—do not obey the principle.[49] Two acts can each be good in one of these ways, we might say, and yet not be good in combination, since their goodness rests on reasons that cancel each other out. But this argument has force only for a use of "ought" whose link to "good" makes it weaker than the imperatival sense that is in question here for cases of action-guiding dilemma. It suggests just the sort of quick departure from duty ethics in the face of moral conflict that my overall argument here is meant to resist. For the sort of ought that rules out alternatives, agglomeration does seem plausible: If anything *but* a certain act is *unacceptable*, and the same is true of another act, how can it not be true of the two in combination?

Since conflicting positive all-things-considered oughts have been eliminated from our picture of dilemmas, our problem is now with agglomeration in negative form. The reformulated principle tells us that FA and FB imply F(A v B), but in a case of exhaustive prohibition the latter formula cannot be action-guiding since its disjunctive object holds necessarily. It disobeys the negative correlate of the principle that "ought" implies "can": that "ought-not" implies "can avoid." However, we should now raise a more general question about what the apparent reference to agency here can amount to on an "ought-to-be" interpretation of the principle—and how much action-guidance it really involves. Interpreted in terms of ideal worlds the principle that "ought" implies "can" essentially guarantees that a deontically perfect world is also a possible world, but it does not ensure that action is needed to bring such a world about. So it allows for ought-judgments without any action-guiding point, such as a judgment that one ought to obey the laws of logic.

Odd consequences of this trivial sort are often tolerated in the interests of systematization.[50] "Ought"-implies-"can avoid" (as opposed to "can"), though presupposed by the Kantian approach from which we get "ought"-implies-"can," is not assumed in standard deontic logic. Requiring the inevitable is thought to be harmless enough, since conformity to it is automatic. But of course this sort of failure with respect to action-guidingness may not be so harmless to whatever claims deontic logic makes to represent ordinary moral discourse. An ought that gives reasons for action, rather than just for preferring some independent outcome, would apply only to states of affairs that depend on what one does.

However, the main variant of deontic logic for "ought-to-do," Castañeda's system, with O applied to "practitions" (intentions or prescriptions), allows for logically harmless but practically pointless uses of "ought" to the extent that it still makes out obligation as a kind of moral necessity.[51] Castañeda also accepts the principle of agglomeration, which he at one point defends in "ought-to-do" terms by appeal to a view of ought-statements as restricting an agent's freedom, since the extent of the restriction on freedom and the reasons for it would have to be the same for O(A & B) as for OA & OB.[52] My remarks here suggest, though, that one should consider the point of such a restriction—its importance, or what it achieves—as part of what is meant by the reasons for it and hence as determining whether it constitutes a real or a tenable restriction. There might be a separate point in each of the restrictions on action whose combination turns out to be pointless in cases of dilemma—to move now beyond logically harmless cases on the assumption that there is also no point in requiring the impossible. By analogy, there might be two restrictive dietary regimens, each offering certain health benefits in return for forgoing certain foods but jointly ruling out so much that the combined regimen would be unhealthy.

We can think of Castañeda's restrictions on freedom as based on a practical interpretation of "ought" in terms of reasons for action-guidance that improves on Williams's reference to desires and related notions of the good. Castañeda seems to be on the right track, moreover, in switching deontic logic to "ought-to-do." However, I think he still retains too much of what is wrong with standard deontic logic by retaining its Kantian basis in moral necessity. One reason he may need to do so, apart from his emphasis on systematic simplicity, is that he does make reference to desires insofar as he makes out the truth of an ought-statement in terms of its relation to the agent's optional ends.[53] The strength of a requirement in contrast to a desire—the binding force of "ought," in other words—has to come from something other than its source, on this sort of end-based account; the usual alternative is some sort of structural feature analogous to logical necessity as on Kant's view.

The intermediate "escapist" account I have suggested in this chapter essentially replaces the model of necessity with that of *needs*, strengthening desire by reference to some sort of harm or bad state of affairs as contingent upon nonfulfillment.[54] The change allows us to continue to speak of oughts as imposing restrictions on an agent's freedom—a moral ought may be said to leave one with no real alternative in moral terms to its fulfillment—but we now lack the unifying assumption that the agent must be left with something he *is* free to do. Needs can quite conceivably be unsatisfiable in combination, that is, as things work out in some particular situation, though they still press just as urgently for satisfaction when they conflict. They do not seem to undercut each other in felt practical force, one might say, even where they cannot both result in action.

Considered individually, needs of the sort in question here would seem to imply "can" at least in the sense of holding out hope of avoiding the harm in question if they are satisfied. Since a set of needs does not imply a corresponding ability to satisfy all of its members in conjunction, however, this version of escapism provides us with a reasonable parallel to "ought" that may indeed violate the principle of agglomeration. Needing each of two things does not imply needing both of them, if only because the harm each averts might conceivably be allowed or even brought on by the pair. Consider, for instance, a patient with two disorders who needs two medications that interact badly, so that the result of taking both medications to avoid ill health would be ill health.

When we switch to the negative version of agglomeration, we can see essentially the same thing in terms of the model of perceptual dominance of reasons *against* various alternative acts—the negative basis of the sanctions-model, in effect—that I appealed to earlier. There may be strong enough reasons against each of two exhaustive alternatives to rule out each of them—from moral consideration, let us say—even if we deny that it makes sense to speak of ruling out the pair of them, or all possibilities, in a single breath. This supposes that the notion of strong enough reasons for ruling something out rests on a figure-ground relation: selection from a background of further possibilities, so that any given act of selection has to leave something over.

That two figures each may be capable of standing out against the background, in short, does not imply that they can do so in combination, just because there may be no further background to contrast with them; each may serve as background for the other, as one's view undergoes gestalt shifts. The "figures" here amount to acts ruled out by strong enough reasons, or forbidden with sufficient strength—on the assumption required by agglomeration as interpreted in "ought-to-do" terms, that acts related by disjunction or the like can be thought of as forming compound acts.

In "ought-to-be" terms, agglomeration may be dealt with differently. Strong enough reasons against doing some act need not be seen as implied by the reasons why it (or the state of affairs that consists in doing it) ought not to be, if the strength of reasons for a prohibition depends on its practical point, as I have suggested. An act that is inevitably going to be done, say, might on this account be one that ought not to be—even though there cannot be strong enough reasons for prohibiting it, since no possible reasons could satisfy the point of a prohibition by keeping it from being done. In application to dilemmas, then, where the overall choice-situation ought not to be, the disjunction of exhaustive alternatives the situation allows for may be thought of as forbidden in ideal terms. In practical terms, the same prohibition would violate agglomeration: There will be strong enough reasons to prohibit each of the alternatives but not their disjunction.

To allow for agglomeration of nondilemmatic oughts, we would need to complicate deontic logic further by qualifying the principle—adding a clause, say, that restricts it in positive form to oughts with compatible objects. For dilemmatic cases, on the other hand, we have to deal with a kind of deontic fragmentation that is evidently not limited to cases of incommensurable value, if there are balanced cases like Sophie's in which only one morally relevant value is at stake. However, as we saw earlier, a more pervasive sort of fragmentation into subsystems already results from the attempt to represent conflicting oughts within an "ought-to-be" version of standard deontic logic as provided by the dyadic system.

The same may now be said of Castañeda's "ought-to-do" system with its assignment of conflicting oughts to different subscripted contexts of ends. Castañeda's approach makes at least initial sense for many of the standard cases of dilemma, which involve a clash between different sorts of values, principles, or the like. However, if a basis in different ends is enough to insulate oughts from each other, we would seem to have a distinct subsystem for every distinguishable source of obligation.[55] Thus, in Sophie's case obligations to different children might be assigned different subscripts to avoid intrasystematic conflict, even though they are grounded in the same moral concerns. But just because they both are grounded in *moral* concerns, it is unclear that this move excludes dilemmas from morality. In any case, by disallowing logical interaction between conflicting oughts, Castañeda's approach would apparently keep deontic logic from capturing the problematic aspect of dilemmas.

This is not to say that a logical system or set of subsystems purporting to represent ethics can be expected to capture everything interesting about real-life ethical cases. As a proposal for structuring deontic logic, Castañeda's treatment of dilemmas seems to me to be on the mark as long as it is not taken as ruling them out *except* from a certain version of deontic logic. His own view in fact seems to be that morality essentially *is* an attempt to resolve conflicts, in the first instance between oughts arising from different agents' ends.[56] At least in rough terms, his approach resembles the account of morality as a social artifact that I shall go on to defend in chapter 3. However, in setting up moral sub-systems in terms of contexts of ends that can be "harmonized" into a single system, as he assumes, Castañeda essentially begins with a general ban on moral conflict.

What I have tried to do in this chapter is not to give a detailed defense of a new approach to deontic logic but simply to show how an adequate approach would seem to split into subsystems in the attempt to capture the notion of practical "ought." This notion allows for dilemmas on the view I have outlined by virtue of its relation to the reasons for and against action. I have used a perceptual analogy to understand the comparison of reasons that all-things-considered practical "ought" presupposes. In the first instance, the notion requires suffi-cient reason for ruling out alternative actions; and I have maintained that this core element of its meaning may be separately applicable to all alternatives in a given situation.

This is enough to provide a rationale for dilemmas in negative form, as cases of exhaustive prohibition. In positive form, as cases of exclusive requirement, they seem to be ruled out by the stipulation that positive or prescriptive "ought" also implies "permissible," understood as the absence of sufficient reason for ruling out its object. To allow for the distinction, I have suggested that deontic logic be founded instead on *proscriptive* "ought." The real complications this change would introduce seem to me to be not much worse than those required in any case in order to shift from the ideal notion of "ought" that the standard system covers to the ordinary practical notion that underlies action-guiding ethics.

We can now understand why agglomeration fails for practical "ought" by noting that the perceptual account of reasons allows for a kind of "split image" in certain cases: Sets of reasons may each be important or serious enough to stand in light of each other, even where they cannot stand together in the way that might seem to be required by a picture of ethics as harmonizing different ends. On the perceptual picture, reasons sometimes compete for dominance, prompting gestalt shifts in our view of the evidence, as captured by the sort of division into subsystems that Castañeda uses to avoid dilemmas. I take this alter-native picture instead to indicate in evidential terms what it means to say that dilemmas are possible. Deontic fragmentation, in short, does not undermine the coherency of ethics but just its unifiability at the level of particular action-guiding oughts. To the extent that the moral code can be seen as a product of potentially conflicting (social and individual) needs, it provides an intelligible basis for dilemmas.

The main point of my treatment of dilemmas in connection with deontic logic in this chapter was to allow for the coherency of practical "ought" in dilemmas—the sort of ought that is intended to motivate and that therefore would seem to fall subject to the problem of motivational force outlined in my preceding chapter. I did so by defending the negative conception of dilemmas. On this conception, which I introduced in section 1 as a way around Williams's denial of practical "ought," dilemmas are thought of as prohibitions of all alternatives open to the agent under the circumstances rather than as conflicting requirements or positive ought-judgments.

I defended the positive/negative distinction in the first half of section 2 with reference to the perceptual picture of the weighting of practical reasons as evidence for an all-things-considered ought, or one that holds in light of all the evidence, as distinct from one that is "overriding" in the sense of being strong enough in practical weight to cancel out competitors. This amounts to a figure-ground notion of reasons that pass a certain threshhold of seriousness as standing out against the general background in a way that allows for gestalt shifts. It allows us to think of negative dilemmas as involving exhaustive all-things-considered prohibitions, because the reason against any given alternative open to the agent may be strong enough in absolute terms to pass the threshhold, even though it cannot be said to cancel the force of opposing reasons, which also pass the threshhold. The notion applies to weighted as well as balanced dilemmas—to cases like Agamemnon's as well as Sophie's—on the assumption that even reasons of lesser weight in comparison with competing reasons may still be strong enough not to be canceled.

Another central idea of this chapter emerged from the comparison of all-things-considered "ought" with the stronger term "must," which apparently is not subject to dilemmas even in negative form. As an alternative to Williams's interpretation of "must" as implying "will" in accordance with a model of necessitation by character, I suggested a strengthened version of the "escapist" or sanctions model that some deontic logicians have applied to "ought." To say that one ought to do something is on this account to say that it is necessary to avoid some sanction or bad state of affairs—perhaps just something on the order of moral wrong, as the general sort of sanction associated with moral "ought." Accordingly, to say that one "must" do something is to refer to a sanction so bad as to blot out opposing reasons for action. This is not to say that there are no such opposing reasons—and statements framed in terms of "must" and related notions do seem to apply naturally to cases of dilemma— but just that they do not persist in view in the way that the perceptual picture of reasons allows with respect to ordinary ought-judgments. What the stronger term rules out in such cases is the inclusion of all of the agent's reasons for action within a single background of evidence bearing on an ought-judgment. It therefore might be said to capture the illusion that the moral sanction is avoidable—the assumption built into standard versions of "escapism" which my account rejects for cases of dilemma.

My ensuing defense of the logical coherency of my account and its implications for deontic logic applied the sanctions model to an interpretation of ought-judgments in terms of *needs*, as an alternative to Kantian "moral necessity" for understanding the imperatival force of moral "ought." A need involves the threat of a sanction that is avoidable by satisfying it, though perhaps not avoidable *simpliciter* since there is no guarantee that a set of needs will be jointly satisfiable. One might think of "must"-statements accordingly as statements expressing the dominance of some particular need or consistent set of needs—perhaps only a limited subset of the overall set of practical requirements imposed by the situation.

On the way to this application of the sanctions model to needs, my argument dealt in somewhat more detail with both the assumptions of cases of dilemma and some central assumptions and principles of deontic logic, in defense of my negative conception of dilemmas as cases in which nothing is permissible. In the second half of section 2, I maintained that dilemmas on my account come out as irresolvable in the sense of not being settled by appeal to any morally acceptable considerations, even if one accepts a stronger disjunctive ought prescribing the satisfaction of at least one of the oughts in conflict—or, in negative terms, forbidding the violation of both prohibitions. In Sophie's case, for instance, this amounts to a weightier prohibition on letting both children be taken to the gas chamber. With a certain allocation of harms, moreover— for instance, if saving one child could be accomplished only by inflicting something worse than death on the other—the disjunctive ought might come out with the same weight as those in conflict, for a case of exhaustively *balanced* prohibition.

I then turned, in section 3, to the logical underpinnings of the positive/negative distinction, beginning with problems about the application of the principle that "ought" implies "permissible" to negative oughts or prohibitions. In nontechnical terms: One might object that my defense of the principle in application to prescriptive "ought" would seem to apply to proscriptive "ought" just as well, as a practical ought enjoining the failure to perform a certain action. I essentially removed the parallelism by distinguishing between a negative ought and an ought that enjoins some negatively specified action. The former does not point the agent toward some indefinite alternative to action but rather just away from action, with no implication that there *is* a real alternative. My argument dealt with the distinction by way of a proposal for a version of deontic logic that takes the operator F (for "forbidden") as primitive in place of O or P, building "ought"-implies-"permissible" into the definition of O so that it covers only positive ought-judgments.

In response to Fregean objections to building negation into the operator, I argued that the very real complications the move would introduce make sense in light of the complicating role of permission as a third possibility between obligation and prohibition in deontic logic. The appropriate analogy to obligation versus prohibition is not really assertion versus negation but rather the more complex array of possibilities that emerge if we consider the alternatives to actively entertaining a proposition—or "thought," in Frege's own mentalistic terms—besides actively blocking it out.

An important result of my suggestions for deontic logic is the retention of the principle of closure: that OA and ~M(A & ~B) imply OB. My view avoids any conflict between closure and "ought"-implies-"permissible," of the sort that has been held to result from dilemmas, since it restricts the latter principle to positive "ought" and rejects positive dilemmas. However, I noted independent problems with closure as applied to ordinary ought-judgments. The principle seems to hold reliably only for statements phrased in terms of "ought," since "obligation" is more sensitive to the wording of particular commitments, principles, and the like, at any rate as applied via an infinitive phrase to some required action.

On the other hand, standard deontic logic is not really set up to capture ought-judgments about action, with its reading of the operator O as "it ought to be the case that" (used interchangeably with "it is obligatory that"). I argued that its claims to represent practical "ought" depend on capturing "ought-to-do" (in Castañeda's terms) as opposed to the statements of "ought-to-be" corresponding to ideal-world semantics. In the second half of section 3 I considered the extreme complication of deontic logic that would result from the modifications needed to extend it to dilemmatic "ought-to-do." I provided a rationale for rejecting the principle of agglomeration—that OA and OB imply O(A & B)—which dilemmas bring into conflict with "ought"-implies-"can" as a principle governing practical "ought." My claim was that ought-statements do not count as practical unless they actually have some point as pieces of action-guidance, and that two statements with such a point considered individually may lose it when agglomerated. But without agglomeration—or with the principle limited to different practical contexts in the manner of Castañeda's "ought-to-do" version of deontic logic—oughts seem to fragment into logically isolated subsystems. So, again, deontic logic fails to capture practical "ought."

The model of *needs* for interpreting practical "ought" comes up in illustrating the failure of agglomeration. It—or the sanctions model generally—yields a way of understanding oughts in terms of negative reasons, with motivational force provided by a threat, the prospect of some sort of sanction on nonperformance. So my argument here extends beyond the issue of the logical structure of dilemmas, to suggest a conception of moral "ought" that might begin to answer the more general problems raised in chapter 1. The model of needs has an obvious subjective interpretation corresponding to my perceptual analogy in this chapter, with *felt* needs taken as involving emotional awareness of the cost of doing without some object. In the case of action-guiding moral needs, this would seem to amount to anticipatory awareness of a sanction on nonperformance. Now I want to ask whether the sort of view suggested by the model can accord dilemmas and ethics generally any "real" basis in the sense of one that is not merely subjective.

3

Motivational Foundations of Conflict

With dilemmas now formulated negatively in terms of practical "ought"—in terms, that is, of prohibitions that are meant to guide action in some appropriately strong sense—I want to take a closer look at their implications for the question of moral realism. Williams's treatment of dilemmas as analogous to conflicting desires rather than beliefs was supposed to indicate, in effect, that ought-statements cannot describe moral facts: facts about the world, independent of our moral judgments and accounting for their truth as on standard definitions of realism.[1] But Williams does not take account of *evaluative* facts: facts about the goodness or badness of some object. To exclude these from the realm of facts is to beg the question against realism before the issue of conflict even comes up. Evaluative beliefs can certainly attribute the sorts of properties that Williams cites as nonagglomerative—properties described by variants of "good" like "desirable" and "prudent"—to contingently incompatible objects without more than pragmatic conflict about which object to choose. It would be another story, of course, to apply the corresponding overall assessments to incompatible objects—to pronounce each of them *best* or *most* desirable, say, or the *only* prudent object of choice under the circumstances.[2] But unless we assume noncognitivism, evaluative beliefs still seem to provide at least a small foothold for conflicting ought-judgments within the category of belief.

This is essentially a version of Philippa Foot's counterargument to Williams.[3] But Williams's problem for belief might seem to re-arise in application to the motivational aspects of dilemma. Capturing the difficulty of dilemmatic choice as something imposed on the agent by the ought-statements in conflict seems to require an internalist view of moral motivation, according to which it is impossible for a rational agent to hold a moral belief without being motivated to act on it. In the case of dilemmas, though, the attempt to act on *all* of one's moral beliefs would be self-defeating. So conflicting all-things-considered ought-judgments would seem to be irrational in combination; with motivational "vectors" thought of as part of the world such judgments describe, they would also rule out the sort of independent reality presupposed by moral realism.

Foot's comments on dilemmas seem to be limited to a fairly weak sense of action-guidance that escapes this problem at the cost of failing to support an account of the motivational force of moral "ought."[4] However, I think that Foot's remarks elsewhere on moral teaching contain materials for an intermediate position on internalism that combines with realism to yield a defensible answer to the problem of dilemmas and motivation. In this chapter I extract that view from Foot along with some other recent authors on metaethics—none of whom, it seems to me, can account adequately for dilemmas as things stand.

I begin by using Foot's comments on moral teaching to identify a version of externalism that ties motivational force in general terms to the moral import or function of an ought-statement, though not to its specific meaning (section 1). This view might be thought of as "general internalism," though it would be classified as a form of externalism as these terms are usually defined. Like standard externalist views, it allows for the coherency of motivational "amoralism," a hypothetical moral stance that involves holding a moral belief without being motivated to act on it. On the other hand, like internalist views, it provides a nonaccidental connection between the meaning of moral terms and their motivational force.

I shall go on to illustrate this nonaccidental connection by offering a speculative account of the teaching of "ought" by reference to emotion. In phenomenological terms my suggestion will be that the "demand quality" associated with action-guiding moral "ought" rests in part on a tendency to generate anticipatory guilt feelings—broadly construed as self-directed emotional discomfort at the thought of responsibility for a wrong. This sort of reference to feeling might seem to violate realist assumptions; but my view is meant to allow for a subject-independent account of the content of any given moral judgment and hence for a variant of moral realism in conjunction with a subject-*dependent* account of motivational force. It thereby solves a problem for current conceptions of realism, which seem to force a choice between dismissing amoralism and slighting the motivational purposes of moral judgment.[5]

I attempt to make a space for this intermediate view by examining the versions of internalism that we find in the writings of two contemporary authors, John McDowell and J. L. Mackie, whose positions roughly reflect the Kant/Hume contrast on motivational force set up in chapter 1. I exhibit problems with both views but also extract from them some elements of an alternative position in section 2. I then fill in my own proposed view and defend it against some objections, with special attention to variants of the charge of subject-relativity in section 3. What I hope eventually to put together, beginning here and continuing in my final chapter, is a view of the basis of morality in a set of socially instituted norms enforced on the individual level by a link to emotion. Despite a conventionalist element—and a partial basis in emotion, something usually associated with subjectivist approaches—I think there is an argument for taking this view as a version of moral realism.

1. Moral Realism and Practical Phenomenology

At least three kinds of force come up in the literature on moral motivation: motivational, practical or action-guiding, and reason-giving force (sometimes referred to as "normativity"). A (first-person) moral judgment with motivational force is one that actually moves the agent who accepts it to act, providing that she is rational. On the other hand, a judgment with practical force is *meant* to get her to act, and one with reason-giving force offers her a reason for action. Anscombe called into question the motivational force of moral "ought" on the grounds that, as currently understood, without reference to a divine lawgiver, it is merely psychological. Foot, on the other hand, takes aim in some of her arguments against the reason-giving force of moral judgments, particularly in response to the Kantian insistence on "binding" obligation.[6] However, in a treatment of Hume on moral judgment Foot has some related comments about the notion of practical force,[7] and I think that her arguments in both places have implications for motivational force. In the present discussion, then, I shall blur over the distinctions between these notions, except where they seem to make a difference, in the hopes of using some of Foot's remarks to bring out the point I have in mind.

Anscombe took moral "ought" to be marked off at this point only by its emphatic quality. I shall try to deal with this in psychological terms by way of a related phenomenological property sometimes called "demand quality," a property I actually take to be shared by nonmoral oughts that exhibit a compulsive hold on us, perhaps by reference to a deviation from some aesthetic or other notion of "fitness."[8] (Consider, for instance, the feeling that one ought to straighten a slanted picture on the wall.) The contrast is to oughts that merely recommend some action—as the best way of promoting our aims, say. What is special about the moral "ought" is presumably something about the psychological sanctions such as blame that a violation of it would incur. For present purposes, however, I shall be content to capture something broader: what we might call the strong imperatival sense of "ought," thought of as picking out an ought with demand quality.

Foot's central aim in her work on reason-giving force is to debunk the special bindingness that Kant attributed to moral "ought" as an illusion—an illusion foisted on us by the way we are taught to use moral language. In particular, as a result of what we are taught to *say* about morality, amoralism comes out sounding impossible: It seems to make no sense for someone to acknowledge the truth of a moral judgment and yet fail to acknowledge its force as a reason bearing on his action. However, I want to emphasize the positive results of this and related illusions, including some partially self-fulfilling results for the special force of moral judgments.

Moral Teaching and Illusion

My point about self-fulfilling illusion can be seen by considering Foot's treatment of the overridingness of moral judgments.[9] As with reason-giving force, overridingness may be thought of as an instance of the kind of binding force that Kant had in mind—in this case, involving enough force to win any conflict with nonmoral considerations, however important the latter are thought to be. In both cases Foot wants to say that the property in question is not a necessary property of moral judgments in the sense of applying to any given occasion of their use; to this extent the binding force of morality is an illusion.

However, despite the negative conclusion she wants to draw from it, Foot's explanation of the illusion of necessary overridingness seems to involve the inculcation of habits of practical reasoning that do accord moral judgments a special place or priority. Moral considerations seem to be necessarily overriding, on Foot's account, simply because we are taught to handle moral judgments differently in the face of conflict, modifying the rules to accommodate exceptions rather than treating them as "rigid rules that it is sometimes right to ignore" on the model of etiquette.[10] Thus, if our verdict in a certain case is that an act that would otherwise be morally forbidden is required on nonmoral grounds, we are taught to withdraw the judgment that it is morally forbidden rather than treating the judgment as overridden. The result, of course, is that no judgment *called* moral is ever overridden.

It is important to see that the illusion in question here is not simply the view of moral judgments as overriding—they are effectively *made* overriding, after all, by the way we are taught to handle them—but rather of overridingness as some kind of intrinsic or necessary property of moral judgments. Foot points out that there are deviant cases, as where a code of personal honor such as one that prescribes duelling is given greater weight than moral proscriptions.[11] The special priority of moral judgments is something we accord to them in ordinary cases rather than something we discover them to have; so it is something we can also take back.

Foot does not say that the illusion of necessary overridingness is in any way useful. However, the attribution of a product of moral teaching to morality itself makes sense as a way of strengthening the habits that moral teaching inculcates. The point also yields a defense of practical illusion on Foot's main "bindingness" issue, the issue of reason-giving force: It might well be useful in getting people to obey moral rules without attention to their desires or interests to represent morality as necessarily reason-giving. Foot in fact suggests something of the sort—along with a basis in moral teaching similar to the one she ascribes to overridingness—when she appeals to the social purposes of moral language to explain why "people are taught to *take* moral considerations as reasons for acting, without any reference to what they want, or what their interests are."[12] Again, the upshot of such teaching would seem to be that moral considerations generally do exhibit the property we ascribe to them necessarily, and the illusion of necessity may help make that so.

To extend the point to motivational force, let us take a look at some of Foot's earlier comments on Humean practical force. In arguing against what amounts to an antirealist account of moral judgments as needed to explain how morality is necessarily practical Foot acknowledges a kernel of truth in the claim of necessary practicality:

> It is not that this is false, but that one may easily insist on too close a connexion between moral judgment and the will. . . . [W]e take it as part of the meaning

of what we call 'moral terms' that they are in general used for teaching particular kinds of conduct; though nothing follows about what any particular individual who uses the terms must feel or do.[13]

These comments suggest a view that might be thought of as a general variant
of internalism, though on the usual definition of this contemporary terminology,
it would come out as externalist. Something about their practical force is presupposed by the meaning of moral terms and may even be said to apply to them
necessarily, but only in a collective sense. It concerns a didactic function that
they have on the whole, that is, rather than their effect on any given use. Presumably, it is a condition of meaningful moral discourse that the terms actually fulfill their didactic function with some regularity—enough to ensure that
moral judgments have practical force in general, meaning "by and large." But
"general internalism" (as I shall call this view) still leaves room for Foot's version of the amoralist: an agent who without irrationality claims not to be moved
by moral considerations since they fail to connect with her desires or interests.[14]

I want in what follows to supplement this suggestion by showing how we
might usefully teach moral judgments in a way that assigns them an illusory
kind of compulsive force in individual motivation. Foot's argument against
reason-giving force at one point briefly suggests what I have in mind, albeit
dismissively, with a mention of some illusory feelings. Her point is just that our
sense that "we 'must do' or 'have to do' something whatever our interests and
desires" lacks any basis in belief:

> [J]ust as one may feel as if one is falling without believing that one is moving
> downward, so one may feel as if one has to do what is morally required with-
> out believing oneself to be under physical or psychological compulsion, or about
> to incur a penalty if one does not comply.[15]

However, "as if" feelings of compulsion of the sort that Foot brings in here
would seem to be partially self-fulfilling in psychological terms to the extent
that they impose a penalty of emotional discomfort on noncompliance that
makes it difficult not to comply.[16] Once again, Foot's legitimate objection is to
a claim about necessity—in this case, a literal reading of our feeling that we
"must" comply, or one that makes out compliance as strictly necessary to escape
some external sanction or penalty.

I shall go on to sketch an account of the teaching of practical "ought" that
makes out such "as if" feelings of compulsion in terms of an internal sanction
of anticipatory guilt, taken not merely as an anticipation of (later) guilt at violating some prohibition but also as current guilt at the thought of a future violation "as if" already committed. Even without supposing that such feelings
necessitate action, I think they have an important role to play in filling out Foot's
mainly Wittgensteinian linguistic account of moral teaching with a kind of
Humean psychological glue. It will not be impossible on my suggested account
to resist the force of a moral judgment, but it will be psychologically difficult in
most cases. My account can still leave room, however, for Foot's rational
amoralist as someone who has managed to talk herself out of the feelings associated with moral teaching or someone on whom moral teaching never quite

took emotional effect in the first place: There is also no necessary connection on any given occasion or for any particular agent between moral teaching and the feelings it sets up as part of a general mechanism for eliciting action. All my account requires is that there be some such mechanism in operation most of the time—and that most of the time it operate effectively—as a presupposition of action-guiding moral "ought."

One might be tempted to question, though, whether this requirement really allows for "the" amoralist as someone completely immune to the force of moral considerations, in contrast to the many normal agents who seem to exhibit a kind of local amoralism for certain circumscribed areas of moral judgment. That someone might believe that, say, eating factory farm animals is wrong, without any desire or interest that pulls against it, seems plausible enough, but it does not follow that a particular agent could keep morality on ice, motivationally speaking, with respect to everything it asked of him. A certain degree of moral motivation might be thought to be required by sufficient participation in the institution of moral discourse to be said to hold moral beliefs as opposed to merely parroting moral statements. I shall not take a position on this issue, but I consider it an advantage of the general version of internalism that it can accommodate such limitations on the possibility of amoralism without ruling amoralism out entirely.

Essentially, though, what we have on my account of compulsive motivation in terms of emotional discomfort are short-term psychological needs in place of Kantian moral or rational necessity to supply the "binding" force of moral obligation for individual agents. To say that this glue is merely psychological is not to say that it is only accidentally linked to the meaning of moral judgments; general internalism gets between the alternatives offered us in the standard dichotomy between internalism and externalism by rejecting the assumption that the "force" of a given moral term is either part of its meaning or a mere concomitant of it. Instead, the view holds that motivational force in a general sense is presupposed by a term's *moral* meaning, or its role in a certain norm-governed linguistic institution, as a condition of any specific meaning it may have. We may think of this as analogous, say, to the way the practical implications underlying the legal meaning of certain terms may depend on their role in a legal system. (Consider, for instance, a phrase used to affix legal penalties like "in contempt of court.") Let us now take a speculative look at the way such a link between moral meaning and motivational force may be set up on the basis of illusion.

Teaching Practical "Ought"

In teaching a child moral language we begin with the strongest instances, leaving qualifications and refinements until later. This means that "ought" does not itself figure in the earliest cases I shall consider, which for the most part use "must" ("Mustn't do that!") and straightforward imperatives or imperatival variants ("Don't!" or simply "No!"). "Ought" is reserved for ages at which a child is able to exercise some judgment. Use of the weaker term leaves room for reasons on the other side: "You shouldn't do that" advises against a given action, perhaps emphatically, but even where it may be said to have imperatival force, it does not *mean* the same as "Don't!" On my proposed motivational account, then, "ought" is introduced only after we use stronger terms to establish the initial link to moral motivation. If deontic terms are in question, what we need to see in the first instance is how we teach "must"—or rather, "must not," since the negative formulation also is teachable at a less advanced stage, when a child has begun to exhibit action on its own but cannot yet reliably follow instructions.

On its earliest uses, though, "must not" applies after the performance of a forbidden action. In advance of or coinciding with punishment—or as itself a form of punishment insofar as it expresses disapproval—we tell a child that he "must not" perform the act in question. Before action we might more naturally use the imperative. Both expressions fit cases where the child seems already to be planning to do some forbidden action and we mean to warn him of impending punishment. Imagine a child who seems to be about to touch some delicate or dangerous object. "Mustn't touch that [vase]," say, might be uttered in a singsong, threatening tone at this point. But a warning to the same effect some time in advance of action would seem to be unintelligible at the earliest stage, before the child can even understand positive act-descriptions.

I conclude that practical "ought" (which I shall take as a generic term covering stronger and negative formulations along with statements framed in terms of "should") has its origins in a situation in which temporal distinctions are blurred in the interests of early moral teaching. This fits in with my proposed account of the teaching of "ought" in terms of anticipatory guilt, for the account will depend on blurring the barrier between past and future in psychological terms and extending guilt in a backward direction to a time preceding action.

Another fact that seems to fit is that in the time right before or after action when "must not" gets its primary use we would naturally turn to an evaluation of the agent: "Bad boy!" or the like. Later, in chapter 4, I shall examine in some detail the role of emotional guilt as a link between duty and virtue ethics. For present purposes, let us just note that guilt is normally for an act, but an act seen as in some way "tainting" the person who performs it; it amounts, one might say, to a feeling of *personal* unfitness. We encourage guilt in the teaching situation just described, then, essentially just by telling the child that violating a practical ought has earned him condemnation.

The personal evaluation may be linked to punishment, but punishment of the usual sort might just be seen as accentuating a more general emotional threat conveyed by our succession of verbal utterances. Their tone is one of mounting anger turning to all-out anger with the performance of the forbidden act. But anger is an emotion that itself can serve as a kind of punishment for others to the extent that it involves focusing negative attention on them. The underlying threat here seems to be rejection—exclusion in emotional terms from the family or other social group—as something that prompts acts of expiation of the sort associated with adult guilt: apologies and various compensatory acts in an attempt at reparation. In this case our anger is likely to abate after punishment, or after our expression of anger if there is no other punishment. On the assumption that early emotional learning results from imitation, however, one fairly immediate result would seem to be self-directed identificatory anger as a prototype of guilt.

We may think of guilt rather broadly at this point, picking it out just as some sort of unpleasant reaction to one's own putative offenses. Even when it is refined (both in childhood development and in the fuller version of my argument on this subject in chapter 4), its phenomenological aspect will be various. But the variants all involve self-blame. The scenario just sketched for learning "must not" involves a kind of verbal ritual acting out anger, and my suggestion is that it is meant not just to modify the child's overt behavior, linguistic and moral, but more fundamentally, to modify his emotion tendencies as motives toward future behavior. It elicits guilt as a reflection of the reactions of authority figures or objects of childhood dependency, though the emotion will later take different forms via emotional identification.

A case involving the infliction of harm on another child may help illustrate this last point—and the possible origins of a distinction between "must" and "ought." Consider our likely response when the child hurts his younger brother. If our aim were just to prevent the misdeed in the future by getting the child to exert behavioral control, the "must not" scenario would seem to be sufficient. However, our more likely tack in all but the most extreme cases is to try to instill empathy, or a tendency to identify with the victim of the misdeed that will serve as a barrier to harmful acts in the future.[17] So instead we make a fuss over the child who has been hurt, thereby showing how *we* identify with him. Sometimes this amounts to punishing the aggressor with a two-person form of social exclusion, as we play up the fact that our loyalties lie with his victim; in any case, it reinforces the sorts of direct expressions of anger just described—to instill a variant of guilt involving empathy with the victim's distress.[18]

If our emphasis in the new situation were on blame (after action) or simple prevention (before), we might still use an ought-statement framed in terms of "must": "You mustn't be so rough with him!" This sounds too sharp, though, for the usual sort of case, where our primary aim is to encourage a form of practical reasoning that rests on the ability to see things from another imaginative standpoint. To acknowledge the validity of two standpoints, or the presence of reasons on both sides, a weaker statement framed in terms of synonyms of "ought" sounds more apt: "You shouldn't be so rough."

What one seeks from a child by way of overt expiation in these cases is likely to be an apology, and here it can be directed at an injured party, a victim of his offense rather than an authority he has offended. We rehearse him in certain linguistic rituals after the forbidden action—"Tell him you're sorry"—and in both sorts of cases we thereby encourage a further kind of mentalistic ritual, involving expiation accomplished by undergoing an unpleasant emotion plus a reading back of later emotional reactions into the standpoint of deliberation. The point for present purposes is that, along with simple empathy with the victim in the more complex case, we also prompt a child to feel guilt in advance of action in future situations where he contemplates doing the same thing.

This experience of anticipatory guilt provides a basis for our illusion of practical compulsion on my account. As an unpleasant feeling, guilt can be said to motivate action to ward off a kind of emotional self-punishment to the extent that it constitutes a motive for its own relief. The account is not meant to imply that guilt is the only emotion appealed to in teaching practical "ought" or that practical "ought" in the strong or "binding" sense yields the only or the best or highest form of moral motivation. However, it is worth noting that the account makes out guilt as not so clearly distinct from love and other emotions sometimes ranked higher.[19] With its link to empathy or emotional identification, guilt might be seen as involving a kind of reflection of love in self-directed negative affect. My claim is just that we need some such element of negative affect to supply the demand quality of "ought."

In defense of my suggestion of temporal illusion, note that we have seen two ways in which the emotional overtones of practical "ought" may serve to extend it beyond the earliest cases pairing it with guilt—in the form of "must not" applied to an act the child may already have performed—to ought-statements preceding action, perhaps at some temporal remove. First, the anticipation with an ought-statement of an act the child seems about to perform—the singsong warning followed by anger if he acts anyway—would naturally result in the association of remembered guilt to the temptation to perform future acts of that sort. Second, another way in which "ought" is extended via guilt to acts at some distance in the future extends it also to positive ought-statements but with different objects. I have in mind the sorts of "contrary-to-duty" obligations imposed on the child as expiation for a forbidden action—obligations, that is, to make amends for acting contrary to duty—on the basis of whose fulfillment his punishment may be lifted. These get their motivational force from guilt insofar as they rest on a threat of continued emotional discomfort—anxiety about social rejection or the like—unless and until he fulfills them. On my proposed account, this experience of guilt as a force for future action may be read into the very content of the emotion—guilt becomes anxiety *about* not having yet made amends or the like—and then may be read back into the initial situation of forbidden action. So the two sources of motivational force—anticipatory emotional punishment and contrary-to-duty obligation—combine to yield a single mechanism capable of operating in advance.

The result in adult life is recognizable as an element of anxiety accompanying the thought of unfulfilled obligation. To the extent that this common feeling amounts to anticipatory guilt, it involves a kind of illusion, I want to say, with failure to perform the required act *so far* conflated in emotional terms with failure to perform it. That is not to say that the agent believes he has failed irrevocably, but just that the thought that he has comes to mind as an object of discomfort in moments preceding reflection. On the view I apply to guilt in chapter 5, an emotion with generally beneficial consequences may even count as appropriate with this illusory sort of object.

The illusion here resembles an optical illusion that the perceiver understands as such but still is visually misled by—in the way that one might be said to be kinaesthetically misled by the sense of falling in the passage I quoted from Foot debunking moral compulsion. My suggestion is that guilt in anticipatory form amounts to an "as if" feeling with a beneficial role as a reason for action to the extent that it makes it psychologically harder for the agent to violate an obligation.[20] Thus, for instance, in a case where action is needed to keep a promise, a sense of *having* to act can be seen as painfully absorbing attention—the agent is constantly looking over his shoulder, one might say—in a way that is due to childhood experience of guilt and related emotions. The result is a situation in which failure to act incurs a cost in discomfort—and therefore becomes a less tolerable option, even if still possible—so that the illusory feeling of compulsion fulfills itself to some extent by constituting a penalty for noncompliance.

I should stress that my suggested account of childhood experience purposely lumps together elements of practical thought that are later distinguished. In particular, there seems to be no clear contrast between practical and specifically moral uses of "ought" in the early teaching of the term in connection with guilt. My initial "must not" scenario would work just as well for touching a light plug as a vase, so my account here applies more generally to practical "ought," even though its foundation in identification with authority gives it a primitive kind of moral basis. Since guilt is thought of as a distinctively moral emotion, one might be tempted to ask how it gets extended to nonmoral cases. However, I think we really should say that the feeling is not extended but the reverse: Its moral use is picked out with time from an undifferentiated cluster of cases in which it plays a role in teaching behavioral norms. We initially lump together cases of morality and etiquette, for instance, using the threat of group exclusion to teach both—and using shame as well as guilt for both, ignoring later emotional distinctions.

Apart from refinements, however, the general upshot of this account is the way it connects the force of "ought" to its meaning—nonaccidentally, I want to say, but not by simply building motivational force into the meaning of individual moral terms or judgments as on standard internalist accounts. Reference to guilt and similar emotions is an essential part of the teaching of moral terms, something that underlies their meaning as a precondition of their moral use, taken as their use in eliciting behavior. The result is a picture of the "magnetism" of moral language as action at a temporal distance.[21] Its influence on behavior depends on emotional demands we make in early moral teaching: what we might distinguish from the meaning of a given moral term as its "didactic import."[22]

In light of the way such terms are taught, that is, they retain emotional overtones from the initial teaching situation. But although this penumbra of associated discomfort is essential to the motivational purpose of moral language, it can be canceled—both in cases of defective emotional learning and as a result of critical reflection. In an emotional sense we can easily see how amoralism is possible: A rational agent may grant that she ought not to do a certain act and yet contemplate doing it without guilt or any similar motivating emotion. Indeed, emotion will drop out even in normal cases where one acts morally just out of habit. My suggestion is not that we experience guilt or some similar emotion on typical moral uses of the word "ought"; rather, because of their role in moral teaching, such feelings are normally available as back-up responses in cases where moral action is *not* automatic. As states of emotional discomfort they can function motivationally in potential form, simply by providing a threat. What general internalism tells us, in short, is that this threat is not part of the meaning of a moral term, though it plays a role in setting up moral meaning in the first place and is in most cases carried along with it.

My argument for general internalism is meant to leave room for a version of moral realism that assigns a fundamental motivational role to moral emotion. I would also like to use it to suggest something more general: the reconception of metaethics as a branch of moral psychology. Some recent authors have attempted to locate within the usual boundaries of the subject in metaphysics and epistemology an essentially perceptual account of moral judgment that is realist despite subjectivist elements.[23] Their view makes out moral responses on the model of color perception and thus represents the content of ethics as subject-independent in the sense of being independent of any particular subject, while granting its dependence on the existence of minds generally. Even if we accept something of this sort for basic *value* concepts, however, the analogy to color perception seems not to fit those responses that underlie specifically deontic concepts like moral "ought."

Feelings of guilt, that is, and related feelings associated with the thought of wrong do not appear to exist in unrefined form with a certain set of natural objects on the model of untutored sense-perception in an infant's initial reactive apparatus. If the account I have offered here is even roughly right, such feelings are based on a tendency to identify emotionally with others, including objects of childhood dependency, who therefore have the power to shape the resulting emotions. Moral emotions like guilt thus seem to be subject to social manipulation of a sort that makes cross-cultural convergence on a perceptual model uncertain. However, I hope to have exhibited another way of allowing for a subjectivist element in moral realism by understanding moral emotions as supplying the motivational force of moral "ought."

The view makes out motivational force as indeed something psychological, something distinct from reason-giving force, which I shall say more about later. This means that ethics need not be rationally undermined, though it loses a certain psychological prop, if one sees through the illusions that originally got it going, assuming one has developed sufficient insight by that stage to make out independent reasons for it. On my proposed account, emotions and other motives in the sense of internal causes of behavior often reinforce moral reasons in adult life; and since moral behavior must be taught at a stage before one can adequately discern the reasons for it, this form of motivation has to be taught first, in conjunction with simple rules. At the later stage, however, one can kick away the motivational ladder and still have access to reasons capable of influencing action: the aesthetic reasons for not risking damage to a vase, say, and the social or interpersonal reasons for not causing harm to others. What is illusory according to my argument here is not the force of moral reasons for an agent assumed to be rational but just the impression that it amounts to "binding" force, understood as a kind of extrapsychological compulsion.

My psychological account of motivational force also explains it as something essentially social. It is something with which morality is invested *by* a social group—not particularly society at large but rather the various overlapping face-to-face groups that teach and thereby shape moral emotions. In what follows I use that basic scenario of moral teaching to construct a general metaethical view that is capable of making sense of moral dilemmas.

2. Internalist Dilemmas

Standard approaches to moral motivation seem to be unable as they stand to accommodate moral dilemmas, for reasons that also yield an unsatisfying treatment of amoralism. Externalist views of the usual sort and antirealist views—the approaches I grouped together in chapter 1 as "subject-dependent"—can be said to make dilemmas too easy. Whether the agent in a dilemma is motivationally "torn" by the choice he has to make depends on whether he happens to be moved by both of the oughts in conflict. If someone is not, the fact that others are or even that their motivational propensities are generally of greater moral value than his own (as on Hare's view) says nothing to challenge his response to that particular situation. The fact that we might justify the response, if it did occur, by appeal to its ordinary function does not imply some deficiency where one manages to avoid it. Similarly, on an externalist account, nothing essential to moral belief seems to be lacking to the amoralist: It comes out not just as possible but even as unproblematic how someone can accept an ought-judgment and yet feel no inclination to act on it.

Internalism is linked in the first instance to noncognitivist versions of antirealism, which interpret the content of a moral judgment in terms of its intended practical function and hence in subject-dependent terms. So on standard antirealist accounts, assuming that genuine ambivalence is possible with respect to moral motivation, dilemmas in a subjective sense will come out as possible too. Their motivational opposition, though, will amount to nothing beyond the agent's ambivalence. Since the content and the motivational force of a moral judgment will both presumably be supplied by the same mental state, whether a situation is a genuine dilemma will depend on the agent's reaction to it. This leads us by a different route to the problem just noted for externalism. On the question of amoralism, however, we get the opposite result: Just because the content of a moral judgment supplies its motivational force, it will be impossible to accept one without the other.

There is another sort of antirealist view in the contemporary literature, J. L. Mackie's "error theory," on which dilemmas also come out as impossible—and at the same time, one might still say, as too easy on the agent—just because all moral judgments are taken to be false. On this approach, which assumes internalism, moral judgments do mean something subject-independent *and* action-guiding, but the combination is impossible: All there really is to back them up motivationally is the agent's mental states. The view is therefore subjectivist; I argue that it might be reconstructed as a form of realism, however, by correcting standard internalism to avoid what Mackie's theory takes to be our usual moral error.

I eventually present this move as a way out of the problem set up in chapter 1. First, though, I want to look at some features of the internalist version of realism that now seems to hold the field. This is John McDowell's cognitivism, defended in opposition to the desire/belief model of intentional action insofar as it takes moral belief—rather than belief supplemented by a further mental state, typically desire—as sufficient to generate action.[24] Here too I think that refining the view to make it accommodate dilemmas and amoralism will yield something closer to my own position. In both cases, for that matter, I think that the necessary refinements can be constructed largely out of materials the author provides. McDowell's remarks at one point suggest that it might be belief as an object of current attention rather than belief alone, at least in the ordinary sense, that constitutes the motivating cognitive state he has in mind. This is something that my own view interprets in terms of emotion, via an evaluative analysis that also seems to accommodate McDowell's characterization of moral insight as a special kind of sensitivity. However, my understanding of emotion will depart from McDowell's perceptual model with an account of the tie between emotions and action that allows for moral dilemmas.

Cognitivism and Motivational Sufficiency

Though McDowell's view is developed in a number of articles on different subjects, its main points relevant to motivational issues can be found in an early critical piece on Foot along with a footnote allusion to dilemmas in an account of virtue.[25] As in my treatment of Foot, I shall not attempt a detailed exposition of McDowell's overall metaethical view but instead shall bring in particular points and positions as they affect the issues under discussion. In brief: McDowell defends an Aristotelian notion of virtue as based on a kind of perception of reasons for action in opposition to Foot's view of morality as simply not giving reasons to someone who has no independent motivation to act morally, of the sort provided by desire on the standard model. Reason-giving force on McDowell's account does not depend on desire as an independent factor; rather, it is something that the virtuous person perceives as applying to the particular situation, with desire taken as following from that perception.

McDowell agrees with Foot, then, that an agent who is unmoved by moral considerations is not necessarily irrational but instead makes her out as morally blind: She fails to see the reason that morality indeed provides. What she lacks is an accurate view of the practical requirements of the situation that McDowell identifies with virtue on the assumption that it depends on a similar appreciation of all potentially competing requirements and hence amounts to a general perceptual capacity. It is in reference to his discussion of this version of the doctrine of the unity of the virtues that McDowell includes a footnote relevant to dilemmas.

In defense of a claim that the virtues of kindness and justice presuppose each other, since the agent with either virtue has to be able to pick out situations calling for its exercise from those that call for the other, McDowell notes:

> I do not mean to suggest that there is always a way of acting satisfactorily (as opposed to making the best of a bad job); nor that there is always one right answer to the question what one should do. But when there is a right answer, a virtuous person should be able to tell what it is.[26]

McDowell's first clause here is as close as he comes to taking a position on the possibility of dilemmas. But it might be read as substituting an explanation short of dilemma—that sometimes all alternatives are morally objectionable in the sense of nonideal—for the sorts of cases of impermissible alternatives that a proponent of dilemmas would cite. I take the rest of the passage to imply a rejection of genuine dilemmas. In such cases there might be said not to be *one* right answer (as in McDowell's second clause) to the question what to do, but this may be understood in a way that does not allow for the substitution (in his next sentence) of *no* right answer, meaning no requirement of the sort that a virtuous person apprehends.

McDowell's substitution rests on the assumption that a right answer to the question what one should do amounts to one that specifies a right act. This works well enough for the positive conception of dilemmas on the assumption that a right answer is an ought-judgment prescribing a permissible act. We can now see that the sort of problem about the motivational sufficiency of conflicting ought-judgments that might seem to undermine McDowell's cognitivism—the problem I used Kant's view to illustrate in chapter 1—does not arise for the positive conception. We do not have to deal with cases in which each of two conflicting all-things-considered oughts yields sufficient motivation to act, on McDowell's account or Kant's, since such cases are ruled out by the assumption that "ought" implies "permissible." But the problem can easily be formulated for exhaustive prohibitions.

On McDowell's account, the virtuous agent must be sensitive to any and all act-requirements imposed by his situation, including of course negative requirements or prohibitions; according to standard internalism, his sensitivity would seem to be sufficient by itself to generate action. But then, if there were cases of genuine dilemma, McDowell's notions of sensitivity and motivational sufficiency would apparently imply that the virtuous agent performs two incompatible actions. It follows that McDowell's account cannot accommodate dilemmas set up as cases of exhaustive prohibition unless it somehow modifies standard internalism. His footnote evades this problem, in effect, by putting the question in positive terms and equating the existence of a right answer with that of a right or satisfactory thing to do. With the question set up negatively, however, there will be *two* right answers—two prohibitions—which together yield the result that there is *no* right thing to do.

It might be thought that McDowell does mean to modify standard internalism, though in a way quite different from what I have in mind, insofar as he relies on a notion of motivational force that connects it to the force of reasons. That is, there would seem to be no distinction between motivational and reason-giving force on his view—or on Nagel's Kantian version of internalist realism, though Nagel does accept dilemmas. Perhaps an internalist in this sense can simply deny that motivational force has to involve a push toward action— has to determine the will, in Kantian terms. Instead, in some cases it might just involve appreciating the practical relevance of a reason—or, in the case of dilemmas, its decisiveness. On this account, whether one actually is moved to act would depend on the absence of all-things-considered competing reasons.

Both Nagel and McDowell clearly want motivational force to imply more than an intellectual recognition of the reasons bearing on action, however. The notion is supposed to replace desire in explaining the generation of action by reasons.[27] To withdraw any push toward action, then, in the face of serious moral conflict, would make dilemmas too easy on the agent. That is, the agent's conflicting reasons would apparently just be rendered inert by conflict, reduced to a mere list of negative features of action that leave him with nothing to do. Rather than being motivationally "torn," or impelled in opposing directions, he would seem to be in a condition of practical stalemate and hence simply frustrated at his inability to settle on a course of action.

I shall eventually propose a way of modifying McDowell's Aristotelian view in connection with the issue of amoralism that will yield a preferable approach to moral dilemmas. But let us note first that certain moves that might be suggested for applying his view to dilemmas by requiring a lesser degree of motivational force are not really open to him, given the kinds of demands his view makes on the notion of a virtuous agent. One might want to object, for instance, that the motivational vacillation or even deadlock that would seem to be mandated by cases of exhaustive prohibition could be explained by attributing to the agent motives of less than full strength. We should see the virtuous agent in such cases as moved to some extent by each of two competing prima facie reasons. To say that, however, would just be to say that the case does not constitute a dilemma; we should remind ourselves of the assumption that dilemmas involve conclusive or all-things-considered oughts in conflict. Presumably, moreover, the virtuous agent would have to be sensitive to each of them in a degree that reflects their moral importance in absolute as well as in relative terms. Agamemnon, for instance, falls short of virtue because he does not sufficiently register the moral horror of the sacrifice of his daughter and hence is insensitive to one side of his dilemma. On the other hand, we cannot say that the virtuous person tries but fails to act on two conflicting reasons that she is sensitive to, for she is assumed to be rational, and rationality rules out action at cross-purposes.

I shall suggest a way of handling this problem; but lest it be thought easy enough for McDowell to handle it just by rejecting dilemmas, we should also take note of a related problem with respect to amoralism. McDowell's answer to Foot's treatment of the amoralist in effect interprets the amoralist as something else—something other than the *motivational* amoralist under consideration—by making him out as morally blind, or unable to appreciate moral reasons on a cognitive level. McDowell's alternative to the desire/belief model essentially rests on expanding the notion of what is involved at the cognitive level so that it would not be possible to share the same view of the circumstances as someone who is morally sensitive and yet not be similarly motivated.[28] To the extent that the "view" in question here involves seeing a certain action in a favorable light, it implies seeing a reason to perform the action and hence has reason-giving force.

McDowell does not distinguish motivational from reason-giving force, as I have noted. Presumably he would count it as either impossible or irrational, and hence as impossible for a virtuous agent, to recognize a reason for action and yet not be motivated. But the amoralist no less than the virtuous agent is supposed to be rational. McDowell's answer to Foot, then, essentially involves denying that the amoralist really recognizes the same moral reasons for action as the rest of us—or in the first instance as the virtuous agent, whose reasons we share when morally motivated. This response may be difficult to fault intuitively just because the problem of amoralism as set up in global terms rests on acceptance of a counterintuitive kind of moral personality. To the extent that we can make sense of it (by appeal to literary examples, say), it is sufficiently foreign to put the amoralist's cognitive state somewhat beyond imaginative reach. In response to examples of our own "local" amoralism, however—my earlier example was eating factory farm animals—McDowell would have to say that we could not really share the virtuous person's view of even the isolated sort of situation that is in question. As a moral "blind spot," this also involves failure to see.

An argument over this sort of case would typically focus on the question whether the agent professing motivational amoralism could possibly be acquainted in a full enough sense with all relevant information, especially firsthand or imaginative information such as that giving insight into the misery of animals on factory farms. However, it is important that this line of response would move beyond the specific focus on belief as the bearer of moral knowledge in the desire/belief model from which McDowell pulls away. It is indeed a kind of "perceptual" acquaintance with the facts—but in a more literal sense than McDowell has in mind in his use of perceptual imagery for moral insight—rather than simple intellectual comprehension that is likely to make a motivational difference in the case cited.

McDowell himself might just say that the supposed amoralist about eating factory farm animals—the agent who claims to recognize that it is wrong and yet not to be motivated to abstain—could not really understand what it was to "recognize" a practical reason. The notion entails acknowledging the bearing of some consideration on one's choice of action, which effectively undercuts a distinction between intellectual and motivational acknowledgment. However, it is not clear that the only way to recognize the practical relevance of a reason is to be inclined to act on it. One might simply use it to *judge* action—acknowledging that eating factory farm animals is morally substandard, say, without feeling impelled to live up to a moral standard so rigorous as to demand that one abstain. To capture the decisiveness of a serious moral reason, we could understand the relevant sort of motivational amoralist as measuring his own and other agents' virtue in light of the standard, deferring to vegetarians as moral exemplars but still without motivation to join them.

Besides dropping desire, then, I think McDowell's exclusion of amoralism must turn on an expansion of the sorts of cognitive possibilities allowed for by the desire/belief model. "Cognitive" comes out, in short, as a broader category than "intellectual" on an approach that would support his talk of moral sensitivity and the like. The move is masked by McDowell's use of the standard terminology: He evidently wants to include some conative elements within belief rather than questioning whether belief in the usual sense is sufficient. To discuss the move in terms that relate it to my own treatment of emotion, I shall use "belief" in what follows more narrowly than McDowell, though one might also substitute some more qualified notion such as "belief in its judgmental aspect" for the sake of faithfulness to McDowell's preferred blurring of the standard distinctions.

McDowell's inclusion of extraintellectual elements within cognition is in fact suggested by some brief comments on incontinence at the end of his reply to Foot.[29] Since he no longer has a purely conative category like desire available to explain continence, McDowell has to make use of the cognitive, and here he appeals beyond belief to *attention*, which he interprets as part of the continent person's "conception" of the situation—the most intellectual of the terms replacing "belief" in his substitute for the desire/belief model. (He sometimes uses "perception," apparently without distinction,[30] but his most common term, encompassing both, is "view.") Of incontinent or weak-willed agents he writes:

> Their inclinations are aroused, as the virtuous person's are not, by their awareness of competing attractions: a lively desire clouds or blurs the focus of their attention on "the noble."[31]

The comment harks back to McDowell's preceding account of Aristotle's virtuous person as exhibiting temperance or single-minded moral motivation—as distinct from mere continence, or strong-willed triumph over contrary motivation—by "silencing" immoral inclinations.[32] In McDowell's example in that discussion the virtuous person simply lacks any desire for illicit sex rather than manages to overcome one. In a case of weakness, then, desire can be made out as an interfering factor, though McDowell's cognitivist view deprives it of any independent role in virtuous motivation.

What does it interfere with in cases of weakness, and how? If we remind ourselves of the distinction between a belief and a thought that one actually entertains or holds in mind, we can replace McDowell's Aristotelian talk of attention to the noble with a reference to whatever mental mechanism serves to fix moral judgments in mind. This may or may not be purely cognitive; I take it typically to involve the sort of cognitive/affective mix that we find in moral emotion. At any rate, it need not be seen as involving the sort of separable or independent noncognitive element that McDowell means to exclude in dropping desire. On the other hand, in most cases it involves something beyond belief. Belief is just what the weak-willed agent is assumed to share with one who is virtuous: what the person overcome by adulterous passion loses sight of but still retains. He knows what is right but fails to act on his knowledge just because he does not have it fixed firmly in mind.

This need not mean that the weak-willed agent is not thinking about the moral truth in question, even in relation to the noble; he may very well be acutely aware that he is acting against his beliefs. It is a fuller kind of practical attention that is presumably lacking. Something similar might now be said of the amoralist, however. His moral sensitivity has been "silenced," to use McDowell's term, not by desire but in this case simply by a failure to generate the appropriate moral emotion as needed to supply motivation.

This is not to say that a moral emotion is always needed to motivate. My speculative account of the teaching of "ought" in section 1 allowed that the moral behavior we inculcate via emotion normally becomes habitual. In typical cases habitual moral behavior is not quite automatic but can be said to involve an emotional residue of the teaching situation, in the sense of arousal sufficient to fix a belief in mind, securing attention. However, it need not involve a specific moral emotion; McDowell's "sensitivity" will do. I would also grant that belief alone can motivate, meaning "can in some cases," even without attention—as when the habit of acting on some moral belief becomes so ingrained as to be discharged in rote fashion. Habit in such a case would not amount to a further mental determinant of action needed to supplement belief but just a pattern of action on belief. It need not be taken strictly as "determining" action; the common inference from a claim that some mental state or faculty can motivate to the view of it as sufficient in something like a causal sense is an instance of the Kantian "necessitarian" approach to morality and motivation that my argument here is meant to question. It is not obvious that anything with the power to motivate must do so unless checked, or that ingrained habits are always compulsive. In any case, the amoralist is assumed to lack normal habits of moral behavior; so at least in short-range terms, motivating him requires an emotion.

Whether the amoralist on this account may be said to share the virtuous person's "view" or "conception" of the situation—"perception" in a broad sense, roughly equivalent to "apprehension," without any sensory overtones—depends on whether we interpret such notions as covering the full range of cognitive and auxiliary responses to the moral facts, including attention and emotion, or as limited to belief. At any rate, the notion of emotional appropriateness that I explain in chapter 5 will allow for the failure to feel an appropriate emotion compatibly with rationality. Appropriateness does not *mandate* feeling, in short. But this point will effectively drive a wedge between reason-giving and motivational force.

Although McDowell does not explicitly question the standard categories for explaining action that he has inherited from the philosophers he criticizes, many of his comments in his reply to Foot and elsewhere suggest my broader interpretation of the cognitive. Here, for instance, he at one point brings in our understanding of the "meaning" of some morally significant circumstance as illustrated by a statement we might make in trying to get someone to share the requisite view of things: "You don't know what it means that someone is shy and sensitive."[33] Someone who made this statement would typically be claiming not just that the hearer lacked some factual information about the behavioral or other implications of shyness but rather that he had no idea what shyness was like. This is what shyness means to the one who is shy, and the reason why it inhibits him behaviorally. Without experiencing shyness "from the inside," one is at least arguably unable to understand its outer meaning in the sense of its behavioral significance. Real knowledge of this sort, however, seems to require imagination and emotional empathy as part of the recommended "cognitive" view of things.

More generally, meanings in the sense indicated include saliences of the sort that emotions register: the notion of what is important or significant about a situation, or in cognitive terms, what is worth attention.[34] McDowell hastens to point out that the appeal the statement about shyness makes is not to "passion as opposed to reason," or to feeling taken as something "quite over and above one's view of the facts,"[35] the sort of independent element of desire that he wants to eliminate. My suggestion here, however, is just that emotional evaluations are part of one's view of the facts. On the account of emotions I defend later in application to guilt, emotions include evaluative thoughts as objects of comfort or discomfort. In McDowell's perceptual imagery of silenced and unsilenced reasons, they may be thought of as an important mental mechanism for *amplifying* reasons, or for amplifying and recording them for future reference—registering them as objects of practical attention by loading them with positive or negative affect.

We can now see how my account might let McDowell handle cases of dilemma. Here, on any adequate picture, we have two emotionally amplified reasons as a norm for the appropriately sensitive moral agent, not just as a description of how some agents happen to react. Of course, it is impossible to act on two conflicting moral beliefs, but the possibility of emotional ambivalence allows for a form of practical attention to both of them.[36] With the agent's conflicting reasons for action seen as given in the evaluative content of the two emotions, we can make him out as motivated by both of two conflicting ought-judgments. Action on one of them will be blocked, of course; but a "residue" emotion such as guilt will remain as a sign of its motivational force deflected onto emotion. I shall later argue that this function of guilt depends on its component of negative affect.

Making McDowell's view accommodate dilemmas requires modifying his commitment to the motivational sufficiency of cognitive commitment to an ought-judgment, if that means its causal sufficiency for action. My account accomplishes this by abandoning strict internalism in favor of the general version defended in section 1, according to which an agent can understand an ought-judgment and fail to register it motivationally. My account takes emotion as the primary bearer of motivational force and hence introduces a further element besides belief to explain moral motivation—something added onto belief in typical cases and potentially detachable from it, even if not quite independent of it on the model of desire. Belief may fail to motivate either because this further element is missing or because its motivational influence is blocked—the latter pertaining to cases of dilemma, where not all oughts can be satisfied, so that emotion serves as a second-best substitute for action.

A version of McDowell's personal moral standard might be said to play a role in my own view to the extent that the weaker normative link my view sets up between moral judgments and emotion still depends for its application to dilemmas on the possibility of conflicting emotions in a rational agent. However, my account of the role of guilt in chapter 4 will depart from the Aristotelian standard of perfect virtue on which McDowell relies. In any case, rather than presupposing a form of virtue ethics of the sort McDowell has in mind—I shall later make some alternative suggestions—my defense of dilemmas admits of a coherent interpretation in terms of general principles of duty: the conception of ethics that McDowell's perceptual imagery is meant to replace with a "particularist" moral theory. Let me now turn to Mackie's view for a notion of the rule-based structure of morality, with morality reconstructed to answer Mackie's arguments against realism.

Protagorean "Social Artifact Realism"

The ordinary conception of real perceptual properties associated with McDowell's version of realism actually makes it seem easy to accommodate dilemmas. In cases of exhaustive prohibition, all we need are noncomparative negative properties that apply to all alternatives, and the list of possible parallels is a long one. Consider the properties of being horrible or hideous or revolting—or even (on certain assumptions) the sort of thing that would disgust an ideal observer. A moral term with similar visceral overtones that would fit my perceptual treatment of sufficient reasons against action in chapter 2 is "intolerable." The possibility of dilemmas as expressed in such terms just means that every option in some cases can fail to meet some minimal standard of moral acceptability.

What threatens the intelligibility of this view is the presumed action-guidingness of moral judgments, as attributed to the moral facts to which they refer on an internalist version of realism. This is essentially the basis of Mackie's "argument from queerness" to the denial of the objectivity of moral values.[37] Mackie uses the term "objective prescriptivity" for the "queer" combination of claims that he takes to be implied both by moral discourse of the ordinary sort and by the writings of most moral philosophers. Prescriptivity or action-guidingness is a property of moral language, but insofar as we use moral language to describe something objective, Mackie's account makes us out as attributing prescriptivity to something in the world. The account therefore amounts to an "error theory": In contrast to noncognitivist accounts that deny moral statements descriptive meaning it interprets them as meaning something false.[38]

However, Mackie's comments at some points suggest that the error might be removable: Ordinary moral discourse could be revised to stick to the facts (as Mackie conceives them) essentially by canceling its prescriptive force. Rather than dropping internalism, as this entails, Mackie evidently means to revise ordinary moral discourse in the direction of noncognitivism. But an alternative

move of the sort I have in mind is suggested in his discussion of naturalist definitions of moral terms with reference to an assumed set of purposes, which is
essentially a reworking of Foot's treatment of "good."[39] Mackie himself bypasses the suggestion for all but a few cases involving fixed standards of evaluation; values would apparently be less than fully objective in the sense he has in
mind to the extent that the determination of standards rests on potentially variable purposes. His own eventual definition of "good" makes indefinite reference to the satisfaction of requirements, and he insists that statements of moral
value must be taken as ascribing "intrinsic requirements" to the world: "requirements which simply are there, in the nature of things, without being the requirements of any person or body of persons, even God."[40] This is the assumption I
want to challenge, for "ought" rather than for "good," along with Mackie's
general assumption of internalism.

Mackie often refers metaphorically to the question of objectivity as the
question whether moral values are part of the "fabric" of the world; his description of behavior as part of its "furniture" suggests that he has in mind a spatial
network of relations among solid objects.[41] Instead, we might think of moral
values as analogous to the weave in a woven fabric—something inseparable from
its threads, after all—and at the same time as relating behavior to persons or
minds to the extent that morality rests on a relation to their purposes, or their
harm and benefit. I take it that this latter sort of dependence on minds does not
undercut realism—does not constitute "subject-dependence" in the relevant
sense—if it leaves intact the role of minds as knowers of moral truths. Mackie
uses the term "objectivity" for the view he means to attack, and he attributes
the view to philosophers who base moral value on subjective states like pleasure/
pain, as well as to Plato and Kant.[42] What moral realism rules out, however, is
subject-*relativity*, meaning relativity to the putative subject of knowledge of a
moral judgment as opposed to the various subjects of experience the judgment
might be thought to be about.

A realist view can even make moral value depend on the existence of minds
as knowers of *some* judgments of the sort that is in question, as long as it does
not make a given judgment depend for its truth on someone's current commitment to it. Since Foot's naturalist definition of "good" appeals to a standard
set of purposes, not necessarily those of a given subject, it would seem to come
out as realist on this account. Moreover, McDowell's treatment of moral value-
properties on the model of perceptual properties is interpreted as realist, though
it makes moral judgments depend in a general sense on our possession of the
capacity for moral sensitivity.[43] I want in what follows to suggest a further level
of general subject-dependence for specifically deontic properties as compatible
with moral realism. If we take for granted either of these other accounts in
application to evaluative properties—making them out as "subjective" only in
a metaethically harmless sense—then I think we can also understand moral requirements as requirements of persons rather than intrinsic requirements without departing from realism. On the sort of interpretation I shall suggest, they
depend on prior social requirements within certain constraints imposed by con

siderations of social value, including both rational and moral value as applied to the comparison of alternative moral institutions.

What I have in mind are the various social choices and attitudes that underlie the adoption and maintenance of a moral code. I shall go on to extract my proposed version of realism, which I refer to as "social artifact" realism, from the picture of morality given in Mackie's own transition to his account of normative ethics. But my extension of Mackie's view should also apply in general terms to rather different conceptions of the basis of morality, such as a version of divine command theory that takes God as the source of moral ought-judgments (perhaps with human welfare in mind) but not of judgments of good. The view also might be taken to yield a contractarian basis for morality that avoids Kantian presuppositions.[44] It combines elements of virtue and duty ethics, as we shall see. I put it forth as a way of reconfiguring the structure of ethics, with a different metaethical basis insofar as it departs from standard positions on the question of internalism.

After denying moral judgments objectivity, Mackie proceeds to a treatment of normative ethics in terms of the function of morality as a system of constraints on conduct designed to protect others' interests.[45] Morality on this account is needed to counteract limited sympathies, or a tendency toward self-interest, and its content depends on what will best promote that cooperative social end. But this suggests that evaluative judgments of a sort that Mackie apparently finds unproblematic, about the effectiveness of means in promoting ends, might help provide an objective basis for *some* moral judgments even if not those in ordinary moral discourse.[46] If so, morality could presumably be reconstructed to avoid the error of attributing action-guidingness to something external.

Perhaps Mackie did not think of this position as "objectivist" just because it assigns an important role to moral emotion. The mythical account of the historical basis of morality that he takes from Plato's *Protagoras* splits it into two elements: *aidōs* (shame or respect; a word with broader implications that Mackie decides to translate as "moral sense") and *dikē* (law or justice).[47] Mackie interprets *dikē* to cover formal rules and politico-legal "devices" set up to secure the aims of morality, but the term would also seem to apply to various informal social practices with the same end, such as promising, that his preceding argument includes under the umbrella term "institutions." These come up as central devices of morality when Mackie fills in the Protagorean view with critical discussions of Hobbes's contract and Hume's artificial virtue of justice, concluding with a rejection of the suggestion that ethics abandon rules in favor of virtues. We might think of *dikē*, then, on Mackie's interpretation, as the basis of morality in rules.

Mackie seems to restrict *aidōs*, on the other hand, to the sources of motivation to conform to rules, dispositions to act as well as emotions. But it would be natural—and consistent with Plato's use of the Protagorean view—to extend this term to the looser sorts of emotional and behavioral habituation that underlie moral virtue. I shall chop things up somewhat differently from either Plato or Mackie, however, by also allowing for an extension of *dikē* to looser norms or standards of behavior of the sort that virtue ethics stresses. On this reading, *dikē* and *aidōs* amount to external and internal aspects of morality—sanctions, standards, or what have you—corresponding in my own account to the subject-independent and -dependent components of moral meaning.

On a less mythological historical account than we find in the *Protagoras*, perhaps the two notions should initially be taken as combined in some more primitive idea such as that of a "taboo," understood as a particular emotion-laden rule. For my purposes here, what is important is just that both play an essential role in morality as it has developed; *dikē* is conceptually distinguishable at an advanced stage as a moral code (broadly construed) and *aidōs* as the source of motivation to act on the code, which cannot be objective in Mackie's terms since motivating states are subjective. Mackie's internalism—his assumption that motivation must be built into the content of moral judgments—keeps him from accommodating the Protagorean account within a version of morality that would escape his charge of error. However, without that assumption, Mackie might be seen as allowing for a form of moral realism in his own remarks on the aspect of morality that he takes to be worth pursuing further.

The Protagorean account would fit in with Mackie's earlier attempts to understand the basic moral terms in a way that cuts across positions on the issue of objectivity. We can see how it might be defended as an externalist form of realism in connection with his comments on "ought." His first use of the notion of an institution comes from John Searle's attempt to close the Humean "is/ought" gap with an argument,[48] via "institutional facts" about promising, from the fact that someone has made a promise to an ought-statement requiring its fulfillment. In answer to Searle, Mackie distinguishes between the mere reporting of facts about an institution such as promising, or describing it from the outside, and on the other hand, speaking from within it, thus in effect endorsing it, as in Searle's conclusion. The distinction is presented as independent of any belief in objective prescriptivity, so it amounts to a way of understanding the prescriptive force of "ought" without attributing any queer combinations of properties to objects. Instead, the motivation to act on an ought-statement apparently comes from involvement in an institution—something it is logically possible to opt out of, thereby blocking the inference from "is" to "ought."

On Mackie's later extension of the notion of an institution to any kind of group practice, these remarks apply beyond promising to morality in general—and we might also say, to the use of terms like "ought" in moral teaching. Mackie himself presumably thinks of an amoralist as someone who rejects the institution of morality altogether, though he is sufficiently aware of it in reference to other people's behavior to be able to describe it from the outside. But on my general version of internalism, there is room for a *motivational* amoralist conceived as someone with one foot in and one foot out of the moral institution to the extent that he uses moral language with a meaning set up by childhood moral teaching. The latter on my account amounts to the practice of loading moral terms with emotional sanctions. The sanctions themselves can be dismissed as "kid stuff" in adult life without abandoning some or all of the other habits they were used to teach—at a minimum the linguistic habits that support the meaningful use of moral terms in the case of the amoralist.

In his account of "ought" in terms of reasons, Mackie applies the notion of an institution to the practice of taking other people's interests as reasons for action, which he represents as "an established way of thinking, a moral tradition" that makes certain demands of an agent.[49] Institutions *create* moral reasons, then, and though Mackie's discussion makes it clear that they are not therefore "artificial" creations in all cases, his later account of Hume in connection with the Protagorean myth indicates that they sometimes come under Hume's "artificial virtue" of justice. They are to some extent products of social convention, that is. But the flourishing of a social group that he mentions here briefly as a kind of overarching group interest—he apparently equates it with survival—would seem to count as a further source of reasons promoted by the link between *dikē* and *aidōs*, between rules favoring cooperation and the moral sentiments that motivate action on them. To reject the link is essentially to opt out of human society by refusing to share its aims.

Or so one might add on Mackie's behalf; he unfortunately fails to connect his treatment of "ought" and institutions with his later Protagorean account of the function of morality. I shall have more to say in the next section about how the notion of group flourishing might be made to yield a realist account of the sort of binding force he attributes to "ought." For the moment, the thing to note is that the resulting view does not involve ascribing any special motivational properties to situations in the world around us. Both *dikē* and *aidōs* can be described from without simply by describing natural and artificial (socially created) facts about the world, in a sense that covers human behavior and responses—including the kinds of nonmoral evaluative facts that Mackie would accept as objectively based, such as facts about the "best" means to one's ends. "The facts" on a Protagorean version of realism, then, will be the same as those in Mackie's subjectivism but with a connection to moral emotion explaining their prescriptive force as something that pertains to statements made within the social institution thus described.

The resulting view, social artifact realism, allows for an understanding of morality as real even though invented—that is, for Mackie's own understanding of it as essentially man-made to fulfill a certain purpose. For artifacts surely deserve a place in the fabric of the world—or even as part of its "furniture," like the tables and chairs we point to in classroom discussions of the reality of physical objects. Morality or the moral code is real on this account in something like the way that an artifact is: It is dependent on minds for its existence and purpose and therefore at least to some extent for its form; on the other hand, it is subject-independent in the sense of not being malleable at will. It can even be viewed as imposing requirements on minds in a way analogous to the postural demands made on the body by a certain kind of chair. But we need to ask whether this is enough to answer the charge of subject-relativity with a notion of the authority of ethics of the sort that Mackie faults naturalist accounts for not being able to provide.[50] Let us now take a step back from the view that has emerged from discussion of Foot, McDowell, and Mackie to see how the result can be reshaped to give us what we want from moral realism.

3. Between the Horns

With its assumption of general internalism, social artifact realism promises a solution to the problem of action-guiding dilemmas because it affords a sense in which the normal agent's emotional reactions are imposed on him by the situation of conflict rather than simply being accidental features of his response. Its two components in the Protagorean story were already in play in the account of the teaching of moral language via emotion that I used at the beginning of this chapter to establish a motivational link between ought-judgments and guilt. My notion of "didactic import" should now enable us to make out guilt or some similar moral emotion as justified in cases of dilemma in a sense that is strong enough to meet reasonable versions of the charge of subject-relativity, as well as being weak enough to allow for cases of abnormal moral response on the order of amoralism.

One way in which my proposed account is not subject-relative, we should now note, amounts to a departure from Foot's version of externalism: An agent's reasons for action do not depend solely on his own desires and interests. At any rate, the social artifact view allows us to say that they do not, since it allows us to appeal to the notion of a group standpoint, with group flourishing as a further end and a source of further interests beyond those of individual members but requiring action of them in at least some cases. Morality on this more thorough-going version of externalism may "give" me reasons that I do not accept—that I choose to look away from or simply miss, in the way that one might fail to take a hint. It may give me reasons to act on others' behalf for the sake of social harmony, say—much as an appeal to group interests might be thought to give me reason to enlarge the gene pool by having children, even if that would in no way promote my own interests, real or perceived. We can still say that reasons are motivationally sufficient on this account in the sense of being able without supplementation to give rise to the requisite behavior, while denying that they *must* do so, even on the part of a rational agent who is aware of them and has no countervailing reasons.[51] Instead, they are available to motivate behavior if the agent attends to them in emotional or other practical terms—if he sees things from the standpoint of the whole.

This yields a version of McDowell's view of moral insight but without the interpretation of motivational sufficiency that keeps his view from accommodating dilemmas. On my account, dilemmas arise because the code of rules best fitted in general terms to the social and individual aims of morality is simply not adequate to all possible cases; but it is not therefore superseded, at any rate within the moral point of view, when it yields a conflict. Though man-made, the rules of morality are not like rules of a game that can be tinkered with to correct any defects, or abandoned along with the game if they turn out not to be perfectible. They sometimes result in deadlock, with emotional response a substitute for action on them, as provided by their general motivational underpinnings. The view drawn from Mackie makes ethics subject-dependent to the extent that it does interpret motivational force in terms of a link to emotion. We now need to ask both how the view can be seen as a form of realism and whether it can stand up to the complaint that a subject-dependent view is too easy on the agent in a dilemma.

Constraints on Moral Codes

What we mainly want from realism, I take it, is a reasonable basis for the authority of ethics. The point of distinguishing the two components of the Protagorean account is to separate out such a metaethical basis from the subject-dependent elements of morality. I take them to correspond roughly to the stages of developing moral consciousness produced by Aristotelian habituation in early moral life, as a child is made to follow rules in rote fashion, on the basis of which, in conjunction with reward and punishment, he learns moral emotion tendencies—the latter in turn yielding moral motivation at a more advanced stage.[52] More fundamentally, though, *dikē* and *aidōs* represent not temporal stages but components of my proposed explanation of moral meaning in terms of the institution of a moral code: the social creation of the code itself and the provision of psychological backing for it by connecting it to emotions. Though they are distinguishable for explanatory purposes, however, it is important to see how the two components interact. The content of the moral code will be influenced by a requirement of teachability, most notably, that brings in the general facts of individual psychology. So the order of developmental stages in individual psychology may be reversed on the social level or in relation to questions of explanatory priority.

On the other hand, the content of the moral code should not depend on individual psychological variations; an agent cannot just opt out of the moral rules by appeal to a deviant or deficient conscience or moral sensibility. This gives in a nutshell the sense in which ethics may still be said to be subject-independent on the Protagorean account, as I shall continue to think of it despite differences from historical Protagoreanism, differences exploited and expanded in my ensuing discussion.

We still need to ask whether the view is undermined by the social variability it presumably allows for. What is to keep it from applying to just any socially accepted code of rules that might be used in moral teaching? Since the result of moral teaching via emotion would seem to be a sense in which socially induced emotion gives us access to moral truths—having been taught to us in conjunction with them and indeed in conjunction with the use of moral language—this amounts to a social version of the charge of subject-relativity. Is the Protagorean view viciously subject-dependent, after all?

Interestingly, the same sorts of social facts may be used to support another objection pulling in the opposite direction. The extent to which individual conscience depends on social indoctrination might seem to undermine the autonomy we expect of a moral agent. This amounts to the independence of the mind from external forces, including social forces. The objection may be compounded by a common philosophical view of emotions themselves as alien psychological forces—as standing outside the mind or self, adventitious additions to it implanted by external objects of desire or by social training or suggestion.

Both of these objections, from subject-relativity and from autonomy, raise questions about the content and interaction of the two components—questions about the role played by moral emotions, along with more general questions about the presuppositions of the moral code. At the outset, though, we should note that it is not so obvious that emotions are in any worse position than beliefs as bases of conscience. Mackie's interpretation of *aidōs* in terms of emotions presumably has to do with their general usefulness as a motivational mechanism; on my own account, emotions like shame and guilt effectively punish a failure to act with discomfort. But this is part of what seems to put them outside the agent's control: They are typically less malleable than beliefs in response to either individual deliberation or the particular features of the agent's situation. For much the same reason, however, emotions may in some ways be better insulated than beliefs against the kind of social manipulation that is now in question. They may also have a biological basis in innate responses that sets more limits on early childhood training.

On the other hand, even my realist version of the Protagorean view is meant to allow for some degree of relativity to social convention as the source of the basic social arrangements presupposed by justice. I do not want to insist that it restricts us to a unique outcome in the choice of a moral code; to count as a version of realism, however, it has to constrain the choice sufficiently to preserve a sense of the authority of ethics.[53] Let us ask, then, whether we can find something in the two components of the view that might serve to keep the choice of codes within reasonable bounds—that might impose limits, for instance, on the fairness of an acceptable moral code. I shall consider the question in illustrative form by asking what might prevent a society from allowing or encouraging indifference to the welfare of a certain subclass of its members. Why not have an "outcaste" group, in short?

A full treatment of issues of justice is of course beyond the scope of my argument here. What I want to argue is that a realist version of the Protagorean view allows for the usual sorts of moves on the subject—plus one that is somewhat different—within a broadly "communitarian" framework. These moves have well-known limitations, but my aim here is just to indicate how a socially based view can avoid any special problems associated with communitarianism. Though derived from Mackie, my own suggested version of the view rests on a use of the notion of group flourishing as a kind of social parallel to Aristotelian happiness, providing a standard for the correction of moral codes. Following Aristotle on individual flourishing, I interpret the notion in a way that allows it some moral or other evaluative content—so that it is not a strict welfare notion but also a notion of group excellence or virtue. This may require departing somewhat from Mackie's metaphysically austere presuppositions, but I think the deviation will turn out to be minimal—and largely defensible in terms of moves that Mackie seems ready enough to allow.

Mackie himself, despite his own use of relativity as an argument against objective values, attempts to handle fairness issues by modifying the principle of universalizability.[54] The first thing we ought to note is that there is nothing about a realist version of the Protagorean view to keep us from simply accepting some such principle as a basic constraint on moral codes. It is specifically moral properties—the requirements of particular situations as in McDowell's version of realism; what Mackie thinks of as "intrinsic requirements"—that apparently would violate a Mackiean ban on "objective prescriptivity." But what about *rational* constraints, such as those set by facts about the best means to group flourishing on Mackie's own view?

Even if universalizability or some other principle of fairness cannot be completely justified in instrumental terms, we might take it as a kind of constitutive constraint on groups we would think of as flourishing. Our preference for groups that satisfy the constraint might be compared to our preference for simplicity in the comparison of rival scientific theories.[55] We might think of universalizability, in fact, as a moral version of simplicity to the extent that it involves treating similar cases similarly. To take this line is to think of fairness in the first instance as a feature we value in groups, whatever its consequences for "prescriptivity," as a source of principles of action. Or better, perhaps: It is a feature we value in moral codes, allowing for their nonarbitrary extension to new cases.

With fairness taken as a property of codes, universalizability also comes out as promoting some independently defined purposes of morality. Besides accommodating unforeseen circumstances, a moral code governed by some such principle will provide a way of resolving interpersonal conflicts that is defensible to all parties.[56] Even with fairness applied directly to groups, universalizability can be seen as promoting social harmony and stability to the extent that it makes the group standpoint attractive to its members and hence more likely to serve as a source of individual motivation.

However, even if it served no further purpose, moral simplicity of the sort that rules out arbitrary distinctions should not be dismissed as something we just happen to value. One might ask at this point whether the appeal to simplicity in the choice among scientific theories would be seriously undermined if we came up with people or cultures with a taste for complexity and epicycles. I take it we would say that people with deviant preferences of the sort suggested just do not participate in the scientific enterprise; a mode of explanation that stresses elegant complexity would be put into some category other than "scientific." To say something similar of "moral" codes would not be to rule out moral diversity. For that matter, it would not rule out caste systems, since moral codes may be conjoined with religious and other nonmoral requirements. My suggestion is rather that fairness may be taken as a norm of social rationality and to that extent—possibly along with competing norms—as governing the construction of moral codes.

Morality on this account involves assessment in light of certain basic rational values governing the aim of promoting group flourishing such as social harmony and stability. If one thinks of the notion of flourishing as applied to plant life, it seems plausible to suppose that it builds in certain basic evaluative constraints such as symmetry or balance, other things being equal: A plant whose lower leaves all fall off, say, might be thought of as a healthy specimen if it is the standard specimen of its kind, but presumably not if others commonly flourish in a more robust sense. Or consider preferences in the human form: The bizarre things that other cultures and our own have done in the interests of physical attractiveness or to mark differences in status need not make us hesitate about the very basic value assumptions implicit in the ideal of a healthy body. Similarly, our notion of a "viable" moral code, meaning one that adequately promotes group flourishing, may rely on certain basic constraints as presupposed by social rationality without thereby imprinting our full set of moral values on the world or imposing them on other cultures.

Constraints of ordinary instrumental rationality of the sort with which I began—our preference for the most effective way of promoting an end (rather than the subtlest, say)—should themselves be viewed as evaluative. Taking a straight line as the "best" way of connecting points requires deciding against various alternative values that favor indirectness. But we can also move beyond the instrumental model in the way I indicated, by including moral constraints on flourishing: not further constituents of the social end, to be promoted as part of it, but minimal standards it has to meet in order to be worth promoting.

Despite its general teleological structure, then, the social artifact view should be able to accommodate nonconsequentialist theories of normative ethics. It is not necessarily utilitarian—any more than Aristotle's view is egoist. As with Aristotelian happiness, the relevant constraints on the moral end may be thought of as built into the notion of flourishing rather than as imposed on it from without. Thus, a condition on group flourishing as the defining purpose of a moral code might be held to be due regard for social subgroups—so that a caste system could be rejected on moral grounds as "unbalanced," like otherwise healthy physical growth that is stunted in one area.

The particular lines of argument I have brought in so far to handle fairness, from universalizability and from social symmetry or balance, still might allow for a moral justification of caste systems as ways of assigning different sorts of people different functions in a well-arranged social order. But the justification will be made no easier by the social basis I have assigned to ethics. As I intend the notion of group flourishing, it does not refer simply to the flourishing of a group in the sense of a collective entity distinguishable from its individual members; it also and primarily entails the flourishing of group members, of individuals *in* a group. On any account I would find acceptable, this is what social groups are for, though once set up they may take on purposes of their own, sometimes in conflict with individual interests. My view counts as "social" because it takes social norms as basic elements of morality; it does not take notions of social value as prior to individual interests.

Division according to function would thus require a defense addressed *to* group members in an attempt to satisfy reasonable demands of a scheme designed to promote their good. An argument on these normative issues might assume ignorance of an individual's place in the social order, of the sort associated with Rawlsian contractarianism; or it might consider features of the social order as "collective goods" of value to group members on the whole, for a teleological defense of basic social values.[57] The usual strategies of both duty and virtue ethics will be available as resources, since my view essentially supplements agent-based virtue ethics with a social notion of virtue, as a source of rules of duty.

I have more to say in defense of social artifact realism in chapter 6. Though I want it to accommodate different approaches to normative issues, the view has general implications for both the structure and the content of normative ethics, some of which will come out in what follows. Indeed, in chapter 6 we shall begin to have a glimpse of some ways in which the view might even affect practical issues. Its main implication for metaethics (narrowly construed) is that an argument in terms of group flourishing relocates the area of potential moral disagreement to the level of basic values. It is here that one might have to appeal to one's own moral perception as in McDowell's version of realism. But we can at any rate limit such appeal to abstract discussion of the elements of moral code construction and other higher level social norms—both norms of instrumental rationality and constitutive constraints on the moral enterprise—as distinct from specific requirements of action. This has the advantage of making the fact of moral disagreement more intelligible and of avoiding the application of special motivational properties to situations in the world around us— the sort of thing that Mackie finds "queer." Instead, our fundamental moral disagreements concern personal and social ends: envisioned states of self and society, whose properties are quite reasonably seen as motivational.

This is not to say that their motivational force is irresistible, even assuming rationality. In fact, there is a further kind of instrumental argument besides those commonly noted that ought to be brought in at this point as a way of limiting the appeal to moral perception. The project of constructing a viable moral code, that is, will be subject to material limitations, as well as to formal constraints like simplicity, to the extent that viability depends on a connection to individual motivation. To strengthen the case for basic moral values such as fairness, I suggest that we supplement the perceptual model of realism with some reference to the emotional mechanism that underlies moral teaching.

The Role of Moral Emotion

The main point to note is that moral emotions seem to be formed from other responses on the basis of natural identificatory processes that are not directly sensitive to social or socially marked distinctions among people—or even to differences in natural endowment of the sort that might be used to support social stratification according to function. Instead, on the sort of picture I relied on earlier in my speculative account of the teaching of moral "ought" in conjunction with guilt, our inculcation of moral emotions presupposes sensitivity to personal and behavioral similarities and relationships such as contact and personal dependency.

Early on, infants exhibit a crying response to the sound of another infant crying.[58] One can see how some general tendency of the sort, to imitate the emotional behavior of other species members, might be useful in an animal herd as a way of communicating a quick response to a threat to the group perceived by one of its members. In humans the empathetic response serves as the foundation for a way of communicating different sorts of emotion—new feelings built on an infant's original stock of emotional responses, as associated with the behavior it imitates. A kind of "imprinting" of emotional behavior—and with it emotions themselves—from the mother or other object of dependency reinforces the infant's natural responses and regroups them into new ones. The infant's natural sympathy in this initially behavioral sense is shaped into the adult tendency to take on others' emotions partly by seeing others imitate its own feelings, with imitation cultivated as a kind of imaginative play. The result is a quick way of communicating more complex feelings, including specifically moral feelings (for instance, guilt), by initiating the game in situations that prompt the child to entertain certain thoughts.

On this rough account of emotional learning as founded on imitation and imagination, identification is not itself an emotional response among others from a certain putative range of sensibility but a mode of communicating responses from preexisting ranges and constructing new responses on the basis of them. The important question in connection with moral teaching, then, is not one of natural convergence of emotional response on the model of perception—or even of "corrected" response on the model of perceptual judgment—but rather of its feasible allocation to objects in support of a moral code.

Behavioral similarity would seem to be enough to set off the mechanism, so the attempt to limit it to members of a social subgroup—or to check it with some opposing tendency, even one that is arguably natural such as fear of the stranger—might be taken as yielding an unstable combination. It is not at all an impossible combination, but its two elements are apparently in tension, and the more inclusive element would seem to be the one that determines the scope of emotional interaction.[59] A rigid stress on the exclusive element thus may be challenged as impeding the construction of a viable moral code.

My claim about caste systems is not that they are ruled out by human emotional nature but just that a basis in social exclusion pulls against our natural response tendencies in a way that tends to undermine moral code construction. Agents would risk acting at cross-purposes in not taking adequate moral account of the sufferings of people they understood to be human. At the very least, then, human emotional nature affects the social and psychological costs imposed by alternative moral codes.

This approach to moral psychology might be thought of as "bottom-up" since it assigns emotion a role in determining the shape of a viable moral code rather than simply tacking it on to a predetermined code as a source of moral motivation. My account therefore differs from other motivational accounts, most notably Mill's utilitarian appeal to "internal sanctions," as well as from the perceptual or aesthetic model that we find, most notably, in Hume.[60] Moral emotion as I conceive it does not just register in affect an independently grounded (or an ungrounded) moral code but is part of the system of penalties and payoffs that makes a code operative in the first place. It plays a special role even among features of individual psychology insofar as occurrent emotion provides the sort of controllable episodic basis that allows for the teaching of moral language.

On my account, negative moral emotions such as guilt may be thought of as felt needs registering in affect our morally "binding" reasons for action. But they are in many cases artificial or manufactured needs set up to reflect the group standpoint in individual response tendencies. Their purpose, in short, is to harness egoistic energies to moral ends. So their nature as the available support mechanism for a moral code also imposes limits on the nature of a viable code: The code must be such as to allow for support from a manageable extension of our natural stock of emotions.

Is it odd to think of this view as realist? The term may seem to presuppose a perceptual model, but a moral code is of course not something "out there" to be seen. Besides being instituted by minds, it now appears to be constrained by their response tendencies. In any case, on reasonable versions of the view I have offered, the standard appealed to may not be the actual code in force but rather one that is corrected in certain ways as needed to promote group flourishing.[61] So it is an idealized artifact of human choice and emotion. But I take it that the hypothetical fact that the actual code would promote group flourishing if corrected in certain ways is "real" enough for our purposes and is connected clearly enough to human harms and benefits to count as a "moral" fact.[62] I shall allow the term "realism," then, for views that answer the charge of subject-relativity by appeal to such facts, seen as governed by constraints of the sort just indicated.

The term has a number of misleading connotations, but it seems to be the term in use as a single expression summing up the alternative to both metaethical noncognitivism or nondescriptivism and Mackie's "error theory," two ways of denying that moral judgments state facts: the former by denying that they purport to be factual; the latter by denying their truth. My two-component view essentially serves to separate the factual content of morality from the question of its force over behavior. It is not put forth as realism in the metaphysical sense that would make out moral judgments as ascribing special properties to objects.[63] Rather, its conception of moral facts as hypotheticals about unrealized states of affairs on the order of group flourishing suggests a way of reinterpreting the notion of "moral observation" that is often assumed, by analogy to perceptual judgment, to amount to acquaintance with particular moral facts of the sort given by "This is wrong."[64] Moral error and disagreement will be easier to understand—and for that matter, a certain degree of skepticism will be reasonable—if we relocate the observation level in ethics (in contrast to science) to that of abstract imagination.

Though morality on this two-component version of realism may depend on the actual moral code as something set up and held in place by minds, its content will not be determined by the desires or decisions of any particular agent or even those open to the group as a whole at a particular historical moment. The notion of a constitution as a written code of rules that constrains further legal decision but is itself subject to correction in light of its general social purposes provides a helpful legal analogy for understanding the authority of a moral code, as a product of human will and invention that nonetheless constrains human choice. To grant it authority in that sense, however, is not to suppose that it somehow has the power to compel obedience, even among agents assumed to be rational; it constrains choice only within the relevant framework. For morality (as opposed to a constitution), the relevant framework is not simply the particular code or system of norms in force but also something more general backing it up: the standpoint of group flourishing. It also involves something more particular that can be harnessed to the social code in psychological terms: guilt or some similar motivational mechanism involving moral emotion. An individual may have to pay a price for abandoning the group standpoint, in the manner of an athlete who risks her health in pursuit of more specialized self-development.

I should note that the social artifact view is not put forth as a thoroughgoing analysis of moral terms or judgments. It is meant to capture only the descriptive content of ethics, at this point considered as a whole: the social practices, behavioral and emotional, by virtue of which a moral code may be said to be "in force" as a way of promoting the characteristic end of life in groups, along with corrections and extensions of the code in light of that general end. This amounts to the backing for our moral judgments, but it leaves out their prescriptive force as something that depends on adopting the normative standpoint that it tries only to understand from outside. An interpretation of what we say from the inside would of course have to do more, and the view is meant to be compatible with different ways of attempting to do more. It provides only a rough account of morality as a social institution, plus an indication of the role of emotion as its link to individual motivation.

Norms of emotional response are fundamental to morality, then, insofar as they regulate the internal sanctions and some of the chief external sanctions that actually keep the moral code in force. I tried to illustrate with my earlier remarks on fairness how they play a role in determining the nature of a viable code. They are essential to it in general terms because they build the group standpoint into individual psychology, providing the individual with a way of accessing it from his own immediate psychological reactions. This yields a sense in which moral emotions let us "perceive" moral facts, but it is an indirect sense, parasitic on their primary role as motivators.

As the basis of moral teaching, norms of emotional response set up a particularly exacting standard of individual moral sensitivity. However, the standard in question need not be seen as an ideal of individual virtue on the Aristotelian model. It would make amotivational uses of moral terms count as in some way deficient though not therefore deviant in meaning, and not in all cases a bad thing. There are times calling for action—even moral action—when the demands of perfect moral sensitivity would get in the way; political "dirty hands" cases provide important examples.[65] But there is another point to be made here: Perfect virtue in fact might be said to require the ability to free oneself in moments of adult reflection from the emotional baggage of childhood moral instruction in order to take a critical look at the accepted moral code.

This point rests on some assumptions worth noting. It places a value on the capacity for moral growth, on the assumption that a perfect moral education of the sort Aristotle describes, say, may or may not yield perfect moral sensitivity, depending on the surrounding society's code—as witness, of course,

Aristotle's views on women and his acceptance of slavery. A "blind spot" may be held in place by emotional distractions, including those set up by the moral code. In fact, as I argue in the next chapter, Aristotle's treatment of shame in connection with the virtues suggests that his view makes insufficient accommodation for personal moral imperfection as something an otherwise virtuous person might be called upon to change. When the moral code itself is in need of improvement, though, its underlying system of emotional response may constitute an inertial force against reasonable change.

A side effect of allowing for detachment from moral emotion is the possibility of amoralism: the rationally intelligible use of moral language without its usual motivational props. Another side effect is the possibility of a kind of emotional self-criticism that can be used to reconcile emotion-based ethics with the value placed on autonomy. One can rise above one's personal system of emotional response, as well as the system set up by the moral code, even supposing that it constitutes an integral part of oneself. Indeed, the point is to ask whether it constitutes the self one wants to be. Thus, we might discourage certain emotions in ourselves, perhaps on moral grounds—and perhaps including the very emotions that allowed us as children to perceive moral grounds: fear of social disapproval, say, or an eagerness to be accepted. Emotional self-criticism may itself be seen as emotion-based—as motivated, for instance, by admiration or disdain for one's current self, as something partly constituted by certain emotions.[66] However, my suggested account of the emotional basis of ethics is not meant to yield a monolithic view of its foundations but to accord emotions a serious place among them, despite the notorious pitfalls of emotional motivation. At least in some cases, emotional self-criticism conceivably involves rising above emotion. I do want to deny, though, that this means rising to a level where the usual emotional support for ethics is annulled.

The Intractability of Wrong

One might think that a corrected version of the actual moral code of the sort that is now in question could not contain conflicts. In defense of universalizability or some similar principle, I appealed to simplicity considerations as favoring a code that can be extended readily to new cases. But surely, it might be said, the need for "in principle" decisions uniting different cases counts against a code that allows for irresolvable conflicts of the sort at issue in dilemmas. In the face of conflict, what we ought to do is to detach ourselves from the emotional reactions that support our ordinary set of moral rules and bring in some alternative principle that yields an acceptable resolution.

This way of ruling out dilemmas is associated with Hare's account of moral thinking as taking place on two levels: the "intuitive" level, consisting in our everyday stock of emotion-based rules, and the "critical" level, a higher court of appeal for deciding what rules to put on the lower level and how to resolve cases in which the rules turn out to be inadequate.[67] On Hare's view what we appeal to is a single principle that he takes to be derivable from universalizability: the principle of utility. But Hare's approach to normative ethics need not concern us here; we may grant for purposes of argument that the *practical* resolution to a moral dilemma should involve "acting for the best"—as Williams puts it in considering the case of Agamemnon[68]—and that this means maximizing utility. The question raised by dilemmas is whether the moral rule that we thereby act against must be seen as superseded. What I need to argue here is just that we may still take it to be in force compatibly with a coherent view of ethics, on assumptions like those just defended as yielding a version of moral realism.

The question of realism initially came up in negative form in connection with dilemmas: Williams's account of them was presented in part as a way of undermining realism. But if I am right, the view turns out to play a positive role in defense of dilemmas. Realist assumptions allow us to put a limit on the responsiveness of our intuitive principles to considerations of simplicity: to distinguish the sorts of corrections to the actual code that are needed to promote its general practical purposes from others that might be introduced solely for the sake of various theoretical ends such as systematic neatness.

In contrast to Hare's prescriptivism, social artifact realism does not make out moral principles as simply chosen by us within certain logical constraints. Our corrections to the moral code that is socially in force are meant to let it capture something subject-independent, even if not unique: a version of the actual code that would do an adequate job in promoting the end or complex of ends summed up as "group flourishing." On this account, a viable moral code is constrained by the nature of its defining social end as well as by the means to it, including most notably its motivational basis in emotional learning. By contrast, Hare claims that reasoning at the critical level permits no appeal to substantial moral intuitions but only to logical intuitions such as universalizability.

With regard to dilemmas, I think there is reason to insist against Hare that the emotional underpinnings of a viable moral code would in fact be undermined by canceling the application of its principles to cases of conflict. In a word, it is important to the general purposes of the code that a morally sensitive agent both register emotionally the principle he has to act against and be seen as responding thereby to a practical requirement imposed by the situation. This point rests on an account of moral education outlined previously that is not unlike Hare's, except that Hare apparently relies solely on considerations of personal virtue to make room for our intuitive emotional responses, as needed for his account to cover responses that may not be justified in utilitarian terms. In a case of conflict, Hare's account allows us to say that a person who experiences no guilt or remorse for violating the overridden intuitive ought would be a morally worse person—or a morally worse educated person, as he also puts it [69]—whom we reasonably think less well of for the lack. But Hare's account apparently does not let us say that one morally ought to feel guilt or remorse in such a case as a substitute for action, or to satisfy a "contrary-to-duty" obligation, perhaps even in contexts where the emotion would do more harm than good. Nor does it let us think of the emotion as rationally appropriate.

Of course, considerations of virtue and the Aristotelian picture of virtue as based on general habits of emotional response also underlie the notion of the ideally sensitive agent that my own discussion took from McDowell. I attempt to show how guilt fits into this picture at the beginning of chapter 4, and my own account will diverge further from both Aristotle's and McDowell's. It has already begun to pull away from them by setting up a special standard, more exacting than normal, for moral teaching. An important point of agreement with them, however, is the view of an ideally sensitive agent as responding to something real—to morally significant features of the situation rather than merely to features that are in general morally significant. It is Hare's willingness to drop this point, I want to claim, that keeps him from making adequate sense of dilemmas.

Consider one of Hare's illustrations of the role he assigns to guilt in moral thinking: On a visit to Czechoslovakia at the height of the cold war, he says, he would have lied to avoid being expelled if he had been asked by officials about the purpose of his visit; despite the belief that he *ought* to lie, he would have felt guilty. Hare handles the case by allowing for conflict on what he elsewhere distinguishes as the intuitive level of moral thinking; he here refers to "a sense of 'thinking that I ought' in which . . . [f]eeling guilty is inseparable from . . . thinking that I ought not." But on the critical level, there is no moral duty to back up this conflicting thought; it is justified simply as something expected of a morally good agent: "I should be a morally worse man if I were not affected in this way."[70] Note that this justification is not utilitarian: Though there might be generally beneficial consequences of emotional sensitivity on moral issues, those agents who would be able to forgo it in this case without effect on their general tendencies would be well advised to do so.

Now contrast the case with that of Agamemnon. Agamemnon is indeed considered morally deficient for failing to be affected with guilt or some similar emotion by the sacrifice of his daughter. But to say only this is to treat the case as fundamentally indistinguishable from one that involves an act that would be wrong under other circumstances but is not wrong under those that obtain, as with Hare's imagined lie to an official of an unjust government. The ideal response on Hare's account is treated as appropriate not to the situation but rather for a person——as in this case *failing* to fit the situation in a way that is characteristic of someone with a good moral upbringing, given the fact that emotions rest on general habits of response.

Hare is willing to apply his position to some morally serious cases, but they all involve slighting some members of a group in order to fulfill a more basic responsibility to the group as a whole.[71] These are what Williams calls cases of "moral cost," without the sort of unanswered claim that is at issue in Agamemnon's sacrifice of his daughter. In all the cases Hare deals with, then, the ought that is not acted on is on his account clearly overridden. His reason for expecting a morally good person to react to it has to do with the limitations of human psychology—the need to construct our everyday moral sensibility from the limited materials provided by general emotion tendencies—considered as distinct from the morally significant features of the situation.

My own approach to morally serious cases appeals to an ideal of moral sensitivity not just as the product of the right sort of upbringing but also as a

standard of correct response: the more exacting didactic standard that underlies moral teaching. This may be thought of essentially as a standard of due
attention to what one is talking about, as registered in emotion. I do not hold
that an agent has to conform to it insofar as he holds moral judgments but that
otherwise his responses are in a certain sense deficient. They do not count as
full responses since they fail to express the motivation to act—though in normal cases it is enough that the agent does act, as he may do automatically. In a
case like Agamemnon's, however, the emotional components of a full response
will be morally required as a substitute for action on one of the oughts in conflict. This was my suggested modification of McDowell's cognitivism in order
to allow for dilemmas.

The point of the further departures from McDowell's view that I took from
Mackie but defended as compatible with the aims of realism is just that we can
still insist along with McDowell that Agamemnon's requisite emotional response
is one that is merited by features of his choice-situation, as opposed to simply
being meritorious on his part.[72] Guilt or remorse is justified or appropriate in
Agamemnon's circumstances, not just understandable or even admirable as the
result of a good moral upbringing. However, I do not want to say that the
emotion amounts to a perception of some special motivational property of
the situation; it is enough that it be backed up by subject-independent facts in
the relevant sense. This sense allows for facts about a code of rules set up and
sustained by minds for subject-dependent purposes. What it excludes is relativity to minds as knowers—or as the source of the prescriptions that substitute
for knowledge on Hare's noncognitivist account.

In short, the moral code is not simply stitched together case-by-case, and it
cannot be tailored to fit the requirements of a particular case as on Hare's
account of dilemmas. Where conflicts occur, we may indeed have to appeal to
considerations of utility. I count this as a moral appeal, but it does not yield a
moral resolution of the conflict on the view I have defended: It leaves intact the
intuitive judgments that Hare would dismiss as lower level. Given the interaction
of the two components of morality that my own view takes as elements in its
explanation, we can rest this refusal to rise above emotion on the general moral
importance of registering the standpoint of the ought that loses out.

Indeed, we may even appeal to utilitarian considerations in support of this
departure from Hare's utilitarianism. In part II I shall use the example of guilt
to defend a notion of appropriate emotion that builds in appeal to considerations of general adaptiveness. It is not limited to a utilitarian reading, as we
shall see. At this point, however, let me confine myself in arguing against Hare
to an example of the general utilitarian benefits of emotion in cases of dilemma.
In a case like Agamemnon's, guilt or remorse as an identificatory response can
be said to exhibit the agent's moral convictions in feelings and acts of expression that are superior to statements of belief to the extent that they are beyond
full voluntary control and hence harder to simulate. They therefore are able to
reassure us about the agent's general response tendencies more than any claims
he might make about his preference for avoiding the conflict and the act he would
have chosen in its absence.

The agent can also be said to subject himself to discomfort by undergoing guilt or remorse, to the extent that his emotions are under some voluntary control. I shall later supplement the picture of emotions as useful for purposes of communication with an appreciation of the motivational and symbolic significance of self-subjection to discomfort. For our present purposes, we can already see that expressions of belief of the sort just indicated would also be oddly remote under Agamemnon's circumstances—"hollow" or "wooden" in a way that contrasts with the immediacy of emotion. The agent brings the situation home to himself and gives others a reason for taking his response seriously insofar as he manifests some emotion on the order of guilt. The emotion serves to dramatize his commitment to ends that his action in this case cannot serve. The fact that it is unpleasant both fits the negative content of the moral belief it expresses and counts as a reason against undergoing the emotion in its absence.

The conclusion I want to draw from these points is that a moral code that yields a dilemma on the level of intuitive moral thinking should not be corrected in the way Hare suggests, by anulling the application of the rules to that case in favor of critical thinking. It is not enough to base the same emotional requirements on considerations of virtue, as Hare has in mind. To see this, let us take another look at what an agent might reasonably think or feel *about* his emotional responses in a situation of conflict of the sort that Hare imagines on his trip to cold-war Czechoslovakia. It would be compatible with the good moral education evidenced by the guilt he feels about a lie that is in fact justified simply to "laugh off" the feeling, dismissing it as a representation of the real moral requirements of the situation, perhaps even with a degree of pride for his advanced moral sensibility.

This is not what we want from Agamemnon, needless to say. Nor could he delude himself about the situation and still be capable of critical thinking. I conclude, then, that the appeal to simplicity as a reason for limiting the number of rules relevant to the case would be undercut by the need to explain what the agent in it ought to feel. In any case, the sort of simplicity I appealed to earlier had a practical justification as allowing for a comprehensible method of extrapolating from the preexisting rules to new cases. What is in question here is just an attempt to sweep away moral clutter in the interests of metamoral neatness. The problem with its application to dilemmas is that it also seems to discard our sense of the intractability of moral wrong.

I brought up this notion earlier in connection with my claim that a moral prohibition is not erased by considerations on the other side, in favor of action. At that point I had in mind nonmoral or positive considerations; but what is in question here is something like higher level considerations: the view of things from an impersonal standpoint of judgment, to be distinguished from both the all-things-considered and the group standpoints that have come into my argument. The notion of intractability will have further, more particular applications later, but in the present context, it can be used as a general way of summing up my answer to the problem I began with about dilemmas and motivational force. It is what makes our moral intuitions resist the kind of systematization that many philosophers would impose on them, by ensuring that a sufficiently serious moral reason against some act is not blotted out by a stronger reason in favor of it. At bottom, then, it involves a kind of intractability to argument that keeps an appeal to critical thought from doing what Hare wants.

The notion of intractability connects my account of dilemmas to specifically moral or deontic notions, as distinct from Hare's account of their emotional basis in terms of virtue and other authors' attempts to explain them as clashes of incommensurable values. The claim that an agent must do something wrong in a case of moral dilemma adds something to the claim that he must forgo some good. It even adds something to the claim that either choice he makes is *bad* insofar as the link to emotion ensures that "wrong" is not just a motivationally inert label—or perhaps even one with positive force on the model of the African-American slang use of "bad" in American English or of the tongue-in-cheek extension to adult behavior of "naughty" and similar terms for reproving children.

This is to say that a use of "wrong" without motivational force is a substandard use, not just that the speaker falls short of a standard of perfect virtue, though depending on the reasons for it the use may be morally substandard and the speaker more than linguistically deviant. In application to dilemmas, this means that it is not left to an agent's psychological makeup to tell him how to react—whether to feel "torn" or simply to grant that both alternatives are wrong while responding to one of them with indifference. To be unmoved by either alternative is to violate a norm of full response; since being moved requires at least undergoing an unpleasant feeling, we have a sense on this account in which a dilemma is hard on the agent but still possible. The agent in a dilemma is torn between two alternatives that are both in emotional terms bad for him. This yields a solution to the problem posed in chapter 1.

Or rather, it yields the outline of a solution. The summary of my results in this chapter raises in rough form a set of further questions more specifically about guilt and other moral emotions: about the response mechanism I want to use to explain moral motivation, its assessment for appropriateness, and its relation to judgments of responsibility and wrong. These include questions about the moral worth and the practical usefulness of guilt as a source of moral motivation but also more general questions about norms governing emotional response and their relation to moral action.

I want to treat guilt in dilemmatic cases essentially as a substitute for action rather than as a way of registering the perception of moral wrong, or a mark of moral virtue or a good moral upbringing, at least in the first instance. But it may seem to be a rather poor substitute for any number of reasons. One that might come up here, in light of my criticisms of Hare's account, is its degree of self-focus: An agent who is motivated by guilt might be said to be acting out of concern for his own moral worth—or even for his own state of emotional comfort or discomfort—and hence to be no less morally deficient than one who dismisses his guilt feelings in a case of conflict.

Moreover, an account of such feelings as appropriate in cases of dilemma might seem to compromise the notion of intractability just defended. It would apparently make out guilt as justified on general utilitarian or other practical grounds in at least some cases where the corresponding evaluative belief—that the agent is responsible for wrong—would not be warranted. But if this is true, it would also seem to detach guilt from a judgment of wrong. Instead, the emotion might be seen as requiring only prima facie evidence of wrongdoing. In that case, the claim that guilt is appropriate no matter what the agent does in a case of dilemma stops short of giving us what it seemed to just above: a view of the agent as responding to something real in the situation. Let us now attempt to deal with this question by way of an extended look at guilt.

II

SENSIBILITY AND STANDPOINTS

4

Moral Residues

Guilt came into my argument in part I in two connected roles: in its primary form, following action, in response to a contrary-to-duty obligation to feel some appropriate emotion, and in anticipatory form, in advance of action, as the emotional strut of the motivational force of moral "ought." I have maintained that the two roles allow the emotion to serve as a kind of substitute for action in cases of dilemma. It is by no means an adequate substitute in moral terms but is enough to answer metaethical worries about the sense in which both of the oughts in conflict can be practical. The motivational role of the emotion also serves to justify it as a sometimes problematic after-the-fact reaction—an affective residue of moral failure that persists even when failure is unavoidable. My treatment of dilemmas as cases in which guilt is warranted for all alternatives is essentially a modification of Williams's claim that their practical resolution leaves a moral "remainder," not itself a feeling but marked by moral feelings of regret, along with other ways of acknowledging that the act the agent has to perform is still wrong. However, along with most philosophers, Williams has little to say about guilt.

Williams's "agent-regret" might be thought of as a general category meant to include guilt along with other emotions, though it suggests a more passive variant of sadness.[1] But Agamemnon's case counts as a genuine dilemma for Williams just because the sacrifice of Iphigenia is still morally wrong under the circumstances, even though it is required by Agamemnon's duties as military commander. It does not just involve a regrettable wrong done *to* his daughter that is analogous to the "moral cost" of the things a politician may be over-ridingly required to do. Rather, its wrongness is serious enough not to be erased by the balancing of obligations that makes it come out at the same time as required, perhaps even with stronger practical weight. My view is that guilt is needed to capture the force of "wrong" in this account as something more than a motivationally inert label.

At the outset, however, I want to continue to work with a broad interpretation of guilt as an "internal sanction" of the moral code involving some form of discomfort at the thought that one is responsible for a wrong—a feeling that may be covered by other emotion concepts, most notably shame, in other cultures. A distinction between guilt and shame with some reasons for preferring guilt, plus an explanation of the pitfalls of the emotion, will emerge as this chapter proceeds. In chapter 5 I argue that the standard way of distinguishing guilt from various other self-directed contrary-to-duty feelings in our own culture—by limiting its object to voluntary action—does not really fit the facts of emotional life or even the norms of emotional rationality. Williams bypasses guilt in favor of regret at least partly because he relies on this distinction in his treatment of dilemmas. In fact, though, on Williams's account the substitution of obligation for practical "ought" in dilemmas would apparently allow blame, the third-person counterpart of guilt in emotional terms, for the violation of moral obligation in such cases.[2] But appropriate blame no less than guilt seems to be limited to voluntary action. My own view will allow instead for weaker grounds for guilt than for blame on the basis of the special motivational role of the first-person emotion.

In this chapter, before attacking the question of voluntariness, I want to fill out the account of guilt that began to emerge in my discussion of its role in childhood moral teaching. My treatment of the moral significance of the emotion in adult life (section 1) will initially focus on the link it provides between the ethics of virtue and of duty. Insofar as it captures the intractability of moral wrong—its resistance to the balancing of obligations—in a case like Agamemnon's, it expresses the sense that some acts are intolerable. In Agamemnon's case it essentially serves to direct feelings of "taboo" onto the self, as tainted or stained by wrong action. It thereby provides an element of moral self-threat that is not present in more passive reactions like regret or shame or in less self-oriented feelings like remorse. It also provides an alternative to a strictly Aristotelian approach to virtue by making room for serious lapses from it within a notion of flawed or imperfect virtue.

I eventually bring my remarks on guilt and virtue to bear on two general contrasts that seem to underlie the motivational significance of guilt: between positive and negative and between self- and other-directed emotions and other attitudes. My argument for an asymmetrical treatment of emotions in each pair will lay the basis for my later defense of weaker grounds for guilt than for blame. Here I shall use it to help answer questions raised by a problematic case for the connection between guilt and perfect or ideal virtue, of the sort that seems to be possible in genuine moral dilemmas, understood as cases in which the agent is not responsible for the situation of conflict and assuming that he does the best he can to act in light of it. The discussion will lead to my account, in section 2, of guilt in the narrow sense as an identificatory mechanism: a general reaction pattern sometimes encompassing the other feelings typically contrasted with guilt but distinguished by a different sort of connection to the self.

I expect my remarks to support a distinction between guilt and shame, in particular, that favors guilt as a moral motivator. But I shall mainly be considering guilt in reasonable doses and with reasonable objects, in sharp distinction to a common view of the emotion as an overwhelming and uncontrollable inhibiting factor. The pitfalls of the emotion will come up in my argument as side effects of its valuable features and as reasons for denying that a requirement to feel guilty provides a way of resolving a dilemma. In a defense of "ought-to-feel" (section 3), I address the general problems raised by requiring *any* feeling, on the usual assumptions about emotional control. I also consider a second-order dilemma raised by the possibility that guilt in a case like Agamemnon's might interfere with effective action on the stronger ought in the conflict. At best, if I am right, a requirement to feel guilty resolves the metaethical problem of dilemmas and practical "ought." It cannot be taken as offering a way out to the agent in a dilemma or as preserving the ethics of virtue from moral luck.

1. The Moral Significance of Guilt

Guilt is usually thought of—by those philosophers who mention it at all—in connection with the ethics of duty, which takes acts as the primary objects of moral evaluation.[3] It is meant to attach to an act viewed as wrong, or a violation of moral obligation. However, within duty ethics it is treated as a secondary matter, a question to be postponed until after the determination of the right act. I want to argue that the moral significance of guilt begins to come out when we consider it as an element of virtue ethics, or the earlier (and recently revived) approach that instead emphasizes the evaluation of persons and personal traits in connection with notions of character and personal moral perfection.

Guilt can be seen as linking the ethics of virtue to that of duty more firmly than is accomplished, for instance, just by listing conscientiousness among the virtues or by laying special stress on the virtue of justice. If conscientiousness is just one virtue among others, its requirements may sometimes be slighted in favor of others compatibly with overall virtue. If justice, on the other hand, is the essential virtue, a single lapse from it presumably takes an agent out of the running for overall virtue. Even if virtue is subject to degrees, its degrees are not calculated act by act, so a serious lapse may make it unclear what motive is left to the agent for future virtuous action. By contrast, taking justice to involve a requirement of guilt for wrong action as a precondition of overall virtue has the effect of imposing a repeatable emotional cost on lapses from virtue.

It is important to this suggestion that guilt both ascribes something negative to the self and is itself a negative state of feeling. It is not itself a virtue—nor is feeling it or having a tendency to feel it—but rather a requirement of imperfect virtue and a goad to future virtuous action. I shall be thinking of it here as an emotion, not a state of affairs or a personal trait. To that extent, my treatment of guilt will be roughly in line with Aristotle's remarks on shame in the *Nicomachean Ethics*; since the Greeks did not have a shame/guilt distinction, I shall take Aristotle's remarks as applying to both emotions.[4] Aristotle apparently considers shame important enough in connection with the virtues to be included in his account of them, but at the same time he acknowledges that it does not really belong on the list. As a correlate of imperfect virtue, shame—meaning the sense of shame, or shame as a dispositional emotion, a tendency to feel certain occurrent emotions (including both shame itself and fear of disgrace) under the right circumstances—may be seen as a virtue in children. For adults, it is neither a virtue nor a part of virtue on Aristotle's account, which at that stage of development rules out serious lapses from perfection.

My own use of "guilt" is meant rather broadly at this point, in a way that does not distinguish it from moral shame, or shame felt for an act viewed as wrong. Even that limitation might seem to introduce a difference from Aristotle's notion insofar as it connects guilt to duty ethics. Though Aristotle's shame does extend to lapses from duty—indeed, he ties it explicitly to voluntary actions[5] —it more directly concerns the personal disgrace to which they subject the agent. One's self is viewed as diminished by the shameful wrong it does, in short, whereas for guilt, we may say by contrast, the self may merely be threatened with diminution: Wrong acts "taint" the agent, but, in normal cases he can erase the taint through reparative action.

In what follows I argue for the importance of guilt even within virtue ethics as a negative response to wrong action; I thereby resist both Aristotle's insistence on perfection and a certain use of Aristotle in contemporary moral philosophy as a model for isolating virtue ethics from the modern ethics of duty. Williams, most notably, favors dropping strictly moral notions in favor of a broader category of the ethical, which is not based on blame.[6] While I welcome the move away from a narrow concentration on duty, my aim here is essentially to help keep the ethics of virtue moored to that of duty—to keep it, as I would say, from drifting out to sea. I also turn to a case of moral dilemma to illustrate an important distinction *within* virtue ethics introduced by the extension of emotional guilt to putative instances of moral perfection.

Guilt and Imperfect Virtue

Let us first note that we are not simply returning to duty ethics when we refer to guilt as *required* by imperfect virtue (in the ordinary sense of flawed as opposed to ideal virtue, with no reference to the Kantian distinction between perfect and imperfect duties). Our claim at this point need not be that guilt is obligatory in the usual sense—a possibility I shall in fact defend later in this chapter —but rather just that undergoing the emotion is a precondition of such virtue as is still achievable under the circumstances. From the standpoint of duty ethics, this claim would seem to amount to a hypothetical imperative—"Feel guilty if you want to be virtuous" or the like—and guilt would not be *commanded* by such a principle, except as supplemented by a duty to exhibit virtue. Within virtue ethics, by contrast, the claim just serves to recommend guilt as one of the necessary ingredients of virtue in the case in question, with virtue assumed to be a state we want to exhibit. It is a question, of course, what force the claim would have against someone who does not much care whether he qualifies as virtuous; an answer might overlap with duty ethics—by appealing, for instance, to the claim on others' respect that virtue entails. But let us limit attention at this point to agents who do have an ideal of overall virtue, though they may not act in accordance with it on all occasions or even bother figuring out what it requires.

The question of overall virtue, as I interpret it, asks whether someone is an admirable person, or admirable on the whole, as opposed to being admirable only with some qualification—in certain respects or in a certain role; as an artist, say. Moreover, an answer to the question involves more than simply summing the more limited sorts of virtue that an agent may display—even with due weight assigned to their importance, the degree to which they involve a display of virtue, and so forth. Thus, for instance, we might deny that Richard Wagner was an admirable person in view of his anti-Semitism or his betrayal of his friend Von Bülow, even granting that he was a very admirable composer, and even with some inclination to say that his achievements as a composer were important enough to outweigh moral failings. His moral failings may be outweighed in some general scheme of things, that is to say, but not in the determination of overall worth as a person on this account.

Indeed, a similar point might be made for cases in which only moral virtue is under consideration at every stage. If a moral lapse is sufficiently serious, it will not be enough to make up for the lapse with good deeds; rather, the agent must appreciate its seriousness, in a sense not unlike aesthetic appreciation to the extent that it rules out being left cold. A Raskolnikov, say, who goes on to become a major philanthropist without a moment of remorse for his murder of the old lady would not thereby have met the demands of overall virtue, even if he also managed to convince himself intellectually that the murder was wrong. Indeed, even a religious conversion would not be *morally* satisfying unless it involved an appropriate element of discomfort about his crimes. We might be willing to infer this from the strength of his later motivation to do good, taken as an instance of the reparative tendency associated with guilt. But at least some postulated negative feeling seems to be needed to assure us that the agent's negative evaluation of his act affects him personally.

Some such argument is familiar from discussions of legal punishment, rehabilitation, and surrounding issues. The hypothetical rehabilitated mass murderer who goes on to lead an exemplary life but never feels remorse gives pause, quite apart from deterrence considerations, even to those of us who would like to do without revenge. No doubt we insist on feeling, in real-life cases of the sort, partly just to help us determine whether any observed changes in personality and mode of life are genuine and reliable, on the assumption that feeling is one of the less malleable signs of belief and behavior tendencies. But we insist on guilt feelings in particular (taking guilt broadly to include remorse and moral shame) because it is also important to us that such changes rest on emotional self-reflection.

For practical purposes, it would presumably be enough if we could get a mass murderer to feel horror at her past acts, pity for the victims, and other alternatives to self-directed discomfort—supposing, for instance, that we had some method of rehabilitation that resulted in her ceasing to identify with her past self. Psychosurgery—or, for that matter, religious conversion—might have that result, but I take it that in moral terms we would not be satisfied. The discontinuity between the agent's past and present selves would seem to undercut any judgment of *overall* virtue—by substituting two selves for one, as it were—rather than justifying a judgment of imperfect virtue. To the extent that we care about the moral worth of persons, we prefer a method of rehabilitating someone that does not essentially involve giving up on her. Other things being equal (as of course they may not be), we want the agent to redeem her old life rather than simply to launch a new one.

It may be that wrongs as serious as those now in question have to be said to rule out anything worthy of the name "virtue," even qualified. Guilt may not be sufficient, that is, even in combination with good behavior in the future, for a judgment of imperfect virtue that applies to the agent's life as a whole in such cases. However, guilt still seems to be necessary to something we think morally valuable—and something that falls within the scope of virtue ethics to the extent that it involves a judgment of persons and their characters and lives rather than being adequately handled by claims about what acts ought to be done. The result may be said to be a "graded" notion of virtue, taken as covering diverse notions of personal moral worth, not all of them covered in ordinary language (or standard philosophic usage) by the term "virtue." Even in a case in which real redemption is impossible, that is, we still seem to place a value just on facing up to the past. We admire someone who insists on doing so at some cost to his own peace of mind—and perhaps even to his effectiveness as a moral agent in certain cases. The notion of a noble character seems to include a kind of heightened sensitivity to one's own moral wrongs. We sometimes think of this as a nobler ideal than moral purity, for that matter, so that imperfect comes out as better in a way than perfect virtue. Other terms might be substituted for "virtue" —"moral decency," for instance—where "virtue" on its ordinary use does not quite apply.

Our ideal of moral self-sensitivity can give rise to duty/virtue conflicts— potentially dilemmatic choices between doing the right thing and displaying the requisite emotional reaction—because of the crippling effects of guilt in some cases. There may even be cases in which overall virtue is not achievable, even with qualifications, because of a conflict within virtue ethics, which on this account will be influenced by the contingencies of the agent's record of moral action to date. Also, of course, our ideal leaves open many questions about the type and degree of wrong for which guilt is required—whether just for "in-character" violations, say, or rather for any major lapses from virtuous character on the part of the agent.

Even with some very rough edges, though, the ideal manages to fill two gaps in standard virtue ethics. First, it yields a "time-bound" view of virtue that allows us to ask what is still achievable in a life that may already include some serious and irrevocable deviations from perfect virtue. By contrast, Aristotle's dismissal of shame in virtuous adults underlines the uncompromising quality of his conception of virtue. The list of virtues derived from Aristotle is not really well designed, one might say, to advise an agent *in medias res*—an agent deciding what to do at some particular point in his life—as opposed to an educator or someone else who is in a position to plan lives from the outset or to judge them as a whole. By supplying a notion of imperfect virtue that includes some negative feelings about oneself, we modify Aristotle's essentially prideful ideal by building in serious gradations, instead of simply balancing it with an indiscriminate ideal of humility as on some standard religious extensions of the Aristotelian model.

Second, as a corollary of the time-bound view, our ideal of moral self-sensitivity provides a way of representing within virtue ethics the stricter action-guiding status of certain ought-statements thought of as commands rather than simply recommendations. That is to say, it lets us preserve some normative notion of binding "ought," conceived as a requirement that the agent cannot get out of—by developing himself in other dimensions of virtue, say, or by compensating within the moral sphere. The ideal accomplishes this within virtue ethics by insisting on a kind of emotional reparation for more serious violations as a condition of such virtue as is still achievable. From among the many things that a virtuous person would not do, that is, it singles out some as incompatible even with imperfect virtue unless the agent pays a certain affective price. By thus allowing for a wrong act's conditional compatibility with a lesser degree of virtue, it keeps virtue ethics from pushing the agent in such a case beyond the ethical pale, declaring him incapable of any morally estimable life by dint of his future behavior. It ensures that even the morally flawed agent will be subject to some personal norms, if only norms of imperfect virtue, in what he goes on to do.

Someone might suggest that the Aristotelian model can secure this result just as well by appealing act by act to the standard provided by the perfectly virtuous person. That is, what an imperfectly virtuous person ought to do on any given occasion will be just what the perfectly virtuous person *would* do, even though it is no longer possible to attain perfect virtue by so acting. However, I think we can see that different norms sometimes apply to the imperfectly virtuous. For one thing, consider the Aristotelean ideal of proper pride that was just mentioned: If nothing else, Aristotle's own picture of what this requires will have to admit of gradations he fails to recognize: some alternatives to the sort of lofty self-regard he expects of the virtuous person. Besides this, there are specific "contrary-to-duty" obligations—obligations to apologize or to make amends, most notably; but also other obligations based on changes in the situation resulting from the agent's deviations from ideal behavior—that would not apply to the perfectly virtuous agent. Perhaps Aristotle could accommodate these under "rectificatory justice,"[7] if the category were stretched to cover states of mind. My point here is just that guilt as a requirement of imperfect virtue amounts to a compensatory state of feeling that does not fit the Aristotelian model without some stretching.

Guilt and Perfect Virtue

I now want to switch to a different sort of case, in which guilt seems to be required by perfect virtue. This is a case of moral dilemma, where the agent's record of moral action is necessarily imperfect, since the circumstances leave him no choice but to do something wrong, even though he is not to blame for the circumstances and does the best he can to resolve the dilemma. Let us for the moment ignore the various questions raised by insisting particularly on guilt in such cases and note that our intuitive treatment of them does seem to require some moral emotion of the sort. A nice case for discussion is provided by a passage from Bertrand Russell's autobiography cited by Marcia Baron in an argument for the inadequacy of Williams's "agent-regret."[8] Russell limits himself in the passage to an expression of sorrow—no guilt or other emotion concerning the moral quality of his act—for a time when his activities as a pacifist during World War I required him to jilt an American woman he had promised to live with if she persuaded her father to bring her to England.

The case as it stands may seem to be what Williams calls a case of "moral cost"—of wronging someone but without doing something wrong under the circumstances—though Russell's description of it provides enough raw material for a full-scale dilemma. Even without modification it allows us to raise some important questions about just how much our ideal of moral sensitivity might require. Russell writes:

> When she arrived I could think of nothing but the war, and as I had determined to come out publicly against it, I did not wish to complicate my position with a private scandal, which would have made anything that I might say of no account. I felt it therefore impossible to carry out what we had planned. She stayed in England and I had relations with her from time to time, but the shock of the war killed my passion for her, and I broke her heart. Ultimately she fell victim to a rare disease, which first paralyzed her, and then made her insane. . . . Before insanity attacked her, she had a rare and remarkable mind and a disposition as lovable as it was unusual. If the war had not intervened, the plan which we formed in Chicago might have brought great happiness to us both. I feel still the sorrow of this tragedy.[9]

The case is conceived as one of clear moral choice: Russell's obligation to work effectively against the war is presumably strong enough to make it right to break a private promise. But even assuming that the promise itself was blameless— along with Russell's later behavior toward the promisee—the promisee still has a right to feel aggrieved. The case at least resembles a dilemma to the extent that it involves an unmet claim: The wrong done to the woman is from her standpoint not really canceled out by the importance of Russell's antiwar activities. We may grant that the latter are important enough to make the promise relatively trivial and Russell's act permissible, however.

As Baron points out, Russell's reaction still seems disturbingly impersonal. It is not quite a cold reaction; rather, I would say (modifying Baron), it is warm in a suspiciously sentimentalized way. What sounds like some sort of hereditary mental illness is inserted into the tale as if it resulted from a broken heart. Such regret as Russell attributes to himself does not seem to be agent-regret, since it is not directed toward his action. He says he feels the sorrow of the tragedy that befell the woman, but presumably he has in mind the tragedy of her overall life rather than particularly his own contribution to it, which did not itself result in tragedy. Williams would surely accept Baron's claim that our ideal of overall personal virtue requires more than this.

Does it require guilt, at least in a broad sense—of discomfort at responsibility (leaving it open what sort of responsibility) for a wrong? As the case stands, we might want to say that Russell really ought to feel a twinge of guilt or remorse, perhaps just as a stage on his way to overall sorrow, while thinking of the woman

and his behavior toward her as vividly as he is now doing in writing his autobiography. But he is under no obligation on other occasions to dredge up those
thoughts in the first place—or to consider the situation from the woman's standpoint. Love may require this, but that is another story, irrelevant to the present
question, unless we suppose that it obligates the agent to remain in a state of
love. From an all-things-considered *moral* standpoint, it seems, the woman's
claim on Russell was relatively unimportant, and his behavior toward her was
justified. At any rate, let us grant this point for purposes of argument along
with others that might be questioned in Russell's own understanding of the case,
since our question is what emotion is called for by the case as Russell understood it.

The case could amount to a full-blown dilemma, as I understand the term,
only if by jilting the woman Russell had done something harmful enough to
count as wrong even all-things-considered. A different sort of case in which she
had already disrupted her life seriously in light of the promise (ruined her repu-
tation by living with him, say) might yield a pacifist parallel to Sartre's case.
Another, more fanciful possibility is suggested by the link Russell may be imagining between his act and the woman's later illness. If heartbreak or something
similar had really helped cause the degree of harm that later befell her—
particularly supposing that the link could have been foreseen—we might indeed
hold that an adequately sensitive moral reaction on the part of the agent in the
case would have to include some element of guilt.

This is not to say, of course, that the reaction has to last forever. Let us get
away from the question of what Russell should be feeling many years later while
writing his autobiography and just note that we do now seem to have a case in
which even perfect virtue requires feelings of guilt, as against what Aristotle
suggests about shame when he limits it to children. Either that or our notion of
virtue has to be modified—made "extensional," as it were—to take in the moral
quality of an agent's life, the record of what he does in life, along with his personal qualities of character. If Russell in this hypothetical case had been able to
pursue his antiwar activities only by doing serious wrong—but on the assumption that this was the best choice available to him under the circumstances—
such wrong as he had to do would not have been chargeable to flaws of character. Indeed, one might say, it sometimes takes strength of character in such
cases not to be inhibited from action by moral squeamishness. At the same time,
it seems that a truly noble character would lead the agent to reflect on his past
act at some time or other and undergo some variant of guilt.

Thus modified, Russell's case (as I shall still call its modified version) brings
out a number of important points and questions about our ideal of moral sensitivity. As we just saw, it suggests that we need an extensional reading of the
notion of virtue—as the agent's record of moral merit, let us say—in order to
accommodate our expectations of an agent in a dilemma. Or better, perhaps:
There are two possibilities to be distinguished here, one of them in conflict with
the claim that perfect virtue in such dilemmatic cases requires guilt—though
both of them in different ways might seem to constitute departures from
Aristotle's assumptions. On the one hand, we might think of merit as a distinct

notion from virtue proper—the alternative I have proposed. A judgment of merit might be said to involve an assessment of the agent's life story, or his life story insofar as it is active, in contrast to both his character and the record of things that happen to him. For we seem to need two notions of personal excellence to capture what we want to say about Russell's case—namely, that virtue in its standard sense, or noble *character*, requires guilt on Russell's part in response to a blot on his record of action as measured by our nonstandard alternative notion of virtue as moral *merit*.

On the other hand, if we think of merit as replacing the standard notion of virtue, we apparently have to drop the claim that perfect virtue requires guilt— welcome news, perhaps, to those who find the claim odd in its mixture of notions of virtue and duty. Merit, it might be said, is simply virtue conceived as subject to moral luck, including a further sort of luck besides that recognized on the standard conception of virtue, which does not allow for dilemmas.[10] Perfect merit simply is not open to an agent in the unlucky circumstances of Russell's case, where through no fault of his own he has to do something wrong. If merit amounts to virtue, this just means that, in describing such dilemmatic cases, we need to retreat to the claims made earlier about gradations of imperfect virtue. In the end, though, I think that an appreciation of the emotional requirements of Russell's case will tell in favor of retaining a conception of virtue as itself untouched by dilemmatic luck and in more general terms will shed some light on the appropriate connection between virtue ethics and the modern ethics of duty.

Up to this point my argument on guilt and virtue has essentially bypassed duty ethics by treating the requirement to feel guilty as ideal rather than prac- tical. The contrasted terms correspond to two alternative readings of ought- statements: on the one hand, ranking something highest, or commending it to choice, and on the other hand, commanding an agent to choose it or bring it about. An ideal ought evaluates but does not prescribe its object, in other words—except on condition that the agent wants to fulfill the ideal. So in application to Russell's case it tells us only what he would feel if he were per- fectly virtuous, not what feelings (if any) are required of him *simpliciter*. One might want to say that from a general moral standpoint—as opposed to one required by love, say, or some similar ideal that calls for imaginative participa- tion in the standpoint of the woman with whom he was involved—guilt feel- ings on Russell's part would be supererogatory. Self-subjection to them consti- tutes a condition of special merit or virtue, beyond what duty commands. My own view, to be defended in section 3, is that in typical cases of dilemma guilt feelings are indeed obligatory and that a reading of "ought" that prescribes them is part of what keeps dilemmas from undermining action-guiding ethics.

My full argument for this last point will depend on the general account of guilt I go on to give in this chapter and the next. In response to those (perhaps Russell himself) who would argue that guilt is irrational or unnecessary for an act of perfect virtue, it is possible to appeal beyond intuitions on specific cases to a general view of the function of the emotion. Morally speaking, emotions like guilt have a special role to play in an approach to ethics that gives serious attention to personal standpoints in the way recommended by many of the current proponents of virtue ethics.[11] In Russell's case, guilt serves essentially to register the standpoint of the woman he had to jilt—her justified resentment of his action—alongside the overarching moral standpoint that determined his decision.

In the end, then, what counts in favor of guilt in a case like Russell's will be its fit with an intelligible overall account of morality and emotion. For purposes of my more limited argument in this section, however, let me end with an attempt to defend my treatment of Russell's case by detaching the claim I mean to make about it from various more questionable claims that might be thought to follow. The claim that Russell ought to feel guilty for having jilted the woman in the case does not mean, first of all, that a reasonable person would encourage Russell to feel guilty. Even from a moral standpoint (and there are others), we may recognize overriding reasons to forgo that often debilitating emotion; as mentioned earlier with reference to other cases, feeling guilty might undermine an effective decision to avoid the other horn of the dilemma by keeping Russell from concentrating on his antiwar activities. Feeling guilty later might not be an option, moreover. For one thing, guilt might conceivably just be crowded out by other appropriate feelings once the woman's horrible fate has over-shadowed any immediate harm done by jilting her.[12]

Secondly, a deeper point to note is that Russell's case seems to involve a basic asymmetry between guilt and other-directed emotional blame as responses to a less than perfect moral record. When we say that Russell ought to feel guilty (or ought at some earlier point to have felt guilty) about jilting the woman, we do not mean to recommend blame or personal anger toward someone who acted as he did, however understandable it may be on the part of the woman. Under the circumstances (on our assumptions about the case), his action toward the woman was morally required, and he was not at fault for the fact that it was. In requiring that he also feel guilty about his action we would not be assessing him negatively for it in emotional terms but rather insisting that he so assess himself. Nor would his self-assessment commit him to a similar emotional assessment of others in his position. He would be committed only to holding that they too ought to feel guilty for acts of the sort—not to a view of them as in fact guilty and hence appropriate objects of third-person blame. To the extent that a feeling of guilt on Russell's part involves a past practical ought, then—directed toward the act that he holds himself responsible for omitting—we might seem to be recommending that it be limited to his own case in a way that the logic of duty ethics is thought to rule out.

Even from the standpoint of virtue ethics considered in isolation, the case serves to highlight the self-directedness or reflexivity of the content of a first-person ideal ought requiring guilt. The expression "holds himself responsible" just applied to Russell is significant because it brings out the fact that what we are demanding of him is the imposition of some sort of moral burden on him-self. This does not imply that we (or he) would have a right to impose that same burden on others—to hold them responsible directly, that is, as distinct from expecting them to take that stance toward themselves. It is important, too, that we do not think of those who satisfy the ideal of perfect virtue just as persons of whom *we* expect something. Our notion of perfect virtue is specifically a notion of emotional or other burdens self-imposed.

We need to retain a distinct notion of virtue, then, as unaffected by dilemma in order to capture within virtue ethics our sense that the agent in a dilemma acts blamelessly. Aristotle's notion of virtue is picked out by its connection to praise and blame. What my discussion here indicates is that due attention to the special features of guilt as the first-person counterpart of blame introduces a further notion of virtue—an extensional notion subject to moral luck and hence more tightly tied to happiness than virtue in Aristotle's sense seems to be.

More fundamentally, the guilt/blame contrast in Russell's case seems to rest on *two* asymmetries with important bearing on questions of moral motivation. It depends not only on the fact that one of the two emotions contrasted is self-directed but also on the fact that both emotions are negative—bad states of feeling, that is, directed toward states of affairs evaluated as bad. The contrast would apparently be reversed if the two could be seen as emotional rewards rather than essentially punishments, given the same sort of difference in reflexivity. Consider how we would react to a positive self-directed feeling in Russell's case: pride, say, at having been able to resist romantic temptation in the interests of the antiwar cause. Even if a parallel feeling of admiration for Russell would be justified on our part, we would no doubt think less of him for reflecting positively on the same facts. An emotional reaction to the case, in short, involves taking a kind of position on the agent's moral record whose own moral assessment depends not just on accuracy but also on what it does for the agent—whether it inflates or diminishes him—and on whether the agent or someone else undergoes it. In the end, then, the importance of guilt to virtue depends on the fact that it is itself something bad.

Two Asymmetries

Let us at this point pause to consider in their own right the two asymmetries that seem to cut off guilt from either pride or blame in Russell's case. Their general importance, I want to say, lies in their link to the two sides of emotional justification: the "backward-looking" assessment of emotions as appropriate or inappropriate to the surrounding situation and their "forward-looking" instrumental assessment in relation to action.[13] What I shall call the "qualitative" asymmetry (positive versus negative, as illustrated by pride versus guilt) bears on our treatment of guilt as a reason for action and hence on its forward-looking justification, as I shall indicate. On the other hand, what I shall call the "directional" asymmetry (self- versus other-directed, as illustrated by guilt versus blame) bears more immediately on the noninstrumental reasons we expect to find for guilt, or its backward-looking justification.

I shall begin with the qualitative asymmetry, since its explanation in general terms seems to focus on norms of individual rationality in contrast to the social norms that underlie the directional asymmetry. However, applying it to the rational assessment of emotions will be a complex matter that also brings in social norms; and the more telling contrast for present purposes will turn out to be not rational but moral. The effect of the two asymmetries in combination—to make a long story short—will be a tendency to justify guilt on rather slim grounds in contrast to either pride or blame. But its explanation will make reference to the moral role of emotions insofar as it involves assessing them as rewards or punishments.

Consider first the motivational significance of the qualitative asymmetry— in the present case, the greater force for action of a negative emotion like guilt than a corresponding positive emotion such as pride. Intuitively it seems that pursuing and attaining some positive goal is optional in a way that the drive to escape something negative is not: The latter serves not just as a goal of action but also as a goad to it. However, we should note that this way of putting things blurs over a certain ambiguity in the classification of emotional states as positive or negative. It assumes that the relevant classification is affective—dividing good from bad *feelings*—so it may not fit certain emotions whose quality as feelings seems to clash with the evaluative points they make.

Love is commonly thought of as positive, for instance, because it says something positive about its object, not because it necessarily feels good. However, my assumption is that an emotion like love can be analyzed into several pairs of affective and evaluative components in a way that yields a qualitative match for each pair.[14] An apparently positive emotion may thus turn out to be negative because it depends on desire, with desire taken as involving discomfort at a negative evaluation of the current situation—of distance from the object, in the case of love—but as yielding comfort when satisfied, so that the emotion may sometimes still be pleasurable overall.

The two levels of qualitative assessment, affective and evaluative, will match up readily enough for guilt and pride. However, distinguishing them brings out another possible source of confusion in understanding what I want to say about the qualitative asymmetry. That is, insofar as its motivational significance rests on the contrast between positive and negative affect, the qualitative asymmetry might seem to presuppose the directional asymmetry rather than operating independently: The greater force for action of a bad feeling depends on its being bad *for the agent*. However, for "self-directedness," in the sense at issue in the directional asymmetry, the emotion in question also has to be *about* the agent— to evaluate him positively or negatively in the way exhibited by guilt and pride. The qualitative assessment of emotions is necessarily self-involved, one might say, but whether a feeling is self-directed is a distinct question that depends on its evaluative content, not just its element of affect, or "feeling" in the narrow sense.

Considered in isolation, then, the qualitative asymmetry amounts to an imbalance in motivational force between positive and negative feeling states whose quality is assumed to coincide with their value for the agent. The asymmetry concerns *rational* motivation to the extent that it is attributable to a difference in the force of positive and negative affective reasons for action. It is often taken for granted, as I noted in chapter 3, that a reason (or a good or sufficient "all-things-considered" reason) for action amounts to a consideration in light of which it would be irrational *not* to act. But the assumption seems really to hold only for negative affective (instrumental) reasons in my sense—the sense that implies affective badness—at least from the standpoint of basic or minimal (as opposed to perfect or ideal) rationality. It seems to be quite compatible with basic rationality to ignore the corresponding sort of positive reason for action: a positive feeling state seen as requiring action for its perpetuation or attainment.

Thus, for instance, to say that pride offers me a reason for moral behavior might just be meant as a claim that I can attain or sustain a certain particularly good state of emotional self-assessment only (or most effectively) by moral behavior. We need not suppose, that is, that in the absence of moral behavior I would feel particularly bad. If not, though, my reason for action need not be viewed as one I would be irrational to ignore—or not unless we supplement our intuitive conception of basic rationality with something more demanding, most notably one that insists on maximizing the good. If rational intelligibility is in question, that is, turning down something good requires no instrumental justification—it is enough to say "I don't need this"—whereas putting up with something bad makes sense only on the assumption that the costs of changing it would be too high or that it is likely to improve things overall.

Again, these points are meant to be limited to things perceived as good or bad for the agent, in particular the agent's affective states. However, the qualitative asymmetry will extend to nonaffective reasons that refer to an agent's interests by way of future feeling states. An agent's recognition that moral behavior is a presupposition of his future *moral* good, or virtue, may indeed provide him with a rational goad toward action, depending on how he feels about a lapse from virtue and on how he thinks he would feel if he exhibited one, assuming a rational requirement to take into account future feelings.

Alternatively, an agent may simply choose to act to achieve a positive goal of moral virtue; but he will not be rationally *compelled* to do so, even on the assumption that he has such a goal and that it does demand action on his part. At most, rationality will require that he either act on the goal or abandon it.[15] By contrast, a goad toward action of the sort that negative affect provides—perhaps just as part of the desire to achieve some goal or of the state in which one envisions it or of some later state one envisions if one does not achieve it—is not subject to the agent's will in quite the same way. One cannot simply get rid of a goad, as opposed to a purely positive end or goal, by focusing on something else; so rationality requires attention to it in practical terms as well—if only to indirect means of getting rid of it—even when it stands at some distance in the future. By contrast, the natural urge to sustain a present state of positive feeling—assuming no negative element such as that introduced by a threat of loss or withdrawal—seems to be optional from the standpoint of basic rationality.

In short: Goals are optional; goads compel. We may still say that a goal provides "sufficient" reason for action in the sense explained earlier—meaning that no further reason would be needed to justify action on it, but not that action must occur in light of it, even assuming all-things-considered status and practical rationality. The qualitative asymmetry emphasizes the bad over the good, then, as providing the kind of "compulsive" motivation that undermines freedom by making it difficult to do otherwise.[16] We recognize it, in effect, when we focus on internal sanctions as motivational props of the moral code.

The significance of the qualitative asymmetry in relation to dilemmas begins to emerge when we consider how the instrumental role of guilt as a source of moral motivation might also affect our assessment of the warrant for the emotion. We seem to adjust the standards of backward-looking justification to reflect forward-looking considerations: An emotional response may be encouraged for its general social (or other practical) adaptiveness, essentially by relaxing the evidential demands we would make on a corresponding judgment.[17] In the case drawn from Russell's autobiography, if guilt as opposed to pride is generally useful as a moral motive, that might explain why we expect Russell to feel guilty about a wrong essentially forced on him by the moral demands of the case rather than proud of himself for satisfying those demands.

However, the pride/guilt contrast does not work out quite so neatly. First, it seems to be only in moral terms that we rule out pride on Russell's part. If we distinguish rational from moral or social appropriateness, pride seems a perfectly appropriate reaction to the case, providing it has the right sort of object. Pride at having jilted the woman would not be appropriate, just because its object is not itself praiseworthy, but pride at having resisted romantic temptation in favor of duty (or something similar) might be sufficiently justified by the evidence. We do not *tighten* the standards of evidence, at any rate beyond a certain point, for an emotion that is *not* to be encouraged on grounds of general adaptiveness. According to the rather generous "perspectival" account of appropriateness that I defend with reference to guilt in chapter 5, sufficient evidence for a judgment of guilt according to the usual standards of warrant for belief will always be enough to warrant the corresponding emotion. So assuming that Russell's antiwar activities were important enough to make his act praiseworthy—as it might be even on a dilemmatic construction of the case, where it also counts as all-things-considered wrong—pride will be rationally even if not morally appropriate.

Second, however, questions about any simple denial of motivational force to pride seem to me to shift attention to the directional asymmetry as the main source of our weaker evidential standard for guilt. We may begin by granting that pride does not motivate action in quite the same "compulsive" sense as a negative emotion like guilt. But this assumes that the form of pride in question contains no element of psychological *need* of the sort that can sometimes make positive emotions hard to suppress. For instance, such pride as Russell might feel for his resistance to romantic temptation in favor of duty must be thought of as a "quiet" variant of the emotion that would not make him at all likely to boast about his deed or about his impersonal cast of mind or the like. But spelling out this assumption suggests that the reason pride is not encouraged in Russell's case is not necessarily because it lacks motivational force but rather at least partly because whatever force it has would tend to make it socially maladaptive.

On the other hand, "quiet" pride may seem to be adaptive to the extent that it lends a kind of passive reinforcement to an urge toward action—in this case, an urge toward moral action. The contrast with guilt turns out to be undercut, that is, by a different way in which pride can have practical consequences—not precisely by "motivating" action, if that means providing a reason that makes the agent act, but rather by putting the agent into a state of mind that facilitates action. It is useful for its mood-lifting and other energizing effects as an enabling factor in the background of action even if not a cause of action in any stronger sense. Even without the admixture of negative feelings, then, pride will have a role to play in moral (and other rational) motivation distinct from its role as an end of action or positive goal. So the qualitative asymmetry need not make pride less practically useful than guilt, despite its less compelling force as a practical reason.

In any case, we also relax the standards of evidence for guilt on the basis of certain noninstrumental considerations—of how one has a right to treat oneself versus others—that my later perspectival account will allow for, along with considerations of general adaptiveness. Let us therefore now bring in the directional asymmetry, initially by comparing pride on Russell's part with a positive reaction to him on the part of someone else. Even in moral terms it would presumably be open to us as readers of Russell's autobiography to admire him for doing what he had to do in the service of the antiwar cause. One wants to say that we have a right, in a way that Russell himself does not, to ignore the harm his act involves for others and react positively to him as its agent just on the basis of other features of it that in this case are assumed to be more important. In making this comparative judgment, we rely on the directional asymmetry, essentially by demanding that a self-directed emotion be more responsive to significant subsets of the available evidence than is expected of its other-directed counterpart.

By contrast, we do not have the right to react negatively to another person—to condemn someone, emotionally speaking—on the basis of a limited subset of the evidence bearing on his act, however significant evidence of that sort may be in general terms. So blame for Russell—the other-directed counterpart of the guilt we expect of him—apparently is ruled out. Indeed, it seems to be ruled out rationally as well as morally in backward-looking terms—unlike pride, which, as noted just above, seems to be ruled out only morally. Rather than being insufficiently warranted by the overall facts of the case, pride apparently rests on shifting attention away from a partial subset of them—the facts about the harm Russell's act does—to which a virtuous agent would be sensitive, even where something else is morally more important.

The problem with blame, understood as other-directed personal anger, is not that it plays a lesser role than guilt in moral motivation. At least insofar as it is negative, it plays a roughly commensurate role as a motive for acting to change one's interpersonal environment. To the extent that it involves a negative evaluation of someone else, though, there are also noninstrumental reasons that count against relaxing the standards of backward-looking justification as with guilt. From the standpoint of minimal charity it would be too much to expect others to live up to the higher standards of behavior that one may justifiably impose on oneself—and that the virtuous person on the view suggested here *must* impose on himself.

In short, the view holds that the demands of perfect virtue include a kind of moral fastidiousness: painstaking attention to morally significant detail. Subjecting oneself to negative emotion as a way of focusing attention on a corresponding evaluative proposition serves to meet these demands in circumstances that do not allow for action. In defense of dilemmatic guilt, then, reacting with discomfort even to partial evidence of responsibility for a wrong may be taken as showing special concern for its victim at the cost of some emotional harm to oneself. But moral fastidiousness as a requirement of perfect virtue would seem to yield just the opposite result for blame insofar as it is other-directed and hence involves subjecting someone else to a negative evaluation. Indeed, I take it that emotional blame is ruled out by our normal expectation of charity toward others, not just by the more exacting demands of virtue, at any rate for those not in the position of victim.

On the social view of ethics and emotion defended here, the quality and direction of these and similar emotions gives them a significance as rewards or punishments for action that can be used to provide motivational backing for the moral code. Guilt and blame both come out as "punishing" to the extent that they direct negative attention toward their objects, whereas pride and admiration count as emotional rewards. It is the fact that pride is a self-administered reward, then, that would seem to make us morally wary of it in a case like Russell's, even granting it sufficient backing to count as rational. At the very least, a self-administered reward is unseemly under circumstances in which one's good deed depends on doing serious wrong, even apart from the instrumental danger of encouraging future indifference to the harms one's actions cause. So we have a kind of reverse parallel of my treatment of guilt as a morally encouraged self-subjection to punishment for harm caused, but with complications introduced by our differential treatment of evidence for and against rational appropriateness.

I have more to say in chapter 5 about the guilt/blame asymmetry in strictly rational terms, but at this point we can already see how the notion of guilt as a self-imposed emotional burden gives it a special moral role to play in cases like the one drawn from Russell's autobiography. It captures our ideal of the noble character as requiring more of itself, in short. But it combines this element of moral self-sufficiency with a sense of connection to others, of sharing in the harms one does to them, to the extent that it involves emotional identification with the victim of wrong. It is this that seems to be missing from Russell's sorrow at the unfortunate demise of the woman he jilted. I now want to go on to argue, however, that something more like guilt in the narrow sense is best suited to supply this lack.

I shall leave off further discussion of Russell's case until I have set forth my account of guilt. In advance of the account, I would expect some readers to recoil at the suggestion that guilt best fits the case. I indicate a number of reasons for this in my next section, but one rather obvious reason I want to dispel at the outset has to do with the sexual overtones of guilt in popular culture. This may suggest to some readers that guilt is to be imposed on Russell for sexual misconduct, but nothing of the sort is intended. At any rate, shame, the main competitor to guilt among after-the-fact moral emotions, would seem to be in even a worse position in that respect—and also to be ruled out by our assumption that Russell acted honorably in the case. He would also have acted nobly, my claim is, if he had allowed himself a twinge of guilt. Remorse might seem initially to be less objectionable than either shame or guilt, but one of my central aims in what follows is to undermine the view of these emotions as necessarily distinct.

2.   Guilt as an Identificatory Mechanism

On a standard philosopher's picture, emotional guilt is contrasted with alternative reactions such as shame and remorse on the basis of the way its evaluative content brings in the self and connects the self to its acts and to other agents. On Rawls's account, guilt is said to be directed in the first instance toward an act viewed as wrong rather than some bad trait of the self as with shame.[18] Its content is seen as essentially moral in a way that is not true of shame, which may sometimes rest on nonmoral traits, including one's relation to the traits or acts of other agents. However, for purposes of setting up a neat contrast in this discussion, I shall restrict myself to a subtype of shame with the same sorts of grounds as guilt—what might be called "moral shame." Thus limited, shame seems to focus more closely on the self than does guilt insofar as the self rather than an act is its primary object of negative evaluation.

Like moral shame but apparently unlike remorse, though, guilt does represent the self as somehow affected (tainted, stained, tarnished, or the like) by the wrong act attributed to it. As a practical motive—via the desire for reparation that seems to separate guilt and remorse from shame—guilt may therefore seem to be self-regarding in a way that remorse is not.[19] Perhaps partly because of this contrast, guilt-motivation is sometimes taken to fall on the egoistic side of the current debate about egoistic versus altruistic sources of moral motivation.[20] The usual emotional alternative considered in the debate is love, whose object is another person viewed positively; but even among negative contrary-to-duty emotions there may seem to be more altruistic possibilities.

Indeed, the point may be applied even to guilt versus shame, though in one sense (as just noted) shame seems to involve a closer focus on the self than either remorse or guilt. A common contrast between guilt and shame links guilt to approaches to ethics based on a notion of individual responsibility for action, or autonomy. Shame is tied more closely to the ethics of virtue—not particularly to the good opinion of others, as was maintained in earlier versions of the contrast but rather to something more like status in a moral community.[21] Both emotions rest on the internalization of others' reactions, but shame seems to involve a thought of being viewed by others with scorn, whereas guilt involves accusatory anger.[22] However, the two emotions are necessarily mixed together as a result of overlaps in childhood teaching: Guilt is often inculcated by a form of group rejection, for instance, to the extent that disapproval involves at least a qualified withdrawal of love.

For that matter, any neat egoism/altruism contrast is further undermined by some other important ways in which guilt may seem to be tied more closely to regard for others than shame is. Its characteristic desire for reparation may be said to move the agent *toward* others insofar as it prompts him to make up for any harm done them, in contrast to the desire to hide from others that is linked with shame. In fact, the connection to egoism/altruism just described may seem to be reversed by Rawls's account of guilt versus shame in terms of the agent's concern for the welfare of others as opposed to his own state of moral perfection.[23] Though Rawls sees shame as a higher moral motive than guilt to the extent that it prompts acts of supererogation, guilt comes out on his account as a more directly altruistic motive: an emotion built on concern for others.

Rawls's view seems to accord with recent research in developmental psychology linking guilt with empathetic distress.[24] In what follows I want essentially to suggest a reconception of the nature of guilt that incorporates a version of this approach, but broadened to cover recalcitrant cases in light of an older tradition of understanding guilt in terms of anger. A version of the latter that brings in a form of empathy can be found in Jonathan Edwards's account of "natural conscience."[25] The view I derive from Edwards's account essentially interprets guilt not as a distinct emotion on a par with shame, remorse, and the like but as a particular emotional mechanism, or a pattern of emotional reaction, making use of these more basic reactions among others. I take this to allow for overlaps between guilt and shame of a sort that will bear on the dispute among anthropologists and others about the difference between cultures that rely on guilt versus shame as instruments of moral control.[26] My more general aim in this section, though, is to tie guilt to the self in a way that explains both its special force and its peculiar pitfalls as a motive for action on behalf of others.

Guilt and Empathy

The current trend among psychologists attempting to understand guilt in individual development bases the emotion on empathy, usually conceived as identification with others' sufferings, or empathetic sorrow or distress.[27] We might be tempted to see this work as providing empirical confirmation for the connection Rawls sets up between guilt and concern for others, but in fact it rests on similar definitional assumptions that deserve some scrutiny. Since "guilt" is essentially a made-up emotion term in the first place, arising in English originally by mistake, it would seem to be fair game for artificial line-drawing, even more than the other elements in our disorderly stock of emotion terms.[28] But we do at this point have some firm intuitions about its use that ought to be respected. In particular, a wider notion of empathy seems to be needed to cover the cases of guilt for simple rule infraction without envisioned harm to others that we often take as prime examples of the emotion.

One might feel at least somewhat guilty, for instance, about various violations of the duty of fidelity—from flattering someone to revealing a confidence to misrepresenting one's political opinions for the sake of social harmony—that do no damage to anyone affected by them and in some cases even are performed just in order to benefit those affected. The sort of reference to general harm— to the usual effects of such behavior—that we might be tempted to make here would apparently limit the emotion to agents who accept a utilitarian justification for the rules they feel guilty about violating. But surely it is at least conceivable that someone might undergo the emotion without theoretical commitment on the subject, and also for acts that seem to do no harm to others even in general terms such as violations of certain rules of religious obedience. On a definition that builds in reference to harm, guilt about victimless sexual behavior, say, would require either attributing to the agent a mistake about the consequences of his act or extending "harm" to cover cases of offense, conceived as involving distress about the rule violation per se.

In any case, there is still a question whether empathetic distress is sufficient to capture the evaluative content of guilt—what the emotion says about its object—where the act in question is reasonably seen as harming others. Something else seems to be needed, that is, to distinguish feeling guilty from just feeling sorry for the person one has harmed, or even sorrowful or distressed on his behalf, perhaps to a degree that is heightened by the recognition of one's own causal role but without any element of emotional self-reproach. Consider what one might feel, say, about the other side's casualties in a war. Adding in a mere belief that one is responsible or even blameworthy might or might not affect the content of one's emotion, turning sorrow into guilt. Even with a shift of emotional focus to the agent's action (as with Williams's notion of "agent-regret") we might just have a kind of self-directed sorrow or some other emotion such as anguish that intuitively seems to fall short of full-fledged guilt.

If we add in a further emotion, though—self-anger or some other negative self-directed emotion—it might seem unclear why we should not take this as the core element of guilt, detachable from empathy and sufficient for guilt in its own right in the cases of simple or victimless rule violation just cited. Empathy could still be seen as playing a critical role in the development of guilt because it serves to extend the emotion beyond such cases, even if we do not make it out as part of the very concept of guilt, let alone the essential part, or as necessarily present in the earliest cases in childhood emotional experience.

However, I think that the notion of guilt as based on self-anger may in fact allow for a broader account of the emotion in terms of empathy. Consider Jonathan Edwards's use of the elements of empathetic anger along with a notion of emotional consistency to make sense of conscience:

> [W]hen a man's conscience disapproves of his treatment of his neighbour, in the first place he is conscious, that if he were in his neighbour's stead, he should resent such treatment from a sense of justice, or from a sense of uniformity and equality between such treatment and resentment, and punishment. . . . And then in the next place, he perceives that therefore he is not consistent with himself, in doing what he himself should resent in that case; and hence disapproves it, as being naturally averse to opposition to himself.[29]

At the initial stage of Edwards's two-stage account, the agent identifies with the resentment of the person he harms or otherwise treats unjustly. It is clear from a preceding passage that Edwards means to say here that the agent actually puts himself imaginatively in the other person's shoes in understanding his resentment.[30] We can think of an agent at this first stage, then—resolving some ambiguities in Edwards's account—as reproaching himself from the standpoint of the victim of a moral wrong he has committed. The second stage essentially combines this element of empathy with the agent's sense of his own contrary motives as the basis for a second-order emotional reaction of "aversion to self-inconsistence and opposition" that Edwards equates with uneasy conscience and takes to be at odds with self-love.[31] We may simplify this for our present purposes to the agent's uncomfortable awareness that his first-order empathetic emotion is self-directed and negative.

Emotional guilt of the sort in question here seems to belong at the first stage of Edwards's account, as the basic empathetic ingredient of an uneasy conscience, involving self-opposition but not yet the second stage of emotional reaction to the awareness of self-opposition. As Edwards describes it, this stage seems to involve a form of anger (as I take resentment to be) based on the agent's imaginative participation in the standpoint of those affected by his action. The account can be stretched to cover psychologists' accounts of guilt as based on empathy in the narrower sense—the sense suggested by Rawls's talk of concern for others —if we grant that anger may be projected onto the persons affected by one's act. That is, empathy in the narrower sense may sometimes come to include anger by considering what one might feel if one were in someone else's position, even if the other person is not perceived as angry on his own behalf. This rests on understanding empathy as emotional identification—which I interpret to cover any emotions based on sharing the evaluative standpoint of another person, as distinct from the tendency to take a particular person as an overall model for one's own experience that psychologists sometimes have in mind by the term. We may speak accordingly of guilt as an identificatory mechanism with a different particular basis in empathy in different cases, some involving self-anger added onto a more sorrowful (or other negative but passive) view of things from another's standpoint and some involving other self-directed negative emotions.

This view also seems capable of covering cases of guilt for victimless wrongs, if we allow for an independent source of self-anger or some other self-directed negative emotion that is empathetic in a broader sense, since it is based on identification with authority figures or with objects of dependency in early life. Empathy on my speculative account of guilt and "ought" in chapter 3 is encouraged in children essentially by linking emotional imitation with the conditions of social acceptance or acceptance in the family group. Disapproval of a forbidden act may be communicated at a stage before the resentment of any victims of harm is in question, with the role of the victim as a source of anger assumed instead by something on the order of a judge. My proposed account of guilt is not meant to settle the ultimate origin of the emotion, however; nor would I want to exclude any possibilities by conceptual line-drawing. Rather, my suggestion that we understand guilt as an identificatory mechanism is supposed to allow for emotional variations as long as they all exhibit an element of Edwards's "self-inconsistence and opposition"—what we may think of as "self-alienation," borrowing a term from Gabriele Taylor.[32] That is, the guilty agent is assumed to be emotionally at odds with himself as a result of the kind of identification with others that we find in the first stage of Edwards's account. This is the basis for the aversive reaction to the awareness of self-opposition that yields conscience in Edwards's second stage.

In the typical sort of adult moral case, guilt rests on identificatory self-anger. I interpret this broadly to involve discomfort at the thought of oneself as responsible for a wrong (with the latter term taken to include both unjustified harm and simple or victimless rule-violation), typically as a basis for a reparative urge that provides a parallel to the desire for revenge characteristic of other-directed anger. This urge may be absent in some cases that we still count as cases of guilt—what I call "deficient" (as opposed to "full-blown") cases.[33] Its presence in typical cases, however, yields a further, forward-looking sense in which guilt is action-oriented in contrast to shame, besides being based on the evaluation of a past action and of the self only in relation to that action rather than as the bearer of a certain trait.

In other cases, though—including many of the sorts of cases psychoanalysts handle—guilt may involve some other self-alienated emotion, something more passive though still negative and self-directed, of the sort that would result from identification with a victim seen as reacting with a passive sense of grievance rather than active blame. Other forms of emotional self-reproach include self-hatred (in the sense of self-aversion) or even self-horror (at one's role in causing the other's suffering, say). What is important is that the reaction involves the kind of emotional self-punishment on behalf of others that Edwards's account captures in terms of the sense of justice. This is to be distinguished from internalized fear of punishment *by* others, as on Freud's account of the origins of the superego, though in fact my account seems to fit Freud's comments on remorse.[34] Its central feature for our purposes is that it makes guilt out as including remorse, along with other negative emotions, where they are used as ways of inflicting punishment on oneself as part of the general sort of identificatory mechanism that we find in Edwards.

This account seems to me to be the one that best explains the overlaps we find in our intuitions about cases. It is not just that emotions like shame, guilt, and remorse have indefinite boundaries or that our ideas of them are obscure or ill-defined. In my own experience of testing out the standard distinctions in application to imagined cases, it often seems clear that both guilt and shame are in play: I find myself more or less wincing and hanging my head at the same time, say. Nor does it seem to be enough to say that guilt and shame or guilt and remorse coincide in application to cases, as they would if they both independently applied; rather, there are at least some cases in which they do not really seem to be distinct. All three may be part of the same emotional reaction—or, more precisely, shame and remorse may be part of guilt—in a case where an appropriately sensitive person with certain moral expectations of himself finds that he has accused someone unjustly, for instance. On the account suggested here shame and remorse, or self-alienated versions of them, may be part of the very punishment that guilt inflicts, in contrast to the usual treatment of these alternative emotions as either interchangeable or quite distinct.

My account also applies to forms of guilt that psychoanalysts have distinguished as "survivor('s) guilt" or "separation guilt" and that our culture seems to have in common with others that mainly impose shame for moral breaches.[35] Guilt at some form of benefit over or separation from the other members of a group with which one identifies may serve as a mechanism of group control in a way that includes moral control, but that also seems to represent at least one strand of development of the notion that is not based on ideas of sin or pollution.[36] The biblical sources of our own culture's emphasis on guilt actually deal explicitly only with sin; to locate emotional guilt in the Bible[37] we seem to need to apply the general sort of identificatory mechanism that we find in Edwards's account to the relationship between man and his *divine* judge. What these different cases have in common seems to be an inner conflict that may be multiplied by the multiplicity of objects of identification—from other people to the group as a whole to God—as reasons for self-alienation that are themselves capable of conflict and hence can generate dilemmas.[38]

I shall deal in my next chapter with the questions raised by dilemmas as cases of unavoidable wrong. For the moment, I should note that the account of guilt I have outlined here is not put forth as a definition in the sense of an analysis of the content of the emotion. We may retain the standard definition in terms of self-attributed responsibility for a wrong. By explaining guilt as an identificatory mechanism, I am in effect adding to this a certain view of how discomfort comes to be directed toward that thought, thus constituting guilt as an emotion. What I have picked out as essential to the development of the feeling is the sort of self-opposition that Edwards interprets in terms of identificatory resentment. Typically this arises from some form of anger, though it also may be based on a range of other emotions serving to distance the self from its act in response to grounds for anger. In any case, it is phenomenologically distinct from standard self-anger to the extent that it is identificatory and hence self-alienated.[39]

Even allowing for the phenomenological range of guilt feelings, I think we can see that mere acceptance of others' anger without some identificatory emotion would not be sufficient. Consider the stock example of a wayward husband who accepts his wife's anger as valid from her standpoint, which is one he has to put up with (even meekly, perhaps) for his own ends, though it is not a standpoint he shares in emotional terms. I think we have to say that his acquiescence in her anger as a punishment imposed from without—even if registered in some sort of counterpart emotion—falls short of felt guilt, though he may of course have a reason to obscure the distinction. Felt guilt seems to be more likely, in fact, in cases where it is clear that others will not impose punishment from without by feeling anger.

More generally, the account of guilt as an identificatory mechanism will help us distinguish what intuitively seem to be genuine cases of the emotion from other possible "fixes" on the thought of responsibility for wrong: satisfaction, say, at being the focus of others' angry attention. By itself, a definition of guilt would limit the relevant cases to uncomfortable emotions but still would allow for emotions other than those we intuitively classify as guilt: simple resentment on one's own behalf, most notably; or self-pity at social rejection (perhaps with a content that acknowledges its justification—something on the order of "I can't do anything right.") I shall also go on to show how the account drawn from Edwards lets us explain guilt-motivation—both its advantages and its pitfalls—in a way that depends on its basis in self-alienation.

A Puritan divine may seem an unpromising choice to appeal to, even with modifications as indicated, in attempting to convince contemporary moral philosophers of the value of guilt-motivation. One reason for the aversion to talk of guilt, along with objections to the Freudian account, is of course its religious overtones: In its more overwhelming forms the emotion is associated with a particularly self-punitive extreme of Puritan religious consciousness. However, it should be clear from the passage quoted earlier that Edwards's treatment of guilt is philosophical rather than religious. In fact, Edwards reverses the usual link to religion by considering conscience as a "natural" motive, meaning pre-religious: a motive that is present in us before our souls are saved. As such, of course, it is not the highest motive on his account; the motive required for Edwards's notion of "true virtue" is benevolence or love—just what some of the current opponents of guilt-motivation have in mind. Moreover, Edwards's (and the common) characterization of bad conscience as "uneasy" stands in contrast to the familiar picture of overwhelming guilt that we find in certain depictions of Puritan religious consciousness—or, for that matter, in psychoanalytic case histories or the modern novel. Guilt on the picture Edwards offers us is or can be a moderate emotional reaction and seems perfectly sensible in affective terms as a way of registering self-attributed wrong. Let us now see what else might be said in its favor.

In Praise of Guilt

On the identificatory account just presented, guilt is sometimes a passive feeling, as I think we have to say in light of the full range of cases. But in the central moral cases, its tie to anger makes it active—if not affectively, in the sense of being aroused in feeling tone, then at any rate evaluatively, to the extent that its evaluative component typically supports an urge toward reparative action: discomfort at the thought that one ought to make up for a wrong. This means that guilt exhibits motivational force to a degree that is not true of shame. Shame—meaning occurrent emotional shame, not just the general sense of shame, or a disposition to exhibit the emotion—is an inhibited or "downcast" feeling in phenomenological terms. So cases of motivation by shame turn out for the most part to be cases of motivation to *avoid* shame, based on (if any emotion) fear or even pride. By contrast, though guilt may be incapacitating in excessive doses, the agent in a state of feeling guilty is typically motivated *by* that state to *escape* it—in a way that makes guilt provide a potentially powerful moral motive even after a moral lapse. It has a special role to play, then—

which is not to say that it leaves no room for shame—in a morality built on a view of human nature as imperfect but improvable.

For a nonmoral example, one might consider what one would be likely to do out of guilt versus shame in response to a bad piece of work one had to publish: On the standard picture, someone motivated by guilt would get to work on something else to make up for wasting his talents or his colleagues' time on the last effort; someone motivated by shame would typically try to hide or obscure the object of his emotion. He might also try to make up for it, but it would not seem to matter to the effectiveness of such compensatory action whether it is connected to the object of shame in a way that would make it count as "reparative"—as repairing what was broken by the violation of professional standards. That is, the agent who is ashamed of his past performance might make up for it, not by improved performance in the same area, but just by stressing other areas in which he already shines.

Guilt in contrast to shame, we might say, is intractable to summing. One might indeed attempt to work it off by performance in other areas, but guilt for a serious moral wrong will be expiated—if at all—only by action (including mental action) that addresses the wrong done. In sublimated form, then, with the thought of wrong hidden from consciousness, it yields a particularly powerful motive because it is unappeasable. For much the same reason, it may sometimes be overwhelming. There are cases of wrong so serious that guilt is inexpiable: Agamemnon's sacrifice of his daughter and many of the other standard cases of moral dilemmas would seem to qualify. On the other side, though, psychological studies indicate that shame is particularly incapacitating in extreme form, at least as induced in children.[40] Someone overwhelmed by either shame or guilt, of course, will not be motivated to do much at all—at any rate, will not be effectively motivated—except to the extent that undergoing the emotion itself counts as a kind of partial or substitute action. Shame involves lowering oneself, or taking the submissive posture, we may say—hanging one's head—whereas guilt involves a kind of emotional self-punishment.

The structure of guilt-motivation is worth exploring further in these terms, since the emotion itself counts as a form of the punishment it demands. One way of making up for a serious wrong, that is, involves anticipating others' reactions by inflicting punishment on oneself. So at least to some extent, the desire for reparation characteristic of guilt may be satisfied just by undergoing that unpleasant self-directed emotion. This gives the emotion a special motivational role as a kind of ritual act of emotional self-punishment. Psychoanalysts see self-punishment of various sorts (self-destructive behavior, most notably) as a defense against guilt in certain cases.[41] But the account suggested here builds this function into guilt itself by way of its self-referential quality.

The point has complex motivational possibilities that seem to pull in both directions—reinforcing guilt as a motive but also explaining some of the pitfalls of guilt-motivation. Though guilt is unpleasant, it seems to be one of a number of unpleasant emotions that we characteristically "wallow" in, with a need to dwell on their negative thought content. In anticipatory form, then, as an attempt to head off further or worse guilt by self-punishment, it may very likely fail. It often has the opposite result, in fact—"feeds" on itself in a way that can compound its motivational force but also constitutes a powerful motive for avoiding the emotion just by shifting attention. Whereas shame incapacitates by inhibition, the arousal often linked to guilt may involve *hounding* oneself to a degree that also interferes with action. There are cases in which one avoids even entertaining the thought of action—of writing a letter already too long postponed, say—out of an inability to face the emotion. On my account, we may say that a tendency toward compulsive repetition of ritual self-punishment sometimes undermines its motivational effectiveness.

This complex account of guilt-motivation with its basis in talk of emotional self-punishment gives rise to questions of voluntariness that I shall postpone to my next section. For the remainder of this section, I want to exhibit some further pitfalls of guilt as a motive, along with some of its advantages in comparison to shame, remorse, and the various other reactions to moral wrong that might be substituted for it. The central point that distinguishes guilt from shame—to focus first on its main competitor—seems to be self-alienation. Shame does not seem to divide the self against itself in the way that guilt does on the account drawn from Edwards. Though it may be seen as based on the expectation of contempt or the like from others—perhaps only hypothetical others (or even just one's hypothetical ideal self) in the case of an action hidden from view—it does not amount to *self*-contempt. The agent does not identify with his judges, that is, in feeling what he feels; he is solidly in the inferior position of the person judged—not at all a comfortable position but one that at least assigns him a definite place. If he did identify with his judges, to the extent of feeling things (at least ambivalently) from their standpoint, his emotion would also come out as part of the guilt response, on the account suggested here of guilt as an identificatory mechanism that sometimes uses other emotions as materials.

With attention confined to cases in which the two emotions are distinct, then, there seems to be one way in which guilt may be worse than shame in motivational terms: Both emotions obviously interfere with self-esteem, but guilt may be said to do so in a "conflicted" way that is arguably more incapacitating than simple inhibition. However, we have begun to see how this element of inner conflict as the basis for the self-referential quality of the emotion also makes it potentially more powerful as a motive. Guilt may play an irreplaceable moral role, in short, to the extent that it yields a self-perpetuating motivational mechanism.

On most of the other comparisons I can think of between guilt and shame, we seem to face a choice between different sorts of advantages and disadvantages. Sometimes it is a value-laden choice: For instance, it might be said that guilt at least accords the self a kind of dignity insofar as it is identified with its judges rather than simply being confined to the position of the person judged. The function of the sense of shame seems to include keeping people in their place—it amounts to the knowledge of one's place—in a way that links the emotion to social stratification and group conformity. Similarly, moral shame may sometimes be incapacitating to the extent that it favors acknowledging imperfections as characterizing oneself in global terms rather than just in connection with a past action.

Moral guilt is also commonly said to be tied to individualism because of its reference to specific acts as falling within the agent's sphere of responsibility.[42] I raise questions in chapter 5 that undercut this point somewhat—it introduces further issues of voluntariness of the sort that the present discussion is meant to bypass—but my account still yields at least a rough contrast with shame on the question of individual responsibility. Still, to the extent that the guilty self identifies with the victims of the wrong it does, as well as with its judges, its responsibility ties it to others; and the connection is reinforced, of course, for nonmoral variants of guilt such as survivor's guilt that are imposed for benefits distinguishing an individual from other members of a group. As a reaction to someone else's plight or disadvantages, guilt is owed *to* others in a way that shame is not.

In different ways, though, both guilt and shame involve negative evaluations focused more or less explicitly on the self. I take it that this is what sets them apart from alternative reactions to moral wrong. Variants of regret, for instance, even if directed toward one's own past acts, on explicitly moral grounds, do not involve any kind of threat to the self—to the estimation of character or merit—on the basis of past acts, but on the contrary seem to use negative feeling simply to distance the self from its past acts without any intervening stage of self-punishment. In affective terms, regret may be unpleasant, but it lacks the element of negative self-evaluation that supports my motivational account of guilt.

The same might also be said of remorse, however, even though this involves a wish to undo the wrong one has done (as guilt may not) along with the need to make up for it by future action. In cases where it is distinct from guilt, remorse is more tightly tied to a specific past action: Its associated reparative desire does not amount to the sort of general need to clear the self—to expiate a wrong, thereby erasing a "taint"—that accounts for the motivational power of moral guilt in anticipatory form. The possibility of "free-floating" guilt, though a source of some devastating psychological problems, at the same time gives the emotion a practical scope that does not characterize its alternatives.

Thus, in my earlier example of publishing a bad piece of work, neither regret nor remorse would seem to motivate later work in the way that we typically see guilt as doing. The same seems to hold for the various other after-the-fact "taboo-feelings" (as I think of them) that might be suggested as alternative emotional residues of moral ought-violation: horror, say; or a kind of moral anguish that amounts to a variant of grief. On the other hand, a feeling of "compunction," which is sometimes mentioned as a less problematic alternative to guilt in cases of moral dilemma, would not really seem to be after-the-fact—or at any rate, it would not admit of the same after-the-fact temporal distance—and thus is naturally interpreted by Hare as a variant of fear.[43]

I conclude, then, that guilt is the best candidate among these negative emotional reactions for supplying the motivational force of moral "ought." It can also cause motivational problems insofar as it sometimes involves an obsessive inability to "let go"—of acts one cannot make up for, relationships one cannot improve, or tendencies one cannot bring under control—but it seems to share at least some of these problems with moral obligation. It therefore seems well suited to help explain the sense of compulsion we associate with "ought." What guilt has over other emotional candidates on the account I have given is a potential future-orientation mediated by its identificatory focus on the self.

For the same reason, of course, we might question its application to Russell's case and other moral dilemmas. There seems to be no need for the agent in such a case to make up for the wrong he has done by his future behavior in other areas of life beyond doing what he can to mitigate the effects of that particular action, as he would if he felt only remorse. Presumably the wrong in question is something he should have done overall. Why not say, then, that Russell ought to have felt remorse at jilting the woman but not the sort of negative self-evaluation involved in emotional guilt? My answer to this question will ultimately depend on a fuller account of the standards of emotional appropriateness. Before we get to that issue, however, we need to ask what is meant by saying that an agent in a dilemma *ought* to react with one emotion or another. My view, in brief, is that the agent ought to feel something like guilt and that guilt in the narrow sense just distinguished is appropriate; but it remains a question whether the agent ought specifically to feel guilt in that sense. Let us now look at some of the more general problems raised by "ought-to-feel."

3.   Contrary-to-Duty "Ought-to-Feel"

Both my account of guilt and the role I assign to it in cases of dilemma rest on a view of emotions as able to serve as substitutes for action. I speak of them in some cases as self-imposed and as indirect ways of satisfying obligations to take action—and for that matter as objects of obligation in their own right. Because of both their motivational force and their independent symbolic significance as rewards and punishments for action, they may sometimes be required to express evaluative standpoints or commitments that an agent cannot express more directly, through action, under the circumstances. By contrast, the recent resurgence of interest in emotions in the ethics literature seems for the most part to limit their role to virtue ethics. They serve alongside action on an Aristotelian account as objects of long-term training in virtue, commendable both in their own right and in support of dispositions to virtuous action but not in any stronger sense required.[44]

The exclusion of emotions from duty ethics is typically traced back to Kant; Ross, for instance, in extending one of Prichard's arguments, appeals to the Kantian principle that "ought" implies "can" as a reason for denying that action from a particular motive (in a sense that includes virtuous feelings) can be obligatory.[45] His argument, along with Prichard's, apparently drives a hard wedge between duty and virtue ethics. In fact, though, elsewhere in the same work Ross provides the reader with sufficient materials for a response to the argument. I shall begin my treatment of "ought-to-feel" by constructing a response from Ross's comments as supplemented by my own view of emotion. What I hope to show is that emotions have an important role to play, albeit a complex role, as objects of obligation alongside action in the general approach to ethics derived from Kant, despite any excesses of Kant's own version of it.

My response to Ross's argument will turn on the way we rely on voluntary action to generate emotion in standard cases. It will eventually be put to work in defense of an interpretation of dilemmatic ought-judgments as guiding action indirectly insofar as they imply various contrary-to-duty obligations, including those prescribing guilt and similar moral emotions. This view involves assigning to action-guiding "ought" a kind of conditional imperatival force in application to feeling, in addition to its literal or direct force as commanding action. However, some care is needed in interpreting this view. For one thing, a major pitfall of guilt-motivation not previously discussed seems to be a tendency to substitute the emotion for right action. "I'm such a miserable sinner" as a way of fending off reasonable change can be sincerely felt as a more or less automatic response to well-rehearsed cues, but this is obviously not what one has in mind in requiring guilt. The requirement to feel guilty if one cannot manage to act must not be taken as implying a permission to omit action and feel guilty instead.

Nor should "ought-to-feel" be taken as resolving dilemmas. It is important in any case to distinguish the practical and normative ethical problems raised by dilemmas from the metaethical difficulties to which my argument here is addressed. A wrong plus guilt will not make a right on any view I would find plausible in answer to those difficulties. But further, "ought-to-feel" will not always yield a way out of them. In some cases, like the one drawn from Russell's autobiography, possible conflicts between required feeling and action might give rise to second-order dilemmas. If the normative point of the required feeling is to protect virtue from the effects of moral luck, my discussion will indicate that this role is also subject to important limitations.

Requiring Guilt Feelings

In the passages that bear on "ought-to-feel," Prichard and Ross are mainly concerned to deny the possibility of being obligated to act from a certain desire or motive—as opposed to simply possessing it, or exhibiting it in some way or other, which is what concerns us here. They do so, moreover, partly on the grounds that requiring act-motive compounds rather than simply acts would involve a regress if applied to the sense of obligation, the desire to do something *because* it is required, or Kantian conscientiousness.[46] However, Ross also brings in an argument from "ought"-implies-"can" that would seem to count against requiring a motive in itself, and Prichard's argument apparently comes up in defense of a general limitation of "ought" to "ought-to-do," taking it as applicable to "actions and actions alone."[47]

I want to look closely at Ross's use of the Kantian principle. He writes:

> It is not the case that I can by choice produce a certain motive (whether this be
> an ordinary desire or the sense of obligation) in myself at a moment's notice,

still less that I can at a moment's notice make it effective in stimulating me to act. I can act from a certain motive only if I have the motive; if not the most I can do is to cultivate it by suitably directing my attention or by acting in certain appropriate ways so that on some future occasion it will be present in me, and I shall be able to act from it. My present duty, therefore, cannot be to act here and now from it.[48]

Our question (to modify Ross's last line here) is whether it can be someone's present duty to have or display a certain motive—and even to display it "here and now" in some wide enough sense of that expression to accommodate acts of the normal sort, as the normal objects of duty. I shall argue that it can be. Though I shall not take the point further here, moreover, I think we could easily extend it to yield the claim Ross explicitly wants to deny: that one can have a duty to act from the motive in question. We just cannot take this to rule out a duty to perform the act in itself, or regardless of motive.

The object of the duty to act from a certain motive, that is, should be understood as *being moved by* that desire, emotion, or whatever it may be, with the duty to perform the act in question seen as independently fulfillable, not as replaced by the duty to display a certain act/motive compound, as on the Prichard/Ross interpretation of Kantian conscientiousness. If acts alone could not be required, we might just avoid the worries these authors raise by substituting motivational prohibitions for requirements. A prohibition of all less-than-virtuous motives would on this account be taken as ruling out any acts the agent would do out of those motives, even if that means ruling out all possibilities for performing those acts. On the supposition that at least some acts are required *simpliciter*, however—if only acts of omission like refraining from murder—we need a more plausible response, in positive terms, to Ross's arguments against obligatory motives.

The relevant sort of motive for our purposes is not a long-term character trait on the model of the sense of duty but a short-term emotional state, including certain motivating states of felt desire. These are clearly covered by Ross's argument, despite its focus on the sorts of motives Kant favored. However, the argument apparently limits our control over such states to the long-term strategies for cultivating them in ourselves that come up in relation to the Aristotelian picture of training in virtue. By means of acts of attention or overt acts that we *can* control, we can manage to produce a certain feeling or other motive in ourselves—but perhaps not "at a moment's notice," or with the kind of *immediate* control that Ross in the quoted passage takes "ought"-implies-"can" to imply.

Ross's denial that we can produce a motive "by choice" suggests that he may also be interpreting the principle as insisting on direct control of a sort that is unlikely: On the Aristotelian picture, one becomes conscientious or courageous, say, not simply by aiming toward being so but instead by directing attention toward something else, such as the actions these motives require on particular occasions. However, we might begin by raising some questions about this interpretation of "ought"-implies-"can" that will also bear on the issue of temporal immediacy and on probable further background assumptions of the Kantian principle.

Are *acts* required only if they can be accomplished directly by choice? Presumably they must depend only on choices one can manage, but must these be choices to perform the acts in question under the descriptions under which they are required? I do not see why we should say so, particularly if we remember some of the differences between "ought" and "obligation" that emerged in chapter 2 and concentrate on "ought," the term for which closure over causal relations holds. There seem to be cases in which our required ends have to be promoted indirectly, that is, by means that entail shifting attention to something else. For instance, perhaps I ought to help a friend who will be able to benefit from what I do for him (so that I will indeed be helping him) only if I do not see myself as helping him but rather as participating in a joint project for its own sake. We might suppose that he needs help because of a loss in confidence that would just be made worse by too much overt concern from others—and that if I thought of myself as helping him, my concern would be evident in what I did.

It may be important to this sort of case that there is something I can do directly—namely, whatever overt acts are required to help my friend. But even supposing that this exhausts my strict obligations in the case—if indeed the term "obligation" applies to it strictly—the claim that I ought to help him seems acceptable. Similar cases might be constructed for various activities that require intellectual absorption, sometimes to the point of blotting out full consciousness of one's motives. Indeed, a similar point is often made about the pursuit of happiness, as a background requirement of either morality or prudence. And there are examples of specific behavior required by morality or prudence—often described by reference to motives or other states of mind—that would tend to be undermined by direct aim. Consider the command to show respect say, or the advice to be assertive, and imagine how likely one would be to satisfy either of them adequately by just trying to.

So intuitive cases do not bear out an interpretation of the Kantian principle as limiting oughts to acts one can perform at will, if that means by willing those acts as such—one way of taking "by choice" in Ross's argument. What about "at a moment's notice"? There are certainly examples of overt acts that are fit subjects of obligation and yet require preparation—or time for completion. Some of these involve long-term cultivation of an ability to act, of the sort that is suggested by the Aristotelian picture of training in virtue: Consider, for instance, my "time-bound" extension of Sartre's case in chapter 2, where the agent's ability to discharge his obligation to support his mother depends on ten years of savings. But there are other examples shorter term than this, particularly where the act itself takes time.

Ross provides at least one good example, in fact, when he turns to an extended discussion of the nature of right acts, or the question how much is to be included in the description of an object of obligation.[49] Of a case in which returning a borrowed book can only be accomplished by mailing it, he concludes that fulfillment of the obligation to return it requires actually getting it to the other party, not just dropping it in the mail.[50] At the very least, if the mails go astray, one owes the other party an explanation of one's failure to get the book to him. Of course, in that case, the object of obligation is not something that can be done "at a moment's notice." One can initiate action at a moment's notice, perhaps, but only in a sense that includes such preparatory mental acts as planning to buy some wrapping paper and the like. In normal cases, however, the same can be said of the processes that give rise to a certain kind of motivation—to an emotional reaction like guilt, say—if one allows for the point about indirectness that came out just above.

Let us take a look at the question of how we generate emotional motivation. For instance, consider how I might get myself to feel guilty about something I took to require the emotion. Suppose I find myself indifferent to some harm I have done to X—or perhaps to some harm that has befallen X as a result of my actions or in comparison to some benefit that comes to me. What might I do to generate guilt? Note that we do not have in mind here the general tendency to feel guilty, or proneness to guilt, even just with respect to X; perhaps I have no deficiency in that regard, or perhaps there are reasons against the general tendency. In any case, what we want is just a feeling of guilt on some particular occasion with an object that is limited accordingly.

One thing I might do and might well be advised or advise myself to do is to think about certain aspects of the situation—to attend to or even to dwell on the harm done to X from X's standpoint, its connection to my own action, and the various things that connect me to X, such as benefits I have received from him in the past. Emotional discomfort essentially serves as a way of directing or sustaining attention toward some negative evaluation and arises naturally (albeit not inevitably) in the act of fixing attention on the thought in question. An attempt to generate it more directly—just by telling oneself to feel guilty— would be inefficacious or even counterproductive, in part because it directs attention to something else.

We should be careful to cancel out any suggestion that generating emotion or emotion itself amounts to an act that is within the agent's control—any more than it is fully within the control of the agent in Ross's case to get a book to someone through the mail. The indirect methods for generating emotion may be no more reliable than the mail. If the mail does go astray, of course, we might withdraw the claim that the agent really *ought* to have returned the book, on the grounds that "ought" implies "can"; but that does not mean that the claim should be withdrawn for all similar cases in which the mail does not go astray but might have. "Ought" holds on the assumption that "can" does; but "can" is adequately fulfilled by doing the act (or exhibiting the emotion or other motive) in question. It does not imply "by some generally reliable method"—in other words, that the agent possesses a general capacity to bring about the object of obligation—any more than it implies "at a moment's notice."

Our uncertain control over our emotions and other motives and states of mind may be indirect in a further way besides that indicated, because the exercise of it typically runs in reverse temporal order from means-ends calculations, as well as depending on the substitution in attention of another end. That is, one may sometimes generate a required emotion by aiming at performing an act—including an act of attention, as in the example just given—which in fact, if performed, would be motivated by the emotion in question. Though the temporal reversal pertains only to occurrent motivation—by emotions and similar episodic states rather than long-term dispositional motives—it is illustrated by one of Prichard's comments about courage. Prichard allows that one may be required to do something that involves action from courage, a particular dangerous act that one can perform only by working up some courage, compatibly with his exclusion of an obligation to act from that motive.[51] However, Prichard's point depends on interpreting courage as the suppression of an occurrent emotion, namely fear.

It is worth taking note in general terms of the sort of negative control of emotions to which this example appeals: our ability to *block* emotions, so that we can also be said to allow them to occur when we do not block them. But it might be thought that guilt admits of this less than other emotions; in any case, it should be clear from my previous discussion of the pitfalls of guilt that I do not mean to deny that one can be overwhelmed by guilt feelings. Indeed, it is possible (and compatible with anything I want to say about emotions generally) that a degree of "uncontrol" is built into the very concept of emotions: that what unites the states we think of as emotional is in part their resistance to full control. More or less by definition, that is, they are states that we cannot just put ourselves into either directly or by entertaining certain thoughts. My claim here is that they are not therefore disqualified as objects of obligation—of practical as opposed to ideal "ought"—given the range of acts that have that status.

Emotions might be said to be midway between belief and action in the degree of practical control they allow for. Belief is typically harder to control, and our claims about what beliefs one ought to have are presumably commendatory for the most part. But "ought-to-think" also applies to occurrent acts of attention—of fixing a certain thought in mind—and through them (in the way just indicated) to emotions. Acts of sustained attention are of course not fully controllable either: One cannot simply command oneself to concentrate on something undistracted. More precisely, such a command may not be possible to satisfy—or may in the next moment go unheeded. We do not therefore hesitate to issue such commands, though—to require someone to pay attention—in cases that allow for the ordinary sort of qualified control. Directing and sustaining attention seems to count as a long-term act on the model of getting that book back through the mail to its rightful owner. It is similarly recalcitrant to full control, despite the fact that in this case the interfering factors may all be internal.

Our even more qualified control over the emotional states that arise from such acts of attention is sufficient reason not to count the generation of emotion as an act: Though the concept of action extends beyond intentional action to behavior that occurs more or less automatically (an example might be tapping one's fingers while thinking), presumably this has to be behavior of a sort that one *could* produce at will. My claim here is simply that, even if emotions are not like this, they are still controllable enough by way of acts of attention to be suitable objects of practical "ought" in at least some cases.

This does not mean we would issue such a practical ought in conversation, even mental conversation. Ordering oneself or someone else to feel guilty might defeat its point by its very directness, according to the argument I have outlined here; more than that, it would seem to undermine the moral significance of the emotion. Guilt in the cases where it is required is supposed to be automatic; only as an automatic response, unmediated by practical reasoning, can it give us the kind of evidence of moral motivation that we want in cases of dilemma, most notably. Russell, for instance, in the case previously discussed, would not be fully admirable in the terms we require if he had simply managed to make himself feel guilty in response to the knowledge that guilt was required by perfect virtue. So virtue imposes a kind of paradoxical limitation on practical "ought-to-feel." The same sort of paradox is abundantly illustrated by "ought-to-think," though, in the sense that involves attention: Consider the self-defeating results in many cases of explicitly urging intellectual absorption on oneself as a necessary means to satisfying the requirements of one's studies or one's job. I conclude that the parallel problems for emotion do not limit it to virtue ethics in the way that the arguments in Prichard and Ross seem to show.

Indirect Action-Guidance

It is important to bear in mind that "ought-to-feel" in a case like Russell's or even Agamemnon's is not quite on the same level as the all-things-considered practical oughts in conflict in a dilemma, despite my argument for taking it as analogous to "ought-to-do." I shall illustrate in a moment how, besides being conditional on the failure to satisfy one of the dilemmatic oughts, the requirement to feel guilty may conflict with the other ought in certain cases. This means that my suggestion that emotions serve as act-substitutes in such cases is not put forth as a way of resolving dilemmas. Emotions do not provide a fully adequate alternative for satisfying the ought the agent fails to act on but serve instead to exhibit its motivational force, along with other signs of its importance to the agent, by exhibiting the internal sanctions on moral failure.

My crucial claim is that this is enough to make the dilemmatic ought in question adequately action-guiding for our purposes: It is meant to guide action directly, though of course it cannot do so in combination with the other ought in conflict; it may still guide action indirectly, however, to the extent that it tells us as a second-best alternative to feel some appropriate emotion such as guilt. According to my preceding treatment of "ought-to-feel," this amounts to telling us to allow ourselves to feel the emotion—if necessary, to get ourselves to—by performing a mental act: directing attention in such a way as to generate the feeling. In short, practical "ought-to-feel" amounts to a kind of indirect "ought-to-do" with another object.

On this account, emotions can be seen as "residues" of moral choice in a fairly literal sense: They embody what is left of action on a moral ought when direct action is blocked.[52] However, they are themselves subject to ought-conflicts. Indeed, I want now to consider what to say about cases in which they seem to allow for higher order dilemmas. Up to this point, for instance, I have been working with an understanding of the case drawn from Aeschylus' *Agamemnon* that takes for granted some assumptions inherited from the literature on dilemmas. In particular, I have assumed that Agamemnon unproblematically ought to feel guilt or some similar moral emotion and that, insofar as the case amounts to a dilemma, this would have been true even if he had chosen differently. However, I think there are problems lurking in any easy resort to "ought-to-feel."

For instance, now that we have distinguished some of the emotions that might be urged on Agamemnon, a question might be raised as to whether the dilemma Aeschylus depicts is genuinely moral. I take it that Agamemnon indeed ought to feel guilt, at least prima facie, as a self-directed variant of remorse for the murder of his daughter. The crime is serious enough to be personally "tainting," in short, even if in a larger sense he had to commit it. But it is not so obvious that Aeschylus represents the necessity in question here as moral or that he takes some moral variant of agent-regret to be appropriate for Agamemnon's other alternative, which involves failing in his duties as military commander (and more fundamentally as his brother's avenger).[53] The conflict might also be interpreted as a clash between moral and nonmoral requirements, with the latter taken as imposed by something like social or religious roles and expectations—or better, perhaps, by an older ethical system now uneasily superseded by specifically moral norms, in a sense that entails regard for the welfare of other agents.

The murder on this account of things is *the* morally wrong act in question, but Agamemnon's alternative might still be thought of as more important to avoid—for instance, on a view like Williams's that questions the finality of moral norms.[54] If this is true, we might want to say that shame or some other contrary-to-duty emotion rather than guilt in the narrow sense would have been appropriate had Agamemnon refused to sacrifice his daughter. The case might still be a "tragic" case to the extent that it pits morality against another powerful system of norms—pre-moral religious norms, say—with no satisfactory resolution possible. But it would no longer seem to be a moral dilemma in our terms. I shall therefore ignore these problems of interpretation in what follows and continue to work with what we might call "the philosopher's Agamemnon": the received picture of Agamemnon as an agent in the grips of a moral dilemma, with both of the choices he faces assumed to be morally wrong.

The received picture also apparently has it that Agamemnon ought to feel something appropriate for the wrong he has to do. One might think of the case, however, as involving another dilemma on the level of "ought-to-feel"—in the first instance a conflict between feeling and action, the result of mixing "ought-to-feel" with "ought-to-do." There are cases, that is, as I noted earlier in discussing the pitfalls of guilt, where the emotion would be so overwhelming as to undermine any possibility of effective action. Surely this is likely in Agamemnon's case: If he allowed himself an appropriate reaction to the murder of his own daughter, one might suppose, he would be unable to function in his role as military commander and hence would be failing to act consistently in light of the very reasons for the sacrifice. But then the ought requiring him to feel guilty, no less than the ought he has chosen to violate, would conflict with the ought he means to act on in performing the sacrifice.

If the result amounts to a further moral dilemma, I take that to show that "ought-to-feel" leaves intact the problems of choice raised by dilemmas and makes clear their unhappy upshot for both duty and virtue ethics. Feeling guilty might itself come out as wrong—or as emotionally self-indulgent, insofar as it interferes with required action—so substituting emotion for action in such a case will not provide an effective way of erasing the moral stain on the agent's character. Guilt will still count as appropriate to the case on the view of appropriateness I shall go on to defend, which builds in reference only to general adaptiveness in the sense that involves fulfillment of some moral or other function in standard cases; but in this case its usual function will be undermined. If we also say that the agent morally ought to feel the emotion, the case might seem to yield a higher order dilemma that rules out perfect virtue no less than perfect performance of obligation.

There are ways around this conclusion that involve denying, after all, that Agamemnon in our variant case really ought to feel guilty. However, on my account of the moral significance of guilt in connection with virtue, the most obvious move would still leave virtue ethics with the problems of moral luck raised by dilemmas. We might take "ought-to-feel" in the case as prima facie only—at least supposing that we also take it as practical, as we need to do to establish the link between virtue and duty. Apart from considerations of virtue, that is, Agamemnon might not seem to have a moral reason against failing to feel guilty that is strong enough to stand in light of the reasons against failing in his duties as military commander in the way explained in chapter 2 in defense of dilemmas. So on this account "ought-to-feel" would not yield a further dilemma within duty ethics, though by the same token it would not afford a way of preserving virtue against the problems raised on the lower level by "ought-to-do." Agamemnon presumably ought to forgo virtue in favor of right action, if he has to choose. Moral sensitivity as a requirement of virtue will make virtue unachievable, in short, even with the "time-bound" imperfections I allowed for in section 1.

A possible way around this conclusion might involve a return to the broad sense of guilt, with the suggestion that the agent substitute some less incapacitating emotion such as remorse to avoid a further conflict. Guilt in the narrow sense would still be made out as appropriate (in the sense of rationally acceptable), no matter what the agent does, but it would not therefore be required by perfect virtue. Remorse could still serve to clear the agent's character to the extent that it is a negative feeling even if not self-directed in quite the same way as guilt, and the requirement to feel it might be said to be in force "all things considered." However, remorse might also be maladaptive in some cases— enough so to give rise to a second-order conflict of the sort just outlined. Though it does not have the self-focus of either guilt or shame and hence might be thought to interfere less with activities requiring self-assurance, the mere fact that it is normally a downcast feeling might inhibit effective action. For that matter, its focus on a particular act in the past and on acts of reparation specifically related to it might distract attention from the agent's other obligations in an unhelpful way.

All that such second-order dilemmas would do to undercut virtue ethics is to limit achievable virtue to something even further from moral perfection than we saw in section 1—even on the level of sensibility, our substitute for action in light of first-order dilemmas. They do not exhibit any sort of incoherency in virtue ethics but simply subject it to problems of moral luck similar to those that apply to the ethics of duty. The point is simply that virtue ethics would seem to be in no better position than duty ethics with regard to moral dilemmas, at any rate if we rise up a level and consider possible conflicts involving "ought-to-feel."

This point rests on a suggestion for avoiding second-order dilemmas within duty ethics, however, by taking the requirement to feel guilty as prima facie only, which now deserves scrutiny. The suggestion presumably would be meant to save the claim that the statements of "ought-to-do" in dilemmatic cases guide action indirectly via "ought-to-feel." Otherwise, that is, we could not make out indirect action-guidance, or the substitution of emotion for action, as yielding a conflict-free manifestation of motivational force for the oughts in conflict on the lower level. So duty ethics would still seem to be threatened with incoherency. In fact, though, I think this misconstrues the relevance of "ought-to-feel" in a way that would leave us with problems of explanatory coherency.

We can see this by considering the connection of all-things-considered status to the strength of reasons, and hence to reasons for attention, as the foundation of "ought-to-feel." On the perceptual model of reasons for prohibition defended in reference to dilemmas in chapter 2, our assignment of all-things-considered status to a statement such as "Sacrificing one's daughter is prohibited" would amount to a claim that the moral reasons against sacrificing one's daughter are strong enough to stand in light of opposing reasons. But this is essentially a claim about "salience," or the appropriate allocation of attention. The strength or seriousness of a reason in comparison to others amounts to its moral or other practical importance. It is important enough to bear in mind as a reason for action, in short—and hence there is reason to load it with affect, thus giving rise to emotion on my account as the normal way of fixing attention on some appropriate object of thought.

Now, this latter reason—the reason for emotion—might sometimes be balanced by stronger opposing considerations. There are many quite ordinary cases in which emotion is not the best way of directing attention, despite the fact that this standard function is what sets it off as a distinct mental category. Emotion can sometimes undermine action or even distract attention from the need to act. If we consider cases of the sort that came into the preceding subsection, where moral action is best promoted by looking away from the moral reasons for it, it seems that a prohibition might be outweighed in some cases even as a reason for attention, since there may be stronger reasons for attending to something else.

I have been following Williams, however, in interpreting overriding status

as implying more than this: that all claims on the other side will be met by acting on the reason in question.[55] But surely Iphigenia, as the victim of
Agamemnon's sacrifice, has a claim on his attention that would not be met by
single-minded devotion to his duty as Greek commander. In something like
McDowell's terms, her claim is important enough not to be "silenced" by any
allegedly more pressing obligations to others. I prefer the visual metaphor of
figure/ground: From a certain standpoint of moral evaluation, her claim stands
out against the background of countervailing considerations. So it counts as
all-things-considered, even when we grant that there are stronger reasons for
directing attention elsewhere.

According to much the same argument as we applied to first-order dilemmas, then, we do seem to face further dilemmas of "ought-to-feel." Despite
appearances, this will not really compromise my proposed resolution of the
metaethical problem of dilemmas. The keystone of the latter was the general
version of internalism, according to which moral language by virtue of its meaning has motivational force in general terms but not necessarily in any particular case. Emotion came in at this metaethical level as the initial vehicle of
motivational force, relied on in early moral teaching to connect "ought" and
similar terms to tendencies to required action. My current argument shows how
"ought" may extend to emotion tendencies too, and in particular to guilt, as a
way of exhibiting the motivational force of the first-order ought that the agent
has to violate in a dilemma. We should not expect in this case either, however,
that the usual role of emotion would be fulfillable in every instance. There may
be cases like Agamemnon's in which the agent also has to violate "ought-to-
feel." What this possibility undermines is not the overall coherency of ethics in
the terms explained above but the agent's personal record of action—and his
virtue, which at this level is not so clearly distinguishable from it, as we can
now see in application to some of the normative problems raised by cases of
dilemma.

Making Up for Moral Luck

Even if dilemmas do not pose a threat to the coherency of ethics, they still are
troubling as cases of moral luck, or responsibility for factors beyond the agent's
control. In chapter 5 I extend the guilt/blame asymmetry to show that they do
not thereby undermine the coherency of the notion of responsibility, which can
be made out in terms that do not imply blameworthiness. My emphasis in my
overall argument here is on the metaethical problems raised by dilemmas. But
within normative ethics, dilemmas are problematic insofar as they indeed saddle
an agent with a form of responsibility that undermines her efforts to make something morally worthy of her life.

Even without blame, that is, the agent in a dilemma will have to live with a
blot on her moral record. My defense of "ought-to-feel" effectively extends her
moral record to include her record of emotional reaction and thus has normative implications. It casts guilt in a positive role as a way of making up for moral
luck: Because the emotion serves as a way for the agent to distance herself from

the wrong she has to do via mental self-punishment, it effectively insulates her character, or virtue proper, from her record of moral action, or what I distinguished as "merit" in section 1.

In the first instance, then, what dilemmas of "ought-to-feel" tell us is just that even this second-best substitute for action may sometimes be morally ruled out. So it will not work as a practical response to moral luck in all cases. More generally, however, the explanation of why it fails seems to me to bring out what is fundamentally at issue in the problem of moral luck: the fact that the self to which we attribute responsibility, conceived as what causes action, is really a construct from our actions (along with the other things we take as basic expressions of moral character) and hence in a certain sense is a fiction. It is fictional as the sort of separable entity on which we can pin responsibility—in a sense that requires a determinate moral character.

Kant of course assumed the existence of a separable noumenal self when he made out a good will as compatible with thoroughgoing moral failure.[56] Even without Kantian metaphysics, though, the ordinary notion of responsibility that is threatened by moral luck seems to trade on an artificial notion of the self as something one could in principle characterize independently of what it does. However, this is particularly questionable when we get to the level of feeling, understood according to my present argument in terms of acts of attention.

Consider Russell's case once again. According to my argument in section 1, the act that he had to do in response to his first-order dilemma, jilting the woman, could be taken as affecting his record of moral action but not his character. However, if he also faced a second-order dilemma, we would have to give a similar treatment to something that intuitively seems more central to his character: his emotional responses in morally momentous circumstances.

One might attempt to cordon off the circumstances of dilemma, at any rate for agents who do not exhibit a similar general pattern of response. However, if we really suppose that the circumstances in Russell's case are morally serious enough to yield a dilemma—that jilting the woman would cause her serious harm (or we might turn back to Agamemnon's case for a deed that wears its seriousness on its face)—it begins to be unclear how we can form a notion of the agent's moral character that does not include his emotional act in the particular instance. The act in question involves a kind of refusal to feel—shifting attention away from any objects of thought that would tend to generate the required emotion—rather than simple affective numbness, in response to a morally momentous occasion. And it is a long-range act, extending beyond the occasion in temporal terms. Withholding the response for a short period, that is, would not be enough to allow the agent to satisfy his primary obligation in the case. Nor could he detach himself from his refusal to feel, on our understanding of the case, by rising to yet a further level and punishing himself with guilt for it—or not until so much time has passed that the result would seem to count as a change in character. So at this level, apparently, one is more or less what one does.

That is why it can also be appropriate to blame someone who is simply prevented by his own emotional incapacity from satisfying "ought-to-feel"— not necessarily an agent confronted with a dilemma but a sociopath, say, who does not have it in her to feel remorse for a vicious murder; or for that matter, the real-life Russell. My asymmetrical treatment of guilt and blame along with various other "reactive attitudes"—to use Strawson's term in bringing them to bear on free will issues—will therefore not yield any sort of uncomplicated overall asymmetry as applied to moral responsibility.[57] On the level of "ought-to-feel" the guilt/blame asymmetry may in fact be reversed: It may be socially adaptive on the whole to blame others for certain morally crucial feelings they cannot help, just because it expresses our own standpoint and commitments as moral agents. By contrast, guilt for one's own unavoidable feelings or refusals to feel might seem to have lost its usual moral point: By shifting attention away from the object of the required feelings to one's own failure to have them, it would simply set up another form of distraction.

The result of some personal deficiencies, in short, is a deficient person, even if he had no chance to be other than he is. What we feel in response is rightly thought of as blame, moreover, in the sense of personal anger—not just hatred or some other emotion that focuses on the person as distinct from what he does. On the account defended here, the agent does something morally condemnable in such a case: He violates a statement of "ought-to-feel." Even in cases of second-order dilemma, where we can presumably assign the cause of the agent's emotional deficiency to the moral demands of the situation rather than to personal moral coldness, we would typically feel an aversion to the cold-blooded agent of harm that might be seen as an emotional correlate of "tainting."

If I am right, then, an understanding of moral luck and related free will issues ultimately requires coming to terms with what amounts to something like a Humean version of the moral self: a fictionally independent entity, invented to serve as a stable object of praise and blame.[58] If this notion raises problems for the coherency of ethics—if its fictional status means that we have to retract in moments of reflection what we need to say as functioning moral agents—they are at any rate not problems special to dilemmas.

For present purposes it will be enough to make clear with reference to concrete cases like Russell's that claims about reactive attitudes like guilt and blame will not yield any simple way out of the problems raised by moral luck. We can find some further important complications in variants of Russell's case that do not amount to dilemmas in my terms but instead raise issues of whether and how action and its consequences "stick to" the moral self. Suppose we alter the case as I have interpreted it and assume that Russell was guilty of some element of negligence—perhaps he inappropriately led the woman on, to get her to come to England—that makes the case fall short of perfect virtue. It would then amount to a dilemma of the sort that Aquinas recognized, a result of the agent's own wrongdoing, even if wrongdoing of a relatively minor sort that does not typically have such devastating consequences.

I take it that in such a case we would hold Russell at least partly responsible for the consequences of his action, even if our blame is mitigated somewhat in degree by the fact that they were completely unforeseeable. We would blame him for causing the woman's demise, that is—not just for leading her on, and not just to the limited extent that we *would* blame him if he had led her on without such extreme consequences. The case would resemble one in which driving home from a party slightly intoxicated results in a car accident—a variant of the case of an unavoidable car accident that I deal with in chapter 5, but one that is avoidable in long-range terms in the sense that the agent could and should have prevented the accident by refraining from driving while intoxicated.[59] The point for present purposes is that the agent's fault as we conceive it in such cases does spread to the consequences of her action, so we think it reasonable to blame her in light of the harm she actually causes. We do not just expect her to feel guilty about it herself in order to distance herself from her record of action and thus preserve virtue—even whatever imperfect virtue she can still claim compatibly with what she did—as in my treatment of cases in section 1. She is damned by the harmful consequences of her deed. The point also holds for Russell's case, supposing that harmful consequences would result from a morally mandated response to the first–order conflict.

One might be tempted to correct for the oddity of these ordinary judgments of responsibility by subtracting out moral luck factors, but any such attempt to tidy them up for theoretical purposes would throw them out of line with our intuitive assessment of the corresponding reactive attitudes. Consider, for instance, the suggestion that an agent guilty of minor negligence without harmful consequences ought properly to feel just as guilty as if she had caused major harm, since her character would be no different from that of the agent who did. This amounts to another way of separating virtue from merit. It seems unreasonable, though, where the harm in question is not even foreseeable in general terms as the sort of thing that might well happen if one commits the minor misdeed in question. This is how Russell's case differs from the case of minor negligence that might have caused a car accident but did not. In the latter case, guilt is warranted not just by the possible consequences of such negligence but also by their likelihood—the risk the agent actually (and knowingly) took by drinking while intoxicated, say. The standard way of generating guilt for something of the sort is in fact to imagine the possible consequences as if they were actual, and we can reasonably demand that the agent do so—vividly enough to induce greater care in the future. But that is nothing to what we would expect of her if the consequences actually occurred, and she did in fact kill someone through negligence.

So the real-life Russell who treated the woman he jilted somewhat badly, but with no very bad results, ought presumably to feel *some* guilt in light of the normal sorts of wounds that can be inflicted by such behavior—not just for a violation of gentlemanly honor or the like. Some guilt may be in order on the same grounds, in fact, even in a case where the woman turns out to suffer nothing at all—because she immediately takes up with someone else, say—though here I think the demand for self-punitive emotion would again be mitigated in degree, this time by events as they actually ensued. However, it would be unreasonable to expect Russell in either of these cases to feel what we would expect him to feel in the case of catastrophic moral luck.

That there are such cases is something I take to be a fact of moral life, to be understood but not made any easier, even in a theoretical sense, by appeal to our reactive attitudes on the sort of account proposed here. For emotions also reflect moral luck. My account of guilt for the unavoidable in chapter 5 will be relevant to the question, then, insofar as it lets us extend the emotion and even appropriate instances of it beyond an agent's morally culpable acts. But it will thereby offer a way of accommodating the phenomenon rather than attempting to dispel it or to reinvent ethics in light of it; for the Humean self that picks up its character from its consequences is not simply a philosopher's notion that might be rejected while maintaining the social practices that constitute morality. I take it to be our ordinary notion, underlying our ordinary treatment of the moral sentiments.

5

Unavoidable Guilt

Several recent authors on guilt and related notions apparently allow for the rationality of guilt feelings in at least some cases of unavoidable wrong. Their views yield different decisions on some troubling real-life cases ranging from the case of an unavoidable car accident that, without any fault on the part of the driver, results in the death of a child to cases of survivor's guilt and vicarious or collective guilt. I now want to take a new look at these cases and others—and a critical look at some of the views of guilt proposed—in an attempt to work out an understanding of the content of guilt and the grounds for its appropriateness that will better support the general conclusion that detaches grounds for guilt from grounds for blame.

This project rests on a rejection of the standard view of guilt as involving a corresponding evaluative judgment that we find, most notably, in Rawls.[1] On this "judgmentalist" account, emotional guilt—what we may distinguish as "subjective" guilt—requires a judgment (in the sense of a belief) that one actually is guilty, a judgment of "objective" guilt of the sort that implies moral responsibility. Views differ on whether this requirement is to be imposed only on appropriate instances or on all genuine instances of the emotion, as Rawls apparently has in mind. At any rate, there is a way of accommodating guilt for the unavoidable that remains within the judgmentalist framework but weakens the content of the requisite judgment to an attribution of *causal* responsibility that extends to cases like the accident case while apparently ruling out survivor's guilt and other disputed cases as impossible.

What I want to defend here in opposition to this account is a nonjudgmentalist view of guilt that sees the subjectively guilty agent as "feeling as if" he were *morally* responsible (section 1). On my own view, guilt amounts to discomfort with a certain evaluative propositional object and hence may be said to correspond to a judgment, though one can undergo the feeling without holding the judgment. Indeed, one can even undergo it appropriately, as I argue in section 2. My view will allow us to interpret survivor's guilt and other disputed cases as having the same sort of content as moral instances of guilt; it will also give us a framework for finer grained consideration of questions of emotional appropriateness in application to the full range of cases.

My view takes guilt as adequately warranted by a partial subset of the total body of evidence bearing on its corresponding judgment—a perceptual "slice" of the evidence, one might say, that on practical grounds is seen as sufficient to warrant holding in mind the evaluative content of the judgment. We may think of this as a "perspectival" account of emotional appropriateness. The general idea behind the view is that emotional discomfort serves as a way of holding an evaluative thought in mind—as distinct from putting it into storage, as with belief—so that warrant for an emotion is properly affected by nonevidential reasons for attention to its evaluative component. These include various instrumental functions that such attention serves, including social or moral functions, along with any noninstrumental moral or other norms that affect its value under similar circumstances. I argue that the view therefore supports an asymmetrical treatment of guilt and blame, as forms of emotional punishment whose practical effects differ because guilt imposes the punishment on the one who undergoes the emotion whereas blame imposes it on someone else.

In a word, guilt is sometimes appropriate, in contrast to blame, when we do not have adequate warrant for the corresponding judgment. After defending this point in general terms, I attempt to tease out some of its implications for our disputed cases of guilt for the unavoidable. I then turn to problems that arise in applying the view to cases of moral dilemma, as cases in which guilt is unavoidable because the agent must do wrong, though any particular wrong he does will be avoidable. The guilt/blame asymmetry explains our reluctance to blame the agent in a dilemma, but it also seems to exhibit the inadequacy of a subjective definition of dilemmas, as cases in which either alternative warrants guilt. The argument allowing for guilt without moral responsibility also apparently supports at least some cases of guilt without *wrong* as perspectivally appropriate. A subjective definition of dilemmas would therefore seem to imply only the prima facie wrongness of either alternative. However, I shall try to show how we can extract an objective notion from my treatment of appropriate guilt (section 3) by way of the reference to "tainting" that comes into our explanation of the desire for reparation characteristic of the emotion.

My account of guilt will have to be complex enough to yield plausible distinctions between dilemmas and other cases, including our initial cases of perspectivally appropriate guilt, where we want to deny that the agent really is guilty. However, I shall begin by narrowing attention to the question of the content of guilt in cases of the latter sort, especially the familiar case of guilt for causing the death of a child in an unavoidable car accident. In effect, I shall be arguing that the simplest ways of responding to such cases are too simple: Either they rule out guilt as something other than the emotion it appears to be or they accept it as unproblematically rational in a way that seems equally counterintuitive. I shall eventually argue that it is rational—but on the basis of the more complex "nonjudgmentalist" account I shall defend here, first in application to guilt itself and then to the grounds for its appropriateness.

1.   Subjective Guilt and Responsibility

How should we analyze emotional guilt? The feeling would seem to rest on self-blame, but we should note first that it does not always have the active or aroused quality of anger. Following the rough lines of Aristotle's definition I take anger—meaning personal anger, the variant of the emotion that amounts to other-directed emotional blame as opposed to mere frustration—to involve a desire to inflict some sort of punishment on its object for a wrong.[2] I would analyze the emotion further into affective and evaluative aspects by taking the desire for punitive action as involving discomfort at an unfulfilled action requirement—at the thought that the agent, or the subject of emotion, ought to punish its object, meaning that action on her part is still needed to effect punishment.

Anger thus is seen as an aroused feeling at least partly because of its essential orientation toward action—its threat of continuing discomfort unless and until the agent does punish the object—even though it may sometimes be satisfied without action, or without action on the part of the agent, perhaps by an apology from the object. An apology might be seen as a kind of self-punishment to the extent that it involves self-abasement, so it seems to count as an active expression of guilt. For that matter, emotional guilt involves a kind of self-punishment in cases in which the agent has some control over whether he experiences that unpleasant feeling. But it is important that, if anger is thought of as originally grounded in an animal urge to attack, guilt comes out not as a self-directed version of the urge—an urge to attack oneself—but as a less aggressive counterpart of it, requiring in the first instance reparation, or some way of making amends. Guilt may thus involve self-punishment as a form of reparation along with the readiness to submit to attack or to other punishment from others; in developed form, though, it is not simply inwardly directed anger.

One might still say that the different desires for action essential to guilt and (personal) anger both have the same general end: a state of affairs in which the perpetrator somehow "pays for" a prior wrong. They differ in where they place the burden of active responsibility for accomplishing that end, each assigning to a different agent a requirement of action enforced by discomfort until the job is done. This difference of course amounts to a limited structural similarity: The agents in question here are different in relation to the prior wrong, but they are both subjects of the relevant emotion. On the other hand, anger has a personal object, viewed as the perpetrator of the wrong, whereas guilt also assigns this prior sort of responsibility to the subject. Insofar as they both hold some such guilty party to account, though, both emotions ultimately rest on the attribution of responsibility for a wrong. So on the assumption that emotional evaluations amount to judgments—the assumption I call "judgmentalism"—one might look for the basic content of both emotions in a judgment of responsibility. The judgment yields emotional guilt and blame as different specifications of the urge to right a wrong depending on the agent's practical standpoint.

I now want to consider problems with this view and ways of defending it in application to some familiar cases of guilt in which we do not seem to have a judgment of moral responsibility: cases of guilt without fault. I shall work with the case of guilt for an unavoidable car accident and construct a variant of it that seems to involve guilt without *agency* to show the inadequacy of a recent attempt to defend judgmentalism by framing the account of guilt in terms of causal responsibility. I think we can see that this move commits the agent in such cases to a counterintuitive degree of irrationality. I shall attempt to show that a nonjudgmentalist account that preserves the reference to moral responsibility would square better with intuition, particularly as extended to more standard cases of guilt without agency that another recent author makes out as rational but nonmoral. I shall end this section by extracting from the cases some features of the practical role of the emotion that seem to yield a rational basis for cases of guilt without blame.

Guilt without Fault

On the view of the content of guilt just described, the emotion is *sui generis*, though its evaluative structure links it closely to anger, with differences in desire content but the same evaluative basis for desire in a judgment of responsibility for a wrong. It seems natural to think of the latter as a judgment of moral responsibility, for a version of this view that I shall call "naive judgmentalism." A naive judgmentalist analysis of guilt makes feeling guilty rest on a straightforward belief that one *is* guilty, a judgment simply asserting the evaluative content of the emotion. But this analysis seems immediately to be called into question by cases of guilt without fault—clear-cut cases, in which the agent may be assumed to know that he is not at fault (an assumption I shall often take for granted in what follows)—such as guilt at causing the death of a child in an unavoidable car accident. Even supposing that the feelings in such cases are irrational, it seems undeniable that they occur, and *almost* undeniable that they amount to guilt feelings.

The denial that they amount to guilt is suggested by the responses of naive judgmentalists to another sort of case, in which the agent does not believe that some act of his was wrong, though he does accept full responsibility for it. A standard example, found in Rawls, involves the violation of a religious taboo in a religion the agent was taught as a child but now rejects.[3] What the agent now feels when he violates the Sabbath, for instance, may be a feeling of discomfort persisting from childhood experiences of guilt, but on this view it cannot be a genuine case of guilt.

It may seem that we need some view of this sort to distinguish guilt from various other emotions that might be confused with it, such as fear of punishment or other forms of anxiety that might be thought of as its childhood predecessors. Even as supplemented by a desire to head off or appease the punishment—by performing some act of the sort that amounts to reparation where we do have guilt—this feeling needs to be conjoined with a view of the punishment as somehow justified, to amount to (subjective) guilt. Built into the notion of guilt, that is—as distinct from, say, fear of persecution—is a kind of acknowledgment of grounds for punishment as given in the corresponding judgment of fault.

In general, it seems that emotions have an evaluative content that determines their classification—distinguishing guilt from fear and various other unpleasant reactions that may not always be so distinct from it in affective quality. I take this to be the main point in support of a judgmentalist analysis, though I think it can also be used to construct an evaluative view that does not require the content of an emotion to be an object of strict belief. But before we abandon judgmentalism, we might try making room within it for cases of "emotional inertia," or the lag of feelings behind their corresponding beliefs, as in taboo cases of the sort just illustrated.

In an attempt to accommodate taboo cases within a version of judgmentalism, one recent author, Gabriele Taylor, seems briefly to bring together two such strategies.[4] First, the naive judgmentalist analysis of guilt might be retained by simply weakening the notion of judgment or belief, taking it to cover any thoughts that come to mind, even if they are immediately rejected by "considered judgment." Thus, Taylor says that the act forbidden by a taboo retained from childhood still "presents itself" as wrong in the circumstances of action, though not when the agent considers it "from a more rational point of view." Her introductory remarks on emotions and belief[5] indicate that she would interpret the notion of belief to include the sort of mental state suggested by "presents itself" in this passage: what is sometimes called an "as if" feeling. An agent's residual feelings from childhood religious belief would still count as involving beliefs on this account as long as they have the thought content required for feelings of guilt.

Second, one might also allow for taboo cases by weakening that evaluative content, the content of the judgment in question, allowing for something like a conventional interpretation of "justified" punishment. Punishment might be thought to be justified in some sense, that is, as long as it is imposed for violating an authoritative rule, meaning one whose authority is generally accepted, even if the agent questions the reasons for it himself. What one feels guilty for, on this view, is just the violation of a taboo—not necessarily a moral wrong and hence not enough to satisfy the naive judgmentalist analysis. Though Taylor apparently combines a move of this sort (I have restated her version of it to apply more clearly to rules) with the weakened notion of belief that was just noted, it would seem to be sufficient on its own to allow for guilt in taboo cases.

Both of these two general judgmentalist strategies—weakening the notion of belief or the evaluative content of the belief required for a guilt feelings— may be extended to the cases with which we are concerned. Here the agent's responsibility is in question rather than the moral evaluation of his act, or whether it amounts to a wrong in the sense of something forbidden as in the taboo cases. A different version of the second strategy, yielding what might be called a "weak" judgmentalist analysis of guilt, stands behind Taylor's own treatment of such cases. I want to consider it here at some length, since it represents a possibility intermediate between naive judgmentalism and my own view.

Taylor interprets emotional guilt in terms of a weaker sort of judgment of responsibility than that involved in ordinary judgments of fault: causal rather than moral responsibility.[6] As applied to the accident case, this notion apparently would make guilt feelings unproblematic, though it would also leave one puzzled as to how their rationality could be called into question. If subjective guilt implies only the self-attribution of causal responsibility, feelings of guilt at causing the death of a child, however unavoidably, would seem to be clearly appropriate as well as authentic.

Of course it is not unthinkable that the analysis of such complex emotions as guilt might yield a few conceptual surprises. But the only advantage of the weak judgmentalist analysis seems to be its straightforward treatment of this and other putatively rational cases of emotion as cases of rational belief. For an idea of the problems it faces in application to irrational cases we might compare the usual version of the accident case with one not even involving causal responsibility. Consider what the weak judgmentalist account would have us say about the distinction between the usual version of the case, in which harm results from something the agent does (albeit unavoidably), and a case in which the chain of causation leads back without interruption to some prior cause. For instance, what if the agent's car had simply been propelled into a nearby child by another vehicle that hit it—and that would have hit the child, had his car not been there—so that the accident in no way resulted from his agency? Here Taylor would apparently have to dismiss guilt as unintelligible—at any rate, in an agent assumed to be otherwise basically rational—since the emotion could not have even the weaker belief content required by her suggested modification of its standard judgmentalist analysis.

Intuitively speaking, however, I think we have to say that such cases are possible. We can imagine someone going over in memory the sequence of events leading up to the crash, pulling out a subset of them to focus on that is compatible with the usual scenario, the one that does involve responsibility, and feeling guilty. His reason need not be uncertainty about what happened but rather, say, some irrational tendency to fix on the worst possible interpretation of events from the standpoint of self-esteem. Perhaps he was taught to blame himself excessively as a child. I take this sort of tendency to be compatible with overall cognitive rationality: The agent one has in mind here is not cognitively confused in the usual sense—his system of settled beliefs is not disrupted—but instead is subject to a relatively localized disruption of the normal response tendencies. However, in order to accommodate such cases within judgmentalism— to preserve a foothold for real but irrational guilt feelings—we apparently need to bring in a version of Taylor's first strategy for handling emotional inertia in taboo cases, with a notion of belief weak enough to allow for cognitive delusion.

Further weakening the content of belief would make the case come out as rational, that is; so to explain it as a case of irrational emotion on this account, we apparently have to ascribe to its agent an irrational causal belief. We have to grant that the agent in the case believes himself causally responsible for the accident. The agent clearly feels as if he were responsible—at any rate, off and on, or at those times when he focuses on the subset of his memories that suggests that interpretation of events—even though he knows he is not and dismisses the feeling as deluded. But the judgmentalist account of the case insists that the feeling implies a deluded belief.

If we have to allow this much cognitive delusion, however, why not attribute to the agent a deluded belief in *moral* responsibility? The strategy of weakening the naive judgmentalist analysis of guilt—the strategy that yields weak judgmentalism—might seem to be unnecessary, in other words, when one considers the weak sense of "belief" the analysis still presupposes. We might extract a similar point from the taboo cases: An agent might sometimes feel lingering guilt about the violation of a religious rule that is not actually accorded much authority in his adult life even in conventional terms, though it was in force during childhood. Particularly clear-cut examples might be drawn from rules of conduct meant to be limited to children, such as prohibitions of naughty words and the like, to show that the weakening of belief content to handle irrational cases does not really represent a distinct alternative to the reliance on a weak notion of belief.

At most, the weak judgmentalist strategy serves to contain the extent of the cognitive delusion that the naive judgmentalist strategy attributes to the agent in such cases. It makes out the first version of the accident case as undeluded, that is, and hence as clearly rational; on the other hand, it seems to yield a treatment of the second version of the case as involving a deeper kind of delusion: delusion as to the facts. Rather than merely being confused about the standards for moral responsibility or something similar, the agent must on this account mistakenly believe that he somehow caused the accident after all.

More precisely, he must both believe this and believe it to be false, either at the same time or with no good reason for a change of mind, since on our hypothesis he knows he is not responsible for the accident, though he feels compelled to dwell on the subset of events that suggests that he is. The case thus requires logical conflict; so the extent of delusion required by weak judgmentalism still seems excessive. It is minor only if one considers how little may be built into the notion of belief on either version of judgmentalism: Any stray thought would seem to have to qualify, if all of the cases in question here are to count as cases of guilt.

On the assumption that belief interpreted in any reasonably strict sense is governed by a principle of logical charity, I would turn instead to a nonjudgmentalist analysis of emotion.[7] Whereas the weak judgmentalist analysis of guilt allows for a weaker judgment than the judgment of moral responsibility required by the naive analysis, my approach would allow for something weaker than a judgment but still framed in terms of moral responsibility. In general, instead of claiming that emotions entail evaluative beliefs, I take them sometimes just to involve evaluative thoughts held in mind by intentional states of comfort or discomfort. Thus, when an agent feels guilty about the death caused by an accident he was involved in, he need not actually assent to the evaluative basis of his emotion—the thought of himself as responsible for a wrong—but he does have to be discomfited by it in a sense that involves entertaining the thought as an object of discomfort.

This is not to say that the agent merely "entertains" such a thought; its status as an object of discomfort (with discomfort taken as a general state of feeling of a sort one would naturally want to escape) is essential to the motivational cast of my account. Nor do I want to say, on the other hand, that the agent has to entertain such a thought explicitly. Let me very briefly try to cancel out some misleading suggestions of my account and to indicate the general rationale for it before considering its application to cases. First, the agent's discomfort about a certain evaluative thought is understood to be directed toward the propositional content of the thought, the state of affairs it concerns, not toward the fact that it occurs to him or some logical or other feature of it as an object of contemplation. Second, my analysis is meant to allow for unconscious emotions, as involving conscious states of affect (comfort or discomfort) but with evaluative objects that the agent cannot identify correctly.[8]

Further, though the analysis is understood to be limited to occurrent emotions, so that guilt amounts to occurrent discomfort at a certain evaluative thought, the thought content of an emotion need not itself be taken as occurrent. There need be no episode of mental utterance corresponding to an unconscious thought; and even on the conscious level, talk of thoughts might be replaced by statements describing relations among hypothetical objects of attention. The claim that an agent's discomfort in a case of guilt, say, is occurrently directed toward a thought of himself as responsible might be understood as meaning that attention to his discomfort would lead to awareness of that thought in the absence of various barriers to attention—including barriers of the sort that presumably make guilt unconscious.

It is tempting to equate a dispositional mental state of attention to a proposition, of the sort here in question, with a belief. However, I take the relevant disposition to be tied in a special way to prereflective features of "mental set," as part of a preparatory form of practical reasoning that sometimes turns on remaining subliminal, immune from the intellectual criticism that belief is expected to withstand.[9] Emotional evaluations, in short, amount to patterns of attention, without the stability we expect of beliefs. That belief implies a degree of logical coherency is suggested by some recent treatments of more straightforwardly cognitive influences on behavior. Stephen Stich, for instance, interprets the less logically structured behavioral dispositions of nonhuman animals as "subdoxastic states," and in a treatment of developed practical reasoning Michael Bratman uses the term "acceptance" for a state of taking some proposition for granted without belief relative to a given practical context.[10]

What Bratman has in mind is the sort of assumption—about the likelihood of an earthquake, in one example—that it is rational to make in some contexts and not others (depending, for instance, on the practical costs of error) in deliberating about what to do. It would not be rational on Bratman's account to let belief vary with the context—an instance of the principle of logical charity, I take it, based on the primary tie of belief to theoretical contexts. I want to suggest, further, that what I have called "as if" feelings in my argument above may be picked out on the model of Bratman's states of "acceptance" by their role in practical reasoning. Their role is of course somewhat different; but like Bratman, I shall be content to characterize them in terms of it—in terms of a kind of idealized or normative functional role, in effect—without attempting to say anything about their nature in themselves except that they otherwise resemble beliefs.

Generally speaking, on the account I have applied to guilt, emotion adds motivational force to our explicit reasoning from judgments insofar as it directs attention to certain thoughts by loading them with discomfort. The usual practical point of guilt, after all, is to motivate action on a moral ought-judgment by inflicting emotional punishment for the failure to act. As we have seen, the mechanism can operate in advance of action as applied to the mere anticipation of moral failure: the thought of oneself as already responsible for a wrong, even when this does not amount to a belief. What it amounts to is a momentary object of (dispositional) attention, held in mind and allowed to influence thought and behavior as if it were believed, though unlike belief it would be discarded upon a moment's reflection.

The point is to generate a readiness to act that resists reflection, along with the ability to ignore or explain away the practical urgings of judgment. Emotional motivation on this account reinforces the usual model of practical reasoning with the need to discharge discomfort as a reason for action beyond what is provided by the evaluative content of emotion, which may or may not be an object of belief. Like Bratman's "acceptance," an emotional evaluation is treated temporarily or for certain purposes as if it were believed. This means that, in discussing cases of the sort at issue here, we cannot take at face value the various thoughts that might occur to an agent: Some mental contents that could be seen as self-ascriptions of responsibility—the agent's reflection that he should never have gone out that night, for instance—would be most charitably interpreted on that account as nonjudgmental. They may sometimes just amount to questions the agent puts to himself or thoughts he considers and rejects; or they may be held in mind on something other than a literal reading as responsibility ascriptions.

On some such assumptions, at any rate, we may say that guilt does involve a thought of oneself as morally responsible but that it need not always involve the corresponding belief. The nonjudgmental analysis will therefore allow for guilt without cognitive delusion even in the second version of the accident case, in which the agent feels guilty just as a result of passive causal involvement in a child's death, though he knows he lacks even causal responsibility for it. In effect, the analysis limits his disturbance to the level of emotion by detaching emotion from belief. It also has the advantage, as I shall argue, of allowing for guilt in some cases where one might be tempted to detach the emotion even from a thought of moral *or* causal responsibility.

Guilt without Agency

A crucial test of my nonjudgmentalist analysis will be its ability in the next section to provide a foundation for some defensible distinctions on the issue of emotional appropriateness. For present purposes, however, let us just attempt to use the analysis to accommodate some apparent cases of guilt. First, in what follows, I show how the analysis allows for clearly irrational cases like the one just discussed (but without yet defending their classification as irrational). Then I apply it to some arguably rational cases that even the weak judgmentalist analysis in terms of causal responsibility would seem to rule out. In effect, then, in the remainder of this section I shall be extending my defense of the nonjudgmentalist analysis to a widening circle of cases—and to another possible way of weakening the notion of responsibility—with implications for the justificatory question of guilt versus blame.

My analysis differs from the judgmentalist analyses considered so far in allowing guilt to take on objects other than the agent's acts—or things he does, if that should be taken more broadly; or even, perhaps, events involving him—for a less clear-cut dividing line than is usually drawn between objects of guilt and shame. On the usual view, only shame applies to personal traits, thought of as distinct from conformity to rules. But if there are norms imposed on children's personal development that a child might be expected to come to live up to without necessarily doing anything, then one might very well grow up to feel guilty about violating them. An example might be guilt about not being very bright or ambitious—not having what it takes to succeed in the way that one's parents may have had in mind. The object of guilt here amounts to something over and above any definite omissions one might be said to have performed—omissions sufficiently localized in time to count as objects of guilt on the usual account. It need not be seen as reducible, say, to a failure to go through some particular stage in development that was supposed to involve doing something: perfecting one's talents, working hard, or the like. Intuitively speaking, it seems possible, whether or not it is rational, to feel guilt, not just shame, about all sorts of uncontrollable inadequacies, inabilities, and traits of character or temperament discouraged by parents and others but extending as far back in one's history as the claim to a distinct personality or self.

This means that the objects of guilt in certain cases will violate the assumptions of Taylor's analysis by failing to allow for reasonable causal attribution to the agent in terms of either event-causation of the usual (Humean) sort or an indeterministic notion of "agent-causation."[11] I shall come back to these two alternatives for making out causal responsibility in a moment, but first let me introduce another sort of case that might tempt us just to abandon reference to responsibility or at any rate to weaken the sense of the term further—the approach taken by Herbert Morris in his defense of "nonmoral" guilt.[12]

Morris marks off as nonmoral a subtype of guilt that does not involve culpability; he explains it instead, in effect, as a form of "separation guilt," based on the severing of personal ties to members of a group with which one identifies. Although Morris's argument focuses directly on the notion of appropriate guilt rather than starting from an analysis of the content of the emotion, it is relevant to my discussion here because it yields a kind of opposite pole from Taylor's account in application to cases of guilt without agency. Unlike my own view, it does not require even the thought of oneself as somehow in the position of an agent.

The cases just cited of guilt for personal shortcomings might indeed seem to involve another sort of responsibility besides the sort at issue in moral blame. Children growing up are more or less held accountable by their parents for living up to parental expectations. I would treat this as sometimes giving rise to a tendency (short of belief) for an agent to think of himself as if he had done something to make his personality what it is; but Morris would say that moral responsibility is not necessary even in thought for a genuine (or even an appropriate) case of guilt. By failing to conform to the norms of the family group, a child may in a certain sense be breaking away from the group independently of anything it does, just in virtue of basic temperament or personality; and this is all that a judgment of nonmoral guilt asserts on Morris's account.

Morris does not apply his view to cases of guilt for traits. However, these may not be the strongest cases in favor of either Morris's view or my own. One might object that their intuitive plausibility as cases of guilt rather than shame seems to depend on whether they involve behavioral shortcomings—as opposed to the failure to meet norms of attractiveness and the like—and hence on a kind of general reference to agency. But there is another set of examples among those discussed by Morris, of guilt for an undeserved benefit[13]—ranging from survivor's guilt to guilt at being favored economically over others—to undercut the suggestion that an object of guilt must at least be manifested in behavior.

An agent might know that there was nothing she could have done, for instance, to keep from being favored over a sibling in her childhood—and nothing she omitted then or since in attempting to make up for the inequality. But the inequality itself seems to be a possible object of guilt. At most, the object of guilt in such cases would seem to involve a passive event—being benefited over others, say. But this is something that happens to the agent, as in the second version of the accident case.[14] Responsibility for the unequal state of affairs that results from it would seem to shift back to its own causes, then, with no causal role for the agent.

It may not be easy, though, even to find an event involving the agent that can serve as part of a causal chain leading to the object of guilt in such cases, if we follow Hume's insistence on logically distinct cause and effect.[15] In some cases, it may not be possible to pick out any very definite event. Consider, for instance, guilt for one's beliefs: Common talk of guilt feelings for a failure of religious belief would seem to apply to a case in which the agent discovers that she never did have the kind of faith that is required of her. But then her guilt will not be attributable to an event of ceasing to believe—or even, given the sort of belief that is in question here, to a failure of belief formation at some particular time when belief was called for. Perhaps she might see herself as involved in some sort of ongoing act of omission of belief formation throughout her life. But although some move of this sort might serve to locate within the agent's history a Humean event-cause of her lack of faith, it could not give us the two events we need for a Humean claim of causal connection. That is, a second application of the move would not seem to pick out a distinct event to serve as the object of guilt in this case. What the agent feels guilty about, if it does amount to an act, seems to amount to the same act: that lifelong omission of belief. But then she would not come out as causally responsible for it in Humean terms, so the case would still pose a problem for the weak judgmentalist account.

Similar cases are brought up by Morris under the heading of guilt for thoughts, as reasons against requiring culpability.[16] By "thoughts" Morris has in mind mainly wishes, but it is worth noting that the strength of such cases depends on assigning them something like the dispositional structure of belief in the cases just considered. Actively entertaining a wish, that is—an occurrent thought of the sort that typically involves an act of attention—may be voluntary and hence avoidable. At any rate, it is subject often enough to some voluntary control that my nonjudgmentalist interpretation of guilt as involving an "as if" attribution of responsibility seems to fit. On the other hand, the sort of evil wish about someone that an agent might discover in himself—perhaps as something he has carried around for years—may also be an object of guilt, whether or not harm actually befalls the other. Since the problem just noted about distinguishing cause from effect would seem to apply to it, though, it would seem to count against weak judgmentalism in the way explained with reference to beliefs.

An alternative strategy for handling the various cases of guilt without agency that have surfaced so far might involve appeal to a notion of substantial *self*-causation that is broader than agent-causation. Agent-causation is supposed to be limited to free acts, but perhaps some other things about me are importantly attributable to *me* in a sense that appeals neither to some distinct event involving me nor to my agency. To say this would not be to deny that there are event-causes to be found for character traits, beliefs, and dispositional wishes—any more than for our status in relation to other members of the various groups that define us. But just because of the way such notions as character are constructed, this consequence of determinism might be held to be compatible with the view that certain traits and patterns of action, including especially mental action, are attributable in a special sense to the self. They help define its individual nature, one might say, along with the sorts of morally self-defining acts that surfaced in chapter 4, but in contrast to passive processes like the workings of the digestive tract that do not express some basic property of the agent, though they may admit of indirect causal control.

This move beyond agent-causation would not solve all problems for the weak judgmentalist view, however. On Taylor's causal version of the view, for instance, only shame, not guilt, is thought to make sense as a "vicarious" emotion, in response to acts ascribed to others—for the behavior of one's children, say, or one's fellow citizens.[17] And it is important to note that the view entails not just that vicarious guilt is irrational but that it is conceptually impossible without at least a deluded judgment of indirect causal responsibility: the belief that one's failings as a parent, for instance, must have been responsible for a child's later misdeeds.

Intuitively speaking, however, such cases seem to be even more common, if anything, than those resembling the accident case with which I began. Whether rationally or not, we sometimes feel as if we were responsible for the acts of others whose doings would be said to reflect on us just by virtue of common group membership without really acknowledging any causal connection. A case in point might be white American guilt about slavery or guilt felt for various other national misdeeds that occurred before the birth of those who feel guilty.

At least sometimes, moreover, such feelings seem to be accepted as appropriate or reasonable. Morris devotes considerable attention to cases of guilt felt in response to the acts of one's nation as cases in favor of his own account, which might be set up as an alternative version of weak judgmentalism.[18] In place of a judgment of responsibility in the sense that involves culpability, Morris appeals to our identificatory ties to other group members. Even without a judgment about the latter, though, if we allow for emotional reactions based on imaginative identification with others, we can make out vicarious guilt as no more problematic than a host of vicarious emotions, including the empathetic reactions to harm done to others that underlie ordinary guilt on the account I gave in chapter 3.

Taylor's sharp contrast between guilt and shame on this question actually seems to rest on a misunderstanding of the notion of vicarious emotion. Shame is commonly felt for acts of others in a way that is not true of guilt. But strictly "vicarious" shame would amount to shame from the other's imagined standpoint; it is "for" another agent in the sense of being felt on his behalf. If I feel shame in response to the misdeeds of my brother, say, normally my feeling will not be vicarious; what I am ashamed of is something connected to myself in real-life terms. My own status is assumed to be diminished by what my brother does even without the assumption that I am responsible for it but just by virtue of the fact that status is partly a product of interpersonal ties.

Identification of course plays a role in determining interpersonal ties. Whether I feel shame, for instance, at the misdeeds of a colleague in ethics depends in part on the importance others assign to our common category but also on my own tendency to group myself with colleagues in my field. However, a similar point applies to guilt in cases in which one feels guilty about activities attributable to a group to which one belongs: family, profession, nation, race, or world. In fact, there is a further way of generating vicarious guilt in such cases that is worth distinguishing from the usual mechanism of identification with other individuals. On the assumption that responsibility can sometimes be assigned to a group considered as a whole, not just to its other members, what one feels may depend on a general kind of group identification, or imagining oneself as participating in the group's *collective* actions. "Collective" guilt in this sense amounts to the feeling of guilt for involvement in a case of collective responsibility.[19] It is a prime case, though not the only case, of vicarious guilt, but it seems to rest on the same general identificatory mechanism that can also operate in extending the bases for shame.

What is the function of guilt in such cases? It can sometimes just amount to an unavoidable cost of basing individual identity on group membership, as Morris wants to say.[20] However, one can often manage to drop out of a group in imagination. Particularly when the group acts in ways one is fundamentally opposed to, it might seem unclear what the point is of feeling guilty on its behalf. Why should I punish myself for something I would never do—for wars and witch trials I know I would have resisted? Does the pride or other pleasure I take in group involvement at other times somehow commit me to feeling guilty in a case where the group goes astray—as a matter of emotional "logic" or perhaps as a kind of recompense for the benefits of group membership?

Morris's comments elsewhere suggest grounds of general moral solidarity,[21] but it is important to note that the acceptance of guilt as appropriate in such cases falls short of a strict requirement to feel guilty. I may be required on moral grounds to feel *something* for the American internment of Japanese civilians during World War II, say; and perhaps my feeling should in some way reflect my membership in the group that committed the crime. However, it is unclear why its very content must reflect that fact. Assuming that I am myself unlikely to participate in such collective acts or even to allow them, it might be enough just to feel sympathy and outrage, perhaps to a degree augmented by my ties to the event. The point is to detach myself, after all.

However, I think we can make out vicarious guilt as having a point, even if not as specifically required, in just such terms. In cases where the identificatory bases of the emotion admit of control, it can be seen as a way of clearing oneself of involvement and at the same time expiating the deed on behalf of others by a kind of ritual self-punishment. One identifies with the perpetrator, whether a group one belongs to or some other individual member of it, simply to distance oneself and the group as a whole symbolically from the deed by submitting in emotional terms to the punishment the deed merits.

Identification with the victims, that is, does represent an alternative way of exhibiting moral solidarity in response to the case. What distinguishes the function of guilt is its self-punitive aspect as a negative self-directed emotion. Though sympathy and outrage may involve an initial layer of negative feeling, they need not feel bad overall in the way that guilt does. I take it, then, that my nonjudgmentalist account serves to supplement Morris's appeal to identificatory ties in explaining the distinctive role of guilt in such cases. The "as if" feeling that one is morally responsible for a wrong and therefore deserves punishment—at any rate, the emotional self-punishment of guilt feelings—seems to make more sense here in intuitive terms, moreover, than Morris's denial that guilt in such cases counts as moral. Morris's distinction between moral and nonmoral guilt allows for a univocal account of the emotion insofar as moral guilt on his account is understood to rest on separation from the moral community.[22] But by a kind of transitivity of identification, this would seem to make vicarious cases of moral guilt come out as moral too.

My suggested moral-but-nonjudgmental account of the various cases Morris considers seems to me to be compatible with the substance of his view; it rejects only his classification of separation guilt as necessarily nonmoral. I do recognize cases of nonmoral guilt—guilt about going off one's health regimen and similar examples—in which the rules the agent violates are in fact nonmoral, though he treats them in emotional terms as if they had moral force. But the distinction does not turn on the issue of culpability. The hardest cases to interpret plausibly as moral might seem to be cases of survivor's guilt. These may involve an undeserved benefit that the agent clearly did nothing to gain and can do nothing to make up for; so on the assumption of basic rationality, one might want to question how he could see himself even in "as if" terms as morally responsible. Morris in fact suggests something of the sort himself, though, when he includes these and similar cases in his discussion of guilt about "unjust enrichment."[23]

My own proposal for handling such cases can be strengthened by appeal to the self-referential character of guilt. To the extent that guilt functions as a kind of emotional self-punishment, that is, it goes some way toward fulfilling its own characteristic desire for reparation. But in that case, the failure to feel guilty counts as a possible object of guilt itself. This effectively redoubles the motivational force of anticipatory guilt—guilt about one's failure (so far) to make up for a wrong, as the basis for a forward-looking variant of the emotion that Morris also wants to recognize.[24] On my account of it in terms of an "as if" feeling, the emotion is sometimes self-generating in anticipatory form: One feels as if one already has done something wrong simply by failing to feel guilty (or guilty enough) yet.

This way of compounding guilt may seem a fiendish trick. In fact, I think it helps explain some of the pitfalls of the emotion, in particular its obsessive or unappeasable quality in many cases. But can it serve as a foundation for guilt, or must one assume a more basic negative self-evaluation as a reason for the emotion? In cases of guilt for an undeserved benefit, I think we might well begin with anticipatory self-referential guilt, if we appeal to a demand for "leveling": a requirement that the agent bring himself down to the level of others in a group with which he identifies, if only by subjecting himself to emotional self-punishment for exceeding the norm. What he should punish himself with, according to this suggestion, is discomfort at the thought that he has done something to deserve punishment—though all he really may have done is to fail to inflict it so far. Indeed, some demand of the sort—requiring in the first instance unconscious self-referential guilt, which then may be masked by guilt with some other (perhaps indefinite) object—may seem on occasion to be imposed by others as a condition of participation in the groups to which we are bound by mutual identification. Breaking away from the family, for instance—whether by one's own efforts or by the death of parents or other misfortunes of family members that do not befall oneself—is a prime source of separation guilt and can sometimes be encouraged by family members.

Morris's discussion brings up resentment and indignation as appropriate reactions on the part of others (along with self-reproach on the part of the agent as involved in feelings of guilt) only in connection with moral guilt.[25] But others' reactions in nonmoral cases may also include other-directed forms of blame of the sort that demand guilt of the agent, sometimes in no less fiendish forms than the one suggested. Part of showing that one identifies with others in a way that makes inequalities unwelcome involves the willingness to make up for inequalities with self-inflicted emotional distress. But this is an unachievable aim in many cases, and according to the account I have offered, it is based on an illusory feeling of responsibility. I now want to argue, however, that there are some cases in which guilt may be rationally appropriate even without adequate grounds for other-directed blame.

2. Perspectival Appropriateness

Understanding the grounds on which we take some cases of guilt to be acceptable in rational terms while dismissing others as unreasonable or unwarranted
"emotional reactions" means taking at least a brief look at the general notion
of emotional appropriateness. The term "appropriate" is semitechnical: an
artificially regimented refinement of our looser and more varied talk in common speech of particular emotions as reasonable or unreasonable in "backward-
looking" terms—as fitting the agent's situation, accurately representing its salient
or significant features to the extent that he is aware of them. It is a notion of
justification relative to reasons rather than a truth-value of emotions, but it is
meant to serve as their primary representational value in a sense that implies
adequate performance of representational function.

Emotions are taken to have a representational function on the sort of account
I favor insofar as they are made out in terms of evaluations—meaning evaluative thoughts, possibly unasserted. I take these as belieflike states or propositional attitudes with a content given by an evaluative judgment that might be
thought of as corresponding to the emotion in question, though it need not
always accompany the emotion. The evaluative thoughts may not be connected
logically to our other settled attitudes, that is, in the way that serves to pick out
judgments as thoughts expressing belief, or attitudes of assertion; they are held
in mind in a more temporary way, but one that allows them a significant influence on behavior. Normally they are objects of attention, though the account
also allows for unconscious emotions as cases in which the agent misidentifies
the content of the evaluation. What holds the content in mind in the relevant
sense is emotional comfort or discomfort—something that can also be seen as
having a representational function to the extent that it reflects the positive or
negative aspect of an associated evaluation.

It is essential to this account that comfort and discomfort are taken as general intentional states—states of positive or negative affect directed toward
evaluative propositions—rather than amounting merely to affective symptoms
of emotional evaluation, as in the usual list of sensory states characteristic of
emotions. Thus, guilt amounts to discomfort at or about the thought of oneself
as responsible for a wrong—not just to the thought *plus* an accompanying pang
of discomfort. On the other hand, it is also important that in justifying guilt all
we have to justify, at least in the first instance, is something on the order of a
"pang" of guilt: a momentary state of discomfort tending to convey attention
to its evaluative object in more or less immediate terms rather than the sort of
settled behavioral tendency linked with belief.

Further, justification of the emotion makes reference to its motivational
function, with discomfort seen as a state from which an agent would naturally
want to escape.[26] In justifying guilt, what we are justifying is essentially an escape
tendency: to change one's affective state by acting to falsify its evaluative content, or the self-attribution of responsibility for a wrong, seen as imposing a
requirement of reparative action. That is, the point of the emotional reaction is
to set up a need to act in certain ways that make up for and in some sense miti-

gate responsibility. But I take this to mean that the representational rationality of guilt (along with other emotions) will be properly influenced by instrumental considerations: The standards of emotional appropriateness will be adjusted to reflect facts about the general practical adaptiveness of a given emotion tendency, or its value as a motivator. For guilt, my account will have the effect of extending the emotion beyond the corresponding judgment of fault—and beyond other-directed emotional blame, as we shall see, for an asymmetrical treatment in rational terms of guilt and personal anger.

Emotions and Cognitive "Fit"

The account just outlined might be said to make out emotions as "evaluative affects." Comfort or discomfort and the thought toward which it is directed are not really separable parts of emotion, but I still speak of them as affective and evaluative "components," worth distinguishing conceptually in order to concentrate on the latter in considering justificatory questions. My strategy for considering emotional appropriateness involves packing the qualitative content of an emotion into its evaluative component—including its positive or negative aspect, even though this might seem to repeat information given by the affective component—to permit an analogy to belief warrant, or evidential justification for the corresponding judgment.[27] The central aim of this approach, though, is to bring into sharper relief some of the limitations on the analogy. Let me try to capture these now at least roughly by appeal to a distinction in current philosophy of mind between "directions of fit."

The distinction arises in Searle's account of intentionality as a point of comparison between beliefs and desires (along with analogous speech acts) that applies only in a derivative sense to emotions.[28] A belief exhibits "mind-to-world" fit insofar as it is supposed to correspond to the world. By contrast, the point of a desire is to get the world to conform to *it*; its direction of fit is "world-to-mind." Thus, in the event of a disparity, a belief counts as deficient in fulfilling its function, or in the usual terms false, whereas the onus normally falls on the world (including the agent) for failing to satisfy a desire.

Emotions do not seem to fall neatly into either category. They are assessable in rational terms as appropriate or inappropriate—what I take to provide the analogy to belief warrant—but these terms normally build in reference to the adequacy of the reasons for an emotion, not just the sort of fit to the world that may be accidental. We may think of such reasons as facts about the agent and hence as included in "the world," at least if we take them as limited to noninstrumental or backward-looking reasons that are assumed to characterize things as they are independently of the mental state in question to allow for our initial contrast between states of belief and desire. A desire is also supposed to fit instrumental or forward-looking reasons, that is, insofar as these count as reasons for thinking its satisfaction good. This is not fitness to the world, though, in the sense that applies to beliefs. In any case, emotional appropriateness still resists characterization in these terms. Even assuming that it is rational appropriateness that is in question—as distinct from the various moral and quasi-moral or social versions of the notion to which one might appeal—it may not be clear that an emotion that fails to fit the world is rationally deficient.

Our assessment of states of sadness, for instance, to start with a simpler example than guilt, will not be based solely on whether they correspond to the facts of the case as measured by a single evaluative standard. The further fact that sadness tends to inhibit corrective action makes it a sometimes unhelpful response to misfortune. For practical purposes, then, we may be justified in withholding the emotional response in circumstances that warrant it. But this point also affects our view of things from a representational standpoint: Forgoing sadness is taken as rationally appropriate in a case in which sadness would also be appropriate, so that we have an important contrast to the assessment of belief warrant.

On certain assumptions, the same may be said of substituting a contrary emotion such as joy. Just to be happy about the same misfortunes described in the same way would of course be unreasonable; a certain caricature of an Eastern mystic might be able to manage it, but she would presumably be sacrificing reasonableness to something else. What is not so unreasonable, or unusual, though it also requires some mental self-trickery, is to focus attention instead on a different perceptual "slice" or cross-section of the information available in order to generate a positive emotion with preferable motivational effects. To the extent that the feeling thus generated involves attention to a thought that is reasonably picked out from the background of evidence for evaluation, the emotion will count as appropriate. The point is that this justification rests on the assessment of a mental act—an act of attention—and hence is quite properly influenced by practical considerations.

What emotions are supposed to represent on this account is the importance of certain pieces of information—reasons of a certain sort, including reasons for attention, rather than directly "the facts" in some distinct sense. But attention is another element of cognition besides belief and is also subject to a kind of evidential assessment. Fitness to the salient facts is enough to warrant even a maladaptive emotion. Accordingly, we may say that an appropriate evaluative object of affect—what my account represents as the content of an emotion—amounts to one that on a reasonable view of things stands out against the background of evidence. Gestalt shifts are possible—there may be more than one reasonable view of things—so the notion is a tolerant one. It also has to be left somewhat fuzzy to correspond at least roughly to our intuitive judgments: What constitutes a reasonable subset of the evidence to pick out for attention— a reasonable perceptual "slice," as I put it—will often be a matter of debate. It is subject to moral and social norms in a way that allows for some degree of relativity to time and local convention. Consider, for instance, how we would classify sadness in the middle of a happy event at the thought of man's ultimate death and decay. The thought makes sense in a certain kind of religious culture but under other circumstances might be a matter for psychiatry.

The variability of the cases I have cited should indicate that we cannot expect an account of emotional appropriateness to provide firm answers to the many questions such cases raise. What I hope to provide is just an explanation of some of the relevant questions. Our reason for picking out "slices" of the evidence for purposes of emotional reaction (and hence for its assessment) has to do with the function of emotions in directing attention: They serve to hold in mind reasons of potentially immediate or isolated significance—by contrast with evaluative belief, which essentially involves putting the same sorts of propositions into storage, connecting them with our other beliefs as settled response tendencies. As I noted earlier, this means that we need only justify something short term in justifying an emotion—at any rate, if we limit ourselves to its basic qualitative justification, ignoring many important questions of degree.

The same point also seems to help explain why warrant for emotion and belief will be affected differently by the practical adaptiveness or instrumental value of a given evaluative thought. One should expect emotion with its basis in attention to be sensitive, most notably, to facts about the usefulness of a thought in motivating action. As a quick response in many cases, however, it cannot rest on any sort of calculation of consequences in the case at hand but at most can come to register the general value of the kind of thought in question. A belief, on the other hand, need not be borne in mind, and the results of including a certain evaluation among the objects of belief will be more unpredictable insofar as beliefs are both less present to consciousness in standard cases and longer term. At any rate, as a normative matter, tied to our acceptance of representation as its defining function, we exclude considerations of adaptiveness from our weighing of the evidence for belief. This amounts to assigning belief its straightforward mind-to-world direction of fit. My alternative suggestion for emotions might be summed up as a claim that emotions exhibit *variable* mind-to-world fit to the extent that their representational function incorporates reference to forward-looking practical reasons along with the sorts of backward-looking reasons that constitute evidence. The standards of evidence are raised or lowered, tightened or relaxed, in light of facts about the general practical adaptiveness of a given response tendency.

The resulting picture of emotional justification ties emotions to something more like perceptual standpoints than a unified conception of "the world." The range of allowable standpoints will be limited by facts of the sort that properly govern objects of attention—facts about the general significance of certain pieces of information—but since these are evaluative, they presumably do not fit into "the world" in the sense intended. Even if one attempted to include them, however—as a kind of "atmosphere" to the world, say—the point for our purposes is that one would have to allow for multiple worlds (or a world with multiple overlapping atmospheres) to capture emotional appropriateness.

The notion of appropriateness that this account yields may be thought of as "perspectival" because it allows for the assessment of emotions in relation to particular subsets or perceptual slices of the total body of evidence, as well as in relation to the evidence overall. It rests on the general point that what we are justifying in justifying an emotion is essentially an affectively mediated tendency to direct attention rather than the sort of settled response tendency that is at issue in assessments of belief. The notion allows for appropriate emotion in cases of what I call "snap" evaluation, where we jump to an emotional conclusion before all the facts are in, as well as in other "parti-resultant" cases, with emotional deviation from warranted belief assumed to reflect the general significance of some part or aspect of the evidence. For guilt, I now want to say, the relevant aspect may amount to something like one's own involvement in a violation of the moral norms, even if the involvement falls short of moral responsibility—and even if the violation is not quite a wrong act—in contrast to the judgment that one is guilty.

My thought is that in general terms the subset of the evidence for the corresponding judgment to which one reacts in these cases is important enough to justify at least an initial outlay of attention. This is what it means to be "sensitive to" the more ramified set of considerations that would ground the judgment. There are further reasons in the case of guilt for thinking that uncomfortable attention, in particular, might be warranted as a way of controlling future behavior, or of making up for past behavior, if only by subjecting oneself to guilt. Guilt seems to be morally useful to us as a motivator, in fact, largely in anticipatory or symbolic forms that depend on perspectival appropriateness. In cases where the emotion is warranted by serious past wrongdoing of one's own, adequate reparation is often just not possible. For that matter, it is questionable how often the emotion is felt in such cases—apart from cases in which the agent unwittingly failed to see things in the requisite light at the time of action, to appreciate the wrong done or his own involvement, and hence might seem to lack the fullest sort of moral responsibility. The point applies to cases of collective responsibility, in which the main moral failing on the part of many agents is likely to be just the sort of failure to pay attention that emotional sensitivity on the account I have outlined is supposed to prevent. It does so, if I am right, primarily by focusing attention on something short of adequate evidence for the corresponding belief.

Detaching Guilt from Blame

I now want to use the notion of perspectival appropriateness to explain why guilt should be appropriate in cases in which blame—personal anger, its third-person counterpart in emotional terms—is not.[29] Guilt functions as a general way of keeping oneself alert to significant subsets of the available evidence, in the first instance for their potential bearing on future moral action. We can therefore justify the emotion as a reaction to subsets of the evidence that do not similarly warrant personal anger. It would be unjust, for instance, to blame someone personally in a case of collective guilt in which the agent himself did nothing wrong. The perceptual slice that he might reasonably focus on—the thought of the deed as chargeable to a group in which he claims membership—does not count as adequate reason for someone else to inflict emotional punishment on him. The aim of keeping him on his toes, morally speaking, would not justify the kind of treatment that one might reasonably accord oneself in a similar case—or demand of him.

The reason is partly just that one is oneself, with more extensive sway over what one may do to oneself in emotional (or other) terms. Guilt also serves a positive function for oneself to the extent that self-subjection to the emotion counts as a kind of self-cleansing ritual: a way of clearing oneself of involvement in wrong by emotional self-punishment. One would not similarly be benefiting another person, helping to clear *him* of involvement, by blaming him for the wrongs done by others in a group to which he belongs. To do so would be to indulge in a mental variant of scapegoating that subjects him to undeserved punishment on others' behalf.

This brief argument rests on understanding emotion as essentially evaluative, with negative personal evaluations seen as unpleasant for their objects, even if their objects do not undergo the associated element of unpleasant affect. The argument does not rest, however, on equating emotional blame with blaming others overtly: There are of course all sorts of moral or social reasons for restraining oneself from overt acts of blame, but even if we limit ourselves to mental acts, blame requires a stronger justification than guilt. Besides the sort of moral reason just given, the asymmetry turns on the wider set of motivationally adequate emotional alternatives to blame. In addition to the availability of a collective object of blame, we ought to take note of a structural difference between blame and guilt that explains why I specify "personal" anger as the third-person counterpart of guilt corresponding to blame. For anger also has an impersonal variant, frustration, whereas guilt is by definition directed toward the self.[30] In combination with my perspectival account of appropriateness, the availability of a less personally punishing alternative for anger means that the standards for justifying its personal variant will be higher.

Frustration counts as a deficient instance of anger, as I put it—in contrast to the full-fledged cases that represent the most fully elaborated instances of the emotion in adult life. So there is something else to turn to when the evidence is not adequate for blame. There may also be deficient instances of guilt—passive cases, say, without the characteristic desire for reparation—but my point here is that these will not be deficient in quite the same way as impersonal anger. They will not be directed toward something more diffuse than their defining personal object, the self; otherwise, they would amount to something other than guilt, perhaps frustration or perhaps a form of sadness with an indefinite object (as on some accounts of depression). By contrast, anger in the sense of generalized frustration, directed toward no one in particular, provides us with an emotional option to perspectival personal anger or blame, anger that targets its object on an inadequate evidential basis for the corresponding judgment of fault. So the standards for imposing blame will not be relaxed as they are for guilt (along with other emotions), assuming that the general practical function of anger would be served well enough by frustration.

There are, of course, cases in which emotional blame without adequate evidence for a judgment of fault is of psychological or other benefit to the agent in the sense of the person undergoing the emotion; cases of scapegoating might be thought to be chief among them. However, this does not affect the justification of personal anger in its representational function; we still speak of anger as unwarranted in such cases. The sorts of facts that affect our weighting of backward-looking reasons for the emotion have to do with its *general* adaptiveness—in the first instance, its energizing function in motivating corrective action. Frustration involves a generalized urge to lash out, corresponding to its diffuse object, that should serve this end as well as personal anger when the evidence does not pick out a specific object. In any case, it is not just benefit to the agent that is in question in considering the general adaptiveness of an emotion. To the extent that personal anger has a role to play as a moral corrective, by inflicting emotional punishment for injustice, any instrumental benefits of scapegoating would be undermined by the fact that it punishes an innocent party.

Guilt seems to be different, assuming that we have a right to scapegoat ourselves—to sacrifice ourselves to some aim of our own—at any rate, up to a point. The emotion has a positive function in defense of moral self-esteem that would not be adequately served by other-directed emotions like frustration, at least in general terms: One might indeed recommend some other-directed substitute on many or even most occasions in the manner of various self-help manuals, but it is *general* adaptiveness that on my account lets us loosen our evidential demands on an emotion. This is meant to be broadly construed, to extend to emotions that offer some unique benefits to the agent or just to people in general, even if they also inflict harms, perhaps even greater harms. Remember that perspectival appropriateness is taken as compatible with the reasonableness of suppressing a given emotion.

Let us now attempt to see what happens to some cases of guilt when we apply the notion of perspectival appropriateness. First, consider the cases of collective guilt that have surfaced at points in my argument. My account of appropriate emotion allows us to grant that no one should be blamed solely for the crimes of others: It would be unreasonable to hold someone responsible in a backward-looking sense (as opposed to insisting that she *take* responsibility) for what her nation or other group may have done in her name.[31] On the other hand, we may also say that she ought to hold herself responsible in the way that is evidenced by emotion. She may be blamed if she fails to manage this—at any rate, in some form; there are emotional alternatives to guilt, albeit more limited than those that apply to blame.

The fact that guilt is appropriate, in the sense of "rationally acceptable," will not be sufficient to mandate that reaction, as I have noted. It does come out as appropriate, though, if we suppose that the agent's involvement in the group that counts as the collective agent in the case naturally sets up enough of a link between her own agency and the act in question to justify directing momentary discomfort toward a thought of herself as responsible for it. The thought may just be brought to mind with a question mark and rejected as soon as she has a chance to reflect on it, but it is appropriate as an object of uneasy attention as long as there is reason for her to raise the question of her moral responsibility. A crime committed by a group in the remote past, say, and clearly excluded from its future behavior by changes in group character over time would not naturally raise the question of responsibility in this sense, though of course a link could be manufactured.

The considerations relevant to deciding such issues are complex, and the relevant concepts are properly fuzzy. I shall be content just to sketch their application to the range of cases at issue. Consider now the case in which one feels guilty for having caused the death of a child in an unavoidable car accident. A central cause of guilt feelings in such cases, or those we are inclined to accept as appropriate, is just the agent's need to reassure himself that he is *not* guilty. That is, after the accident the driver of the car that killed the child would naturally feel impelled to run through what happened, considering vividly his own participation in it, if only to be sure that he did not do anything to cause it. He would do this by confronting himself with various particular subsets of the total body of relevant evidence that considered in themselves would tend to suggest that he is guilty—and to call up feelings of guilt as they come to mind, given the responsiveness of emotions to partial evidence. In each case he would be able to answer any self-accusation by bringing to mind further evidence. This would presumably allay guilt, though it would not prevent the reaction, and it would not prevent the reaction from recurring, at any rate for some time after the accident: A morally sensitive person in a case of such moral consequence could be expected to review the facts repeatedly and in rather exacting detail, focusing first on the memory of this or that act of his that might be picked out as a cause of the accident, then searching again for the reasons for thinking its results could not have been foreseen.

The need to clear oneself of real or objective guilt can in this way generate guilt feelings. Where the need is real, though, in the sense of being supported by more than the facts of the agent's individual psychology, the feelings may well come out as appropriate. It is not irrelevant to the case under discussion that the victim is a child, someone an agent is supposed to take special pains to look after, so that it is reasonable to assume more than the normal amount of responsibility even after-the-fact, and blame cannot easily be shifted to another agent. The agent reviewing his contribution to the case may focus, say, on the fact that he turned the car sharply in a certain direction—then remind himself that it was too dark to see the child—or he may focus on things he could have done differently whose connection to the case is more remote. Going out at all that night or going out with a trivial purpose might well come up as reasons for self-reproach (not just regret), at least until the facts of the case more or less settle in mind. My suggestion here is not that they should settle into a judgment of guilt but that emotional guilt properly precedes adequate evidence for such a judgment. Even when all the evidence is at hand, guilt will be appropriate in reaction to partial subsets of it whose role in producing the reaction serves a general practical purpose—in this case, as a way of assuming special responsibility for those unable to fend for themselves.

The appropriateness of the emotion depends, then, on the reasonableness in instrumental as well as representational terms of focusing attention on certain thoughts, including the sorts of perceptual memories one might well retain from a car accident and other bits of reflective information of a sort that can come to mind, be banished, and then come back again. This picture stands in contrast to the usual idea of even emotional guilt as imposed on the basis of an inner set of courtroom proceedings, deliberating to a final judgment. I would fill it out, moreover, with a parallel in mentalistic terms to the primitive notion of "tainting" in which the agent struggles to clear himself of a connection to some morally disturbing event by holding in mind the various thoughts that seem to link him to it and severing any putative link by means of emotional self-punishment.

What will be in question in disputed cases on the issue of appropriateness will normally be the general adaptiveness of guilt feelings in response to a sub-set of the overall evidence that constitutes prima facie evidence for a judgment of guilt. However, in cases of irrational guilt where the emotion is not based on a natural or reasonable perceptual slice of the available information, we do not have even prima facie evidence for the judgment. This is how I would handle the variant of the accident case in which a memory of merely passive involve-ment—driving a car that was propelled into the child by another car that hit it—is trumped up into a recurring thought of oneself as somehow at fault, just on the basis of a neurotic habit of self-accusation.

Such cases are not so odd, nor are they limited to cognitively irrational agents, if one includes as genuine feelings of guilt the pangs and other momentary sen-sations that might be felt just in raising the question of warrant for the corre-sponding judgment in cases where responsibility has unclear boundaries. The heightened responsibility that adults assume on behalf of children yields a fund of familiar examples, but one might also consider, for instance, the feelings that arise as one asks whether damage to a borrowed book or a sublet apartment was something one ought to have foreseen and avoided. In some circumstances or states of mind—where one expects to be blamed unreasonably by others, say—it would not be unnatural to pay at least momentary attention even to perverse subsets of the evidence, if only to rehearse the arguments against according them prima facie weight. In general, it is important to note that not just any emotional response that might be made out as normal will come out as appropriate on the perspectival account, despite its appeal in standard circum-stances to the notion of a natural object of attention.[32]

Some explanation of irrational guilt along these lines may thus be applied to more ordinary cases of guilt without fault from the literature. Let us see how it fits two particularly problematic sorts of cases. Consider first taboo cases such as those discussed by Rawls: cases of residual guilt for violating prohibitions from childhood or the surrounding society that the agent cur-rently rejects. These resemble the original accident case in not involving self-attributed fault (meaning responsibility for a wrong), though unlike the vari-ant case they do involve agency. Here, however, the stress is on the denial of "wrong" rather than "responsibility." Taylor's inclusion of taboo cases as cases of genuine guilt (contra Rawls) by appeal to conventionally accepted authority for the rule in question would seem to make them appropriate cases, assuming no mistake about the conventions. One might indeed provoke a pang of guilt just by remembering or anticipating blame on the part of others, so the response is in that sense natural. However, on my own account the emo-tion would still come out as inappropriate in a case in which the conventionally accepted rule in question just sets up an artificial way of sorting moral experience.

Proscribing something purely as a matter of convention, that is, without reference to human harms and benefits or other reasonable objects of moral attention (if there are any), does not support the appeal to general adaptiveness that results in our more relaxed standard of evidence for guilt than for blame. The general moral significance of emotion in a broader sense—as a way of enforcing conformity to whatever rule is in place—would seem to be relevant only where moral considerations favor adherence to the particular rule in question. So "mere" taboos in the sense of purely conventional prohibitions whose validity one rejects will not yield even prima facie support for guilt feelings.

We have to say more, though, to handle taboos that may not be purely conventional but arguably have some basis—inadequate from the standpoint of moral justification—in a natural human response. Examples include fear of the stranger as a possible source of racial taboos and the feelings of hostility used to punish deviation from standard sex roles and preferences. On the assumption that a certain behavioral norm ought to be modified, the feelings that serve to enforce it need not come out as appropriate just because it is in fact widely accepted. However, rather than denying that guilt in such cases is based on a natural way of sorting information, we can follow the model of blame and deny the adaptiveness in general social terms of allowing ourselves to react to a certain portion of the evidence in isolation.

On the other hand, there are rules on the order of the ban on incest that are commonly called taboos but are thought of as essential to the foundations of human society, albeit with details subject to convention. Here we may be willing to accept guilt as appropriate even in a case like that of Oedipus, where the violation is involuntary and hence does not merit blame. This sort of extension of appropriate guilt beyond blame has to be limited to the aspect of emotional justification that appeals to the practical reasons for attention to a certain subset of the evidence for the relevant evaluation. The subset itself has to be accepted independently, that is, as a natural or reasonable object of attention—on grounds I shall not attempt to pin down here—in order to avoid the kind of practical gerrymandering that would simply manufacture objects of guilt.

If we now turn to survivor's guilt and similar cases of guilt without agency— cases that might seem to be distinct in kind, involving the thought of separation from a group rather than of moral responsibility for a wrong—we can ask whether there is a way of counting them as appropriate without multiplying senses of guilt as in Morris's account. In fact, many of the moral cases just discussed typically involve a component of survivor's guilt: The justification of collective guilt commonly appeals to benefits received as a result of the harms done to others by one's group; even in the second version of the accident case, guilt might be defended simply for surviving the child that dies. I interpret such feelings as involving a thought of moral responsibility that is not warranted by the evidence as a whole. Rather, on the perspectival account the justification for holding it in mind depends on the practical value of guilt as an identificatory mechanism: its role in promoting the sense of moral solidarity that Morris describes.

This is to say that guilt in the relevant cases functions as a way for the agent to clear himself via emotional self-punishment of any suggestion of benefit from being favored above the other members of a group with which he identifies. It expresses the fact that he does identify with the group by bringing him down to its level in emotional terms. On the perspectival account, his self-attribution of responsibility also has to rest on a natural way of sorting the available information. I think we can say that it does in serious cases of survivor's guilt—as opposed to just any case of guilt for the ills of the world—insofar as the thought arises naturally as a question in others' minds where people are genuinely "in the same boat" in some respect or other.[33] These are cases in which it is natural to resent inequality.

However, the account does not accept others' personal resentment of the agent as warranted in such cases. It matters to the justification of survivor's guilt that it is self-inflicted as a way of expressing identificatory commitments. Others are in no position to decide for the agent what these are to be; the most they can reasonably do is demand that he decide a certain way as a condition of group acceptance. But even this does not pick out guilt in particular: The emotion comes out as optional, morally speaking as well as rationally, to the extent that other feelings such as those involved in humility represent alternatives for accomplishing the sort of leveling in question.

The cases I have brought up so far give us the beginnings of a continuum of cases on the question of grounds for guilt short of belief—and the beginnings of an argument from appropriate guilt feelings to a kind of objective guilt suitable for dilemmas. What varies in the cases is the strength of the reason we have for attention to the propositional object of discomfort involved in guilt feelings: the thought that the agent is responsible for a wrong. In the original version of the accident case, but not in the variant case or the typical taboo cases, we consider it reasonable as well as understandable for someone in the agent's position to raise the question of guilt. Appropriate cases of collective guilt and survivor's guilt seem to involve something stronger, however: Unlike either of the accident cases, they are cases in which the question of responsibility also naturally arises in other people's minds. There is a social as well as a nonidiosyncratic psychological basis for the emotion, that is—a basis for claiming that the agent really is tainted by what his society has done in his name, say; or that there is a real need to make up for inequality of the sort that undermines group solidarity. The other cases that Morris emphasizes, such as guilt for thoughts, seem to me to vary with the particular circumstances in respect to where they fall on the continuum. But I now want to extend the continuum in the direction of greater strength of reasons for attention—to cases in which there is reason not just for raising the question of responsibility but also for reaching a positive conclusion.

3. Objective Guilt and Wrong

Moral dilemmas seem to be cases of appropriate moral guilt without full moral responsibility. They are cases in which the agent cannot avoid doing *something* wrong, even if he can avoid the particular wrong he chooses to commit, since his choice situation offers him only wrong alternatives. So the cases do involve agency—they even require specifically moral agency—but they seem to count as cases of guilt without fault, versions of the original accident case distinguished by the agent's appeal to moral reasons for what he does. I take them to be cases in which each alternative is prohibited on serious enough grounds to make it come out as wrong all things considered despite the lack of permissible alternatives to it. With the notion of perspectival appropriateness on hand and defended in intuitive terms for nondilemmatic guilt without fault, we can see dilemmas as cases in which emotional or subjective guilt is appropriate for either alternative. The thought is that the reasons for prohibiting a given alternative form a morally significant subset of the information bearing on a dilemma: a natural object of attention that is important enough in general moral terms to warrant an emotional reaction even without being balanced against countervailing reasons.

Indeed, we might be tempted to define dilemmas in subjective terms as cases in which either alternative warrants guilt. However, despite my dismissal of rational guilt in taboo cases, my notion of perspectival appropriateness could conceivably allow for cases of guilt without *wrong*. Perhaps guilt is sometimes adequately warranted in light of its general practical function in a case of merely prima facie evidence for counting some act as wrong, as well as for holding the agent responsible for it. If so, what the agent does in a dilemma might not really count as wrong all things considered under the circumstances.

Thus, on this account, we might say that the ban on parricide violated by Agamemnon's sacrifice of Iphigenia has enormous general moral importance that is registered in emotion but is not really in force as a guide to action in the particular situation—assuming that it is even more important to ensure the success of the Greek expedition. Or in a "balanced" case like the one drawn from Sartre, where the agent faces a choice between abandoning his dependent mother and failing in his duty to join the French resistance, we might say the same for a prohibition of either action: Neither is more important, so both have merely prima facie status, and all the agent morally *must* do is choose—though guilt will be warranted whatever choice he makes.

However, if we accept these cases as genuine dilemmas, at any rate as philosophers understand the term, we have to say more than this. My own view is that the violation of prohibition in such cases is serious enough to count as wrong all things considered; it is not in the usual terms *justified*, then, at any rate fully, even if it is excused by the facts of the agent's choice-situation, so that he is not subject to blame.[34] We can now see that the appropriateness of emotional guilt does not imply this view of the wrongs of the case. I shall go on to argue, however, that it does imply something stronger than merely prima facie wrong—something we can understand at least in rough terms by reference to the primitive notion of "tainting." With some further backing, moreover, it can be made to yield a notion of objective guilt suitable for dilemmas.

Real Taints

My appeal to the notion of tainting in explaining the psychological function of guilt in the last section suggested a way of distinguishing among cases of guilt for the unavoidable. What we wanted there was a way of distinguishing between appropriate and inappropriate subjective guilt—on a notion of appropriateness that did not reduce to warrant for the corresponding judgment, of objective guilt or fault. Of those cases that come out as appropriate on the perspectival account it seems that some do and some do not involve what might be thought of as a real taint—a real need to dispel the *appearance* of fault, let us say—as a result of involvement in the act in question. I now want to suggest that this notion is sufficiently objective to allow for a reasonable interpretation of the comments of agents in survivor's guilt and related cases. It also will help us understand what is at issue in cases of dilemma.

I should first point out that the agent in the accident case is not tainted by involvement in a morally offensive act in the way that Agamemnon is, for instance. The case involves a need to clear oneself, in response to a question that naturally arises about one's own responsibility for what happened; but as I understand it, the case assumes that the question does not arise in minds other than one's own. It is taken as obvious, that is, that the agent in the case is not responsible for a wrong; indeed, as the case is set up, no wrong was done. What justifies attention to the question of responsibility and hence makes guilt an appropriate reaction is the adaptiveness on other occasions of the general emotional mechanism guilt brings into play. This is to say that there is no real or objective correlate of guilt in the particular case at hand, though the case has important motivational implications for other cases.

What I want to argue, though, is that more than this is involved in cases of dilemma—and even in the sorts of cases that Morris cites as examples of objective nonmoral guilt. As a first step in the argument, we might say that these cases involve an appearance of fault—something to which others besides the agent might be expected to react, so that guilt functions essentially as a way of heading off others' blame. The agent's need to clear himself is based on something intersubjectively real, that is. I refer to it as a "taint" to mark what I take to be its nonaccidental resemblance to the primitive notion, which involved various punitive or cleansing rituals acted out even on inanimate objects used as instruments of wrongdoing.[35] But my point is not just about what we are inclined to *say* in cases of dilemma. For one thing, the verbal point does not really apply so readily to all such cases, as we can see by considering what we would say about the agent in the case drawn from Sartre. Failure in one's duties as a son or a citizen may not draw the kind of harsh reaction from others that leads us to speak of a taint as opposed to a serious moral shortcoming or other flaw. My point here is just that there is something, whatever it amounts to or should be called, that gives guilt more than individual psychological backing in such cases.

A taint in this sense amounts at least to an intersubjective tendency—to raise the question of responsibility—somewhat on the order of a "suspicion" of objective guilt in the semiobjective sense in which that term is sometimes used. To be tainted is to be "under a cloud" of suspicion, or reasonably subject to suspicion on the part of others, as opposed to just having reason oneself to raise the question of responsibility, which is all we need for appropriate subjective guilt as in the accident case. What we are doing here, one might say, is reinterpreting the primitive notion in psychological terms. An agent is really tainted on this account where he has a real need to clear himself in the eyes of others—not just where others would in fact be suspicious but only where, in light of the facts or the evidence available (assumed to constitute a natural perceptual slice of the overall evidence), they would have real reason to be. At a minimum they have reason to demand an explanation. Emotional guilt is essentially a way of heading them off by raising the question oneself—and reacting to it, as an instance of a general response tendency learned for its motivational usefulness on other occasions that also serves on this occasion as a form of self-punishment, symbolically distancing the agent from even nonculpable involvement in moral wrong.

To see how the notion of a real taint in the sense of intersubjectively warranted emotional guilt applies to cases—filling out the rational portion of the continuum of cases mentioned in the preceding section—we might first consider variants of the accident case in which the agent does have "something to answer for" in others' eyes, even if he would in the end be declared blameless. One might suppose that the agent did something a bit irregular in his car upkeep that required explanation in light of what happened. Perhaps it was not really a factor in the accident; or perhaps its explanation would amount to an excuse. In any case, the very need to supply such a reason is enough to yield a limited objective basis for guilt on the account I have offered.

By contrast, on the usual interpretation of the accident case, the need to supply a reason—to defend oneself against charges of objective guilt—is a matter of individual psychology, albeit by no means idiosyncratic. In general terms: A perceptual slice of the relevant information that counts as a natural object of attention from the standpoint of individual psychology may not have the same status from a social standpoint. In the original accident case, others typically would dismiss the agent's guilt feelings as making no sense to them, simply on the basis of what is immediately evident. In other cases, further questions may be in order—even if we sometimes suppress them to preserve social harmony or the agent's peace of mind. Despite its social reference, that is, the notion of a taint is not merely conventional: An agent may have something to explain independently of whether others in fact demand an explanation; his real appearance of guilt in this sense will not depend on whether he actually appears guilty in others' eyes.

What should we say, then, about survivor's guilt and the other cases that Morris wants to treat as involving real or objective guilt? The word "taint" does not apply naturally to such cases, nor do such cases seem to raise a serious question of moral responsibility. Where they do involve some sort of wrong, as in cases of being favored financially over others, it is something that is clearly not the agent's fault; what is objectionable to others about him is supposed to be just that he benefits from the situation, if only passively. However, I think we can still say that the agent in such a case has a need to prove something to others —to express his solidarity with them, bringing himself down to their level by way of the sort of symbolic leveling behavior described earlier. Guilt here may be seen as a way of keeping social frustration from focusing—as it naturally might—on him. What it serves to erase is a real appearance of indeed benefiting ("enjoying" benefits), or grounds for envy.

The notion of a taint does apply naturally to cases of collective guilt, and it provides a way of understanding the real basis for collective guilt in application to individuals. In popular discussions of the question of German guilt for the Holocaust, for instance, there sometimes seems to be a tendency to dismiss guilt *feelings* as unreasonable to expect from people born after the war on the grounds that it would indeed be unreasonable to hold them personally responsible in a backward-looking sense for what happened. But assuming that there is a real basis for a judgment of collective guilt—in a sense, remember, that need not apply to individuals (as with corporations whose environmental sins cannot be charged to every employee, or in some cases, to any employee in particular)—it makes sense to speak of innocent individuals as tainted by the acts of others. This does not mean that they are themselves morally flawed in some way but that the question of moral responsibility naturally arises on the basis of their group affiliation—with emotional guilt supplying a kind of answer (though not the only possible answer) in practical terms.

The upshot of this discussion of cases—gradually narrowing down my initial cases of guilt without fault by appeal to the perspectival notion of appropriateness—is that there is sometimes a real basis for guilt feelings that falls short of the judgment that one is guilty. I have referred to this as a "taint," offering an intersubjective reading of what I take to be a successor to the primitive notion of tainting. But we might just think of it instead as perspectival guilt. It amounts to something midway between guilt feelings and objective guilt in the usual sense, as implied by a judgment of fault, and it seems to be enough to explain those nondilemmatic cases of guilt without fault in which we would not be inclined to dismiss the agent's claim that he really is guilty. Instead of reconceiving the cases as involving guilt in some other, nonmoral sense, we may reinterpret their claim to objective status in terms of intersubjective backing for guilt feelings.

Real taints in this intersubjective sense would seem to represent the strongest consequence for dilemmatic options that is derivable from an argument from moral feeling, an argument based solely on the appropriateness of guilt or some similar emotion in response to whatever the agent does. However, by adding in reference to the element of voluntary control at this point in the argument, I think we can see that dilemmas also involve something stronger, something closer to full-blown objective guilt, though still perspectival in a way that accords with my treatment of the grounds for the emotion. They involve a real basis for full-blown objective guilt—not just for raising the question of responsibility but also for a positive answer in the form of a judgment of fault, though the evidence for that conclusion is overturned by countervailing reasons. In itself, that is, the evidence is sufficient for the attribution of responsibility just insofar as the agent intentionally did something he knew to be wrong under the circumstances; but since they were circumstances where he *had* to, morally speaking, a broader view would show that he is not really at fault.

Thus, even long after Agamemnon's sacrifice of his daughter, the act requires explanation in moral terms. Objectively speaking rather than subjectively (if he feels nothing), there is a need for Agamemnon to satisfy himself and others that the act was morally required under the circumstances. But we also want to say more than this: that the act left moral traces of a sort that are summed up in the imagery of staining. It is a mark against him, a blot on his record of moral action, and a threat to his character or virtue—unless the wrongness of the deed (from a limited but morally central standpoint) can somehow be "put into perspective" by rehearsing the explanation for it yet again.

The way dilemmas apparently differ from the cases of intersubjectively real taints just considered lies in something like the fact that Marcus notes in defense of dilemmatic guilt:[36] They do involve responsibility for a *particular* wrong, insofar as the agent in them chooses a wrong option in the knowledge that it is wrong and carries through on the choice by voluntary action. Of course the choice is in some sense involuntary or forced on him; he has no control over his range of options, in particular the fact that all of them are wrong. So he is not responsible for doing *something* wrong, or for wrong or wrongdoing as such.[37] But he is responsible for the particular wrong he does in a sense that exceeds mere involvement in moral wrong. We might say that his act is culpable as far as it goes—perspectivally, in other words, or considered from a certain standpoint, a standpoint that is important enough to count as morally significant in itself.

This is more than a claim of general moral significance, of the sort that yields feelings of compunction in response to prima facie wrong. My suggestion in Agamemnon's case is that there are strong enough reasons against the sacrifice of his daughter to make it count as wrong all things considered in the circumstances in which it occurs, even on the assumption that there are stronger reasons on the other side. That these reasons for counting the act as wrong also tend to undermine the agent's moral worth—or metaphorically, that the act stains the self—counts as an objective basis for felt guilt that still makes psychological reference but is not therefore merely intersubjective.

Marcus's own treatment of dilemmatic guilt does not seem to be limited to a first-person standpoint in the way I have in mind. She appeals, as I have just done, to the agent's voluntary control over what he does in support of the attribution of responsibility, but she does not distinguish between grounds for guilt on the part of the agent and grounds for blame, the corresponding other-directed emotion. Our intuitive view, I take it, is that blame in the sense of personal anger is not really warranted in such cases—at any rate, for what the agent does, as opposed to a failure to feel what he ought to feel about his action.

It may be reasonable to *shun* an agent tainted by a seriously wrong act—an act on the order of parricide, say, as in Agamemnon's case—or to feel various related emotions (possibly taken as variants of blame), such as personal aversion or horror. But if we really agree that he made the morally best choice open to him at every stage, it would not be appropriate, though it might be natural, to blame him in the sense that entails feeling the desire to punish him that is characteristic of anger. From a third-person standpoint, on the perspectival account, his act comes out as wrong but excused, even though in emotional terms he should not excuse himself and is therefore subject to blame for not feeling guilty. According to the argument I have outlined, this asymmetrical treatment of blame and guilt rests on the differential practical effects of reacting to a partial basis for assigning fault—assessed in light of the different emotional alternatives to that reaction—in one's own case versus that of another. On Marcus' unamended account, by contrast, an agent in a dilemma would come out as morally blameworthy for his action—for doing what morally speaking he had to do.

To complete the task of characterizing dilemmatic guilt perspectivally, let me now attempt to show how we might replace the metaphor of staining with appeal to reasons, of the sort that would tell us when a taint counts as real. As noted earlier, talk of taints is not quite applicable to cases like the one drawn from Sartre. On the other hand, it does apply to nondilemmatic cases of moral conflict: We speak of money from a bad source as tainted, for instance, even on the assumption that it would not be wrong to make use of it for a good end. To meet the challenge to my account posed at the end of part I, we need to show that perspectival guilt can capture the intractability of wrong. But that requires a notion strong enough to distinguish dilemmas from the various weaker cases of moral conflict that might be confused with them. We are now in a position to approach the task in light of my discussion of the function of guilt in this chapter and the last.

Dirty Hands

If we think of emotional guilt as a self-cleansing ritual, we may say that the agent in a dilemma has real grounds for it to the extent that the ritual is really required to cleanse him of responsibility for a wrong. This means that the reasons supporting a negative self-evaluation, even if evidentially limited, are morally important enough in themselves to affect the assessment of the agent's moral worth unless checked—as they are when the agent subjects himself to guilt. To remove the metaphor of tainting, then, let us stipulate, first, that the reasons are significant enough for the evaluation to register in attention in the way that unpleasant affect allows it to do—thus warding off a more settled negative self-judgment. For dilemmas, however, we need a second stipulation, one that explains why the need for the self-cleansing ritual recurs: From the limited perspective of the act under consideration we do have enough reason for reaching a judgment of fault; the judgment is undercut only in light of the total body of evidence. So attention to the act (which is morally warranted) warrants emotional guilt. What we have in the role of objective guilt in dilemmas, then, is essentially an unsatisfiable need—a need to dispel the appearance of fault, based on a limited subset of the evidence that is important enough by itself to yield moral wrong.

Guilt functions on this account as a way of preserving virtue by providing some further reasons on the other side—balancing those that threaten to undermine virtue with evidence that the agent takes them seriously enough to suffer over them. To the extent that the suffering is in some sense self-inflicted—as we may say in light of our indirect control over emotions via acts of attention—it amounts to a way of bringing oneself down to the level of a victim of the wrong in question. On my understanding of guilt as an identificatory mechanism, it essentially serves to register the standpoint of the victim. But there are other cases resembling dilemmas, sometimes marked off as cases of "dirty hands," where the agent is not required to take that standpoint—perhaps he even ought *not* to take it—not just in order to avoid a second-order dilemma of the sort discussed in chapter 4 but rather because of an obligation to see things from the standpoint of the whole. Or so I want to maintain as a way of distinguishing such cases from dilemmas.

The term "dirty hands," which is based on the metaphor of staining or tainting, sometimes is used as a more general term covering dilemmas, though Williams and other authors use it to mark off cases falling short of dilemma as exemplified by the unsavory compromises politicians sometimes have to make to gain and retain office.[38] The term also extends to more serious cases that arise in the conduct of office; one example is Winston Churchill's reputed decision during World War II to allow the city of Coventry to be bombed rather than reveal to the Germans that the Allies had cracked their code. Like the word "taint" and its derivatives in application to the cases in my last section, the term "dirty hands" does not apply naturally to all the relevant cases at issue here. But I shall take it as a semitechnical term covering all such political and related cases along with genuine cases of dilemma.

Williams's discussion of the range of relevant cases in fact suggests another term to distinguish nondilemmatic cases. The term, which has surfaced at several points in my argument, is "moral cost." Williams uses it in application to cases where, though there is a right thing to do, it still involves "wronging" someone. There is a victim of the action, that is, who has a legitimate complaint—unlike the person whose interests lose out in a case where one ought simply overrides another—though on the other hand, this is not enough to make the action wrong as in cases of dilemma. The notion introduces a tripartite division of cases of conflict—into cases of overriding, moral cost, and dilemma—that apparently rests on a view of certain agents (politicians and others exercising authority on behalf of a group) as licensed to make utilitarian trade-offs. Their duties require sacrificing individual interests to the interests of the group as a whole and hence involve special permission to violate the rights of individuals. But the rights of individuals are not therefore simply canceled; they leave emotional traces on the order of "disquiet" on the part of an appropriately sensitive agent as evidence of the "moral cost attached to letting a right be overridden by consequences."[39]

In short, then, the notion of moral cost amounts to a moral remainder resulting from a clash between utilitarian and rights-based obligations in which rights lose out for certain special reasons but are not therefore overridden on the account Williams wants to maintain. For our purposes, questions about the details of the account can be shelved in favor of the general point that Williams's notion of an uncanceled moral remainder in cases of conflict is not limited to dilemmas. He makes it out in nondilemmatic cases as the remainder of a right, as distinct from an all-things-considered moral reason—a "claim" of the sort that figures in his explanation of the uncanceled element in a dilemma.[40]

The notion also seems to be linked to a distinction between the appropriate emotional residues in such cases, with "regret at the deepest level" reserved for dilemmas, while moral cost cases are characterized by reference to various weaker emotional reactions—as "distasteful," for instance.[41] However, I think it would be a mistake to suppose that the different sorts of cases of conflict may be understood adequately by appeal to different variants of agent-regret—or, on the other hand, in terms of quantitative differences in emotional intensity. I think we can improve on Williams's appeal to the level of emotional involvement with a finer specification of the possibilities in play here, if we think about the way in which guilt and similar emotional reactions are focused not just on action but also on the self.

Consider Churchill's case as described just above, on the assumption that he did the right thing in sacrificing Coventry to the Allies' war aims. If we also assume that the conduct of his duties allows for emotional sensitivity on the question—in contrast to the second-order dilemmas discussed in chapter 4— the requisite reaction will involve discomfort at what he had to do, but not the sort of devaluation of self that is involved in the variants of guilt. Nor need we suppose that the problem with guilt has to do with the crippling effects of self-alienation. Rather, a negative self-evaluation is just not warranted here, as it is in a case of dilemma.

We might sum this up by noting that distaste and disquiet and other emotions of the sort Williams uses to characterize moral cost cases do not impute a stain to the agent's self but at most something more peripheral, as suggested by "dirty hands." They also seem to differ from guilt in not requiring quite the same focus of attention on the wrong in question: It would be correct as a dispositional attribution of emotion to say that someone feels uneasy about something she did in the way these terms suggest even if she managed to avoid thinking about it and hence never felt the relevant emotions. Similarly, a certain kind of avoidance in thought would suffice to discharge an obligation to respond with distaste or disquiet to an unsavory act. One need not dwell on the act and inflict some negative emotion on oneself in occurrent terms. But this is the point of guilt feelings, in virtue of which they are sometimes required, on the account I have offered.

We do sometimes use the very malleable term "guilt" to refer to the agent's feelings in moral cost cases, but I would suggest that what distinguishes genuinely dilemmatic cases is a requirement to feel guilty *simpliciter*—not just on condition that one take a certain limited standpoint but in a sense that implies a requirement *to* take the relevant standpoint. We can sum this up by saying that the standpoint in question, a subset of the evidence bearing on the case, has a claim on the agent's full attention. By contrast, the politician who must wrong someone is obligated to include that person's standpoint within her overall view of things—and hence to qualify any satisfaction she feels on the whole with an element of discomfort. But she is not really obligated—indeed it might seem to be inappropriately "personal" of her, though it is sometimes treated as a mark of noble character—to drop out of the group perspective and dwell on the harm done to individuals. One expects politicians to give consideration in their overall judgments to the harm they have to do to individuals, but not necessarily to give it the sort of isolated emotional attention that Sophie owes, for instance, to the child she cannot save.

In short, then, moral cost cases may be distinguished from dilemmas in emotional terms as requiring only peripheral attention to the wrong in question—something secured well enough by dispositional affect or by mixing discomfort into what one feels toward a more inclusive object. By contrast, dilemmas call for occurrent discomfort as a way of focusing attention on the threat of a negative self-evaluation of the sort involved in guilt. We can illustrate this point by comparing the original version of Russell's case with the dilemmatic case that I constructed from it in chapter 4. The difference between the two cases turned on degree of harm done: In the original version the woman was disappointed and her life was disrupted by Russell's failure to keep his promise, but the connection between his act and her later mental illness and death was merely incidental. However, I take it that with the same degree of political reference (enough, let us grant, to justify Russell in assessing his action from the standpoint of the whole, even though his political role is unofficial)—and without reference to requirements imposed by love—this difference in degree of harm would make the difference between moral cost and dilemma. It would yield a general moral obligation to think about his act from the woman's standpoint and to experience something on the order of emotional guilt.

This is to say that, with the case set up as a dilemma, Russell is required to assume the emotional standpoint of a victim, the one whose rights he has to sacrifice in favor of consequences, as a way of making up for the sacrifice. On a moral cost version of the case, though, if we consider things from a general moral standpoint, he is required at most to feel guilty if he sees things from the victim's standpoint. He is also required not to feel various unqualified positive emotions such as unalloyed pride at his act as viewed from the more removed standpoint. He can get by without guilt in the narrow sense, even on a view of things from her standpoint, if he substitutes a perspectival emotion with less self-focus on the order of remorse, however.

To justify an unconditional obligation to feel guilty in the moral cost case, we would have to bring in the particular requirements imposed on Russell by love as an interpersonal ideal, and I think we would also have to switch to "separation guilt." That is, love for the woman presumably does commit Russell, at least as a requirement of virtue, to seeing things from her standpoint—to identifying with her in a sense that should indeed yield self-alienation if he has to sever the relationship. In contrast to the dilemmatic case, though, where he actually does the woman serious harm, I would not take the real-life Russell as morally tainted by the act required of him.

I conclude, then, that the worries introduced at the end of the last subsection can be met by a subtle enough treatment of the different emotional requirements of different cases of conflict. A "real taint" in the fullest sense involves real self-threat in moral terms from an all-things-considered moral standpoint. But in Williams's cases from political life, the wrongs done to individuals for the sake of more important political aims are assumed to be insignificant from the all-things-considered standpoint and to taint the person who does them only to the extent of making her morally impure. Though she is not a fit subject of perfect pride, she is also not an appropriate target of self-blame like the agent in a dilemma.

The basic point of difference between my own and more standard emotion-based approaches to dilemmas can be illustrated with reference to Russell's case by pausing now to reflect on the epigraph I gave this book: "The fox condemns the trap, not himself." If Russell's case is interpreted as a moral dilemma, one might naturally ask why he should blame himself. After all, our assumption is that he made the best decision he could under circumstances that arose through no fault of his own. If anything was to blame, it was the world for setting up those circumstances, or perhaps the moral code that rejects all responses to them—the trap, not himself.

On the view I have taken, though, what the ideally sensitive moral agent would feel may not quite fit what the fox would believe. Feelings are belieflike but properly part from beliefs insofar as their primary function includes some of the purposes of action. In cases of dilemma, guilt serves as an act-substitute to the extent that it goes some way toward satisfying its associated desire for reparation. Here it would essentially bring Russell down to the position of the person he has to harm, making up to some degree for the deficiencies of the world and the moral code as applied to action. In general, then, moral emotion plays a role within the moral life and does not merely record it.

6

Basing Ethics on Emotion

My argument in chapters 4 and 5 was needed to dispel certain initial objections to understanding dilemmas in terms of emotional guilt. A more fundamental question now remains to be considered, if we widen our focus beyond guilt, which was picked out for central treatment here because of its disputed status in cases of dilemma and its special motivational significance. This is the question of how the acceptance of dilemmas ties ethics to emotions in general terms. An argument to dilemmas from the reactions expected of agents like Agamemnon as suggested by Williams's treatment might seem to take moral judgments as simply serving to record moral emotions.

I proposed a metaethical alternative in chapter 3 that counts emotions among the grounds of ethics in virtue of their role in moral motivation. They constrain the shape of the moral code, that is—the corrected version of the social institution of morality that counts as a real albeit man-made basis of ethics—in virtue of the fact that any viable moral code has to be teachable in conjunction with emotions. But emotions or other attitudes or mental states might seem to *exhaust* the bases of ethics on this account, which I put forth as a two-component variant of moral realism, though granting the oddity of the term. One might say that what it means for a moral code to be "in force" in a given society is just for it to be held in force by shared emotions of moral assessment: An action counts as a violation of the rules, or as wrong, to the extent that it is seen as justifying moral blame or some similar emotion.[1] My guilt/blame asymmetry qualifies an account in these terms but leaves intact its view of ethics as a projection of human feelings onto the world of objects.

This sort of "projectivist" view is often attributed to Hume.[2] On its usual interpretation, however, it depends on a roughly perceptual model of moral sentiment that seems to force a choice between realism and emotion-based ethics. This is what I now want to call into question. My aim in this discussion generally has been to trace a path between the horns of various opposed alternatives in metaethics, and on this issue I want to say that a motivational model of the role of emotion offers a way between standard positions on the question of moral realism. I shall argue this by considering the view put forth by Simon Blackburn as a "quasi-realist" version of projectivism.[3] Blackburn's account comes close to the one I have offered in its resistance to opting for either of the standard alternatives on the question in sharply opposed form. It provides a logical structure for emotion-based ethical discourse that essentially mimics the structure of discourse about real objects. What I propose is a similar sort of intermediate account that does not fit Blackburn's characterization of his own view as a form of antirealism, but that seems to me to yield a better resolution to the problem set up in chapter 1 for "subject-dependent" approaches to moral dilemmas.

I attempt to fill out my explanation of the motivational model in this final chapter by showing how it differs from standard projectivism and by exhibiting its implications for the view of moral emotion as essentially a kind of perception of moral saliences (section 1). My aim is to pull together and to place into perspective some of the diverse points and insights that emerged as my argument here proceeded through the range of issues brought up initially by moral dilemmas. The problem of dilemmas, as I have understood it, centers on a question about the rational coherency of a moral code that generates sets of practical or action-guiding oughts incapable of joint satisfaction. My answer has interpreted moral action-guidance as based on the interplay between individual and group standpoints. Emotion functions primarily on my account as the source of individual motivation to conform to a moral code set up in the first instance as an instrument of group flourishing. It is justified by its general motivational role in a way that allows for unsatisfiability or some other motivational foul-up on a given occasion. On the other hand, its own social sources block any simple foundationalist view of emotion in relation to the content of the moral code.

The metaethical role of emotion is multileveled and complex in ways that I attempt to bring out in this chapter. Among the morally significant aspects of emotion is its capacity to take in other evaluative standpoints via identification. I have made much of this capacity in my account of guilt, as a prime example of a socially constructed emotion. But we may also see identification in more general terms as the source of a kind of emotion-based knowledge, both of other individuals and of the interpersonal standpoint that informs the moral code. This latter is important as providing another way between two horns in recent debate: the personal and the impersonal standpoints at issue in discussions of the value of ethical impartiality.[4] It also lets us characterize dilemmas as a product of the basis of ethics in combining different standpoints. On the account I have defended, these come out not just as conflicting personal standpoints of the sort that can result from different roles or other sources of obligation but more fundamentally as complementary metaethical standpoints—of the individual agent faced with a moral decision and of the social end that governs his behavior as a moral agent—whose interaction can go wrong in the particular case. I end with a discussion of some problems for the general view of ethics (section 2) that has emerged from this attempt to understand dilemmas as conflicts of action-guiding moral oughts.

1. The Motivational Model

On my account of dilemmas, emotions function primarily as substitutes for action, motivational traces of the ought that is not acted on. This stands in contrast to the perceptual model of emotions as putative bearers of ethical knowledge that we find in a number of contemporary authors.[5] On the motivational model, moral emotions may still be seen as yielding a kind of indirect knowledge of ethical properties as an inference from our felt tendency to act in certain ways. But the difference can be brought out by contrasting different possible accounts of an example that comes up in the dispute between intuitionist realists and projectivists: perceiving the sadness in a face.[6] Realists relying on the perceptual model want to say quite simply that we are aware of sadness in such a case as an irreducible property of what we see, though one that depends on our perceptual makeup in the way that color properties do. A standard projectivist account, by contrast, would take us as "projecting onto" a face perceived as contorted in a certain way an associated feeling from our own experience.

Thus explained, our naive view of sadness as something we perceive in the face comes out as a kind of perceptual illusion. Mackie sees an analogous illusion, of "intrinsic requirement" or "objective prescriptivity," as undermining ethical discourse, but on other versions of projectivism the illusion comes out as benign. The point for my purposes is that it still apparently counts as perceptual in a broad sense: Projectivism on its standard construal takes for granted the model of emotion as primarily a mode of apprehension that is assumed by the realist view from which it departs. On the sort of view I want to suggest, though, one might say that what goes on when we see a face as sad is that we respond to its contortions with a trace of empathetic sadness—not a perception, real or apparent, of *its* feeling but a feeling felt on its behalf.

The moral analogue to sadness on the view I shall defend, however, need not be something we can attribute to external objects considered in themselves. We might think of it as a relational property linking an act that is judged wrong to emotional sanctions accepted as part of the institution of a moral code. In any case, it is the tendency to impose the sanctions—a mental act tendency—that we are aware of when we seem to "perceive" moral properties on this view. But we now need to ask how the account differs from more sophisticated versions of projectivism than Mackie's. Blackburn, for instance, at one point characterizes his own account as "conative" in contrast to the realist's perceptual account.[7] The main point of difference in general terms is Blackburn's classification of his account as antirealist, whereas in departing altogether from a perceptual account, I hope to locate an alternative to perceptual realism within a form of realism that assigns emotions a fundamental moral role.

Forms of Subject-Dependence

Blackburn's quasi-realism is essentially a way of reconciling projectivism with the "ordinary language" evidence for realism. We speak of ethical statements as true or false, most notably—as objects of doubt and of knowledge—and we use them in unasserted contexts such as conditional clauses without reference to the speaker's current emotion or other attitude. Blackburn attempts to explain such features of ethical discourse in terms of a complex set of semantical constraints meant to "fulfill the practical purposes for which we evaluate things."[8] These may be said to give ethical discourse the appearance of describing some independent reality, whereas in fact on Blackburn's account it rests on the projection of our own attitudes onto a world of natural or nonmoral facts.

Blackburn's antirealist approach, inherited from Ayer and Hare and ultimately attributed to Hume, starts with a picture of moral judgment as based on an individual's emotional or other practical stance toward the world, though recently Blackburn has attempted to allow for a social version of the picture.[9] Like my own view, Blackburn's projectivist quasi-realism claims a kind of subject-independence compatibly with a basis in emotions or other attitudes—what Blackburn sometimes speaks of as personal "commitments." This is backed up by a refusal to endorse statements expressing subject-dependence,[10] as opposed to my own restriction in chapter 3 of forms of subject-dependence relevant to the issue of realism to those in which the mind in question is seen as the one currently making a given moral judgment. Does Blackburn's theory provide an alternative way out of the problem outlined here for dilemmas and motivational force in chapter 1?

Let us first ask how Blackburn's theory differs from the one I have offered. On a general level, several important differences seem to emerge from the fact that Blackburn's account is set up explicitly as a version of expressivism.[11] That is, although according to quasi-realism moral judgments exhibit belieflike behavior, their primary function on Blackburn's projectivist view is really that of attitudes. Of the sentences expressing them he writes:

> They express something more to do with attitudes, practices, emotions, feelings arising in contemplating some kinds of conduct, with goal seeking, with insistence upon normative constraints on conduct, and nothing to do with representing the world. In the familiar metaphor, their "direction of fit" with the world is active—to have the world conform to them, rather than descriptive or representational.[12]

In other words, the world in itself contains no moral facts against which we might measure our moral statements; a discrepancy does not imply inaccurate description but rather some sort of failure to act properly. Yet it is perfectly apt to speak of such statements as true or false on Blackburn's view insofar as we *construct* truth and similar notions to further the practical aims of moral discourse.

One might want to say that an extended notion of "the world" results from our creation of values on this account. This is essentially the view I have taken, with the moral code seen as a creation of the human mind but once created as taking on a life of its own in constraining further moral choices. The rules it comprises exhibit the world-to-mind direction of fit that Blackburn attributes to our moral statements in the passage just quoted. But moral statements themselves may on this account be understood as having a descriptive function to the extent that they describe the workings of the code. More precisely, they describe human action in terms of its fit to the code—as satisfying or failing to satisfy the moral rules. The code itself may be seen as a kind of projection of our deontic attitudes, but onto an intervening screen, as it were, rather than directly onto objects. The result is an artifact of thought, allowing for a new, relational way of describing natural objects. It is in some respects like the fictional objects that Blackburn discusses along with legal codes as examples of how texts may constrain what we say—except that it does not purport to represent anything. For a legal analogy, as noted in chapter 3, one might consider the way the U.S. Constitution constrains legislation, sometimes in a way that conflicts with the values of current legislators.

Blackburn at one point in discussing subject-dependence speaks of the values we create as taking on a life of their own.[13] However, as I intend this point, it involves a break with the antirealist tradition that Blackburn's view is meant to defend—the tradition from which he derives its classification as "expressivist." On the account I have suggested, the point of moral discourse is to describe acts in relation to the code—to an idealized version of the actual code, corrected in light of the end it is meant to achieve: group flourishing, which essentially replaces Blackburn's appeal to the pragmatic aims of moral discourse. Since the code on this account is not the invention of any one mind—or even of the dominant social sensibility of any one era—it is perfectly possible to get its contents wrong. The overarching end that constrains it is itself made out as something other than a product of human sensibility, though it depends on human ends. By contrast, Blackburn presumably wants to say that his own appeal to pragmatic aims is simply an expression of some more fundamental set of attitudes.

This last point reveals a basic difference between Blackburn's account and the one I described in chapter 3. On the face of them, many of his comments on moral sensibility and the like resemble my characterization of the corrected moral code. In connection with the notion of a "viable" code, for instance, consider what Blackburn says in response to popular associations with "relativism" and "subjective" views of ethics:

> Just as the senses constrain what we can believe about the empirical world, so our natures and desires, needs and pleasures, constrain much of what we can admire and commend, tolerate and work for. There are not so many livable, unfragmented, developed, consistent, and coherent systems of attitude.[14]

However, remarks like these about the "best possible set of attitudes" seem to require interpretation themselves in terms of the speaker's attitudes—as endorsing a certain sensibility—on Blackburn's account of value.[15] Blackburn often brings in higher order emotions and other attitudes *toward* one's moral emotions in his detailed account of quasi-realism. They figure, for instance, in his explanation of the use of moral terms in unasserted contexts, with the speaker understood as endorsing logical and other connections among endorsements.[16] And they also underlie his explanation of moral truth to the extent that seeing our moral judgments as false depends on the notion of an improved standpoint of evaluation from which we may admire or disavow our first-order emotional propensities.[17] Fundamental reference to a judgment of emotional appropriateness taken as descriptive could not do this job without compromising the expressivist cast of Blackburn's theory.

The same must be said, then, of appeals to group flourishing or even to particular moral ends such as fairness as constraints on the moral code. I suggested several alternative ways of making sense of such constraints in chapter 3—in terms of judgments of group value, for instance, on a version of the perceptual model; but also in motivational terms, as supporting the teachability of moral rules. An expressivist account, though, would seem to have to rely on a basic expression of preference at some point in the explanation. If it is expressivist at the level of moral judgments, moreover—and I shall later suggest that it need not be—it would have to do without the separation into two components that allows for a version of externalism.[18] That is, from *within* morality on my own account one has to endorse the sort of cooperative sensibility that is constitutive of the moral enterprise—or at any rate, one has to endorse it by and large— but the content of morality is given independently. So one can withhold the endorsement and still acknowledge moral truths.

For an individual property analogous to group flourishing on my proposed view consider health as an end that might be said to be constitutive of medical practice. The doctor's warnings about alcohol may be understood and acknowledged, with health seen as the standard of adequate functioning proper to the sort of entity that is in question, a body, even by someone whose current commitments lie elsewhere. Similarly, group flourishing may be seen as a normative constraint governing groups, spelling out the elements of group perfection, but assessed from a standpoint the speaker may reject.

It is worth noting that neither of these standpoints, medical or moral, has to be taken as setting up an invariant ideal: There may be internal conflicts among the elements in question, so that an individual might have to choose, say, between high energy and placid endurance, on the model of the choice between societies stressing cultural achievement and those content to make a relatively unperturbed contribution to the stream of life. This may be somewhat weaker than Blackburn's view, with its assumption that moral truth is constructed to serve the pragmatic ends of moral discourse, favoring a single answer to questions set up in moral terms.[19] Blackburn's view apparently builds in the philosopher's concern with dialogue and debate—or perhaps particularly the linguistic emphases of his semantical approach to metaethics. At any rate, on my own account even the overarching end of morality need not be shared by someone who grasps the content of a moral judgment.

Subject-independence on my account rests on more than a higher order positive attitude toward subject-independence as in Blackburn's quasi-realism. It also seems to provide a basis for a descriptivist interpretation of moral language. A moral judgment may be understood, not necessarily as expressing the speaker's attitudes, but as purporting to describe the world in terms of some standard of morality that counts as "real" enough for the purpose, whatever its origins as a projection of attitudes. It is a real invention or artifact, somewhat on the model of a computer program, which once designed constrains what the programmer can do—including his attempts to modify it. But the sort of reality in question here should not be confused with that claimed by metaphysical realism: the view that abstract properties exist apart from the things whose properties they are. Existence apart from the mind of a putative subject of knowledge is all that is in question, as with the color properties discussed in the debate over the perceptual model of realism.

I have suggested "social artifact realism" as a name for this alternative approach to metaethics. However, if the word "realism" poses problems, we might just get rid of it and speak instead of social artifact "descriptivism" as an alternative to the expressivist version of projectivism that Blackburn draws from twentieth-century metaethics in the tradition stemming from Hume. The view still shares with Hume the insistence that moral properties are not simply "out there" as objects of perception, even though our moral language often suggests as much. But neither are many of the acts we describe by reference to such properties. Instead of filling out the Humean account of moral language, the view essentially expands Hume's account of the moral imagination by taking something like the standard to which he appeals in making sense of justice as underlying more basic moral attitudes, to the extent that morality entails a principled extension to new cases.

It is appeal to some such standard that provides the hardness of the moral "must" and that thereby helps make dilemmatic cases hard enough on the agent to avoid the problem I set up for subject-dependent views in chapter 1. Blackburn's quasi-realist projectivism and my own view both see ethics as in some sense subject-independent even though emotion-based. However, it was subject-dependent motivation that was in question in chapter 1. The two-component view allows for a split between content and motivation, so that the motivational force of an ought with all-things-considered rational status need not actually be strong enough to win the day. At the same time, the self-punishing aspect of guilt as a substitute for action and its anticipatory role as a motivator in advance of action may be said to keep the agent on the hook. If we allow for "perspectival" guilt, with a real but limited foundation in a moral "taint" on the agent, the emotion will be warranted by the ought the agent violates in a dilemma.

By contrast, though Blackburn could of course allow for guilt or some other unpleasant residue of moral conflict, he could not provide any firmer foundation for it than how we ultimately happen to feel.[20] That is, a requirement to feel guilty would seem to have to rest on our higher order attitude toward the emotion—toward a certain sort of sensibility in reaction to a dilemma. To avoid my objections to Hare's treatment of moral residues in virtue-ethical terms, the account might endorse anger or some similar emotion toward an agent who fails to exhibit the requisite sensibility. But this would itself express a certain sensibility. At no point could we simply appeal to the moral demands of the case, the content of the practical oughts in conflict, as dictating what to feel.

My own account departs from expressivism in the first instance by analyzing emotions in terms of ought-judgments and other evaluations. This may seem to make moral judgment prior to emotion—with odd results for the attribution of emotions to animals and humans that lack the capacity for moral judgment— but it is important to note that the dependence is not one-way.[21] My detailed account of guilt might in fact be viewed as providing a particular example of how an emotion with a moral content might result by processes of refinement and social shaping from a childhood reaction that is itself not specifically moral. The child in my developmental account in chapter 3 reacts initially on the basis of a pre-moral evaluation of its immediate environment as a source of pleasure or pain—but extended to include social pleasures and pains via the mechanism of emotional identification. The eventual result of the social sources of emotional learning in general terms is comfort or discomfort directed toward fairly sophisticated sorts of propositional objects, including moral act-requirements, so that emotions serve to register the importance of moral reasons for action, as in the picture that emerged from my discussion of deontic dominance in chapter 2. I now want to approach the results of that discussion from another angle, in relation to the question of the sense in which emotions may be said to amount to perceptions of moral truths.

Emotional Perception

A perceptual interpretation of moral emotion may seem to be implied by the role we accord emotional reactions as evidence of the truth of moral judgments. Despite the original use of "intuition" in ethics to stand for an intellectual faculty, the term now often seems to be applied to any gut feeling in response to particular cases. In attempting to systematize our emotional reactions into general principles, it might be said, what we are doing is weeding out illusion by applying a test of coherency. What passes the test counts as a perception of the moral facts.

This account of things also may seem to fit our preanalytic treatment of emotions as a guide to moral decision-making. A feeling of discomfort at some act I have managed to justify to myself or that others are trying to persuade me to do is something we count as a reason for moral mistrust. The act just "feels wrong." However, I would suggest that such appeals to emotion as a bearer of moral knowledge may be understood without the analogy to sense–perception, in terms of the motivational role I have assigned to moral feeling. The use of emotion to motivate moral behavior lets us take emotional reactions as data—in the first instance, as clues to what we really think, to the extent that they involve urges to act. On my account, that is, they have an evaluative content that in ordinary cases is keyed to our moral beliefs rather than directly to the facts themselves, as on perceptual versions of realism. But they may be said to "track" the relevant facts, at any rate roughly, and to provide the bases for an inference to them, insofar as they are taught to us as motivational props of the moral code. They register the values instilled in us as part of the process of setting up the code by linking it to individual psychology.

Emotions may also be said to provide a kind of moral knowledge that short-cuts belief in some cases. Their motivational function depends on directing positive or negative attention toward their evaluative objects, which might not always be accepted as objects of belief. We might think of empathy, for instance, as providing a kind of nonmoral knowledge, of others' mental states, by way of evaluative standpoints understood not to apply to ourselves. But to grant this is not to say that we "perceive" others' mental states via emotion in a sense that implies direct awareness; rather, our awareness is mediated by imagination. In any case, emotional knowledge of moral truths comes out as a much more complex matter on the sort of account I mean to suggest here than it does on a perceptual model. I shall have more to say in my next section about the sense in which empathy may afford individuals a source of specifically moral knowledge via identification with the group. For the moment, let me take a simpler example of emotion without belief.

Suppose I feel uneasy about some action that in fact seems justified—grading a paper I take to be irredeemably bad, say, on the basis of just the first few pages. Emotional discomfort here serves to hold in mind a general rule enjoining punctilious performance of all job-related duties that prescribes completing the paper. The result in this case is a variant of guilt; but the mechanism in play here extends beyond self-punitive or even negative emotions in a way that may indeed make it seem to resemble perception. Perceptual language came into my discussion of the evidential assessment of oughts in chapter 2, where I used the image of figure/ground dominance to make intelligible the persistence of negative oughts in the face of conflict—the source of dilemmas on my account in terms of sufficiently strong reasons. One might suggest, then, that moral emotions amount to perceptions of the force of moral reasons.

There is a kernel of truth in this view to the extent that emotional comfort and discomfort on my own account of emotions might be said to register in affective terms their positive or negative evaluative content. However, we have to be careful not to take "perception" too seriously—even after canceling out any sensory connotations, as I have done. For our emotional access to the facts is typically mediated by beliefs—possibly false beliefs, as my example here is meant to indicate. My "perception" of the importance of completing an irredeemably bad paper is explainable as the residue of an emotion securing attention to a general rule that is thought to be important enough by and large to justify a few spillovers to other cases. Even in veridical cases, moreover, what emotional attention hooks onto in the first instance may be something to be added to the surrounding situation, not something found in it: the act to be done, not some property of the world by virtue of which it demands action. And the emotion may be at some remove from the situation—like an allergic reaction to a food enjoyed at the time but producing hives a few hours later.

One might object that sense-perception also depends on our expectations and other beliefs about the situation. However, to pick out moral emotions I take it that we need to assign them a belieflike *content*, even if it is one that has to be left indefinite in some cases. Consider a case involving more in the way of affective quality than the one just cited: moral horror at the thought of a seriously wrong act such as Agamemnon's parricide. The sensory "feel" of this and similar reactions may be part of what motivates the analogy to perception, but it seems to have sources in imagination that are distinguishable from the simple awareness of moral wrong. I would interpret it as an identificatory response to the victim's pain and feelings of betrayal or to society's feelings of aversion to the perpetrator. To assign the feeling a specifically moral content, though, so that it might seem to count as the perception of a moral property, we need to see it as directed toward an abstract thought: that the act in question is forbidden, say. It is in this sense, conceptual rather than causal, that moral emotions seem to be mediated by beliefs.

On my account, emotions *are* reasons for action—even instrumental reasons, since comfort and discomfort, besides registering the force of evaluations, themselves amount to reasons for sustaining or changing one's present state. To see more concretely how emotions can be understood in motivational terms, we might turn away from the moral cases under consideration to other cases of emotional perception that we would not be so ready to explain by appeal to special properties of objects. An analogy I find useful from detective fiction is the detective's uneasy sense that something "doesn't fit": There is something funny about the facts of the case as she knows them—or perhaps there was something out of place in a room she has just visited—but it is unclear where to locate the problem. We need not explain her perception of "unfittingness" as keyed to a corresponding property of the situation that she somehow is in contact with directly. I would suggest instead that she is more immediately aware of something like the interrupted scanning of her own perceptions or thoughts—her review of the facts of the case or the objects in the room, in contrast to normal cases in her experience or to the room as she saw it before. In short, she is reacting to something irregular about her own mental tendencies, though her attention is focused outward on its causes.

I like this analogy partly because the sense of "fittingness" is sometimes brought in to characterize the positive input of our moral faculties. My own view is that the negative reaction, a "taboo feeling," is more basic—and that it need not have much specific affective content, beyond something like the detective's sense of uneasiness, in order to count as an emotion. It amounts to a socially inculcated or reinforced aversion to certain acts, with an intellectual content whose analysis may require as much special insight and skill as is required of the detective to get at the causes of her uneasiness. In the moral case, of course, in order to be effective the basic reaction has to be widespread. But its analysis involves attention to things too remote to count as plausible objects of perception: the moral code, the ends it is meant to serve, and the ways it has to be corrected in order to serve them.

One need not understand these things in detail to use moral language intelligibly: Our ordinary descriptions of acts as satisfying or failing to satisfy the moral code will be left indefinite. I shall have something to say in my next section about problems the social artifact view faces to the extent that it has a relativist basis—with "the" moral code picked out in some way that implicitly refers to the speaker. At this point, however, I want to raise a related question about the basic value constraints that the view presupposes. These emerged in the discussion of fairness in chapter 3 as possibly importing reference to real value properties in something like McDowell's sense. But the properties were limited to such things as the rational way of assessing means to an end and the proper composition of the social end to be used in assessing the moral code. Should we now accept at least these basic value constraints as indeed objects of emotional perception in the broad sense just indicated? Can one simply *see*, for instance, that harmony and stability are traits of a flourishing group in the way that the detective recognizes the solution when it occurs to her?

The analogy is too simple, I think, for what we have to deal with in the moral case are constraints on what is to count as a solution—as if the detective had to choose between two partial solutions, both with some loose explanatory ends but one yielding a better account of how the deed was done and the other a fuller account of the perpetrator's motive. Suppose she opted for the first explanation on the grounds that a murderer's mental states may not always be open to understanding or scrutiny. If we share her basic explanatory expectations, must we be given pause by the thought that someone else might have different explanatory expectations—might insist, for instance, that understanding an act requires understanding its reasons?

By admitting that the acceptance of a certain solution rests on a basic decision on explanatory issues—rather than on some sort of perception of explanatory adequacy—we would not be taking a statement of the solution simply as *expressing* the speaker's explanatory expectations, any more than a jury in announcing its verdict is simply expressing the presumption of innocence. Similarly, in the moral case, our reliance on a choice of basic values at a certain level need not be taken as undermining descriptivism; our moral judgments may be understood as describing acts in accordance with the values we have chosen rather than simply as expressing the choice of values—even if the choice introduces a relativistic element. This account still gives us what we want from realism as long as our value-choice is implicit in the moral code, as a social/historical artifact that is not modifiable at will. Whether it is thus implicit is a matter for argument on occasions when we encounter a real disagreement about basic values, about which I say more in the next section.

The motivational model defended here as a way of understanding the metaethical relevance of emotion seems to me also to yield a better notion of its normative ethical relevance. It allows for the importance of the "forward-looking" assessment of different emotions in accordance with their motivational effects by letting it influence the standards of emotional appropriateness. By contrast, the analogy of perceptual correction to remove the distortions of perception from different standpoints tends to produce a "disinterested" ideal of moral judgment as something essentially impersonal. One line of argument sparking the current revival of virtue ethics rests on the importance of particular personal standpoints of evaluation.[22] But the motivational model seems to provide a clearer picture of the reasons for the moral assessment of emotions that virtue ethics brings to center stage.

On an account of moral training like the one drawn from Aristotle, emotions are taken as subjects of praise and blame not just because of their tendency to lead to overt action but for their own sake.[23] They are typically understood in terms of character traits, but the motivational model sees them as based on acts of a sort—acts of attention—even where they do not lead to overt action. In admiring someone's courage, say, or his sympathy and concern, what I value in the first instance is his tendency to hold in mind certain thoughts in situations of danger or harm to others, often at some affective cost to himself. Emotional affect is explained as a way of holding thoughts in mind by registering their evaluative features in positive or negative feeling tone. This may seem at first sight to fit the perceptual analogy, but it involves actively entertaining one proposition rather than another, not simply receiving information from external reality.

There are further possibilities within duty ethics, if we accept my defense of "ought-to-feel," for basing ethics on emotion in normative terms: Motives can be seen as the prime bearers of moral value with overt acts judged only derivatively.[24] On the metaethical question of the emotional basis of ethics, though, there seem to be three possibilities to be distinguished, besides of course the denial of an emotional basis as in Kant.[25] Besides the different ways of understanding emotions as registering moral judgments, that is—perceptually or motivationally—there are familiar ways of understanding moral judgments as essentially registering emotions. Views on the metaethical question can be divided according to whether they assign emotions or other motives a place in the semantical analysis of ethical judgments. Blackburn's semantical approach is a new entry in the dominant twentieth-century tradition of inquiry into the meanings of moral terms stemming from G. E. Moore's cognitivist account of "good" as unanalyzable on the model of color terms.[26] I hope to have contributed in this essay the beginnings of both a finer grained understanding of the nature of moral emotion and a way of remaining neutral on the semantical questions that have dominated metaethical discussion until now.

2. Sensibility and Standpoints

One way of basing ethics on a kind of emotional perception has indeed emerged from my argument here to the extent that it underscores the role of empathy in moral judgment. The motivational significance of empathy as a way of binding oneself to others was important to my defense of emotional guilt, which I interpreted as an identificatory mechanism, in response to moral dilemmas. Emotional identification also can be seen as yielding a form of knowledge—knowledge of others' mental states, of the sort that came up in the last section, and also, we should now note, a form of specifically moral knowledge to the extent that it enables us to take a perspective essential to morality, that of the group as a whole.

The picture of morality to which I have appealed rests on this overarching view of things in its reliance on a notion of group flourishing as guiding the correction of the moral code. This ideal is meant to be understood by analogy to the Aristotelian notion of individual flourishing or happiness. Though I have allowed a standard way of referring to our estimates of flourishing in terms of the ascription of value-properties, it is important that the properties in question are often unrealized. The same is true of many of the other properties that we understand via empathy: They involve states of feeling, for instance, that would result from some future action we are contemplating but may not do.

Perception of external objects is not the right model for such cases. In my argument up to this point I mainly took for granted our views about group flourishing and saw moral emotions on my motivational account as imposed on individuals in order to enforce obedience to a pre-existing moral code. But we now might probe deeper, to questions about the bases of the code.

Morality would of course be undermined by a certain kind of basis in emotion, whereas the epistemic role of emotions on the perceptual realist model poses no threat. However, the tendency of this essay has been to uncover various ways in which the motivational role of emotions affects the content of the moral code and to reinterpret their epistemic role in terms of it. I want to complete my argument, in this section, by beginning to respond to some problems that might be raised for the view that has emerged here, indicating how I think they might be handled by extensions of it. In particular, I attempt to show at least roughly how objections concerning the view's reliance on a standpoint that seems to oppose individual autonomy can be countered by a notion of self–identity that brings out its sources in group identification.

A variant of group identification—self-projection into the standpoint of the whole (not to be confused with the impersonal standpoint)—ultimately figures as one of the sources of our insight into group flourishing. We understand what makes a group flourish by analogy to the way we understand individual happiness in the case of another agent, putting ourselves into the imagined position of the group in question. This positive appeal to imagination stands in contrast to the elimination of personal biases that produces disinterested moral emotions on the usual perceptual model, but it can still be seen as involving a correction of individual perspective. On the other hand, it may seem to involve personifying the group in a way that calls to mind the collectivist excesses of nineteenth-century idealism. I want to suggest, instead, that group identification underlies a certain kind of individual self-regard.

The Interpersonal "Ought"

My treatment of "ought" in chapters 2 and 3 essentially explained the sense of obligation as based on the imposition of group needs on the individual, with moral emotions originating as felt individual needs manufactured by the group to enforce compliance. But part I ended with a different sort of appeal to the emotional basis of ethics in response to initial worries about subject-relativity and related issues. Despite the social sources of our adult stock of emotions, ethics on the account I offered has to rely on the shape given to behavior by our natural emotion tendencies. I appealed particularly to our tendency to identify emotionally with others, as a barrier to views that put some subgroups beyond the moral pale—not an insuperable barrier, but one that imposes a social cost on exclusive caste systems.

I now want to add to this some more general reflections on how my view brings together self-regard and concern for others in support of moral motivation. Even apart from the sources of particular emotions like guilt in identification with others, emotional motivation may be seen as linking the self to others to the extent that it focuses an agent's attention on something external to himself while appealing to his concern for his own state of comfort as a further reason for action.[27] By using object-directed comfort or discomfort as a way of holding significant thoughts in mind, emotions can be said to incorporate some other-regarding reasons for action within self-interest.

The stress on social factors in this account fits in with views of the self as essentially a social product.[28] Our first stirrings of self-awareness are plausibly held to depend on identification with the reactions of others—to behavior that from others' external perspective seems to require explanation in terms of a localized set of perceptions and interests or a distinct personality. Given the facts of childhood dependency, our sense of ourselves as having interests—or a self-interest; or a self—requires not just a review of our mental contents considered in isolation but also some awareness of the changes in them consequent on action on our behalf by others. We must come to see such action as originating outside ourselves and in general to distinguish ourselves from the group or groups that provide our initial sources of identity.

Further, even in adult life our sense of who we are is in many ways constituted by our relations to others—by a potentially conflicting set of statuses and roles, from our initial place in the birth order of a certain family to the position we eventually achieve in society at large. But these fairly commonplace observations about the social sources of the self can be made to yield an alternative to the reliance of traditional accounts of the role of emotion in ethics on notions of individual flourishing, even those that build in some moral or social value-constraints on flourishing.

We might think of the self as originally *extended*—enlarged to include various others (in the first instance, the mother)—but with shifting boundaries leading us to distinguish an individual self, over time, as a kind of intersection of its multiple group extensions. On this picture, the other end-point of social composition is also a kind of explanatory construct: The overarching group, the group that yields "the standpoint of the whole," might be thought of as the conflict-free idealization of the various small-group social sources of self-identity. But we have to resist any temptation to see the standpoint of the whole as one among other personal standpoints—a standpoint someone or something might be said to *have* rather than one we ought to strive to take. It need not count as a possible experiential standpoint, a "perspective" in the sense that implies a subjective point of view, but rather just as a limit on our attempt to reconcile the various group standpoints that potentially constitute a self.

Reconciling group standpoints, that is, means reconciling the aims of various competing groups, which presumably means reconciling the desires and interests of the various extended selves that would result from allying ourselves to them. By taking this project to the limit, we remove a kind of limit to individual self-definition by keeping open multiple possibilities of group membership. To the extent that a subjective viewpoint emerges, it is that of imaginary self-projection—in this case into an enlarged view of things rather than into someone else's particular perceptual position. It is a viewpoint that centers on the agent rather than tends toward neutrality. We do have to adjust our individual slant on things to attain it, as on the usual account of perceptual correction. But it is important to the moral cast of mind the account yields that our corrections are not meant to achieve an impersonal standpoint; rather, they aim at a certain overarching pattern of personal standpoints.

The resulting imaginary standpoint, of enlarged self-interest, is a psychologically rewarding one to take. Any barriers to it involve forgoing something personally valuable, if only because they put limits on the pleasures of imagination. I think we can use these reflections to get at some specifically social reasons for adherence to morality—thus in effect expanding the standard notion of autonomy as self-rule to include identification with the moral community. Such an ideal can be made to yield a modern version of traditional Aristotelian approaches to virtue ethics, with their reliance on individual flourishing as an aim that depends on relations to others but can be all too easily limited to an elite subgroup. The aim serves as something that might induce an agent to behave morally without necessarily advancing his welfare. What I think my socially based approach might be able to add to fill this role—particularly in cases where individual flourishing has to be sacrificed, even in a moral sense, as in second-order dilemmas—is a view of group flourishing as affecting individual self-identity and hence the worth or meaning of an individual life in a sense distinct from individual flourishing.

I shall attempt to fill out this suggestion in a moment, but its initial point is to avoid a view of morality as simply imposed on the individual by processes of social engineering—even small-scale engineering, of the sort involved in my account of moral teaching via guilt in chapter 3. The basis of guilt in identificatory processes that I went on to describe in chapter 4 begins to move us away from that model to the extent that it makes out even a socially manufactured emotion like guilt as expressing a natural emotional mechanism that is itself essentially social. My current suggestion involves extending that account to the bases of moral motivation. On the account I have offered, guilt involves the absence of something positive—a sense of community with others, let us say—that in emotional terms may be thought of as a form of pride. Pride in this communitarian form may be seen as a socially based element in our conception of the meaningfulness of an individual life—its worth in a sense that sometimes detaches from individual happiness or even virtue.

To put the matter simply: We derive self-worth in a fundamental way from our identification with various overlapping groups and group projects. Action on reasons given by a particular group standpoint, whatever its instrumental costs or benefits, has a self-fulfilling expressive function for the individual: It enhances the self by identifying it with something larger. Group identification may be psychologically rewarding with respect to all sorts of group affiliations, of course, including bad ones, but as a source of value it presupposes a value-laden notion of group flourishing. It is a further move to *the* group standpoint— the standpoint of the whole, what I think of as the moral standpoint, as opposed to that of some elite group, or even of the various overlapping subgroups an individual in fact belongs to—but I think it can be made easier by understanding what is achieved by social pride.

That is, the value of group identification for the individual self in more mundane cases, such as ethnic pride, lies partly in the protection it offers against contingency, or the vagaries of individual fortune. My ill fate will be less of a loss to me if I can see my efforts as serving some larger effort than my own, something whose success in pursuit of what I value is compatible with my own failure. This sort of self-transcendence, in one form or another, is the point of group membership insofar as it affects self-regard. Groups also have fortunes, however, and their aims may be frustrated or misdirected; for that matter, they can mistreat or exclude some of the individuals who identify with them. So an individual's group commitments can also be failures. Insurance against ill fortune is provided by spreading out one's commitments to various different groups—and is reinforced by commitment to an ideal community, the community of the whole. Taking the moral standpoint in this sense is the best available bulwark against bad moral luck.

There are ways in which the moral project also can fail—I shall bring up a possible metaethical failure in the next section—but it is at any rate cushioned against the usual forms of bad luck, including moral luck, to the extent that it looks beyond individual flourishing, or even the flourishing of a particular subgroup. For instance, in the face of a moral dilemma or other situation in which my own virtue turns out to be irredeemably compromised—a second-order dilemma, say, in which moral sensitivity is no help either—it would still be possible, if I really did act as well as one could under the circumstances, to take pride at least in that achievement. At the very least, pride gives me a reason for not doing *worse*. What I do still matters or has a point—the intended sense of "meaning" here.

In more normal cases where we raise the question "Why be moral?" the answer may be given by appeal to a form of pride—not specifically to the affective rewards of the occurrent emotion but to a presupposition of its evaluative content: the claim moral behavior gives us on other agents' regard. This is supposed to be independent of our actual affiliations with others, and of others' accurate perception of us, as also subject to ill fortune. What one loses by aiming at others' actual regard as opposed to what they would think (or feel) if they knew one's motives, say, is membership in an ideal community as a basis for self-respect.[29]

An overarching group ideal as an extension of individual self-worth might suggest some sort of Nietzschean version of self-perfectionism. But the notion of imaginary self-enlargement I have in mind is not an inflation of self-regard; rather, it amounts to the set of potential identifications with others that results from removing barriers to enlargement of one's own perspective. With the self seen as the intersection of an individual's multiple overlapping possibilities of group membership, any two-person group including oneself counts as a component standpoint in the set that is potentially one's own, the set of communities one might enter into. To slight any one of these standpoints is thus, one might say, to limit oneself by obstructing a possible mental route to imagined self-enlargement.

We can think of the interpersonal standpoint in this sense as a particular kind of group standpoint: a standpoint of the whole that is constructed out of all its parts, since it takes in all the overlapping social perspectives that potentially constitute the self. My suggestion is that this or some similar practical ideal affords a motive toward moral behavior in people whose motivational structure is roughly normal but who might still seek reassurance that they are not losing out by acting morally—as opposed to an amoralist, defined as someone who lacks moral motives.[30] My discussion here is just meant to exhibit a self-regarding motive for seeing things from the moral standpoint, not to present that standpoint as a precondition of rationality, as on Kantian accounts of the moral "ought."

The "ought" that emerges from my account of morality as a social artifact will be normatively "binding" only from the group standpoint; from the standpoint of particular individuals it is binding only in the psychological sense given by my treatment of motivational force in chapter 3. Societies have reasons, that is, why their individual members must do what morality prescribes; their members have those moral reasons only in a weaker sense that allows for a failure to act on them compatibly with rationality. Accompanying psychological sanctions, as instilled by the group to generate conformity to moral reasons, give the illusion of rational bindingness on the individual level and serve as goads to action in the individual case. It is only when an individual takes the overarching group standpoint that he is "bound" by moral reasons. What I have suggested is that we do have a natural motive for taking that overarching view of things, namely pride; but it is not the sort of motive that compels action.

Final Perspectives

I now want to consider some further objections to the social view of ethics I have proposed, on the grounds that its reference to the surrounding community gives it a conventionalist aspect. There are various ways of defusing the threat of relativism.[31] Here I want to show how we might ward it off, at any rate for terms of serious moral condemnation such as "wrong," by appealing to assumptions the social artifact view makes about hypothetical corrections to the moral code in force in a given community. Various ways of avoiding a relativist upshot can be teased out of the reference to a "viable" moral code, particularly as understood in light of possibilities of group overlap. Williams has recently defended relativism for groups that do not come into contact.[32] I shall eventually be using the possibility of group contact as one barrier to relativism on the view I think of as roughly Protagorean: as making man the measure of morality, at least in a collective sense, whether or not it comes out as relativist on all definitions or makes man the measure of "all things."

The relativist element of the view seems to emerge when we call into question the many references I have allowed to "the" moral code. On my proposed interpretation, moral judgments are to be taken as describing contemplated acts in accordance with a corrected version of the code. They therefore essentially extend and apply a man-made standard whose creation amounts to the conventional acceptance within society of certain practices of moral response, including but not limited to moral emotions. But we need to face a familiar problem about the multiplicity of conventionally accepted standards on many issues, even within the same overall group.

The question turns on the possibility of conflicting group practices that can result in basic disagreements over issues such as abortion on which there may be moral subcommunities in opposition. But an adequate answer for metaethical purposes does not require picking out one such community as the source of "the" moral code for a given speaker. The actual code may be thought of as indeterminate in some cases without threat to what is at stake here in metaethical terms—the existence of a right answer to moral questions—with its basis in a corrected version of the code. There might very well be two right answers in the sense of conflicting ways of correcting the code, both making it viable insofar as they both would adequately promote group flourishing. Since viability is a "satisficing" rather than a "maximizing" notion, the criterion it provides might be met in several equally acceptable ways.

On the other hand, this sort of conflict need not entail metaethical relativism—depending on where we locate the initial indeterminacy that gives rise to it and what we take a moral judgment to say. An indeterminacy in the code itself—in our attempt to sum up the moral practices of the overall community—need not imply variation in the higher order standard appealed to in correcting it: what counts as group flourishing or as adequate promotion of group flourishing. On these questions of basic value, as opposed to specifically moral or deontic questions, my view allows for a limited "perceptual" version of realism. But it is one that turns on a complicated feat of imagination (of hypothetical social practices and their effects on the group as a whole) rather than simply on "seeing" moral properties in the world around us. Much error is possible, along with disagreement about how to tell what *is* an error, on such questions as whether a group that restricts reverence for human life to postnatal forms of it would be likely to flourish. But divergent views could be explained either by different hypothetical factual conjectures or by problems in performing the imaginative acts required for moral perception.

However, an explanation of the latter problems might be thought to introduce a higher level source of indeterminacy. There may be no single answer, that is, to the question how one is to consider things from the overall group standpoint. For instance, even assuming that a fetus is conscious at a given stage of development, there will be different ways of weighing its interests against the mother's. Nor is it clear that only a conscious standpoint can matter to the determination of group flourishing. The assignment of independent value to life might be thought to be part of group flourishing in the way that, say, cultural achievement arguably is—not just because of its effects on human consciousness but also for its own sake.

Perceptual realism on the model of G. E. Moore's theory[33] is the standard way of settling such questions of multiple goods, and my view is meant to allow for it as one possibility. We can still minimize the need to accept special moral properties by limiting ourselves to perception of the elements of group flourishing. Value properties on this account would be attributed to hypothetical social practices and situations as seen from a general group standpoint rather than to particular situations in the world around us. They would not be seen as intrinsically motivating in the way that Mackie finds objectionable, for it is left open that a rational agent may not care to promote what she understands to be a requirement of group flourishing. So my suggested version of realism can at least do without any distinctively moral faculties of perception and rely on ordinary interpersonal insight as mediated by emotion and expanded by imagination. At a certain point, however, this version of the view may indeed require insistence on what one "sees."

Still, we can avoid adopting Moore's intuitionist moral epistemology to explain such claims. We may suppose that there is a "truth of the matter" about the constraints on group flourishing—on the model of Aristotelian happiness—without holding that we have access to basic truths of a sort that warrants the term "knowledge." Instead, perhaps, a particular vision of the moral aim can be tested in imagination, either by simple apprehension or by the more complex sorts of operations embodied in Rawls's method of reflective equilibrium, but without any guarantee that imagination is vivid enough or free enough from personal biases to arrive at the right conclusion. With perceptual realism pushed to the level of basic constraints on moral codes, we could thus make better sense of disagreement among moral agents assumed to be rational, educated, attentive, and the like, and at the same time necessarily committed to particular personal standpoints.

As an alternative to perceptual realism, however, I think we could also allow an element of indeterminacy at this level. Different societies and different subgroups within the same society may disagree on basic questions of value without any of them being in error, perhaps because there is no definite answer. We might be tempted to sum this up with a claim that such issues must be decided by convention. But although important social aims will be impeded if we cannot get everyone to agree on a convention, the metaethical result need not be relativism. Basic judgments of value within the range of indeterminacy might be subject to a relativist account, but there may be ways of avoiding that result for particular deontic judgments. I want to end this discussion by sketching one line of argument that attempts to "drain off" an initial element of value-relativism by the way it understands judgments of moral wrong. It is a complex argument that may or may not convince; but I do not put it forth as essential to the defense of social artifact realism. Rather, it suggests a purer form of the view, one that avoids any appeal to moral perception, but that still does not come out as relativist, if the argument is correct.

The argument turns on interpreting moral judgments as general claims about the viability of alternative moral codes, not just the particular code to which the speaker happens to adhere. The result in a case of conflicting codes would apparently favor the more permissive judgment. That is, if we were to grant that there could be a viable society whose code permits an act forbidden by our own, I take it that we would be granting thereby that the act in question—polygamy, say—is not really wrong but just contrary to our own way of life, or "locally forbidden." Similarly, in the abortion case we might be said to have two alternative ways of assigning values, either of which would lead to a viable version of the code, assuming for the moment that we agree on the criteria for viability. But the judgment that abortion is wrong amounts on the present suggestion to a judgment that abortion is ruled out by the corrected moral code—meaning any version of the moral code that would be viable in the sense of adequately promoting group flourishing. This would seem to be false, though, if we suppose that there is at least one viable version of the code that permits abortion. The statement that abortion is morally permissible, which makes this weaker claim, would come out as true whatever the personal values of its speaker.

In that case, however, moral disputes like the one over abortion will turn out to rest on disagreement over basic issues of social rationality: on what counts as group flourishing or as adequate promotion of it. But then we need to complicate the above argument by considering the possibility of higher level conflict over the assessment of viability. For instance, perhaps an abortion foe would insist that the development of fetal life itself ought to count in the determination of group flourishing, whereas others would deny this. Unless the dispute could be attributed to a factual disagreement, the two groups would seem to be talking at cross-purposes in the way that is characteristic of moral relativism.

Whether it really amounts to relativism, however, depends on whether we allow judgments of the viability of a moral code to be settled by personal decision. There may be a truth of the matter on that level—or an indeterminacy that we leave unresolved—compatibly with the interpretation of particular moral judgments as referring to the speaker's moral code. For the social artifact view does not have to take moral judgments as in some sense *about* the different evaluative standpoints from which they are made. Though it gives a descriptivist account of them by reference to a corrected version of the speaker's moral code, it need not interpret them as describing the content of such a code. Rather, a moral judgment may be understood as referring indefinitely to the form or forms the actual code would take if corrected and describing a certain act in relation to it. A judgment of wrong, say, would describe an act as ruled out by any corrected version of the code. So the meaning of its reference to a "corrected" moral code (as understood in terms of viability) would not vary with the speaker in cases of conflicting moral subcultures.

However, what if we were to grant that its truth-value does vary with the speaker: that the criteria for determining its truth-value are open to personal decision on basic questions of value? This sort of subject-relativity (whether individual or social) may be taken as the defining feature of moral relativism, at any rate as applied to cognitivist views of ethics of the sort under consideration. But there is an analogy I brought in earlier to undercut metaethical expressivism that might also be useful in connection with relativism—showing how my view could conceivably incorporate an element of both relativism and expressivism without amounting to a version of either of them.

Suppose we take a basic judgment of social rationality as expressing a certain decision-making stance, on the model of a jury's presumption of innocence in Anglo-Saxon law. This is what determines which corrected version of the code a given speaker has in mind in making a particular moral judgment. So his moral judgment might also be said to express that stance, but only in the extended sense in which a jury's verdict might be thought of as a particular expression of the presumption of innocence. Its linguistic function may still be seen as descriptive: It is meant to describe a certain act in terms of the applicable system of rules, just as a verdict of "not guilty" is meant to describe a certain agent in terms of the applicable system. However, on our present hypothesis of basic indeterminacy, it is as if we were tempted to equate "not guilty" verdicts reached under two different legal systems. The verdicts can be taken as *meaning* the same thing—that the agent did not commit the act she is charged with—but their reference to different ways of weighing evidence undermines the equation.

So moral judgments on this account have to be understood relative to a particular system of basic presumptions and other norms; and it seems that there may be several such systems corresponding to differences in the constraints one recognizes as governing the promotion of group flourishing. But let us ask at this point what the social artifact view could say about two distinct societies with different codes. One test of the viability of a moral code would seem to be its ability to survive contact with other ways of life. If maintaining a certain code in force in a community that has access to alternatives requires changing some of its rules, that change would count as a correction introduced for the sake of social stability. A version of this point also would seem to apply cross-temporally, to codes that develop in ways that can be made out as historically necessary. We might accept a superseded code as a standard for assessing judgments within its limited temporal sphere—and similarly for geographically isolated societies—in the way that Williams suggests; this is essentially the model of alternative frames of reference provided by my jury analogy. But we also have a way of getting beyond this to a more overarching social frame of reference.

In effect, on this account, moral codes will be tested by their tenability from a larger group standpoint in light of the natural conditions of social life. But note that this is a negative test only—there might be a code that could survive knowledge of alternatives yet for some other reason fails to promote group flourishing—so it is compatible with competing accounts of the constraints on group flourishing. The way the test is formulated lets us avoid the conclusion that any culture that in fact wins out over others has the more viable morality. For instance, it would not necessarily rule out cultures or subcultures such as the Amish in American society whose existence depends on protective barriers limiting the contact their members have with the outside world. What it rules out is a society that could not survive contact with others even with the aid of protective barriers compatible with group flourishing on the account suggested in chapter 3. This would disallow unfair barriers such as those singling out a particular social subgroup (for instance, women) for behavioral restriction.

It may still seem odd to count a code or a group adhering to it as morally superior just because it wins a competitive test of viability. But note, first, that a society that does win out over others need not have a morality that itself would pass the test, since the test also implies viability in absolute terms. Some feature of the winning society's code, that is, including the very means by which it won (unfair economic practices with respect to other cultures, say), may be incompatible with group flourishing, at any rate on the larger scale of the group that would be formed by incorporating other cultures as subcultures.

Second, though there may be a sense of "morally superior" in which the term applies to cultures that may not be viable in competitive terms, I think we should consider this as analogous to the case of an individual who exceeds the standards for personal virtue in ways that undermine his personal effectiveness and hence make his conduct come out as wrong. Imagine a teacher, say, who adheres to an ideal code of conduct in relation to students that assumes an unrealistic degree of honesty and reliability on their part—with the result that he is always being taken advantage of and his aid to deserving students is not really helpful. We do sometimes speak of such individuals as "morally superior," though their behavior in fact comes out as morally defective in any but the ideal world it presupposes. It is easier to think of societies than of individuals as operating in isolation, but the point is that this view of things no longer fits the facts of the case and hence never did fit the long-term facts. What is at issue in determining viability is the suitability of a moral code to guiding a society through time. If a code cannot command the allegiance of its members—or if it could not command such allegiance in the face of competition—then whether or not one admires the features of human nature that lead its members to favor alternatives, it is simply defective in real-world terms, on the model of the pedagogical code that makes unrealistic assumptions about student behavior. Like it or not, the function of codes in controlling behavior means that the facts of human behavior impose limits on what they can prescribe.

One might object that moral codes are embedded in a host of other institutions that might influence individuals to opt in or out of a given social group. A particular code may gain adherents, say, not because of its moral content but because it is conjoined with an appealing set of cultural values. However, we should note that the test of competitive viability, despite its basis in real-life patterns of choice, also has a hypothetical element. It is meant to turn on a culture's survivability under conditions of clear-headed choice—ruling out military conquest, say, along with subtler kinds of encroachment, as evidence of moral superiority. On the other hand, if a society's moral code is in some way responsible for its cultural appeal rather than simply being incidentally conjoined with it, then a widespread preference for the cultural values in question would indeed seem to count as a reason in favor of the code. The preference for them would count among the facts of human nature, that is, so that my argument on the issue of the real-life presuppositions of the code would apply, even if the cultural values themselves (ranking Disneyland alongside the Louvre, say) might be faulted on aesthetic or other nonmoral grounds.

In short, the test of competitive viability involves a mix of real-life and hypothetical elements that a fuller treatment would of course have to spend some time sorting out. I think we have them sufficiently in hand, however, for purposes of my present argument. Let us apply the test to the extreme case of cultural contact, where we have conflicting subcultures within the same society.

If a social consensus would naturally tend to develop in favor of one of the views in conflict, on the one hand, that would seem to mean that the other side's version of the corrected code is not really viable, at any rate under present historical conditions. On the other hand, if both sides could manage to coexist, that would apparently undermine the claims of the abortion foes in our example. We again would have to deny, that is, that their version of the corrected code is really viable. It would not yield group flourishing in its own terms, on our hypothesis, where the opposing subgroup is able to follow its own code, so that there are regular violations of the presumption in favor of fetal life. This assumes that the opposing subgroup is sizable, or would naturally become so under the imagined circumstances, which allow for contact with social alternatives. So even if abortion required going elsewhere, the violations would be substantial enough to undermine the abortion foes' standard of "adequate" flourishing—unlike, say, the occasional murders that a society banning murder can be said to tolerate.

What if we conclude that neither version of the corrected code is viable? Or what if neither consensus nor coexistence is possible and the conflict so undermines social stability that the actual code has to be viewed as incorrigible? In that case, a moral prohibition could not hold true, assuming that it amounts to a claim about corrected versions of the code. Abortion would again come out as permissible, but so would everything else. This is a disturbing outcome in metaethical as well as ethical terms. The point for my purposes, however, is just that it is not relativism. The truth of a moral judgment would not vary with the speaker. Rather, judgments of wrong would all be false—as on Mackie's view but for different reasons: because morality has turned out to be a failed project, not because its basic materials were misconceived.

Note, too, that this scenario rules out even replacing the actual code with one that enforces a decision without consensus, as an extreme form of "correction." The abortion example illustrates nicely the possibility that any such ruling would be too regularly violated to promote stability. The alternative in practical terms would seem to be the adoption of a more permissive standard of viability, as setting a threshhold of adequate (rather than requiring maximal) promotion of group flourishing. "Our" moral code, then, can be understood as the code universally in force—potentially, that is; with current indeterminacies where we now disagree, but on the more optimistic assumption that something can be worked out. For the moral aim would indeed seem to be unachievable and the project of morality misconceived if our allusions to the corrected code turned out not to refer to even one possible social construct.

At any rate, the view I have outlined as a version of realism, though set up partly in relativistic terms, on this account manages to avoid thoroughgoing relativism without any element of perceptual realism. Nor does it quite fit into the other standard metaethical categories, though it combines elements of several of them. In particular, it involves a partial basis in emotion that offers an

Notes

Chapter 1

1. See the following selections in *War and Moral Responsibility*, ed. M. Cohen, T. Nagel, and T. Scanlon (Princeton, N.J.: Princeton University Press, 1974): Michael Walzer, "Political Action: The Problem of Dirty Hands," pp. 62–82; Thomas Nagel, "War and Massacre," pp. 3–24; R. B. Brandt, "Utilitarianism and the Rules of War," pp. 25–45; and R. M. Hare, "Rules of War and Moral Reasoning," pp. 46–61.

2. Nagel, "War and Massacre," p. 23.

3. See esp. Brandt, "Utilitarianism," pp. 30–31; cf. Hare, "Rules of War," pp. 59–60.

4. For a general discussion of the notion, see Bernard Williams, *Moral Luck: Philosophical Papers 1973–1980* (Cambridge: Cambridge University Press, 1981), pp. 20–39; and Thomas Nagel, *Mortal Questions* (Cambridge: Cambridge University Press, 1979), pp. 24–38.

5. See the discussion in Alan Donagan, *The Theory of Morality* (Chicago: University of Chicago Press, 1977), p. 144; cf. G. H. Von Wright, *An Essay in Deontic Logic and the General Theory of Action* (Amsterdam: North Holland, 1968), p. 81, n. 1. The reconstruction of Aquinas's reasoning in terms of issues of moral luck is my insertion; one might suggest *grace* as the applicable concept within his own framework.

6. See Immanuel Kant, *The Doctrine of Virtue: Part II of the Metaphysic of Morals*, trans. M. J. Gregor (Philadelphia: University of Pennsylvania Press, 1964), p. 23. Kant allows for conflict between the *grounds* of obligation—which, according to comments he makes elsewhere, apparently are such as to become obligations if certain conditions (presumably including the absence of conflicting grounds) are satisfied; cf. idem, *Lectures on Ethics*, trans. L. Infield (New York: Harper & Row , 1963), p. 19.

Kant's views on the holy will, which I use subsequently to give some internal support for his position on moral conflict, are not explicitly brought to bear on the issue, as far as I know, though the connection seems obvious enough. See esp. idem, *Foundations of the Metaphysics of Morals*, trans. L. W. Beck (Indianapolis: Bobbs-Merrill, 1959), pp. 30–31. But note that the form of necessitation in question would amount to obligation only for imperfect beings on Kant's account; cf. the distinction between forms of necessitation in point of freedom in *Lectures on Ethics*, pp. 27–30.

7. See W. David Ross, *The Right and the Good* (Oxford: Clarendon, 1930), pp. 19–20, 28, 41.

8. See G. H. Von Wright, "Deontic Logic," *Mind* 60 (1951): 1–15; cf. A. N. Prior, "The Paradoxes of Derived Obligation," *Mind* 63 (1954): 64–65. Cf. also Roderick M. Chisholm, "Contrary-to-Duty Imperatives and Deontic Logic," *Analysis* 24 (1963):

33–36, and G. H. Von Wright, *Norm and Action* (London: Routledge & Kegan Paul, 1963). A general account is provided in Dagfinn Føllesdal and Risto Hilpinen, "Deontic Logic: An Introduction," in *Deontic Logic: Introductory and Systematic Readings*, ed. R. Hilpinen (Dordrecht, Holland: D. Reidel, 1971), pp. 1–35; see esp. pp. 8–9, 13, and 23–26.

9. Reprinted as E. J. Lemmon, "Moral Dilemmas," in *Moral Dilemmas*, ed. C. W. Gowans (New York: Oxford University Press, 1987), pp. 101–14; cf. idem, "Deontic Logic and the Logic of Imperatives," *Logique et Analyse* 8 (1965): 45–51, for a fuller account of the implications of dilemmas for deontic logic.

10. See Plato, *Republic*, I, 331c5–9.

11. See Jean-Paul Sartre, "Existentialism Is a Humanism," trans. P. Mairet, in *Existentialism from Dostoevsky to Sartre*, ed. W. Kaufmann (New York: Meridian, 1957), pp. 295–96.

12. Lemmon, "Moral Dilemmas," p. 113; cf. pp. 111–12.

13. Reprinted as Bernard Williams, "Ethical Consistency," in *Moral Dilemmas*, ed. C. W. Gowans (New York: Oxford University Press, 1987), pp. 115–37.

14. Lemmon, "Moral Dilemmas," p. 107, n. 2.

15. See Aeschylus, "Agamemnon," 204–52.

16. See Bernard Williams, *Problems of the Self: Philosophical Papers 1956–1972* (Cambridge: Cambridge University Press, 1973), pp. 204–5.

17. See Philippa Foot, "Moral Realism and Moral Dilemma," in *Moral Dilemmas*, ed. C. W. Gowans (New York: Oxford University Press, 1987), pp. 250–70; also, Samuel Guttenplan, "Moral Realism and Moral Dilemma," *Proceedings of the Aristotelian Society* 80 (1979–80): 61–80, and Walter Sinnott-Armstrong, *Moral Dilemmas* (Oxford: Basil Blackwell, 1988), pp. 189–214.

18. See Bernard Williams, *Morality: An Introduction to Ethics* (New York: Harper & Row, 1972), pp. 92–93, and idem, *Moral Luck*, pp. 60–61, 74, and 78–79.

19. See ibid., pp. 60–63; cf. p. 74, n. 2 (cf. also n. 3 for Williams's identification of "tragic" cases with dilemmas).

20. See Bas C. van Fraassen, "Values and the Heart's Command," in *Moral Dilemmas*, ed. C. W. Gowans (Oxford: Oxford University Press, 1987), pp. 138–53; and Ruth Barcan Marcus, "Moral Dilemmas and Consistency," in ibid., pp. 188–204.

21. See Thomas Nagel, "The Fragmentation of Value," in *Moral Dilemmas*, ed. C. W. Gowans (Oxford: Oxford University Press, 1987), pp. 174–87. For another view of ethics as based on conflicting standpoints, closer in some ways to my own view, see Stuart Hampshire, *Morality and Conflict* (Cambridge, Mass.: Harvard University Press, 1983), pp. 140–69. Cf. also the discussion of incommensurability in connection with dilemmas in Joseph Raz, *The Morality of Freedom* (Oxford: Oxford University Press, 1986), pp. 357–66.

22. See Hector-Neri Castañeda, *Thinking and Doing: The Philosophical Foundations of Institutions* (Dordrecht, Holland: D. Reidel, 1975), pp. 191, 195–201.

23. Nagel, "Fragmentation of Value," p. 175.

24. See Terrance C. McConnell, "Moral Dilemmas and Consistency in Ethics," in *Moral Dilemmas*, ed. C. W. Gowans (Oxford: Oxford University Press, 1987), pp. 154–73; cf. also idem, "Moral Dilemmas and Requiring the Impossible," *Philosophical Studies* 29 (1976): 410–11.

25. See McConnell, "Moral Dilemmas and Consistency," p. 171, n. 2, and Marcus, "Moral Dilemmas and Consistency," p. 190. Cf. John Rawls, *A Theory of Justice* (Cambridge, Mass.: Harvard University Press, 1971), pp. 133–34; David Lyons, *Forms and Limits of Utilitarianism* (Oxford: Oxford University Press, 1965), p. 21; and Donald

Davidson, *Essays on Actions and Events* (Oxford: Clarendon, 1980), p. 34. For more on Davidson's views, cf. Frank Jackson, "Davidson on Moral Conflict," in *Actions and Events*, ed. E. Lapore and B. McLaughlin (Oxford: Basil Blackwell, 1985), pp. 104–15.

26. Marcus, "Moral Dilemmas and Consistency," pp. 194–95.

27. See Alan Donagan, "Consistency in Rationalist Moral Systems," in *Moral Dilemmas*, ed. C. W. Gowans (Oxford: Oxford University Press, 1987), pp. 278–81; cf. Herman Wouk, *The Caine Mutiny* (Garden City, N.Y.: Doubleday, 1952).

28. Donagan, "Consistency," pp. 280–81.

29. See R. M. Hare, "Moral Conflicts," in *Moral Dilemmas*, ed. C. W. Gowans (Oxford: Oxford University Press, 1987), pp. 208–10; cf. also Earl Conee, "Against Moral Dilemmas," in *Moral Dilemmas*, ed. C. W. Gowans (Oxford: Oxford University Press, 1987), pp. 241–43.

30. Further proponents of dilemma include Philip L. Quinn, who extends the notion to conflicts between moral and religious requirements in "Moral Obligation, Religious Demand, and Practical Conflict," in *Rationality, Religious Belief, and Moral Commitment*, ed. R. Audi and W. J. Wainwright (Ithaca, N.Y.: Cornell University Press, 1986), pp. 195–212, and Michael Slote, who extends it to utilitarian cases in *Beyond Optimizing* (Cambridge, Mass.: Harvard University Press, 1989), pp. 99–123; cf. idem, "Utilitarianism, Moral Dilemmas, and Moral Cost," *American Philosophical Quarterly* 32 (1985): 161–68.

Foot, "Moral Realism and Moral Dilemma," does not seem to take a definite position on dilemmas, at least as here interpreted (see esp. pp. 265–66), although her argument does allow for something weaker along the same lines (cf. pp. 254–55, 267–68). I omit a number of other intermediate or hard-to-classify views from this brief overview of central contributions. For a detailed summary of the relevant arguments in the literature along with bibliographical information, see Sinnott-Armstrong, *Moral Dilemmas*.

31. See Henrik Ibsen, *The Works of Henrik Ibsen* (New York: Blue Ribbon Books, 1928), 4: 165–215. Among philosophers' treatments, see esp. Terrance C. McConnell, "Moral Blackmail," *Ethics* 91 (1981): 544–67, and Martha Nussbaum, *The Fragility of Goodness: Luck and Ethics in Greek Tragedy and Philosophy* (Cambridge: Cambridge University Press, 1986), pp. 25–82.

32. Christopher Cherniak and Roy Sorensen (personal communications) have each independently called my attention to the theory of heuristics as offering a similar account of decision-making within cognitive limitations—in that case meant to explain apparent irrationalities in probability assessment; see, e.g., Amos Tversky and Daniel Kahneman, "Judgment under Uncertainty: Heuristics and Biases," *Science* 185 (1984): 1124–31. Sorensen has suggested two nice analogies to my proposed view of dilemmas as a tolerable side effect of man-made (or "man-tailored") morality. First is the practice of overbooking flights, something that airlines do systematically in the expectation that not every passenger will show up—a reasonable expectation, albeit sometimes violated. Second is an optical illusion, which might be considered an inevitable result of what, on the whole, is the ideal visual system. In the moral case, however, I mean to deny that we have the kind of independent standard needed to dismiss such consequences as "illusions"; an appeal to God, say, even if it yielded a religious solution to a dilemma, would still leave it unresolved in strictly moral terms. The same holds for practical solutions on utilitarian or similar grounds.

33. See Williams, *Moral Luck*, pp. 118–19, 124–25; cf. idem, "Ethical Consistency," pp. 134–36. For his views on moral luck and blame, cf. idem, *Moral Luck*, pp. 20–39, and idem, *Ethics and the Limits of Philosophy* (Cambridge, Mass.: Harvard University Press, 1985), pp. 176–77.

34. See, e.g., Foot, "Moral Realism and Moral Dilemma," pp. 251–57, and Michael Stocker, *Plural and Conflicting Values* (Oxford: Clarendon, 1990), p. 124; cf. also Christopher W. Gowans, "Moral Dilemmas and Prescriptivism," *American Philosophical Quarterly* 26 (1989): 187–97, for the defense of a position similar to Williams's, apparently without awareness of the overlap.

35. Nagel, "Fragmentation of Value," p. 175.

36. For the terms "internalism" and "externalism," see W. D. Falk, "'Ought' and Motivation," *Proceedings of the Aristotelian Society* 48 (1947–48): 492–510; cf. W. K. Frankena, "Obligation and Motivation in Recent Moral Philosophy," in *Essays in Moral Philosophy*, ed. A. I. Melden (Seattle: University of Washington Press, 1958), pp. 40–81. A more precise version of the rough characterization of moral realism I rely on here is provided in David O. Brink, *Moral Realism and the Foundations of Ethics* (Cambridge: Cambridge University Press, 1989), p. 17.

Also roughly speaking, internalist realism can be identified with an Oxford school of contemporary metaethics developed most systematically by followers of John McDowell—see, e.g., David McNaughton, *Moral Vision* (Oxford: Basil Blackwell, 1988), pp. 46–50 (cf. p. 15 for the claim to represent McDowell's views, although McDowell avoids this terminology himself).

On the other hand, standard externalist realism seems to correspond to a Cornell school of realism; cf., e.g., Brink, *Moral Realism and Foundations of Ethics*, pp. 37–80. As Brink points out (p. 78), internalism is linked in the first instance with noncognitivist versions of antirealism, for which the practical function of morality or the connection with emotion that supports it actually supplies the meaning of a moral judgment. However, the view has come to be linked with versions of realism that attempt to incorporate a Kantian treatment of practical reason. See, e.g., Thomas Nagel, *The Possibility of Altruism* (Oxford: Clarendon, 1970), pp. 7–14, and idem, *The View from Nowhere* (New York: Oxford University Press, 1986), pp. 139ff; cf. Christine M. Korsgaard, "Skepticism about Practical Reason," *Journal of Philosophy* 83 (1986): 5–25. For the alternative approach, and another version of the internalism/externalism distinction that Korsgaard and others rely on—applied to reasons rather than to moral judgments—cf. Williams, *Moral Luck*, pp. 101–13. I shall rely on Falk's specifically moral version of the distinction in what follows; though it is sometimes explained in terms of Williams's version, the two pull apart for views that allow moral judgments to be true in application to an amoralist or other agent to whom they do not give reasons in Williams's sense. Philippa Foot's view, for instance, which I deal with centrally in chapter 3, section 1, seems to be naturally classified as externalist on moral meaning but internalist on reason-giving force; cf. Brink, *Moral Realism and the Foundations of Ethics*, pp. 39, 43, 61.

37. See David Hume, *A Treatise of Human Nature* (Oxford: Clarendon, 1964), pp. 470–76; cf., e.g., p. 457. Cf. Nagel, *Possibility of Altruism*, pp. 10–11. The classification that follows is designed to avoid problems about the proper interpretation of Hume's view.

38. Kant, *Lectures on Ethics*, p. 20.

39. See ibid., p. 28, for a distinction between two sorts of practical necessitation, *per stimulos* and *per motivos*, with emotional motivation in the former category, and the latter construed as broader, including also the sort of objective practical necessitation that applies to action on obligation. Cf. Kant's comments on moral motives and binding grounds of obligation on pp. 18–19.

This broader notion of motivation clearly extends beyond the psychologist's sense relied on for emotional motivation in P. S. Greenspan, *Emotions and Reasons: An*

Inquiry into Emotional Justification (New York: Routledge, Chapman and Hall, 1988), e.g. p. 153; cf. R. S. Peters, *The Concept of Motivation* (New York: Humanities, 1980), esp. pp. 37–51. I think that the psychologist's sense is at this point the common one, so I shall use Philippa Foot's alternative terminology ("reason-giving force") for the Kantian notion; but note that some current authors, e.g., Korsgaard, "Skepticism," do not make this distinction in discussing motivational force.

40. Cf. Ronald De Sousa's apparent equation of normal and appropriate emotional response in *The Rationality of Emotion* (Cambridge, Mass.: Bradford Books, 1987), p. 202. Hume himself allows only for a limited belief-based distinction between reasonable and unreasonable emotional response that would not supply what we want here; cf. Hume, *Treatise of Human Nature*, pp. 415–16. My argument in what follows will work from my own account of appropriate emotion in Greenspan, *Emotions and Reasons*, pp. 83–107. I reexplain this notion here in simpler terms, however; see chapter 5, section 2.

41. Cf. McNaughton, *Moral Vision*, p, 48.

42. See Hare, "Moral Conflicts," pp. 209–10.

43. For discussion of the textual evidence that the chorus faults Agamemnon for not reacting appropriately, see Nussbaum, *Fragility of Goodness*, pp. 36–37ff.

44. See Williams, *Moral Luck*, p. 27.

45. See Greenspan, *Emotions and Reasons*, e.g., p. 96; cf. Williams, *Moral Luck*, p. 63.

46. See G.E.M. Anscombe, "Modern Moral Philosophy," in *Collected Philosophical Papers*, Vol. 3, *Ethics, Religion and Politics* (Minneapolis: University of Minnesota, 1981), pp. 26–42.

47. See e.g. Philippa Foot, *Virtues and Vices and Other Essays in Moral Philosophy* (Berkeley: University of California Press, 1978); John McDowell, "Virtue and Reason," *Monist* 62 (1979): 331–50; Alasdair MacIntyre, *After Virtue* (Notre Dame, Ind.: University of Notre Dame Press, 1984); Williams, *Ethics and the Limits of Philosophy*; Stocker, *Plural and Conflicting Values*; and Michael Slote, *From Morality to Virtue* (New York: Oxford University Press, 1992). An early influence on some of these writers was Iris Murdoch; cf. Murdoch, *The Sovereignty of Good* (London: Ark, 1970).

48. Anscombe, "Modern Moral Philosophy," pp. 29–33.

49. See Foot, *Virtues and Vices*, pp. 150–51, 162–63; cf. pp. 178–79. The latter term seems to capture current talk of "normativity," as sometimes equated with motivational force, following Kant; cf. note 39 this chapter. In historical terms I take reason-giving force to amount to the rationally "binding" force of obligation, essentially the justificatory force of the moral "ought." For an early contemporary statement in terms of normativity, see Stephen L. Darwall, *Impartial Reason* (Ithaca, N.Y.: Cornell University Press, 1983), pp. 19ff. The notions of reason-giving and motivational force now need to be pried apart in classifying views as internalist; cf. Brink, *Moral Realism and Foundations of Ethics*, pp. 38–40.

50. For an interesting historical overview, see Louis I. Bredvold, *The Natural History of Sensibility* (Detroit: Wayne State University Press, 1962). For the philosophical account I rely on here, see Stephen L. Darwall, "Motive and Obligation in the British Moralists," *Social Philosophy and Policy* 7 (1989): 139–40. A helpful discussion of the relevant conceptual framework is provided in Charlotte Brown, "Moral Sense Theorists," in *Encyclopedia of Ethics*, ed. L. C. and C. B. Becker (New York: Garland, 1992), 2: 862–68. For a historical view that bears a certain structural resemblance to the one I go on to defend, cf. also Jerome B. Schneewind, "Pufendorf's Place in the History of Ethics," *Synthese* 72 (1987): 144–46.

51. See Anscombe, "Modern Moral Philosophy," p. 27; cf. Joseph Butler, *A Dissertation of the Nature of Virtue* (London: SPCK, 1970), par. [2], p. 148.

52. For a fairly standard definition of "metaethics" that would cover relevant issues in psychology and other empirical subjects, see William K. Frankena, *Ethics* (Englewood Cliffs, N.J.: Prentice-Hall, 1973), pp. 4–5.

53. See Jonathan Edwards, *The Nature of True Virtue* (Ann Arbor: University of Michigan Press, 1960), p. 63; cf. the review of recent work in developmental psychology in Martin L. Hoffman, "Development of Prosocial Motivation: Empathy and Guilt," in *Development of Prosocial Behavior*, ed. N. Eisenberg-Berg (New York: Academic Press, 1982), pp. 281–313.

54. See 5d under "guilt" in *The Oxford English Dictionary* (Oxford: Clarendon, 1970), 4: 496; cf. 6a–b under "guilty" on p. 497 for uses of the adjective in application to conscience, mind, feelings, and the like, going back to Shakespeare a century earlier.

55. For a historical account of "tainting" in relation to legal culpability, see George Fletcher, *Rethinking Criminal Law* (Boston: Little, Brown, 1978), pp. 343–50. Cf. the account of religious ideas of pollution in Mary Douglas, *Purity and Danger* (London: Routledge & Kegan Paul, 1966).

56. A colleague at the National Humanities Center, Michael MacDonald (personal communication), brought to my attention an English account from 1621 of the pitfalls of emotional guilt, or the guilty conscience, described in terms of the "sense of . . . God's anger justly deserved"; see Robert Burton, *The Anatomy of Melancholy* (New York: Tudor, 1927), pp. 400–404. Note that Burton declines to attribute emotional guilt to Catholics; despite the gradual internalization of religious feeling throughout the Middle Ages and the influence of the Reformation on both religious traditions, some difference in sensibility might be thought to result from the clearer steps laid out in the Catholic tradition for penance and forgiveness of sin. At any rate, on the account offered here, the mere lack of a word for emotional guilt (in Latin, for instance) will not be decisive.

Thus, Augustine, writing about his adolescent theft of pears, has to work within the confines of a shame vocabulary; cf. *St. Augustine's Confessions*, trans. W. Watts (New York: Putnam, 1922), 1: 77–79. Given that he describes himself as undergoing some emotion associated with the internalized sense of God's anger, my account in what follows will allow Augustine emotional guilt. I have some further comments in later notes on these often fascinating historical and cultural issues, although I cannot attempt a full-scale treatment here.

57. See esp. Sigmund Freud, *Civilization and Its Discontents*, trans. J. Strachey (New York: Norton, 1961), pp. 83–96; cf. Friedrich Nietzsche, *On the Genealogy of Morals*, trans. W. Kaufmann and R. J. Hollingdale (New York: Vintage, 1969), pp. 57–96.

58. See esp. Melanie Klein and Joan Riviere, *Love, Hate and Reparation* (New York: Norton, 1964), pp. 65–66.

59. See Ruth Benedict, *The Chrysanthemum and the Sword: Patterns of Japanese Culture* (Boston: Houghton Mifflin, 1946), pp. 222–23ff.

60. See John Stuart Mill, *Utilitarianism* (New York: Bobbs-Merrill, 1957), pp. 36–43.

Chapter 2

1. See Sinnott-Armstrong, *Moral Dilemmas*, pp. 108–68, for a discussion of two patterns of argument against dilemmas from the two pairs of principles. For our pur-

poses, one fairly compact argument will be sufficient to exhibit both conflicts. If we allow M for physical possibility, the assumption that there are dilemmas as interpreted in terms of conflicting positive ought-judgments comes out as the claim that there are acts A and B such that OA and OB and ~M(A & B). But on this assumption, the principle of closure would yield O~B and O~A. Closure essentially tells us that an obligation also applies to anything required to fulfill it, and dilemmas amount to cases in which each obligatory act requires the negation of the other. So now we have two pairs of ought-statements with contradictory objects: OA & O~A and OB & O~B. Even if they are practically inconsistent, however, neither pair of statements amounts to a truth-functional contradiction. The same holds for the pair that conjoins their objects to yield obligations with contradictory objects according to the principle of agglomeration: O(A & ~A) and O(B & ~B). But the standard system of deontic logic takes impossible states of affairs as impermissible; with P as its operator for permissibility, that is, it lets us conclude for any A that ~P(A & ~A). (Cf. (C4′) in Føllesdal and Hilpinen, "Deontic Logic," p. 13.) The assumption that "ought" implies "permissible" will therefore let us derive a contradiction within the standard system, since in application to each of the conjoint ought-statements just derived it yields a statement of the form P(A & ~A). Alternatively, a contrapositive version of "ought"-implies-"can" yields ~O(A & ~A) for any A and hence a direct contradiction of our derived ought-statements.

2. Williams's position essentially rests on applying to practical "ought," taken as a conclusion of deliberation, a principle of "exclusivity" that combines the two deontic principles he thinks dilemmas force us to choose between: "ought"-implies-"can" and agglomeration (see *Moral Luck*, pp. 118–19). A version of this point occurs in his earlier treatment of what he calls deliberative "ought"; see idem, "Ethical Consistency," pp. 134–36.

However, I shall not deal here with Williams's argument on this subject in full detail, partly because its terms shift in a way that makes it resist perspicuous treatment. Besides equating practical "ought" with "ought" as a conclusion of deliberation (a point I shall deal with later in this chapter), Williams apparently makes different assumptions in different places as to whether a practical ought is by definition "conclusive," or all-things-considered (cf. *Moral Luck*, pp. 118–19, 124, n. 3).

For the defense of a position similar to Williams's on practical ought in dilemmas, see Gowans, "Moral Dilemmas and Prescriptivism," and idem, *Innocence Lost: An Examination of Inescapable Moral Wrongdoing* (New York: Oxford University Press, 1994).

3. See P. S. Greenspan, "Conditional Oughts and Hypothetical Imperatives," *Journal of Philosophy* 72 (1975): 259–79; cf. idem, "Derived Obligation: Some Paradoxes Escaped," Ph.D. dissertation (Cambridge, Mass.: Harvard University, 1972).

4. This depends on a version of the principle of deontic closure, which in rough form tells us that anything necessary to satisfy an ought is itself obligatory. I shall later suggest some limitations on the principle, but even in modified form it should still allow for the inference in question here. In general terms, my present argument brings to mind Nagel's argument on reasons in *Possibility of Altruism*, p. 36. But note that Nagel considers only the direct derivation of earlier instrumental reasons from a statement dated at the time assigned to action, whereas my suggested account dates ought-statements at the time of utterance and allows for distinct dates on their objects, or the acts they require.

5. In Grice's terms, what I ascribe to a general use of "ought" might be thought of as part of its "conventional meaning" as distinct from "conversational implicature," or the shifting commitments of individual speakers; see Paul Grice, *Studies in the Way*

of Words (Cambridge, Mass.: Harvard University Press, 1989), p. 41. An analogy might be the way the word "but" implicates contrast between two conjuncts, except that our example might be said to involve two different conventional uses.

Among examples not related to "ought" itself, the best I can think of have to do with literal versus recognized nonliteral uses of the same form of words. For instance, the expression "God damn!" as used today no longer prescribes divine condemnation but instead functions mainly to express anger. It therefore "implicates" anger on the part of the speaker, as a function of conventional meaning. But it can also be used with almost the opposite intent, in a hoot of victory (when one's team scores a touchdown, say). It might even be thought that this latter use is common enough to count as a further conventional meaning. In either case, the expression serves at least one general emotive function in the language that is distinct from its literal meaning—and possibly from a given speaker's personal intent.

Assuming that practical force involves a similar kind of functional or conventional meaning, we might want to say that it "implicates" rather than *implies* "can" in any strict logical sense. Remember that Grice invented the former term to contrast with logical implication (see pp. 24–25; cf. pp. 121, 341). The important point for our purposes, however, is that this does not make "can" follow simply as a matter of conversational implicature, as Sinnott-Armstrong maintains (*Moral Dilemmas*, pp. 121–26). Rather, the principle would seem to be definitive of practical "ought," as designed to serve a particular (action-guiding) function in the language.

6. See Hume, *Treatise on Human Nature*, p. 457; cf., e.g., Foot, *Virtues and Vices*, pp. 78–80.

7. See, e.g., Williams, *Moral Luck*, p. 119.

8. See, e.g., Hector-Neri Castañeda, *The Structure of Morality* (Springfield, Ill.: Charles C. Thomas, 1974), p. 64; Gilbert Harman, *The Nature of Morality* (New York: Oxford University Press, 1977), pp. 117–19; and Joseph Raz, *Practical Reason and Norms* (Princeton, N.J.: Princeton University Press, 1990), pp. 29–32.

9. A version of this view seems to surface, e.g., in Williams, *Moral Luck*, pp. 109–11; cf. also Nagel, *Possibility of Altruism*, pp. 8–9, and Foot, *Virtues and Vices*, p. 152 (though I gather that Foot would now reject this argument [personal communication]).

10. See Aristotle, *Nicomachean Ethics*, 1147a27–31; cf. idem, *Movement of Animals*, 701a11 *et circa*, and idem, *De Anima*, 433a17 *et circa*.

11. See Lewis White Beck, *A Commentary on Kant's Critique of Practical Reason* (Chicago: University of Chicago Press, 1960), p. 39, for a reconciliation of Kant's references to practical reason as determinant of and as identical to the will.

12. See Davidson, *Essays on Actions and Events*, p. 39.

13. Williams, *Moral Luck*, p. 119.

14. See John M. Cooper, *Reason and Human Good in Aristotle* (Indianapolis: Hackett, 1986), pp. 23–46.

15. See Stocker, *Plural and Conflicting Values*, pp. 51–84, for an argument that Aristotle himself makes room for conflict. However, my use of Aristotle's view of practical reasoning here is not meant to commit him to dilemmas.

16. Cf. Williams, *Moral Luck*, e.g. p. 12.

17. Cf. Alasdair MacIntyre, "What Morality Is Not," in *The Definition of Morality*, ed. G. Wallace and A.D.M. Walker (London: Methuen, 1970), pp. 27–31. See Greenspan, "Conditional Oughts and Hypothetical Imperatives," p. 275, n. 13, for an argument against one natural way of interpreting the results of a first-person ought as binding from a third-person standpoint.

18. See William Styron, *Sophie's Choice* (New York: Bantam, 1980), p. 589; cf.

P. S. Greenspan, "Moral Dilemmas and Guilt," *Philosophical Studies* 43 (1983): 117–25.

19. Williams, "Ethical Consistency," p. 136.

20. Williams, *Moral Luck*, pp. 78–79; cf. p. 74.

21. Cf. Sinnott-Armstrong, *Moral Dilemmas*, for the use of this compound over-ridingness notion in defense of dilemmas.

22. Williams, *Moral Luck*, p. 119.

23. Williams, "Ethical Consistency," p. 123, and idem, *Moral Luck*, p. 79; cf. *Moral Luck*, p. 125.

24. See Slote, *Beyond Optimizing*; cf. Stocker, *Plural and Conflicting Values*, pp. 314–15.

25. The two principles of standard deontic logic that together have this result are given as (C1) and (C2) in Føllesdal and Hilpinen, "Deontic Logic," pp. 8–9; but note that (C2), which denies the possibility of exhaustive prohibition, begs the question for our purposes.

26. See esp. Roger Wertheimer, *The Significance of Sense: Meaning, Modality, and Morality* (Ithaca, N.Y.: Cornell University Press, 1972), pp. 82–83, 110–11.

27. See, e.g., Williams, *Moral Luck*, p. 60.

28. See Ross, *Right and the Good*, p. 28.

29. See Wertheimer, *Significance of Sense*, pp. 117–18; cf. pp. 104, 109.

30. Note that the "total" body of evidence on a standard reading means all relevant reasons—not just all available reasons or all reasons actually held by the agent, as on Davidson's interpretation of "all-things-considered" in *Essays on Actions and Events*, p. 40. Taking the latter notion as evidential thus should not rule out an objective notion of dilemmas. To say that two competing prohibitions hold all things considered on this account will not simply tell us about the agent's epistemic position—that he is not in possession of adequate reasons for choice or the like (which in weighted cases, of course, may well be false)—but rather about the requirements of his situation. My perceptual imagery is meant to capture something about the objective determination of rational weight, not to suggest that it depends on an observer.

31. Cf. Williams, *Moral Luck*, pp. 74, 79.

32. Cf. Marcus, "Moral Dilemmas and Consistency," p. 193; my own view here comes closer to Williams's. Note that the initial examples of conflicting oughts in Foot's critique of Williams seem to be cases of overriding that are better suited to Marcus's view; see Foot, "Moral Realism and Moral Dilemma," p. 251.

33. Lemmon, "Moral Dilemmas," p. 106; Williams, *Moral Luck*, pp. 124–30.

34. Williams, "Ethical Consistency," p. 129.

35. See Alan Ross Anderson, "The Formal Analysis of Normative Systems," in *The Logic of Decision and Action*, ed. N. Rescher (Pittsburgh: University of Pittsburgh Press, 1967), pp. 147–213. Cf. A. N. Prior, "Escapism: The Logical Basis of Ethics," in *Essays in Moral Philosophy*, ed. A. I. Melden (Seattle: University of Washington Press, 1958), pp. 135–46.

36. That is, it denies that the object of permission will incur *any* deontic sanction. Even if OA and OB are interpreted as referring to two different sanctions, S_A and S_B, as needed to allow for an escapist account of dilemmas, fulfillment of either one of these oughts in a dilemma would seem to incur *some* sanction—e.g., since A entails ~B, it would incur S_B—which would seem to be enough to make it impermissible.

37. See Greenspan, "Moral Dilemmas and Guilt," p. 118; cf. pp. 121–22. I pushed the argument a bit further in connection with some assumptions of deontic logic in "Sophie's Choices: More on Exclusive Requirement" (unpublished).

38. See Von Wright, *Essay in Deontic Logic*, pp. 78–81; cf. Peter Vallentyne, "Prohibition Dilemmas and Deontic Logic," *Logique et Analyse* 117–18 (1987): 120, n. 5. The distinction is made more explicitly and defended at length in idem, "Two Types of Moral Dilemmas," *Erkenntnis* 30 (1989): 301–18.

39. This assumes that the tiebreaker does not cancel out any of the original dilemmatic prohibitions and that prohibition applies to all particular acts satisfying a given description, or tokens of a certain act-type. This is another difference from permission, which tells us only that there is nothing objectionable about an act insofar as it satisfies a given description, or amounts to a token of a certain type, so that the particular act in question may still be prohibited.

40. Cf. Sinnott-Armstrong, *Moral Dilemmas*, pp. 121–26, 160–61, for the limitation of the ought-implication principles to conversational implicature as extended beyond practical uses of "ought."

41. Cf. (C2) in Føllesdal and Hilpinen, "Deontic Logic," p. 9.

42. Gottlob Frege, "Negation," in *Translations from the Philosophical Writings of Gottlob Frege*, ed. Peter Geach and Max Black (New York: Philosophical Library, 1952), p. 125.

43. See Michael Dummett, *Frege: Philosophy of Language*, 2nd ed. (London: Duckworth, 1981), p. 317.

44. Cf. ibid., p. 335.

45. Cf. Ruth Barcan Marcus, "More about Moral Dilemmas" (unpublished; delivered at the Chapel Hill Colloquium in Philosophy, 1980), pp. 14–15.

46. See Føllesdal and Hilpinen, "Deontic Logic," p. 17. Note that Marcus's second-order regulative principle to avoid conflicts seems to make best sense in these terms—since at the time assigned to action in a dilemma it may well be too late for the agent to avoid it, though his doing so would still count as the ideal state of affairs.

47. Cf. esp. Chisholm, "Contrary-to-Duty Imperatives." Cf. Greenspan, "Derived Obligation," for my discussion of many of these issues.

48. Cf. Føllesdal and Hilpinen, "Deontic Logic," pp. 26–31. I should note that this seems not to be true of a more recent attempt to handle dilemmatic oughts as cases of defeasible reasoning, by abandoning modal logic altogether (in favor of "nonmonotonic" logic) as the appropriate foundation for deontic logic. See John F. Horty, "Moral Dilemmas and Nonmonotonic Logic," *Journal of Philosophical Logic* 23 (1994): 35–65; cf. idem, "Deontic Logic as Founded on Nonmonotonic Logic," *Annals of Mathematics and Artificial Intelligence* 9 (1993): 69–91. The analogies illustrating Horty's proposal (propositions roughly true but conflicting as stated, such as "Birds fly" and "Penguins don't fly," on the assumption that penguins are birds) suggest that it would not really capture dilemmas, in the sense of specific conflicting directives for action, but rather just general ought-statements whose conflict in application to a particular case presumably would be handled by withdrawing one of them. (We would not conclude, for instance, that Tweety the Penguin does fly *qua* bird as well as failing to fly *qua* penguin, but rather that "Birds fly" is not really applicable to Tweety's case.) Horty's point, as I understand it, is that we cannot appeal to the content of such statements—to built-in exception clauses and the like—to tell us which one to withdraw. His proposed system of deontic logic would cover conflicting rules and hence would yield a logic applicable *to* our ordinary deontic judgments—perhaps one that more accurately reflects our ordinary use of them in moral reasoning. But it would not seem to yield a logical systematization *of* our deontic judgments, or a "deontic logic" in the usual sense, except as limited to the general level.

49. Williams, "Ethical Consistency," p. 132.

50. On dilemmas and simplicity, see Bernard Williams's comments on Isaiah Berlin's value pluralism in his introduction to *Concepts and Categories: Philosophical Essays*, by I. Berlin (London: Hogarth, 1978), pp. xvi–xvii.

51. See esp. Hector-Neri Castañeda, "On the Semantics of the Ought-to-Do," *Synthese* 21 (1970): 451; cf. idem, *Thinking and Doing*, pp. 207–8, 248–53.

52. See Castañeda, *Thinking and Doing*, p. 224.

53. For Castañeda's overall account (whose full complexity I cannot attempt to capture here), see esp. ibid., pp. 154–79. Castañeda's notion of the "Legitimacy" of practitions as the value analogous to the truth of propositions, and of deontic truth as necessary Legitimacy, is summed up in a very helpful overview of Castañeda's views; see Michael E. Bratman, "Castañeda's Theory of Thought and Action," in *Agent, Language, and the Structure of the World*, ed. J. E. Tomberlin (Indianapolis: Hackett, 1983), pp. 152–55; for more on the connection to an agent's ends, including some problems with cause-effect relations, see pp. 155–59.

54. Cf. the account of needs in contrast to desires given in David Wiggins, *Needs, Values, Truth* (Oxford: Basil Blackwell, 1987), pp. 5–16.

55. Cf. Bratman, "Castañeda's Theory of Thought and Action," p. 156, where oughts on Castañeda's account are taken as indexed to a specific promise.

56. See esp. Castañeda's account of the three "dimensions" of morality in *Structure of Morality*, pp. 175–226; cf. his account of the consistency of normative systems by analogy to legal systems in *Thinking and Doing*, pp. 225–28.

Chapter 3

1. Williams, *Problems of the Self*, pp. 204–5; cf. Wiggins, *Needs, Values, Truth*, pp. 87–137.

2. Cf. also P. S. Greenspan, "A Case of Mixed Feelings: Ambivalence and the Logic of Emotion," in *Explaining Emotions*, ed. A. O. Rorty (Berkeley: University of California Press, 1980), pp. 223–50. I there deal with cases that exhibit a logical structure Williams bypasses (see Williams, "Ethical Consistency," p. 117), along with the sort of logical behavior that he takes to mark off desires. That is, the unqualified evaluative beliefs that reflect emotional ambivalence may be said to be retained in residual form by being qualified rather than simply eliminated in the face of conflict.

3. See Foot, "Moral Realism and Moral Dilemma," esp. pp. 254–57, 265–67.

4. Ibid., p. 262; cf. pp. 267–68.

5. See McNaughton, *Moral Vision*, pp. 139–40, 48–50; and Brink, *Moral Realism and Foundations of Ethics*, pp. 43–50.

6. See Foot, *Virtues and Vices*, pp. 157–73; cf. p. 179 for the distinction from motivational force. For a study of Foot that overlaps on important points with the account that follows but without the implications for general internalism, see Simon Blackburn, "The Flight to Reality," in *Virtues and Reasons*, ed. R. Hursthouse and G. Lawrence (Oxford: Oxford University Press, 1995).

7. Foot, *Virtues and Vices*, pp. 74–80.

8. Cf. the account in terms of "fittingness" in Maurice Mandelbaum, *The Phenomenology of Moral Experience* (Baltimore: Johns Hopkins University Press, 1969), pp. 59–71.

9. Foot, *Virtues and Vices*, pp. 181–88.

10. Ibid., p. 186.

11. Ibid., pp. 183–85.

12. Ibid., p. 153.

13. Ibid., pp. 79–80.

14. Ibid., see, e.g. p. 152.

15. Ibid., p. 163.

16. Cf. P. S. Greenspan, "Behavior Control and Freedom of Action," *Philosophical Review* 87 (1978): 25–40.

17. Cf. Ben Spiecker, "Education and the Moral Emotions," in *Philosophical Issues in Moral Education and Development*, ed. B. Spiecker and R. Straughan (Milton Keynes, U.K.: Open University Press, 1988), pp. 43–63.

18. For a review of the psychological literature suggesting a developmental account of guilt as based on empathy (but omitting the earlier stage I include here), see Hoffman, "Development of Prosocial Motivation," pp. 297–305. I discuss this evidence further in chapter 4.

19. See Laurence Thomas, *Living Morally: A Psychology of Moral Character* (Philadelphia: Temple University Press, 1989), pp. 76–80, for a negative view of guilt as a self-interested and hence an essentially antimoral motive. It is compatible with anything I have in mind, I should say, that we would prefer to have children (and friends and others) act out of some motive other than guilt; but I take it that the same holds for moral ought-statements.

20. For my general account of emotions as reasons operating by way of the need to escape discomfort, see Greenspan, *Emotions and Reasons*, pp. 153ff. For an empirical account of emotions that pays less attention to conceptual issues but otherwise overlaps with mine, see Paul L. Harris, *Children and Emotion: The Development of Psychological Understanding* (Oxford: Blackwell, 1989); with reference to the suggestions I develop here, see pp. 44–45, 93–94, 98.

21. Cf. C. L. Stevenson, *Facts and Values* (New Haven, Conn.: Yale University Press, 1963), p. 13.

22. This might be thought of as a variant of Grice's "conversational implicature" but with the ordinary purposes of moral discourse replacing the communicative aims of an ordinary speaker. See Grice, *Studies in the Way of Words*, pp. 26–28. The notion of "didactic import" is not meant to cover just any emotional overtones of a word resulting from the way it is commonly taught, such as shame in connection with words for the genitals, but just those essential to setting up its role in the language. I characterized the latter as its "functional" meaning in chapter 2, section 1; in Grice's terms it seems to amount to "conventional" meaning (see my note 5, chapter 2). There is no institution of genital discourse designed specifically to control behavior. To claim that moral discourse is another matter is not to rule out the possibility of a society—or in a nice example that was suggested to me, some ultraliberal parents in California (presumably speaking their own language)—that did without terms set up for their action-guiding function. The point is just that they would thereby be doing without "moral" language in our (conventional) sense. This is not to say that moral discourse has no further functions that they might retain, as part of an institution that could still be called "moral," albeit in a somewhat different (more "laid–back") sense.

23. See esp. Wiggins, *Needs, Values, Truth*, pp. 185–211; see also John McDowell, "Values and Secondary Qualities," in *Morality and Objectivity: A Tribute to J. L. Mackie*, ed. T. Honderich (London: Routledge & Kegan Paul, 1985), pp. 110–29. Note that Wiggins considers "realism" something of a misnomer for his view, although he would accept McDowell's "cognitivism" (see p. 209).

24. Cf. McNaughton, *Moral Vision*, pp. 21–23, 46–47, 106–13.

25. See John McDowell, "Are Moral Requirements Hypothetical Imperatives?,"

Proceedings of the Aristotelian Society Suppl. 52 (1978): 13–29, and idem, "Virtue and Reason," 331–50. For help in understanding McDowell's view, I am indebted both to McNaughton, *Moral Vision*, and to Jonathan Dancy (personal communication), who provided comments on the ensuing discussion. See Dancy's *Moral Reasons* (Oxford: Basil Blackwell, 1993), which advances a version of McDowell's view but which reached me too late for consideration here.

26. McDowell, "Virtue and Reason," p. 348, n. 5.

27. Cf. Nagel, *Possibility of Altruism*, pp. 29–32.

28. McDowell, "Moral Requirements," p. 16.

29. Ibid., p. 28.

30. McDowell, "Virtue and Reason," p. 333.

31. Ibid.

32. McDowell, "Moral Requirements," pp. 26–27.

33. Ibid., p. 21.

34. Cf. McDowell, "Virtue and Reason," p. 344. Annette Baier, in her comments on my *Emotions and Reasons* (American Philosophical Association Pacific Division meetings, March 1990), noted that the point about emotions can be traced to Descartes's treatment in "The Passions of the Soul"; see *The Philosophical Works of Descartes*, trans. E. S. Haldane and G.R.T. Ross (Cambridge: Cambridge University Press, 1970), Vol. 1, Pt. Second, Art. 74, p. 364.

35. McDowell, "Moral Requirements," p. 22.

36. Cf. my defense of ambivalence as rationally appropriate in Greenspan, "Case of Mixed Feelings"; cf. idem, *Emotions and Reasons*, pp. 109–36.

37. See J. L. Mackie, *Ethics: Inventing Right and Wrong* (London: Penguin, 1987), pp. 38–42.

38. Ibid., pp. 23–24, 40, 35; cf. pp. 23, 40.

39. See Foot, *Virtues and Vices*, pp. 132–47; cf. pp. 100–5.

40. Mackie, *Ethics*, pp. 51–52, 59.

41. Ibid., pp. 15, 16.

42. Ibid., esp. p. 31.

43. See McDowell, "Values and Secondary Qualities," pp. 120–22. McDowell acknowledges the limitations of the secondary qualities analogy on p. 120; the point of the analogy seems to be the distinction between general and particular subject-independence (independence of minds generally vs. the speaker), with the latter taken as sufficient for a claim to be part of "reality." Cf. also McDowell's discussion of related issues in "Aesthetic Value, Objectivity, and the Fabric of the World," in *Pleasure, Preference and Value*, ed. E. Schaper (Cambridge: Cambridge University Press, 1983), pp. 1–16.

44. Cf. John Rawls, "Kantian Constructivism in Moral Theory," *Journal of Philosophy* 77 (1980): 515–72. Since Rawls's later political version of constructivism is set up to accommodate intuitionist realism, it should also be compatible with the alternative I propose; cf. John Rawls, *Political Liberalism* (New York: Columbia University Press, 1993), p. 95.

45. Mackie, *Ethics*, see esp. pp. 106–15.

46. Ibid., cf. pp. 27–29, 35, 48–49, 65–66, 75.

47. See Plato, *Protagoras*, 320c8–323a4, and Mackie, *Ethics*, pp. 108, 113–15.

48. Cf. John Searle, "How to Derive 'Ought' from 'Is'," *Philosophical Review* 73 (1964): 43–58; cf. Mackie, *Ethics*, pp. 66–72, esp. p. 67.

49. Mackie, *Ethics*, p. 79; cf. pp. 73–79, 81, 111–13.

50. Ibid., p. 33.

51. See my discussion of "having" a reason in P. S. Greenspan, "Unfreedom and Responsibility," in *Responsibility, Character, and the Emotions,* ed. F. Schoeman (Cambridge: Cambridge University Press, 1987), p. 75, for a way of retaining the claim that the agent in such a case "has" a reason to do what morality requires. Cf. Williams, *Moral Luck,* pp. 106–7, for the basis of the denial of such "external" reasons in the insistence that a reason necessarily motivates a rational agent. Extending externalism to the version that applies to reason-giving as well as motivational force allows for a fuller answer to Mackie's "argument from queerness"; cf. Richard Garner, "On the Genuine Queerness of Moral Properties and Facts," *Australasian Journal of Philosophy* 68 (1990): 137–46.

52. Cf. Aristotle, *Nicomachean Ethics,* esp. Bk. II, Secs. 1 and 3. Note that ordinary moral consciousness is in question here. For philosophers and others inclined to reflect on and analyze morality, we might of course include a further stage—the evaluation of moral codes according to metaethical norms, which includes standards of viability of the sort I go on to describe.

53. For a recent antirealist attempt to provide a limited kind of objective basis for ethics, with particular reference to the issue of authority, see Allan Gibbard, *Wise Choices, Apt Feelings: A Theory of Normative Judgment* (Cambridge, Mass.: Harvard University Press, 1990), pp. 153–250. On Gibbard's view, however, the authority in question comes out as that of a speaker—or of particular moral utterances—rather than of certain sorts of claims or considerations independently of their source, which I take to be the issue relevant to ethics.

54. Mackie, *Ethics,* pp. 36–39, 83–92.

55. Cf. the discussion of "explanatory values" in Geoffrey Sayre-McCord, "Moral Theory and Explanatory Impotence," in *Essays on Moral Realism,* ed. G. Sayre-McCord (Ithaca, N.Y.: Cornell University Press, 1988), p. 279.

56. Such appeal provides the basis for contractarian arguments; cf. Rawls, *Theory of Justice,* pp. 15, 13.

57. Cf. Raz, *Morality of Freedom,* pp. 198–203, 250–55. Alternatively, to the extent that social groups are susceptible to treatment as moral agents, one might take them as having duties to their members, including duties of fair treatment, perhaps as an element of the sort of social atmosphere of tolerance and similar liberal values that Raz commends. On a contractarian approach, a group's claim on its members' adherence might be based on performance of such duties. An argument along these lines was suggested to me by the treatment of society as the primary bearer of the duty to aid needy individuals in David Copp, "The Right to an Adequate Standard of Living: Justice, Autonomy, and the Basic Needs," *Social Philosophy and Policy* 9 (1992): 231–61. Just as the duty to aid on this account gets parceled out to individual members via taxation, moreover, other social duties to individuals might be held to transfer to them too, for a socially based account of "duties to oneself" and similar issues.

My central argument here is meant to be independent of these suggestions. However, for a systematic defense of some of the social notions I rely on, see Copp, "What Collectives Are: Agency, Individualism and Legal Theory," *Dialogue* 23 (1984): 249–69, and idem, "The Concept of a Society," *Dialogue* 31 (1992), 183–212. In *Morality, Normativity, and Society* (New York: Oxford University Press, 1995), Copp defends a social artifact view that overlaps in many ways with my own. One point of difference, though, is Copp's focus on the overall society as the source of moral norms, as opposed to the various smaller group interactions that support the teaching of morality via emotion on my account.

58. See Hoffman, "Development of Prosocial Motivation," p. 282. My own attempt

to make philosophic sense of empathetic emotion in Greenspan, *Emotions and Reasons*, pp. 62–79, resembles the account of "fellow feeling" in Adam Smith, *The Theory of the Moral Sentiments*, in *British Moralists: 1650–1800*, ed. D. D. Raphael (Indianapolis: Hackett, 1991), 2: 201–6. Recent discussions in cognitive science also deal with the topic under the heading of "simulation"; see, e.g., Robert Gordon, *The Structure of Emotions* (Cambridge: Cambridge University Press, 1987), pp. 149–55.

59. Note that the reference to emotional interaction—meaning *mutual* influence, of the sort that supports emotional learning, as described in section 1—may be used to limit the moral implications of our more extended sympathy with animals. Indeed, emotional identification sometimes extends even to inanimate objects: I cry out in pain when my car hits a pothole, say; see also the findings reported in Alvin Goldman's APA Pacific Division Presidential Address, "Empathy, Mind, and Morals," *Proceedings and Addresses of the American Philosophical Association* 66 (1992): 27–28.

On the other hand, an argument of the sort I offer for not excluding members of a subclass of one's own society from the scope of our moral obligations also may be extended to members of other societies—for instance, by noting that the habits of mind encouraged by subjecting them to hostile treatment would be likely to turn inward when it lacked a target, thus threatening the stability of the moral code. However, these issues (and others I omit) deserve a fuller treatment than I can provide here.

60. See Mill, *Utilitarianism*, pp. 36–43, and Hume, *Treatise of Human Nature*, p. 456; cf. p. 470. Mill holds that human emotional sensibility in no way restricts the content of a moral code. Hume's account, on the other hand, restricts sympathy to a later stage in the establishment of justice as a moral virtue; see, e.g., p. 498.

Cf. also Rawls, *Theory of Justice*, pp. 453–512, for an account of moral emotions relevant to contractarianism that I take to be essentially "top-down." The account presented here overlaps at important points with Rawls's defense of the "stability" of the principles of justice, but Rawls's treatment of moral psychology in connection with stability seems to be intended only as confirmation of the principles, not as an independent basis for them. Thus, on Rawls's view, any feasible principles of justice must be capable of support from a natural set of moral sentiments amounting to our sense of justice; so they would have to satisfy the requirement of teachability and other general presuppositions that may bring in facts about human emotional nature. But the choice of principles in Rawls's "original position" is justified without more specific reference to human motivation—in contrast to my own picture of moral emotions as providing a particular episodic basis for the teaching of moral language and behavior that generates moral norms.

61. Cf. David Wong, *Moral Relativity* (Berkeley: University of California Press, 1984); cf. also Castañeda's appeal to correction of actual moral codes in light of an ideal of morality in *Structure of Morality*, pp. 185–89. See also Richard Brandt, "Toward a Credible Form of Utilitarianism," in *Morality and the Language of Conduct*, ed. H-N. Castañeda and G. Nakhnikian (Detroit: Wayne State University Press, 1965), pp. 107–43, for a similar use of the notion of an ideal moral code, though without the historical reference that these other views presuppose. My own suggestions might be thought of, for that matter, as yielding something like a social version of Brandt's relativist "ideal observer" view in metaethics; see, e.g., Richard Brandt, *Ethical Theory* (Englewood Cliffs, N.J.: Prentice-Hall, 1959), pp. 173–74.

62. A similar basis for a version of realism in facts about social rationality is provided by Peter Railton, "Moral Realism," *Philosophical Review* 95 (1986): 163–207; however, Railton's approach is tied to utilitarianism in a way I want to avoid. I leave it as an exercise to the reader, incidentally, to decide whether my own view also counts

as a version of "naturalism." The issue is complicated by my willingness to grant that the notion of flourishing is partly evaluative, possibly even in a sense we can think of as "moral." McDowell has recently questioned the interpretation of "natural" in relation to Aristotle; see "Reason and Nature" (unpublished; delivered at the meetings of the American Philosophical Association, Eastern Division, December 1992). My own hunch (which I hope to explore in some further work) is that the categories of the natural and the normative are not so distinct at the social level, even with "natural" taken in its more modern sense. In any case, the issue will be affected by the options I leave open for the metaethical underpinnings of social artifact realism in chapter 6.

63. In partial explanation of the tendency of moral philosophers to interpret realism in this way (cf., e.g., Gibbard, *Wise Choices, Apt Feelings*, pp. 33–34), I offer Keynes's observation on G. E. Moore's literal-mindedness: "Moore had a nightmare once in which he could not distinguish propositions from tables. But even when awake, he could not distinguish love and beauty and truth from the furniture" (J. M. Keynes, *Two Memoirs* [London, Rupert Hart-Davis, 1949], p. 94). Keynes's comment seems to be meant admiringly, but one result of Moore's influence is that his hypostatizing tendency sometimes sets the standard for what philosophers have in mind by "realism" and similar terms in ethics—as witness, e.g., the characterization of objectivist ethics as attributing moral values to "the furniture of the world" in Mackie, *Ethics*, p. 16. My own move away from a perceptual model also means giving up a common analogy to scientific realism, but I take it that the convergence of the two sides in the current realism/antirealism debate—e.g., the overlap between my view and Gibbard's— actually serves to undermine antirealism's challenge to our naive phenomenology (cf. Brink, *Moral Realism and Foundations of Ethics*, pp. 23–24).

64. See esp. Harman, *Nature of Morality*, pp. 3–10, for an antirealist argument resting on this assumption; cf. Nicholas L. Sturgeon, "Moral Explanations," in *Morality, Reason and Truth*, ed. D. Copp and D. Zimmerman (Totowa, N.J.: Rowman and Allanheld, 1985), pp. 49–78, for a realist reply.

65. Cf. esp. Walzer, "Political Action"; Williams, *Moral Luck*; and Nagel, *Mortal Questions*.

66. Cf. Simon Blackburn, "Rule-Following and Moral Realism," in *Wittgenstein: To Follow a Rule*, ed. S. H. Holzman and C. M. Leach (London: Routledge & Kegan Paul, 1981), p. 175.

67. See esp. Hare, "Moral Conflicts," pp. 206–19; cf. idem, "Utilitarianism and the Vicarious Affects," in *The Philosophy of Nicholas Rescher*, ed. E. Sosa (Dordrecht, Holland: D. Reidel, 1979), pp. 141–52.

68. Williams, "Ethical Consistency," p. 123.

69. Hare, "Moral Conflicts," pp. 209–10.

70. All quotes this paragraph from ibid., p. 210.

71. Ibid., p. 209.

72. Cf. McDowell, "Values and Secondary Qualities," pp. 118ff.

Chapter 4

1. Though Williams contrasts agent-regret with a number of other contrary-to-duty reactions (see *Moral Luck*, pp. 30–32), as far as I know his published discussions do not connect it to guilt. My remarks here are based in part on some conversations with Williams in 1989, particularly in discussion of preliminary drafts of chapters 2–3 of

Shame and Necessity (Berkeley: University of California Press, 1993); the book itself came out too late for consideration in this argument, however.

2. Cf. Williams, *Moral Luck*, p. 121.

3. See, e.g., Marcia Baron, "Remorse and Agent-Regret," in *Midwest Studies in Philosophy*, ed. P. A. French, T. E. Uehling, Jr., and H. K. Wettstein (Notre Dame, Ind.: University of Notre Dame Press, 1988), 13: 259–60; cf. Herbert Fingarette, "Feeling Guilty," *American Philosophical Quarterly* 16 (1979): 159–64, and Herbert Morris, "Reflections on Feeling Guilty," *Philosophical Studies* 40 (1981): 187–93.

4. See Aristotle, *Nicomachean Ethics*, 1128b10–35.

5. Ibid., 1128b29.

6. See esp. Williams, *Ethics and the Limits of Philosophy*; cf. also Slote, *From Morality to Virtue*.

7. Aristotle, *Nicomachean Ethics*, 1131b25–1132b20.

8. See Baron, "Remorse and Agent-Regret," p. 270. Baron's favored alternative to agent-regret is remorse, although she also acknowledges that guilt applies to many of her cases, at least in a broad sense; cf., e.g., p. 260. Her argument is apparently meant to cut against virtue ethics, however, rather than to support modifications in the standard version of the theory, as suggested here. Note that her definition of virtue ethics is an odd one, since it apparently insists on incompatibility with duty ethics and rules out taking conscientiousness as a virtue; cf. p. 259.

9. Bertrand Russell, *The Autobiography of Bertrand Russell: 1872–1914* (Boston: Little, Brown, 1967), pp. 329–30.

10. But cf. Stocker, *Plural and Conflicting Values*, p. 65, for an interpretation of Aristotle on which base acts, including even acts performed under duress, rule out *eudaimonia*, and with it presumably virtue. Stocker takes the point as applying to cases of "dirty hands"—like my "weighted" dilemmas, except that the alternatives are not said to be wrong all things considered; see, e.g., ibid., p. 10.

11. For examples of this approach, along with the works by Williams cited earlier, see esp. Lawrence A. Blum, *Friendship, Altruism and Morality* (London: Routledge & Kegan Paul, 1980), and Michael Stocker, "The Schizophrenia of Modern Ethical Theories," *Journal of Philosophy* 73 (1976): 453–66.

12. Without our independent information about Russell's somewhat limited emotional range, I should add, this might be a more charitable explanation of his reaction in the passage cited. Perhaps I ought to remind the reader, for that matter, that the case in which I have made out guilt as obligatory is substantially modified from Russell's real-life case. As another alternative in the real-life case, on a view that allows for unconscious guilt as an emotion the agent misidentifies (cf. Greenspan, *Emotions and Reasons*, pp. 25–30), one might instead argue that Russell really did feel guilty on some level, despite the fact that the passage acknowledges only sorrow. The element of irrationality commonly introduced by unconscious emotion might help make sense of the confusion I have noted in Russell's account of the reasons for his feeling.

13. See Greenspan, *Emotions and Reasons*, p. 4; cf. pp. 83–136, for the development and defense of the general account of emotional appropriateness that I begin to apply to guilt in this section, which is preliminary to my argument in chapter 5, section 2, in this volume.

14. See Greenspan, *Emotions and Reasons*, pp. 31–32; cf. pp. 55ff.

15. Cf. Greenspan, "Conditional Oughts and Hypothetical Imperatives," pp. 272–73.

16. Cf. Greenspan, "Behavior Control and Freedom of Action," and idem, *Emotions and Reasons*, pp. 153, 165–66, 173.

17. Cf. ibid., pp. 83–136.

18. The basic account outlined here is culled from a number of sources; see esp. Rawls, *Theory of Justice*, pp. 440–46, 479–85; Herbert Morris, *On Guilt and Innocence: Essays in Legal Philosophy and Moral Psychology* (Berkeley: University of California Press, 1976), pp. 59–63; Gabriele Taylor, *Pride, Shame, and Guilt: Emotions of Self-Assessment* (Oxford: Clarendon, 1985); and Fingarette, "Feeling Guilty." I shall postpone until chapter 5 a discussion of standard assumptions about the connection of emotional guilt to the self-attribution of responsibility.

19. Cf. Taylor, *Pride, Shame, and Guilt*, p. 101; cf. pp. 99–100.

20. Cf., e.g., Thomas, *Living Morally*, pp. 76–80.

21. Cf., e.g., Taylor, *Pride, Shame, and Guilt*, pp. 54–57ff.

22. Cf. Gibbard, *Wise Choices, Apt Feelings*, pp. 136–40.

23. See Rawls, *Theory of Justice*, pp. 484–85; cf. pp. 445–46.

24. See esp. Hoffman, "Development of Prosocial Motivation," for a review of the recent literature.

25. See Edwards, *Nature of True Virtue*, pp. 61–74.

26. See esp. Benedict, *Chrysanthemum and the Sword*; cf., e.g., Millie R. Creighton, "Revisiting Shame and Guilt Cultures: A Forty-Year Pilgrimage," *Ethos* 18 (1990): 279–307.

27. See esp. Hoffman, "Development of Prosocial Motivation," pp. 296–97. Hoffman does not make a clear shame/guilt distinction; but cf. June Price Tangney, "Moral Affect: The Good, the Bad, and the Ugly," *Journal of Personality and Social Psychology* 61 (1991): 598–607, for results supporting his central claims in application specifically to guilt.

28. See *The Oxford English Dictionary*. Other languages apparently have no noun for emotional guilt per se but instead must refer to the sense of guilt or to feelings of guilt—which presumably can include feelings of moral shame—to distinguish the emotion from the state of *being* guilty or at fault. Alternatively, they can use an adjective for "guilty" with "feels," to mean "feels *as if*" at fault.

29. Edwards, *Nature of True Virtue*, pp. 66–67. Edwards's notion of consistency is apparently a "sentimentalist" modification of the then-current "intellectualist" views of Samuel Clarke; see Norman Fiering, *Jonathan Edwards's Moral Thought and Its British Context* (Chapel Hill: University of North Carolina, 1981), pp. 87–93.

30. Edwards, *Nature of True Virtue*, p. 64.

31. Ibid., cf. pp. 61ff.

32. See Taylor, *Pride, Shame, and Guilt*, p. 92; cf. pp. 90, 106.

33. Cf. Greenspan, *Emotions and Reasons*, pp. 48–55.

34. See Freud, *Civilization and Its Discontents*, pp. 85, 94ff. Freud apparently uses "remorse" for guilt felt for an actual deed. In any case, his developed account of the sense of guilt that he takes to precede action seems to me to allow for the identificatory interpretation I give here. In fact, Freud suggests something of the sort in his characterization of the superego in terms of aggression directed toward the ego it develops as a part of; cf., e.g., p. 84. See also p. 95 for the characterization of the sources of guilt in terms of love/hate ambivalence; cf. Klein and Riviere, *Love, Hate and Reparation*.

35. See esp. Arnold H. Modell, "On Having the Right to a Life: An Aspect of the Superego's Development," *International Journal of Psychoanalysis* 46 (1965): 323–31; cf. Takeo Doi, *The Anatomy of Dependence* (Tokyo: Kodansha International, 1973), pp. 48–57, for a Japanese psychiatrist's account of a similar notion of guilt in Japan (at the death of parents and the like) as a reaction to the sense that one is betraying one's group ties. I shall attempt a fuller discussion of such cases in chapter 5.

36. Cf., e.g., Douglas, *Purity and Danger*. What is commonly referred to as "Jewish guilt" seems to me to be in large part a variant of separation guilt with the features I focus on here rather than anything specifically religious as one might suppose. (Note that the notion of original sin is distinctively Christian, indeed Western Christian, due to Saint Augustine) Another element may be something like Nietzschean "debt"; cf. Nietzsche, *Genealogy of Morals*, pp. 62–63ff. The one element I can locate that does seem to have biblical sources is the tendency to explain bad events as results of one's own (or in the biblical case, the group's) misdeeds. According to my argument in chapter 5, even raising the question of (objective) guilt—"What have I done to deserve this?"—can be enough to generate guilt feelings.

37. Cf., e.g., Ezekiel 6:9 and 36:31 for expressions of self-loathing that seem to be plausibly classified as guilt; I owe these references to biblical scholar David Halperin (personal communication).

38. Cf. Sharon Bishop, "Connections and Guilt," *Hypatia* 2 (1987): 7–23.

39. Cf. Gibbard, *Wise Choices, Apt Feelings*, pp. 139–40. Gibbard's own account of guilt as a counterpart to anger is naturally read in the rather weak terms I go on to discuss, but it also allows for filling out in the way I propose here.

40. See, e.g., June Price Tangney, Patricia Wagner, and Richard Gramzow, "Proneness to Shame, Proneness to Guilt, and Psychopathology," *Journal of Abnormal Psychology* 101 (1992): 469–78.

41. See Michael Friedman, "Toward a Reconceptualization of Guilt," *Contemporary Psychoanalysis* 21 (1985): 540; cf. pp. 535, 539.

42. Cf., e.g., the account of the Ancient Greek shift from "shame-culture" to "guilt-culture" in E. R. Dodds, *The Greeks and the Irrational* (Berkeley: University of California Press, 1951), pp. 17f., 28–63.

43. Hare, "Moral Conflicts," p. 208.

44. See, e.g., L. A. Kosman, "Being Properly Affected: Virtues and Feelings in Aristotle's Ethics," in *Essays on Aristotle's Ethics*, ed. A. O. Rorty (Berkeley: University of California, 1980), pp. 103–16. For other treatments of the issue of responsibility for emotion (but mainly in a backward-looking sense of "responsibility"), see Robert Merrihew Adams, "Involuntary Sins," *Philosophical Review* 94 (1985): 3–31, and Edward Sankowski, "Responsibility of Persons for Their Emotions," *Canadian Journal of Philosophy* 7 (1977): 829–40.

45. See Ross, *Right and the Good*, pp. 4–6, and H. A. Prichard, "Does Moral Philosophy Rest on a Mistake?," *Mind* 21 (1912): 33. For a more recent example of the standard view of Kant on emotions, see esp. Blum, *Friendships, Altruism and Morality*; cf. Nancy Sherman, "The Place of Emotions in Kantian Morality," in *Identity, Character, and Morality*, ed. O. Flanagan and A. O. Rorty (Cambridge, Mass.: MIT Press, 1990), pp. 149–70, for another side of this story. However, I take it that Kant's exclusion of emotions from the grounds of moral judgment as required by my own argument remains intact, even if he makes room for them in other ways as components of the moral life.

46. Cf. Prichard, "Moral Philosophy," p. 27, and Ross, *Right and the Good*, p. 5.

47. Prichard, "Moral Philosophy," p. 24.

48. Ross, *Right and the Good*, p. 5.

49. Ibid., pp. 42–43.

50. Note that Ross later changed his mind on this point, holding instead that the duty to fulfill a promise was a duty not to effect a certain result but to try to do so; see W. David Ross, *Foundations of Ethics* (Oxford: Clarendon, 1939), p. 108. The change would reinforce my argument in what follows for treating "ought-to-feel" on the model of "ought-to-do."

51. Prichard, "Moral Philosophy," p. 33.

52. Cf. Marcus, "Moral Dilemmas and Consistency," p. 198.

53. Cf. Aeschylus, "Agamemnon," 217–18; cf. Nussbaum, *Fragility of Goodness*, pp. 35–37.

54. Williams, "Ethical Consistency," p. 135.

55. Williams, *Moral Luck*, p. 179.

56. See esp. Kant, *Foundations of the Metaphysics of Morals*, p. 10; cf. Nagel, *Mortal Questions*, p. 24. What I suggest here is not unlike Nagel's own diagnosis of the problem of moral luck, which he explains by appeal to his distinction between internal and external points of view; cf. pp. 36ff.

57. See Peter Strawson, "Freedom and Resentment," in *Free Will*, ed. G. Watson (Oxford: Oxford University Press, 1982), pp. 59–80; cf. Susan Wolf, "Asymmetrical Freedom," *Journal of Philosophy* 77 (1980): 151–66. The issue is also complicated by features of the rational and moral assessment of these emotions noted elsewhere in this chapter—for instance. in my discussion of asymmetries involving pride.

58. See Hume, *Treatise of Human Nature*, pp. 251–55; cf. pp. 409–10. The fiction I have in mind as bearing on responsibility issues is a bit different from the one Hume discusses in his treatment of personal identity (cf. esp. p. 255). It essentially involves making out the self as distinct from and prior to its actions, in order to cast it in the role of responsible cause. Although a full discussion of these issues is beyond the scope of this discussion, I shall have a bit more to say about them in chapter 5. For related comments on the notion of causation by character, see Greenspan, "Unfreedom and Responsibility"; cf. Adams, "Involuntary Sins."

59. Cf. Greenspan, "Unfreedom and Responsibility," pp. 69–70. Nagel discusses a similar case, of an accident resulting from failure to have one's brakes checked, with reference to moral luck in *Mortal Questions*, p. 29.

Chapter 5

1. See Rawls, *Theory of Justice*, p. 482. For general objections to judgmentalism, see Greenspan, *Emotions and Reasons*, pp. 15–80.

2. See Aristotle, *Rhetorica*, Book II, Sec. 2, 1378a31–1378b5; cf. Greenspan, *Emotions and Reasons*, pp. 48–55.

3. Rawls, *Theory of Justice*, p. 482.

4. See Taylor, *Pride, Shame, and Guilt*, p. 86.

5. Ibid., p. 1.

6. Ibid., p. 91.

7. See Greenspan, *Emotions and Reasons*, pp. 18–20; cf. idem, "Emotions as Evaluations," *Pacific Philosophical Quarterly* 62 (1981): 158–69.

8. See Greenspan, *Emotions and Reasons*, pp. 25–30. But note, in relation to my present argument, the reasons offered against any easy inference to unconscious evaluations on pp. 19, 24.

9. Cf. ibid., pp. 153–62.

10. See Stephen P. Stich, "Beliefs and Subdoxastic States," *Philosophy of Science* 45 (1978): 499–518, and Michael E. Bratman, "Practical Reasoning and Acceptance in a Context," *Mind* 101 (1992): 1–15.

11. For the latter notion, see, e.g., Donagan, *Theory of Morality*, p. 45.

12. See Herbert Morris, "Nonmoral Guilt," in *Responsibility, Character, and the Emotions*, ed. F. Schoeman (Cambridge: Cambridge University Press, 1987), pp. 220–41.

13. Ibid., pp. 232–37.

14. Taylor has a puzzling comment about the parallel sort of economic case: "If I feel guilty about my privileged position in society due to circumstances of birth then I see myself as an agent causally involved: it is *my* birth which has brought about the state of affairs which is my privileged position" (*Pride, Shame, and Guilt*, p. 91). But the agent's birth is no less passive than being benefited economically or the like; it just is less easily distinguished from the person to whom it happens. So it is questionable how this could yield the requisite sort of causal responsibility on Taylor's account without an implausible attribution of delusion to the agent. Presumably, what is in question is causation by the agent in some sense—if not through her act or agency then at least through some other form of activity on her part. But surely birth does not qualify.

15. See Hume, *Treatise of Human Nature*, p. 139.

16. Morris, "Nonmoral Guilt," pp. 226–32.

17. Taylor, *Pride, Shame, and Guilt*, pp. 91–92.

18. Morris, "Nonmoral Guilt," pp. 237–40.

19. Cf. Joel Feinberg, *Doing and Deserving: Essays in the Theory of Responsibility* (Princeton, N.J.: Princeton University Press, 1970), p. 233. Taylor apparently misses this distinction when she cites Feinberg's point that vicarious objective guilt is impossible, in support of her own view that "feelings of guilt . . . cannot arise from the deeds or omissions of others" (*Pride, Shame, and Guilt*, p. 91; cf. n. 5 and Feinberg, *Doing and Deserving*, pp. 231, 237).

20. Morris, "Nonmoral Guilt," pp. 239–40.

21. Ibid., pp. 232, 237.

22. Ibid., p. 226.

23. Ibid., p. 232.

24. See, e.g., Herbert Morris, "The Decline of Guilt," *Ethics* 99 (1988): 66.

25. Morris, "Nonmoral Guilt," 226.

26. See Greenspan, *Emotions and Reasons*, p. 31; cf. pp. 153–62.

27. Cf. ibid., esp. pp. 83–107, for my extended inquiry into appropriateness, resulting in a nonquantitative criterion in terms of belief warrant.

28. See John Searle, *Intentionality* (Cambridge: Cambridge University Press, 1983), pp. 31–35; cf., e.g., p. 8 for his statement of the point as a claim that emotions have no direction of fit—meaning, I take it, emotions themselves as distinct from desires and beliefs. Searle sees emotions as combining elements of desire and belief, with an emphasis on desire (but as only partially characterized by his analysis; cf. p. 36), while making out appropriateness in terms of belief satisfaction (pp. 8–9). Note, however, that he uses the category of desire to capture evaluative content.

29. Cf. Gibbard, *Wise Choices, Apt Feelings*, p. 139. In the ensuing argument I hope to show how the standards for guilt and anger might diverge—compatibly with the value placed according to Gibbard on meshing guilt and anger (cf. p. 299). See Sinnott-Armstrong, *Moral Dilemmas*, p. 107, for the application to dilemmas of a similar claim of asymmetry between *remorse* and blame, though without the explanation I provide here; cf. also Greenspan, "Moral Dilemmas and Guilt."

30. Cf. Greenspan, *Emotions and Reasons*, pp. 48–55, 188, n. 3.

31. Cf. my distinction between backward- and forward-looking notions of responsibility in Greenspan, "Unfreedom and Responsibility," pp. 64, 71. One might be tempted to take personal blame as appropriate just in virtue of its usefulness in getting individual members to exert forward-looking responsibility and reform the relevant group. However, general adaptiveness would seem to be well enough served by blame imposed for failing to *take* responsibility—in that way and also in the emotional terms

that I go on to justify. Something similar applies, moreover, to any independent symbolic function that might be assigned to blame, in expressing a strong stand against the group behavior in question.

32. On the other hand, the standards of appropriateness may incorporate facts about normal emotional development to the extent that these affect both the naturalness of an object of attention and the general adaptiveness of an emotional response to it. This point may afford a deeper explanation of the notion of "paradigm scenarios" in De Sousa, *Rationality of Emotion*, pp. 181–84, as early stages in emotional learning that are given special stress in determining the rationality of an emotion in adult life. In view of facts about emotional "inertia," or the tendency of emotional responses to outlive changes in their corresponding judgments, we would expect some stages in childhood development to affect adult response patterns. For instance, it might be thought that anger in response to injuries to oneself, as the natural childhood strut of the sense of justice, is important enough in developmental terms to warrant blame on the part of the victim in a case like Russell's, even in the absence of adequate grounds for third-person moral blame—a possibility I tried to allow for in chapter 4. But there is also room for a good deal of empirical disagreement on these issues; it should be evident that my treatment of cases here rests on a heavy element of conjecture.

33. Cf. Morris's somewhat less discriminate acceptance of "shared guilt" in *On Guilt and Innocence*, pp. 111–138.

34. Cf. Sinnott-Armstrong, *Moral Dilemmas*, p. 42; unlike Sinnott-Armstrong, I take it that "I had no choice," even if meant as an appeal to *moral* necessity, counts as an excuse.

35. Cf. Fletcher, *Rethinking Criminal Law*, pp. 343–44.

36. Marcus, "Moral Dilemmas and Consistency," pp. 193–94, 198–99.

37. This point distinguishes dilemmas from the cases of responsibility for inevitable states of affairs cited in John Martin Fischer and Mark Ravizza, "Responsibility and Inevitability," *Ethics* 101 (1991): 258–64. Note that the agent in a dilemma would have done otherwise (avoided doing wrong) if he had been able to; cf. the contrasting cases cited on pp. 264–65.

38. See Williams, *Moral Luck*, p. 54; cf. p. 41. Cf. also Stocker, *Plural and Conflicting Values*, pp. 9–19.

39. Williams, *Moral Luck*, pp. 63, 61.

40. Ibid., p. 79.

41. Ibid., p. 63.

Chapter 6

1. See, e.g., Richard Brandt, "The Science of Man and Wide Reflective Equilibrium," *Ethics* 100 (1990): 263. The general pattern of definition derives from Mill, *Utilitarianism*, p. 60—cf. also Gibbard, *Wise Choices, Apt Feelings*, p. 41—though Mill does not single out emotional blame but has in mind also overt acts of social censure and punishment.

2. See esp. Hume, *Treatise of Human Nature*, p. 469.

3. See esp. Simon Blackburn, *Spreading the Word* (Oxford: Clarendon, 1984), pp. 167–71, 181–223.

4. See esp. Nagel, *View from Nowhere*, pp. 171–75.

5. See esp. De Sousa, *Rationality of Emotion*; cf. also, e.g., Morton White, *What Is and What Ought to Be Done* (New York: Oxford University Press, 1981), which

assigns emotions a role in moral knowledge analogous to that of sense-perception in scientific knowledge. McDowell's work also seems to assign emotions a role I think of as perceptual—in the broad sense I have in mind here (meaning, roughly, "representational"), not on a specifically sensory interpretation, as might seem to fit the "secondary qualities" view—despite a very different account of moral knowledge; cf. esp. my discussion of McDowell's *Virtue and Reason* in chapter 3, section 2, in this volume.

6. See Simon Blackburn, "How to Be an Ethical Anti-Realist," in *Midwest Studies in Philosophy*, ed. P. A. French, T. E. Uehling, Jr., and H. K. Wettstein (Notre Dame, Ind.: University of Notre Dame Press, 1988), 12: 365; cf. p. 374, n. 5, for further references.

7. Ibid., p. 365; cf. Simon Blackburn, "Errors and the Phenomenology of Value," in *Morality and Objectivity: A Tribute to J. L. Mackie*, ed. T. Honderich (London: Routledge & Kegan Paul, 1985), pp. 1–22, for a careful account of the ways in which moral judgment fails to fit a perceptual analogy in detail (as on McDowell's "secondary qualities" view).

8. Blackburn, *Spreading the Word*, p. 195; cf. pp. 186, 207.

9. Cf. Blackburn "Flight to Reality." For an explicitly social version of antirealism, cf. Gibbard, *Wise Choices, Apt Feelings*. For simplicity's sake, I shall limit my remarks here to Blackburn, but I take them to apply at least roughly to any expressivist view.

10. See Blackburn, *Spreading the Word*, pp. 217–19.

11. Ibid., pp. 167–71.

12. Simon Blackburn, "Attitudes and Contents," *Ethics* 98 (1988): 504.

13. See Blackburn, *Spreading the Word*, p. 219, n. 21.

14. Ibid., p. 197.

15. Ibid., p. 21.

16. Ibid., pp. 193–95.

17. See Simon Blackburn, "Truth, Realism, and the Regulation of Theory," in *Midwest Studies in Philosophy*, ed. P. A. French, T. E. Uehling, Jr., and H. K. Wettstein (Notre Dame, Ind.: University of Notre Dame, 1980), 5: 357–58, and idem, "Rule-Following and Moral Realism," p. 175.

18. Blackburn at some points seems to be open to a general interpretation of internalism, however; see his *Spreading the Word*, p. 189. But cf., e.g., idem, "How to Be an Ethical Anti-Realist," p. 363, for the more standard view.

19. Blackburn, *Spreading the Word*, pp. 198–201.

20. In a recent paper on dilemmas, Blackburn indeed rests the special nature of moral dilemmas—but set up as positive ought-conflicts and interpreted in terms of quandaries about what to do—on nothing beyond a quantitative difference in residues; see his "What Is Puzzling about Dilemmas?" in *Understanding Moral Dilemmas*, ed. H. E. Mason (New York: Oxford University Press, 1995). I saw an earlier version of the paper, as delivered at a conference on dilemmas at the University of Minnesota in April 1991.

21. Cf. Blackburn, "Flight to Reality." On the social bases of emotion in connection with my own suggestions on this issue, cf. the "social constructionist" views current in anthropology and related subjects, as represented, e.g., in Rom Harré ed., *The Social Construction of Emotions* (Oxford: Basil Blackwell, 1986). However, on some versions the approach apparently rules out any innate emotions, as I do not mean to do; my assumption is rather that innate responses are shaped into new emotions via social learning.

22. See esp. Stocker, "Schizophrenia of Modern Ethical Theories," pp. 453–66.

23. Cf. Kosman, "Being Properly Affected."

24. See esp. Robert M. Adams, "Motive Utilitarianism," *Journal of Philosophy* 73 (1976): 467–81.

25. Cf. Michael Moore, "The Moral Worth of Retribution," in *Responsibility, Character, and the Emotions*, ed. F. Schoeman (Cambridge: Cambridge University Press, 1987), pp. 199–202ff.

26. See G. E. Moore, *Principia Ethica* (Cambridge: Cambridge University Press, 1903), pp. 6–15.

27. Cf. Greenspan, *Emotions and Reasons*, pp. 155ff., and idem, "Fooling the Motivational Meter: A Reply to Roberts" (unpublished). It might be useful to think of emotional affect as also providing a second-order reason for action, in the sense of Raz, *Practical Reason*, pp. 39–40—albeit a positive or reinforcing reason of a sort Raz bypasses—to the extent that it provides a reason for attention to an evaluative reason (the evaluative content of emotion). I read this book too late to influence my discussion here; however, it might also provide some helpful terminology for the ideas about oughts and reasons expressed in chapters 2–3.

28. See, e.g., Josiah Royce, *The Philosophy of Josiah Royce* (Indianapolis: Hackett, 1982), pp. 189–96; cf. George Herbert Mead, *On Social Psychology: Selected Papers* (Chicago: University of Chicago Press, 1956), pp. 39–42, 199–246. The brief reflections that follow are my own.

29. Cf. Royce's ideal communitarianism (e.g., *Philosophy of Royce*, pp. 367–87). For that matter, there are elements of a communitarian view in the Kantian ideal of the realm of ends; cf. Kant, *Foundations of the Metaphysics of Morals*, pp. 51ff.

30. Cf. Rawls's discussion of "congruence" in *Theory of Justice*, pp. 567–77. A more ordinary argument from pride than the one I suggest here, but limited to agents with a certain kind of motivational structure, might point out that whatever one cared to achieve in life on an individual level would be cheapened or compromised by being achieved at the cost of violating moral requirements. Its achievement would be comparable to winning a fight that was "fixed"—as the agent would be aware, even if no one else was.

Note that my argument is not meant to show that morality is *the* overriding end, but just that it is among the ends, of a rational agent with the usual sort of motivational structure. It may have to compete with individual achievement and other forms of value (some arguably moral) whose focus is more directly on the individual.

31. Cf. esp. Wong, *Moral Relativity*, and Geoffrey Sayre-McCord, "Being a Realist about Relativism (in Ethics)," *Philosophical Studies* 61 (1991): 155–76, for recent defenses of the possibility of combining relativism and realism.

32. See Williams, *Ethics and the Limits of Philosophy*, pp. 160–66.

33. See Moore, *Principia Ethica*, Ch. 6.

34. Cf. A. J. Ayer, *Language, Truth and Logic*, London: V. Gollancz, 1946 (rev. ed., Dover, n.d.), pp. 102–13.

Bibliography

Adams, Robert Merrihew. "Involuntary Sins." *Philosophical Review* 94 (1985): 3–31.
———. "Motive Utilitarianism." *Journal of Philosophy* 73 (1976): 467–81.
Aeschylus. "Agamemnon." In *The Oresteian Trilogy*, trans. P. Vellacott, 41–100. Harmondsworth, Middlesex, England: Penguin, 1959.
Anderson, Alan Ross. "The Formal Analysis of Normative Systems." In *The Logic of Decision and Action*, ed. N. Rescher, 147–213. Pittsburgh: University of Pittsburgh Press, 1967.
Anscombe, G.E.M. "Modern Moral Philosophy." In *Collected Philosophical Papers*, Vol. 3, *Ethics, Religion and Politics*, pp. 26–42. Minneapolis: University of Minnesota Press, 1981.
Aristotle. *De Anima*, trans. D. W. Hamlyn. Oxford: Clarendon, 1968.
———. *Movement of Animals*, trans. E. S. Forster. London: William Heinemann, 1968.
———. *Nicomachean Ethics*, trans. D. Ross. New York: Oxford University Press, 1925.
———. *Rhetorica*. In *The Basic Works of Aristotle*, 1325–1451. New York: Random House, 1941.
Augustine, St. *St. Augustine's Confessions*, trans. W. Watts. 2 vols. New York: Putnam, 1922.
Ayer, A. J. *Language, Truth and Logic*. London: V. Gollancz, 1946 (rev. ed., Dover, n.d.).
Baron, Marcia. "Remorse and Agent-Regret." In *Midwest Studies in Philosophy*, Vol. 13, ed. P. A. French, T. E. Uehling, Jr., and H. K. Wettstein, 259–81. Notre Dame, Ind.: University of Notre Dame Press, 1988.
Beck, Lewis White. *A Commentary on Kant's Critique of Practical Reason*. Chicago: University of Chicago Press, 1960.
Benedict, Ruth. *The Chrysanthemum and the Sword: Patterns of Japanese Culture*. Boston: Houghton Mifflin, 1946.
Bishop, Sharon. "Connections and Guilt." *Hypatia* 2 (1987): 7–23.
Blackburn, Simon. "Attitudes and Contents." *Ethics* 98 (1988): 501–17.
———. "Errors and the Phenomenology of Value." In *Morality and Objectivity: A Tribute to J. L. Mackie*, ed. T. Honderich, 1–22. London: Routledge & Kegan Paul, 1985.
———. "The Flight to Reality." In *Virtues and Reasons*, ed. R. Hursthouse and G. Lawrence. Oxford: Oxford University Press, 1995.
———. "How to Be an Ethical Anti-Realist." In *Midwest Studies in Philosophy*, Vol. 12, ed. P. A. French et al., 361–75. Notre Dame, Ind.: University of Notre Dame Press, 1988.

———. "Rule-Following and Moral Realism." In *Wittgenstein: To Follow a Rule*, ed. S. H. Holzman and C. M. Leach, 163–87. London: Routledge & Kegan Paul, 1981.

———. *Spreading the Word*. Oxford: Clarendon, 1984.

———. "Truth, Realism, and the Regulation of Theory." In *Midwest Studies in Philosophy*, Vol. 5, ed. P. A. French, T. E. Uehling, Jr., and H. K. Wettstein, 353–71. Notre Dame, Ind.: University of Notre Dame Press, 1980.

———. "What Is Puzzling about Dilemmas?" In *Understanding Moral Dilemmas*, ed. H. E. Mason. New York: Oxford University Press, 1995.

Blum, Lawrence A. *Friendship, Altruism and Morality*. London: Routledge & Kegan Paul, 1980.

Brandt, Richard. *Ethical Theory*. Englewood Cliffs, N.J.: Prentice-Hall, 1959.

———. "The Science of Man and Wide Reflective Equilibrium." *Ethics* 100 (1990): 259–78.

———. "Toward a Credible Form of Utilitarianism." In *Morality and the Language of Conduct*, ed. H-N. Castañeda and G. Nakhnikian, 107–43. Detroit: Wayne State University Press, 1965.

———. "Utilitarianism and the Rules of War." In *War and Moral Responsibility*, ed. M. Cohen, T. Nagel, and T. Scanlon, 25–45. Princeton, N.J.: Princeton University Press, 1974.

Bratman, Michael E. "Castañeda's Theory of Thought and Action." In *Agent, Language, and the Structure of the World*, ed. J. E. Tomberlin, 149–69. Indianapolis: Hackett, 1983.

———. "Practical Reasoning and Acceptance in a Context." *Mind* 101 (1992): 1–15.

Bredvold, Louis I. *The Natural History of Sensibility*. Detroit: Wayne State University Press, 1962.

Brink, David O. *Moral Realism and the Foundations of Ethics*. Cambridge: Cambridge University Press, 1989.

Brown, Charlotte. "Moral Sense Theorists." In *Encyclopedia of Ethics*, Vol. 2, ed. L. C. and C. B. Becker, 862–68. New York: Garland, 1992.

Burton, Robert. *The Anatomy of Melancholy*. New York: Tudor, 1927.

Butler, Joseph. *A Dissertation of the Nature of Virtue*. London: SPCK, 1970.

Castañeda, Hector-Neri. "On the Semantics of the Ought-to-Do." *Synthese* 21 (1970): 449–68.

———. *The Structure of Morality*. Springfield, Ill.: Charles C. Thomas, 1974.

———. *Thinking and Doing: The Philosophical Foundations of Institutions*. Dordrecht, Holland: D. Reidel, 1975.

Chisholm, Roderick M. "Contrary-to-Duty Imperatives and Deontic Logic." *Analysis* 24 (1963): 33–36.

Conee, Earl. "Against Moral Dilemmas." In *Moral Dilemmas*, ed. C. W. Gowans, 239–49. Oxford: Oxford University Press, 1987. Previously published in *Philosophical Review* 91 (1982): 87–97.

Cooper, John M. *Reason and Human Good in Aristotle*. Indianapolis: Hackett, 1986.

Copp, David. "The Concept of a Society." *Dialogue* 31 (1992): 183–212.

———. *Morality, Normativity, and Society*. New York: Oxford University Press, 1995.

———. "The Right to an Adequate Standard of Living: Justice, Autonomy, and the Basic Needs." *Social Philosophy and Policy* 9 (1992): 231–61.

———. "What Collectives Are: Agency, Individualism and Legal Theory." *Dialogue* 23 (1984): 249–69.

Creighton, Millie R. "Revisiting Shame and Guilt Cultures: A Forty-Year Pilgrimage." *Ethos* 18 (1990): 279–307.

Dancy, Jonathan. *Moral Reasons*. Oxford: Basil Blackwell, 1993.

Darwall, Stephen L. *Impartial Reason*. Ithaca, N.Y.: Cornell University Press, 1983.

———. "Motive and Obligation in the British Moralists." *Social Philosophy and Policy* 7 (1989): 133–50.

Davidson, Donald. *Essays on Actions and Events*. Oxford: Clarendon, 1980.

Descartes, Réné. *The Philosophical Works of Descartes*, trans. E. S. Haldane and G.R.T. Ross. 2 vols. Cambridge: Cambridge University Press, 1970.

De Sousa, Ronald. *The Rationality of Emotion*. Cambridge, Mass.: Bradford Books, 1987.

Dodds, E. R. *The Greeks and the Irrational*. Berkeley: University of California Press, 1951.

Doi, Takeo. *The Anatomy of Dependence*. Tokyo: Kodansha International, 1973.

Donagan, Alan. "Consistency in Rationalist Moral Systems." In *Moral Dilemmas*, ed. C. W. Gowans, 271–90. Oxford: Oxford University Press, 1987. Previously published in *Journal of Philosophy* 81 (1984): 291–309.

———. *The Theory of Morality*. Chicago: University of Chicago Press, 1977.

Douglas, Mary. *Purity and Danger*. London: Routledge & Kegan Paul, 1966.

Dummett, Michael. *Frege: Philosophy of Language*, 2nd ed. London: Duckworth, 1981.

Edwards, Jonathan. *The Nature of True Virtue*. Ann Arbor: University of Michigan Press, 1960.

Falk, W. D. "'Ought' and Motivation." *Proceedings of the Aristotelian Society* 48 (1947–48): 492–510.

Feinberg, Joel. *Doing and Deserving: Essays in the Theory of Responsibility*. Princeton, N.J.: Princeton University Press, 1970.

Fiering, Norman. *Jonathan Edwards's Moral Thought and Its British Context*. Chapel Hill: University of North Carolina Press, 1981.

Fingarette, Herbert. "Feeling Guilty." *American Philosophical Quarterly* 16 (1979): 159–64.

Fischer, John Martin, and Mark Ravizza. "Responsibility and Inevitability." *Ethics* 101 (1991): 258–78.

Fletcher, George. *Rethinking Criminal Law*. Boston: Little, Brown, 1978.

Føllesdal, Dagfinn, and Hilpinen, Risto. "Deontic Logic: An Introduction." In *Deontic Logic: Introductory and Systematic Readings*, ed. R. Hilpinen, 1–35. Dordrecht, Holland: D. Reidel, 1971.

Foot, Philippa. "Moral Realism and Moral Dilemma." In *Moral Dilemmas*, ed. C. W. Gowans, 250–70. New York: Oxford University Press, 1987. Previously published in *Journal of Philosophy* 80 (1983): 379–98.

———. *Virtues and Vices and Other Essays in Moral Philosophy*. Berkeley: University of California Press, 1978.

Frankena, William K. *Ethics*. Englewood Cliffs, N.J.: Prentice-Hall, 1973.

———. "Obligation and Motivation in Recent Moral Philosophy." In *Essays in Moral Philosophy*, ed. A. I. Melden, 40–81. Seattle: University of Washington Press, 1958.

Frege, Gottlob. "Negation." In *Translations from the Philosophical Writings of Gottlob Frege*, eds. P. Geach and M. Black, 117–35. New York: Philosophical Library, 1952.

Freud, Sigmund. *Civilization and Its Discontents*, trans. J. Strachey. New York: Norton, 1961.

Friedman, Michael. "Toward a Reconceptualization of Guilt." *Contemporary Psycho-analysis* 21 (1985): 501–47.

Garner, Richard. "On the Genuine Queerness of Moral Properties and Facts." *Australasian Journal of Philosophy* 68 (1990): 137–46.

Gibbard, Allan. *Wise Choices, Apt Feelings: A Theory of Normative Judgment.* Cambridge, Mass.: Harvard University Press, 1990.

Goldman, Alvin. "Empathy, Mind, and Morals." *Proceedings and Addresses of the American Philosophical Association* 66 (1992): 17–41.

Gordon, Robert. *The Structure of Emotions.* Cambridge: Cambridge University Press, 1987.

Gowans, Christopher W. "Moral Dilemmas and Prescriptivism." *American Philosophical Quarterly* 26 (1989): 187–97.

———. *Innocence Lost: An Examination of Inescapable Moral Wrongdoing.* New York: Oxford University Press, 1994.

———, ed. *Moral Dilemmas.* Oxford: Oxford University Press, 1987.

Greenspan, P. S. "Behavior Control and Freedom of Action." *Philosophical Review* 87 (1978): 25–40.

———. "A Case of Mixed Feelings: Ambivalence and the Logic of Emotion." In *Explaining Emotions,* ed. A. O. Rorty, 223–50. Berkeley: University of California Press, 1980.

———. "Conditional Oughts and Hypothetical Imperatives." *Journal of Philosophy* 72 (1975): 259–76.

———. "Derived Obligation: Some Paradoxes Escaped." Ph.D. dissertation. Cambridge, Mass.: Harvard University, 1972.

———. "Emotions as Evaluations." *Pacific Philosophical Quarterly* 62 (1981): 158–69.

———. *Emotions and Reasons: An Inquiry into Emotional Justification.* New York: Routledge, Chapman and Hall, 1988.

———. "Moral Dilemmas and Guilt." *Philosophical Studies* 43 (1983): 117–25.

———. "Unfreedom and Responsibility." In *Responsibility, Character, and the Emotions,* ed. F. Schoeman, 63–80. Cambridge: Cambridge University Press, 1987.

Grice, Paul. *Studies in the Way of Words.* Cambridge, Mass.: Harvard University Press, 1989.

Guttenplan, Samuel. "Moral Realism and Moral Dilemma." *Proceedings of the Aristotelian Society* 80 (1979–80): 61–80.

Hampshire, Stuart. *Morality and Conflict.* Cambridge, Mass.: Harvard University Press, 1983.

Hare, R. M. "Moral Conflicts." In *Moral Dilemmas,* ed. C. W. Gowans, 205–38. Oxford: Oxford University Press, 1987. Previously published in R. M. Hare, *Moral Thinking* (Oxford: Oxford University Press, 1981), pp. 25–62.

———. "Rules of War and Moral Reasoning." In *War and Moral Responsibility,* ed. M. Cohen, T. Nagel, and T. Scanlon, 46–61. Princeton, N.J.: Princeton University Press, 1974.

———. "Utilitarianism and the Vicarious Affects." In *The Philosophy of Nicholas Rescher,* ed. E. Sosa, 141–52. Dordrecht, Holland: D. Reidel, 1979.

Harman, Gilbert. *The Nature of Morality.* New York: Oxford University Press, 1977.

Harré, Rom, ed. *The Social Construction of Emotions.* Oxford: Basil Blackwell, 1986.

Harris, Paul L. *Children and Emotion: The Development of Psychological Understanding.* Oxford: Basil Blackwell, 1989.

Hoffman, Martin L. "Development of Prosocial Motivation: Empathy and Guilt." In

Development of Prosocial Behavior, ed. N. Eisenberg-Berg, 281–313. New York: Academic Press, 1982.

Horty, John F. "Deontic Logic as Founded on Nonmonotonic Logic." *Annals of Mathematics and Artificial Intelligence* 9 (1993): 69–91.

———. "Moral Dilemmas on Nonmonotonic Logic." *Journal of Philosophical Logic* 23 (1994): 35–65.

Hume, David. *A Treatise of Human Nature*. Oxford: Clarendon, 1964.

Ibsen, Henrik. *The Works of Henrik Ibsen*. 11 vols. New York: Blue Ribbon Books, 1928.

Jackson, Frank. "Davidson on Moral Conflict." In *Actions and Events*, eds. E. Lapore and B. McLaughlin, 104–15. Oxford: Basil Blackwell, 1985.

Kant, Immanuel. *The Doctrine of Virtue: Part II of the Metaphysic of Morals*, trans. M. J. Gregor. Philadelphia: University of Pennsylvania Press, 1964.

———. *Foundations of the Metaphysics of Morals*, trans. L. W. Beck. Indianapolis: Bobbs-Merrill, 1959.

———. *Lectures on Ethics*, trans. L. Infield. New York: Harper & Row, 1963.

Keynes, J. M. *Two Memoirs*. London: Rupert Hart-Davis, 1949.

Klein, Melanie, and Joan Riviere. *Love, Hate and Reparation*, 57–119. New York: Norton, 1964.

Korsgaard, Christine M. "Skepticism about Practical Reason." *Journal of Philosophy* 83 (1986): 5–25.

Kosman, L. A. "Being Properly Affected: Virtues and Feelings in Aristotle's Ethics." In *Essays on Aristotle's Ethics*, ed. A. O. Rorty, 103–16. Berkeley: University of California Press, 1980.

Lemmon, E. J. "Deontic Logic and the Logic of Imperatives." *Logique et Analyse* 8 (1965): 39–71.

———. "Moral Dilemmas," In *Moral Dilemmas*, ed. C. W. Gowans, 101–14. Oxford: Oxford University Press, 1987. Previously published in *Philosophical Review* 70 (1962): 139–58.

Lyons, David. *Forms and Limits of Utilitarianism*. Oxford: Oxford University Press, 1965.

MacIntyre, Alasdair. *After Virtue*. Notre Dame, Ind.: University of Notre Dame Press, 1984.

———. "What Morality Is Not." In *The Definition of Morality*, ed. G. Wallace and A.D.M. Walker, 26–39. London: Methuen, 1970.

Mackie, J. L. *Ethics: Inventing Right and Wrong*. London: Penguin, 1987.

Mandelbaum, Maurice. *The Phenomenology of Moral Experience*. Baltimore: Johns Hopkins University Press, 1969.

Marcus, Ruth Barcan. "Moral Dilemmas and Consistency." In *Moral Dilemmas*, ed. C. W. Gowans, 188–204. Oxford: Oxford University Press, 1987. Previously published in *Journal of Philosophy* 77 (1980): 121–36.

McConnell, Terrance C. "Moral Blackmail." *Ethics* 91 (1981): 544–67.

———. "Moral Dilemmas and Consistency in Ethics." In *Moral Dilemmas*, ed. C. W. Gowans, 154–73. Oxford: Oxford University Press, 1987. Previously published in *Canadian Journal of Philosophy* 8 (1978): 269–87.

———. "Moral Dilemmas and Requiring the Impossible." *Philosophical Studies* 29 (1976): 409–13.

McDowell, John. "Aesthetic Value, Objectivity, and the Fabric of the World." In *Pleasure, Preference and Value*, ed. E. Schaper, 1–16. Cambridge: Cambridge University Press, 1983.

————. "Are Moral Requirements Hypothetical Imperatives?" *Proceedings of the Aristotelian Society* Suppl. 52 (1978): 13–29.

————. "Values and Secondary Qualities." In *Morality and Objectivity: A Tribute to J. L. Mackie*, ed. T. Honderich, 110–29. London: Routledge & Kegan Paul, 1985.

————. "Virtue and Reason." *Monist* 62 (1979): 331–50.

McNaughton, David. *Moral Vision*. Oxford: Basil Blackwell, 1988.

Mead, George Herbert. *On Social Psychology: Selected Papers*. Chicago: University of Chicago Press, 1956.

Mill, John Stuart. *Utilitarianism*. New York: Bobbs-Merrill, 1957.

Modell, Arnold H. "On Having the Right to a Life: An Aspect of the Superego's Development." *International Journal of Psychoanalysis* 46 (1965): 323–31.

Moore, G. E. *Principia Ethica*. Cambridge: Cambridge University Press, 1903.

Moore, Michael. "The Moral Worth of Retribution." In *Responsibility, Character, and the Emotions*, ed. F. Schoeman, 179–219. Cambridge: Cambridge University Press, 1987.

Morris, Herbert. "The Decline of Guilt." *Ethics* 99 (1988): 68–76.

————. "Nonmoral Guilt." In *Responsibility, Character, and the Emotions*, ed. F. Schoeman, 220–41. Cambridge: Cambridge University Press, 1987.

————. *On Guilt and Innocence: Essays in Legal Philosophy and Moral Psychology*. Berkeley: University of California Press, 1976.

————. "Reflections on Feeling Guilty." *Philosophical Studies* 40 (1981): 187–93.

Murdoch, Iris. *The Sovereignty of Good*. London: Ark, 1970.

Nagel, Thomas. "The Fragmentation of Value." In *Moral Dilemmas*, ed. C. W. Gowans, 174–87. Oxford: Oxford University Press, 1987. Previously published in *Mortal Questions* (Cambridge: Cambridge University Press, 1979), pp. 128–41.

————. *Mortal Questions*. Cambridge: Cambridge University Press, 1979.

————. *The Possibility of Altruism*. Oxford: Clarendon, 1970.

————. *The View from Nowhere*. New York: Oxford University Press, 1986.

————. "War and Massacre." In *War and Moral Responsibility*, ed. M. Cohen, T. Nagel, and T. Scanlon, 3–24. Princeton, N.J.: Princeton University Press, 1974.

Nietszche, Friedrich. *On the Genealogy of Morals*, trans. W. Kaufmann and R. J. Hollingdale. New York: Vintage, 1969.

Nussbaum, Martha. *The Fragility of Goodness: Luck and Ethics in Greek Tragedy and Philosophy*. Cambridge: Cambridge University Press, 1986.

Peters, R. S. *The Concept of Motivation*. New York: Humanities, 1980.

Plato. *Protagoras*, trans. C. C. Taylor. Oxford: Clarendon, 1976.

————. *Republic*. In *The Collected Dialogues of Plato*, trans. E. Hamilton and H. Cairns, 575–844. New York: Pantheon, 1961.

Prichard, H. A. "Does Moral Philosophy Rest on a Mistake?" *Mind* 21 (1912): 21–37.

Prior, A. N. "Escapism: The Logical Basis of Ethics." In *Essays in Moral Philosophy*, ed. A. I. Melden, 135–46. Seattle: University of Washington Press, 1958.

————. "The Paradoxes of Derived Obligation." *Mind* 63 (1954): 64–65.

Quinn, Phillip L. "Moral Obligation, Religious Demand, and Practical Conflict." In *Rationality, Religious Belief, and Moral Commitment*, ed. R. Audi and W. J. Wainwright, 195–212. Ithaca, N.Y.: Cornell University Press, 1986.

Railton, Peter. "Moral Realism." *Philosophical Review* 95 (1986): 163–207.

Rawls, John. "Kantian Constructivism in Moral Theory." *Journal of Philosophy* 77 (1980): 515–72.

————. *Political Liberalism*. New York: Columbia University Press, 1993.

————. *A Theory of Justice*. Cambridge, Mass.: Harvard University Press, 1971.

Raz, Joseph. *The Morality of Freedom*. Oxford: Oxford University Press, 1986.

———. *Practical Reason and Norms*. Princeton, N.J.: Princeton University Press, 1990.

Ross, W. David. *Foundations of Ethics*. Oxford: Clarendon, 1939.

———. *The Right and the Good*. Oxford: Clarendon, 1930.

Royce, Josiah. *The Philosophy of Josiah Royce*. Indianapolis: Hackett, 1982.

Russell, Bertrand. *The Autobiography of Bertrand Russell: 1872–1914*. Boston: Little, Brown, 1967.

Sankowski, Edward. "Responsibility of Persons for Their Emotions." *Canadian Journal of Philosophy* 7 (1977): 829–40.

Sartre, Jean-Paul. "Existentialism Is a Humanism," trans. P. Mairet. In *Existentialism from Dostoevsky to Sartre*, ed. W. Kaufmann, 287–311. New York: Meridian, 1957.

Sayre-McCord, Geoffrey. "Being a Realist about Relativism (in Ethics)." *Philosophical Studies* 61 (1991): 155–76.

———. "Moral Theory and Explanatory Impotence." In *Essays on Moral Realism*, ed. G. Sayre-McCord, 277–81. Ithaca, N.Y.: Cornell University Press, 1988.

Schneewind, Jerome B. "Pufendorf's Place in the History of Ethics." *Synthese* 72 (1987): 123–55.

Searle, John. "How to Derive 'Ought' from 'Is'." *Philosophical Review* 73 (1964): 43–58.

———. *Intentionality*. Cambridge: Cambridge University Press, 1983.

Sherman, Nancy. "The Place of Emotions in Kantian Morality." In *Identity, Character, and Morality*, ed. O. Flanagan and A. O. Rorty, 149–70. Cambridge, Mass.: MIT Press, 1990.

Sinnott-Armstrong, Walter. *Moral Dilemmas*. Oxford: Basil Blackwell, 1988.

Slote, Michael. *Beyond Optimizing*. Cambridge, Mass.: Harvard University Press, 1989.

———. *From Morality to Virtue*. New York: Oxford University Press, 1992.

———. "Utilitarianism, Moral Dilemmas, and Moral Cost." *American Philosophical Quarterly* 32 (1985): 161–68.

Smith, Adam. *The Theory of the Moral Sentiments*. In *British Moralists: 1650–1800*, Vol. 2, ed. D. D. Raphael, 20–54. Indianapolis, Ind.: Hackett, 1991.

Spiecker, Ben. "Education and the Moral Emotions." In *Philosophical Issues in Moral Education and Development*, ed. B. Spiecker and R. Straughan, 43–63. Milton Keynes, U.K.: Open University Press, 1988.

Stevenson, C. L. *Facts and Values*. New Haven, Conn.: Yale University Press, 1963.

Stich, Stephen P. "Beliefs and Subdoxastic States." *Philosophy of Science* 45 (1978): 499–518.

Stocker, Michael. *Plural and Conflicting Values*. Oxford: Clarendon, 1990.

———. "The Schizophrenia of Modern Ethical Theories." *Journal of Philosophy* 73 (1976): 453–66.

Strawson, Peter. "Freedom and Resentment." In *Free Will*, ed. G. Watson, 59–80. Oxford: Oxford University Press, 1982.

Sturgeon, Nicholas L. "Moral Explanations." In *Morality, Reason and Truth*, ed. D. Copp and D. Zimmerman, 49–78. Totowa, N.J.: Rowman and Allanheld, 1985.

Styron, William. *Sophie's Choice*. New York: Bantam, 1980.

Tangney, June Price. "Moral Affect: The Good, the Bad, and the Ugly." *Journal of Personality and Social Psychology* 61 (1991): 598–607.

Tangney, June Price, Patricia Wagner, and Richard Gramzow. "Proneness to Shame, Proneness to Guilt, and Psychopathology." *Journal of Abnormal Psychology* 101 (1992): 469–78.

Taylor, Gabriele. *Pride, Shame, and Guilt: Emotions of Self-Assessment*. Oxford: Clarendon, 1985.

Thomas, Laurence. *Living Morally: A Psychology of Moral Character*. Philadelphia: Temple University Press, 1989.

Tversky, Amos, and Daniel Kahneman. "Judgment under Uncertainty: Heuristics and Biases." *Science* 185 (1984): 1124–31.

Vallentyne, Peter. "Prohibition Dilemmas and Deontic Logic." *Logique et Analyse* 117–18 (1987): 113–22.

———. "Two Types of Moral Dilemmas." *Erkenntnis* 30 (1989): 301–18.

van Fraassen, Bas C. "Values and the Heart's Command." In *Moral Dilemmas*, ed. C. W. Gowans, 138–153. New York: Oxford University Press, 1987. Previously published in *Journal of Philosophy* 70 (1973): 5–19.

Von Wright, G. H. "Deontic Logic." *Mind* 60 (1951): 1–15.

———. *An Essay in Deontic Logic and the General Theory of Action*. Amsterdam: North Holland, 1968.

———. *Norm and Action*. London: Routledge & Kegan Paul, 1963.

Walzer, Michael. "Political Action: The Problem of Dirty Hands." In *War and Moral Responsibility*, ed. M. Cohen, T. Nagel, and T. Scanlon, 62–82. Princeton, N.J.: Princeton University Press, 1974.

Wertheimer, Roger. *The Significance of Sense: Meaning, Modality, and Morality*. Ithaca, N.Y.: Cornell University Press, 1972.

White, Morton. *What Is and What Ought to Be Done*. New York: Oxford University Press, 1981.

Wiggins, David. *Needs, Values, Truth*. Oxford: Basil Blackwell, 1987.

Williams, Bernard. "Ethical Consistency." In *Moral Dilemmas*, ed. C. W. Gowans, 115–37. Oxford: Oxford University Press, 1987. Previously published in *Proceedings of the Aristotelian Society* Supp. 39 (1965): 103–24. The version discussed here first appeared in Williams, *Problems of the Self: Philosophical Papers 1956–1972*, pp. 166–86 (Cambridge: Cambridge University Press, 1973).

———. *Ethics and the Limits of Philosophy*. Cambridge, Mass.: Harvard University Press, 1985.

———. Introduction to *Concepts and Categories: Philosophical Essays,* by I. Berlin, vii–xviii. London: Hogarth, 1978.

———. *Morality: An Introduction to Ethics*. New York: Harper & Row, 1972.

———. *Moral Luck: Philosophical Papers 1973–1980*. Cambridge: Cambridge University Press, 1981.

———. *Problems of the Self: Philosophical Papers 1956–1972*. Cambridge: Cambridge University Press, 1973.

———. *Shame and Necessity*. Berkeley: University of California Press, 1993.

Wolf, Susan. "Asymmetrical Freedom." *Journal of Philosophy* 77 (1980): 151–66.

Wong, David. *Moral Relativity*. Berkeley: University of California Press, 1984.

Wouk, Herman. *The Caine Mutiny*. Garden City, N.Y.: Doubleday, 1952.

Index